Made in America

☆
☆

Improving the Nomination and Election of Presidents

Alexander Heard
with
Scarlett G. Graham
and
Kay L. Hancock

For Jean

Sponsoring Editor: Lauren Silverman/Catherine Woods
Project Coordination, Text and Cover Design: Carlisle Publishers Services
Cover Illustration: Carlisle Graphics
Production: Michael Weinstein
Compositor: Carlisle Communications
Printer/Binder: R. R. Donnelley and Sons, Inc.
Cover Printer: New England Book Components

Made in America: Improving the Nomination and Election of Presidents

Library of Congress Cataloging-in-Publication Data

Heard, Alexander.
    Made in America: improving the nomination and election of
presidents / Alexander Heard.
      p.   cm.
    Includes bibliographical references and index.
    ISBN 0-673-46355-9   :
    1. Presidents—United States—Nomination.   2. Presidents—United
States—Election.   I. Title.
JK521.H43   1991   90-41330
324.6'0973—dc20   CIP

90 91 92 93 9 8 7 6 5 4 3 2 1

For Jean

Contents

Foreword

☆
☆

Plato called democracy "a charming form of government, full of variety and disorder, and dispensing a sort of equality to equals and unequals alike."[1] Trying to cope with the variety and disorder, we quickly learn that assessing issues of public policy is a far easier task than designing the institutions of self-government. Political contests are regularly fueled by enormously complex questions, but the controversy is always primarily over the goals advocated and the means for reaching them. When the subject is less *what* government should do than *how* it should be chosen and made legitimate, issues of self interest are seldom so quickly understood and agreed upon.

Suffrage issues connect the means and ends of government. The link between voter participation and public policy is deemed axiomatic. But the consequences of most procedural and organizational proposals are harder to discern. Even when self-interest is involved, changes in the ways politics is conducted often bring unexpected results. The uncertain effects of procedural and organizational alterations on the acquisition and exercise of power, and on the realization of democratic values, easily tempt a preference for the known present over an uncertain future. And so it goes when Americans contemplate proposals to alter the institutions through which they nominate and elect their nation's chief executive. Historically, changes have come about more from periodic outbursts of frustration or ambition than from deliberate foresight and contemplation.

The sources of presidential effectiveness, indeed of governmental effectiveness generally, are deeper than getting good people to seek high office. Every president has had individual qualities that bore on the effective use of presidential power and influence, but the office is also an institution within a vastly complicated, ever evolving constitutional government. This government both empowers and limits its occupant. *How* the office is filled is but one aspect of the ambitious striving for successful self-government by an unprecedentedly complex nation in an unprecedentedly complex age.

My hope for this book is that it will deepen understanding of how Americans actually "choose" their president, and of the consequences that flow from how they do so. The book identifies the related functions served by the electoral process, and in the end discusses feasible changes likely to improve the quality of the nation's self-government. The book is an effort at institutional assessment and design. Yet it acknowledges that more is needed for successful self-government than institutional arrangements and their adaptation to a rapidly changing technological society. As Robert Penn Warren has asked, must we not "face the hard fact that somehow we must, after all, civilize ourselves?"[2] Ultimately, the intellect, vision, vigor, probity, compassion, style, and morality of people are more decisive than procedure and structure, yet the form of government must fit those people, whatever their qualities.

Chapter One addresses frustrations felt with the present means of choosing presidents and defines important functions that the process needs to perform. Chapters Two through Five concern the quality and transmission of *information,* adequate flow of political information being essential to the conduct and durability of democratic government. Chapter Six takes up varieties of individual and group *participation,* other than voting, in nominating and electing presidents. Chapter Seven concerns voting, the factors that affect its exercise, and the long downward trend in general election balloting for president. Chapter Eight examines influences on shaping the public *agenda* exerted by presidential selection practices. Chapter Nine concerns the search through electoral change for better *leadership* in governance, and Chapter Ten examines the limiting circumstances and the possibilities of achieving better *government* through changes in nomination and election procedures. Chapter Eleven summarizes proposals for improving the selection of U. S. presidents, including actions and attitudes that would contribute to the health of American democracy.

The practices of democratic politics are so intricately woven together that most procedures and data that bear on one of the five functions listed above will be relevant to one or more of the others as well. Financial contributions, for example, are a form of participation, but their volume also influences the exchange of information and the recruitment of leadership. As a consequence, references to election finance will appear in more than one chapter. So it is with other topics. When the recommendations are brought together in Chapter 11, however, they are organized into familiar categories: political parties, campaign finance, the general election, and governance.

My associates and I have been conscious that the United States is constantly changing. Yet we have faith in the adaptive powers of the American system, powers that are born of conflicting values and competing initiatives. The proposals in the final chapter, and those referred to along the way, are framed with a distinction between specific actions to be taken and matters to be left to evolve in an environment of political competition. The look ahead is from twenty-five to fifty years.

Acknowledgments

☆
☆

The Alfred P. Sloan Foundation provided the initiative and the bulk of the funding for this look at how Americans choose their presidents. At a late stage, discretionary funds put at my disposal some years before by the Rowland Foundation, on the generous initiative of Edwin H. Land, proved of great value. The Sloan Foundation asked only that the work focus on the possibilities of improving the process of presidential selection. Albert Rees, president of the Foundation when the work began, and his associates, gave me free rein over the character of the inquiry and my choice of colleagues. The Foundation was more than patient as the time required stretched beyond first estimates.

At an early stage, two dozen papers were commissioned addressing topics carefully defined to aid the work. Several were used later by their authors in books or articles. Twelve others were brought up to date and published together in 1987 by the Duke University Press in a volume edited by Michael Nelson and me under the title *Presidential Selection.* That book includes an essay by Allan P. Sindler on presidential disability and the replacement of an election winner in special situations, including the period between the election and the inauguration. The subject is not treated in the chapters that follow here. Nor is the means of selecting vice presidential nominees, a subject Mr. Nelson has written about in *A Heartbeat Away,* a report of the Twentieth Century Fund Task Force on the Vice Presidency, and also in the fall, 1988, issue of *PS: Political Science and Politics.*

The commissioned papers helped in significant ways and I am much obliged to their authors: John H. Aldrich, Herbert E. Alexander, Christopher Arterton, Herbert R. Asher, James David Barber, James R. Beniger and Robert J. Giuffra, Jr., McGeorge Bundy, Harlan Cleveland, William Crotty, Ralf Dahrendorf, Xandra Kayden, John H. Kessel, Theodore J. Lowi, Ernest R. May, Michael Nelson, Gary R. Orren, Thomas E. Patterson, Richard Matthew Pious and Susan Delancey Weil, Richard Rose, Allan P. Sindler, Soedjatmoko, and Robert C. Tucker.

Early in my inquiries the advice and reactions of some fifty politicians and students of politics were sought in four meetings held successively in

Washington, Nashville, San Francisco, and New York. In August 1982 twenty-four persons came together at Montauk Point, Long Island, for five days of presentations and discussions that were timely and useful in developing further guides for the work. Arthur L. Singer, Jr., vice-president of the Sloan Foundation, gave valuable aid at several stages, especially in organizing those meetings, and Stephen White of the Foundation staff helped in the initial activities. I am grateful to them and to Joel L. Fleishman and the late Kingman Brewster who were early advisers to the Sloan Foundation.

In recent years I have been privileged to participate in several deliberations related to presidential selection. Among these were stimulating sessions of the Columbia University Seminars on Media and Society, under the leadership of Fred W. Friendly, and of the Committee on the Constitutional System, chaired by Lloyd N. Cutler, C. Douglas Dillon, and Senator Nancy L. Kassebaum. Along the way, I interviewed a number of persons, including two former presidents of the United States, to all of whom I feel much indebted. Herbert E. Alexander and Erwin C. Hargrove read the manuscript at a late stage and gave much appreciated help.

The work was conducted under the aegis of the Vanderbilt Institute for Public Policy Studies. Professor Hargrove and Clifford S. Russell, successive Directors of the Institute, were generously hospitable and helpful. The experienced aid and counsel of Lottie M. Strupp, Assistant Director for Administration of the Institute, were important at all times. I am indebted for support of several kinds to the president of the Vanderbilt Board of Trust, David K. Wilson, to Vanderbilt's other trustees, to Chancellor Joe B. Wyatt, to Provost Charles A. Kiesler, to Dean Jacque Voegeli, and to other officers of the university.

Nanette B. Fancher worked as administrative assistant and in other capacities during much of the research and writing. Her participation was invaluable. Thomas A. Underwood was research assistant and contributed importantly to the work over two years. Wanda Uselton and Susan Gotwald served as administrative assistants at different times, as did Betty D. Slayden and Susanne N. LaFever for shorter periods. Tamara Hilbert did the final typing and in many other important ways saw us to the end. I am grateful to them all.

As the writing of the book evolved, my senior colleagues, Scarlett G. Graham and Kay L. Hancock, became decisively important contributors to the concept of the work, to the research in which it is grounded, and to its writing. The book is theirs, too. To them should go a majority of the credit for any merit it may have.

All faults are mine.

Alexander Heard
Vanderbilt University

CHAPTER ONE

What's the Problem?

☆
☆

Early in 1988, the year that saw George Bush elected president, *Time* magazine lampooned presidential nominating procedures in a cover story and, in an article with the title, "Oh, What a Screwy System," deplored the factions and interest groups that manipulate the rules, complained that aspirants to the presidency are subjected to a demeaning marathon, observed that the struggle divides rather than unifies each party, that, deplorably, talented leaders won't run, that the press has an unhealthy influence over all of this. The article quoted Congressman Morris K. Udall's belief that the United States has "one of the most unfortunate systems imaginable for electing the leader of the most powerful nation on earth."[1]

Later that year, the general election itself was called a "handlers' handicap" and a technical exercise devoid of content, an extravaganza that merely named the occupant of a rhetorical presidency.[2] The election embodied the latest style of public campaigning for the office and reflected the greatest decline since the arrival of television in the use and influence of developed argument.[3] Multi-second news "bites" dramatized a shift from party democracy to media democracy, a shift that is the most remarked contemporary characteristic of the way Americans choose their president. News coverage "drives the system now," proclaimed Lee Atwater, Chairman of the Republican National Committee in 1990.[4]

But the practices of 1988 did not signal the only recent evolution in the tortuous avenue to the White House. During the previous twenty years the means of choosing candidates had been altered in greater detail, in a shorter span of time, and with more visible effects than ever before. And after two decades of changes there remained widespread and sustained disagreement over the virtues and vices of the American way of nominating and electing presidential candidates.

In a mood notably different from that of *Time's* story, a *New York Times* lead editorial on the eve of the 1988 Iowa caucuses concluded that

it was time to recognize that the campaign, while painfully long, expensive and relentless, has nonetheless had a beneficial effect for the process as well as the candidates. It has made them learn the concerns that animate real people, in local places. . . . Whoever wins tonight, or in New Hampshire or in November, even the losers will have won something of value, for by learning better how to get their messages across, they will one day be better cabinet officers, legislators—or Presidential candidates.[5]

Nonetheless, for half a century the Gallup poll had been reporting that the public was "in favor of major changes in the electoral process." In 1984, two-thirds of the persons surveyed would have done away with the national conventions and chosen presidential candidates in a nationwide primary.[6] Yet *Newsweek* columnist George Will, fully possessed of critical powers, in giving "Two Cheers for Iowa" in 1988, declared that

the presidency is a political job and should generally be reserved for those who have made politics their vocation. If you are reluctant to run, you probably should not; if you lack fierce desire, you probably will not have the political energy to govern effectively. So the presidency is reserved for a small subset of professional politicians—those with presidential ambition.[7]

REFORM AND FRUSTRATION

A long series of first-ballot nominations in both parties had begun in 1956. Campaigning by presidential candidates separate from their party organizations had also developed noticeably in the 1960s. So did the independent soliciting and spending of money for presidential candidates. Television rose dramatically in importance, again especially from 1960 onward, as did campaign expenditures, making many earlier political practices obsolete.

The substance of issues was changing, as were the types and numbers of interest groups. And all this occurred as many traditional societal conformities of the 1950s, shared values and visions, were giving way to irreverent challenges. The general stability in the culture of presidential nominations and elections that had lasted for more than half a century was shaken. The 1968 Democratic national convention in Chicago, surrounded by controversy and violence, provided the drama and catalyst for a subsequent revolution in the way major political parties nominate their candidates and for important changes in some aspects of the general election.

Following 1968, Democratic party rules were amended to assign mandatory quotas in choosing national-convention delegates. This was meant to guarantee levels of participation by women, blacks, and the young. In the Democratic Convention of 1972, the percentages of blacks and women went up about three times over 1968 and the percentage of young delegates (those under 30) even more. High black and female participation continued thereafter.[8] Widespread use of primaries for choosing national convention delegates grew in both parties, and the caucuses in which others were chosen became open to more general participation. In 1968, 34 percent of Republican delegates and 38 percent of Democratic delegates were chosen in primaries. By 1980, those percentages were 74 and 75, respectively.[9] In 1988, even with its cadre of *ex officio* "super delegates," the Democratic proportion was still nearly two-thirds; the Republican proportion was over three-fourths.[10]

Inescapably, nomination campaigns became longer and more costly. In 1976, partial public funding of presidential nomination and general election campaigns was introduced. The maximum subsidy for which an aspirant could qualify in 1988 in pursuit of a nomination had risen to $11.5 million, and during the general election to $46.1 million. The new era saw growing dependence of campaigners on ever more sophisticated public opinion polling, on increasing professionalism in campaign fund solicitations, on computerized mass mailings, and on new political specialists spawned by new technologies. Among these were experts in the ever-growing complexity and potential of "communications." The "boss" of earlier decades was dead. But the many changes in law and practice did little to reduce the cacophony of discontent.

In the Democratic party, after each presidential election from 1968 leading up to 1988, successive rules commissions were created to revise nominating procedures. During the two decades, the changes had many unanticipated effects. A fatalism developed. Experienced Republican analyst John Sears said, in 1988, "After every election we all stomp the ground and say how terrible it is. And by the time we do it again, we've made it worse."[11]

Over the years discontent with government itself had also grown. There is, after all, no guarantee that democracy can survive in the United States. In the middle of the crisis decade of the 1970s, 58 percent of persons polled were found "alienated and disenchanted by the government" and public confidence expressed in the presidency itself had dropped to 23 percent.[12]

In 1983, Seymour Martin Lipset and William Schneider examined a broad range of public opinion polls from the previous two decades and explored the increasing disenchantment of Americans.[13] While Americans still believed their institutions of government were superior to alternative institutions, those authors speculated that sustained dissatisfaction with governmental effectiveness might eventually erode the foundations of institutional support as well. They attributed the public disaffection to real events preceded by political developments that increased public reactions. They argued that political interest was stimulated by the 1960 election and the subsequent Kennedy administration. The 1964 election polarized the nation along rather clear ideological lines. Within the resulting political context—which came to include a newly distrustful, invasive journalism—specific events, notably the unpopular war in Vietnam, an economy seemingly out of control, the Watergate scandals, and continued economic difficulties throughout the 1970s, contributed to public disaffection not only with the performance of government, but with the performance of other major social institutions as well. Regard for the performance, for example, of business and organized labor plummeted along with that for government. People continued to appreciate the important roles those institutions played in society, but the institutions' actions were often seen as detrimental to the public good.

Lipset and Schneider concluded that while Americans were aware of the limitations governments face in trying to master public problems, nonetheless in those years they viewed the performance of their government as unacceptably imperfect. At the same time, even in that period of dissatisfaction, and despite a long tradition of ambivalence toward leadership, Americans also had an ultimate faith in leadership—faith that with the right kind of leadership things could be made better.[14] Getting such right leadership can depend on how the leadership is chosen.

THE PERMANENCE OF CHANGE

Later in this chapter, three assumptions are set forth that underlie the proposals to be made for improving how presidents are nominated and elected. Also proposed are five functions that the process should encourage. The book's later recommendations are offered as a means of achieving these. But first, it has become commonplace to observe that the qualities called upon for gaining nomination, and then election, and subsequently to lead in governing, are not all the same. The subject has a complex and dynamic past.

The freshet of changes since 1968 in federal and state statutes regulating presidential selection, and in party rules and campaign behavior, has been both accompanied and stimulated by a torrent of proposals and analyses. No single component of American government has received greater recent attention than the presidency, and especially the means of filling it. But such attention is not new; it is a response to new conditions, not a creator of them. It continued those "incremental developments through time" that constitutional historian Gordon S. Wood sees as the origin of American institutions, society, and culture.[15]

Starting in 1804, ten of the last fifteen amendments to the Constitution have affected how the United States chooses its presidents. Statutes and political party rules, as well as unregulated electoral practices, have also changed with evolving values, technologies, economic structures, governmental functions, social aspirations, and other fundamental national circumstances.

The nation's founders required much time in the summer of 1787 to agree on a presidential selection process, but they nonetheless addressed it as an adjunct matter. Their attention to it was overshadowed by their concern for the presidency as an institution. In contrast, throughout the country's subsequent history the practices used in choosing presidents have been deemed of high national and partisan political significance. The ramifications go beyond objective assessment of the mechanical means of filling the presidential chair. They reach to *conflicts among personal values and political interests.* These conflicts are major sources of changes in regulations and practices, and they lie at the root of much contemporary complaint. The significance of how presidents are chosen has been considerable because of its perceived importance to the larger contests of American politics.

The practices that have been evolving across two centuries have emerged from philosophical tenets applied in contemporary political conflict. In illuminating the intellectual assumptions out of which the Constitution came, Professor Wood shows sharply that "What men believed ... was what counted,"[16] and what they believed emerged not solely from their apprehension of eighteenth century philosophy and history but also from the immediate problems they needed to solve or ameliorate.

> Since it was the constant and universal principles applicable to solving immediate problems that they were really after, there was always the danger in the delicate balance between historical experience and self-evident truth that the rational needs of the present would overpower the veracity of the past.[17]

In the evolution of American political institutions, philosophical doctrine would ever be influenced by political issues and the conflict surrounding them, and political issues and conflict would ever be shaped by empirical circumstances.

A remarkable quality of the American Constitution and the government it set in motion has been adaptability. The nation's population has multiplied more than fifty times, its geographic expanse has been enormously extended. There have been radical transformations in the economic, racial, social, educational, military, and other characteristics of the nation, including changes in its multiple media of communications, in the characteristics of its competing political interests, and in its relations with other governments and peoples. There have been recent upward surges in random and organized crime, an enormous increase in drug cultures, and increasing evidence of differences in taste, values, and behavior among age and social groups. Yet the government's capacities have kept itself and the nation going with basic liberties not only preserved but extended.

The record offers hope, though not certainty, that the political system can continue viable. The prudent will remember that unceasing evolution has continuously transformed American society in ways that bear on its capacities for self-government. Especially in recent decades has there been an inexorable movement to a multiethnic population, one that in the next century will have a white minority and more diverse cultural memories than Magna Carta, Plymouth Rock, Lexington, and Davy Crockett. The future, as did the past, will test the embracing adaptability of the American system and its capacity to generate hope, rewards, and loyalty among the heterogeneous masses living within it.

The evolution in the presidency itself since the Great Depression and World War II has been striking. Since Franklin Roosevelt's first election, the presidency has become a radically more vivid and consequential source of national leadership. Its occupant now exerts routinely—not just intermittently in moments of crisis—independent initiative, and sometimes decisive leadership, in policy formation and government action. "The White House" has become a huge executive bureaucracy.[18]

The pace of future change will accelerate. There is no plausible way to predict beyond the immediate future the successive shifting characteristics of communications, culture, and values—with their effects on personal behavior and political capacities—in which American democratic institutions will need to function. For example, many of the changes in technology, ways of living, and community standards projected by futurists like John Naisbitt would, if realized, produce expectations and frustrations, leading, in Naisbitt's projection, to an "ethic of participation" that would replace representative democracy and the party system with procedures for participatory democracy.[19] One need not accept such a radical vision of the future to acknowledge the certainty of change, and to recognize that the need will remain constant for American democratic institutions and habits to adapt to an ever evolving context.

Adaptations in the means of presidential selection quickly became a well-established practice. A flaw in the original scheme as well as major changes in the American condition have from the outset stimulated formal and informal modifications. A written constitution was a distinctive American contribution to self-government.[20] Its provisions for choosing a president, however, were found faulty and were altered as early as 1804. The Constitution provided that each member of the electoral college would vote for two persons for president, with the person receiving the largest number, provided it constituted a majority, becoming president. The runner-up, provided his votes constituted a majority, would become vice-president. In 1800 Thomas Jefferson and Aaron Burr, political antagonists, received the same number of electoral votes for president. As provided by the Constitution, the contest was then thrown into the House of Representatives, where each state delegation cast one vote. Only after 36 ballots was Jefferson chosen.

The potential for a tie vote, and alternatively for manipulation, was considerable. It was anomalous that a president's chief rival would become the vice president and hence the possible successor. As the linking of political interests developed into political factions with some continuity and cohesion, the arrangement was clearly unsatisfactory. The Twelfth Amendment to the Constitution, adopted in 1804, provides for the separate election of the president and vice president in the electoral college, thus making factional and later party slates inevitable.

The Fourteenth Amendment invalidates the three-fifths compromise of Article I and apportions United States representatives among the states on the basis of total population, including all former slaves, thereby altering representation in the electoral college. The Fifteenth Amendment declares that the right to vote shall not be denied on account of race, color, or previous enslavement. Women's suffrage is guaranteed by the Nineteenth Amendment.

The Twentieth Amendment changes the ending date of presidential terms from March 4 to January 20, deals with the terms of other elected federal officials, and prescribes for presidential succession under special circumstances. The Twenty-second Amendment declares that no person may be elected president more than twice, or under a certain condition more than once. The Twenty-third Amendment gives the District of Columbia the right to participate in presidential elections. The Twenty-fourth says no person may be prevented from voting for president or vice-president in any primary or other election for failure to pay a tax. The Twenty-fifth Amendment treats extensively and importantly presidential disability and succession, and the Twenty-sixth protects persons who are eighteen years of age or older from being denied the right to vote because of age. These ten amendments, along with constitutional interpretations by the courts, have altered in drastic ways the selection of presidents.

Congressional enactments have also addressed presidential selection. Procedures for selection of a president when the choice fell to the House of Representatives were adopted in 1825. An important statute was adopted in 1887, as a belated aftermath of the controversial Hayes-Tilden election contest of 1876, regulating the counting of electoral votes in the Congress. Congress has also enacted three presidential succession laws—in 1792, 1886, and 1947—prescribing how the office should be filled in the absence of both an elected president and vice president.

State governmental regulation, too, has significantly shaped presidential and vice presidential selection, as has action by political parties at both state and national levels. Especially conspicuous has been the enactment of diverse state presidential primary laws, beginning in Florida in 1901. Their use expanded and contracted twice in irregular patterns during the subsequent decades. The composition and conduct of national nominating conventions and their decisiveness in choosing candidates have seen much change, too. And campaigning has altered with technology, especially changes in transportation, paper manufacture, radio and television broadcasting, opinion polling, and the ability, in making decisions, to manipulate politically relevant data. The cost of campaigning per voter in constant dollars was long generally stable, but rose sharply after the 1950s. Sources of money and the channels through which it flows have changed as the outreach of government has touched more and more segments of society and as legal regulations have been modified.

All of this means that the way Americans choose their presidents has been constantly remade, sometimes intentionally, sometimes spontaneously in reaction to a changing society.

CONFLICTING GOALS

Kenneth S. Davis, biographer of Franklin Roosevelt, wrote that

> obviously the basic causal force operating in Western and thence world, history, from the early 17th century until today, has been the accelerating advance of science and technology and its increasingly strong impact on social, cultural, economic, and political institutions and on the lives of individual men and women.[21]

Continuing evolution in science and technology and in the intellectual and societal forces they produce has molded the American nation and precipitated its multiple competing interests and advocacies. The presidency and the successive modes of filling it across two centuries have been intimately and continuously affected by this cultural evolution, and their shape and viability will continue to be its children.

What the United States needs from its way of choosing presidents and what its citizens in all their variety desire of it animate the complex issues. Clearly, able leaders—by whatever broad and partial definition—must be selected, but beyond that necessity little else about the process is so self-evident as to be universally accepted. As we have seen, the more numerous opportunities for public participation in presidential selection that have developed most recently were accompanied, ironically, by increasing expressions of dissatisfaction with presidential performance. The process of presidential selection itself has become longer, more open, better reported, more expensive, and a larger presence in the nation's political life. And it has stimulated recurring waves of criticism.

Proposals aimed at virtually every aspect of presidential selection have been offered in recent years to remedy its extensive array of perceived defects.[22] Campaign finance, the mass media, and political parties have especially been drubbed as central sources of difficulty. When the many proposed remedies are grouped according to their potential effects on the process, however, they are often found to lead in different directions. They are frequently directed at different goals, in pursuit of different values, and consequently lack conceptual consistency and often operational compatibility.

Some advocates, for example, propose that the vote be further nationalized by abolishing the electoral college or by requiring a single national nominating primary for each party. Yet others argue for retaining federal principles by continuing the electoral college or by strengthening political parties at local and state levels. Some proposals seek more direct voter participation in nominations by increasing the use of presidential primaries. They are countered by strong advocates of greater autonomy for convention delegates in deciding whom to support. Some proposals seek to strengthen political parties; others would weaken them further. Advocates of orienting presidential campaigns more strongly around programmatic issues are opposed by others who favor campaigning to encourage broad consensus formation. Along with proponents of a strong traditional two-party system are now found persons who see merit in multiparty politics.

The lines along which opinions divide generally reflect piecemeal concerns rather than coherent, integrated objectives. The appropriate orienting question should be not "What's wrong with the process?" but rather "What do we want it to accomplish?"

The underlying goal is enhancement of the nation's capacity for effective, durable popular government. That large, complex standard, platitudinous though it may be, provides the beginning point. Such a perspective oriented the founders in designing the institutions they created through the Constitution. Their consideration of individual institutions and the best form each could take was informed by their understanding of the contribution each would make to the totality of political arrangements. And their application of principles was tempered by their awareness of experience and current circumstances. That continues to be the best approach.

There is no sure, widely accepted road to improving presidential selection. In fact, one discovers that often citizens who are influential on federal policy matters have not thought seriously about issues of presidential selection. They focus on presidents as they find them. But that is not true of all. A prominent bipartisan Commission on National Elections reported in 1986 that when it began its work "most of its members were convinced—as is much of the general public—that there are major flaws in the system for nominating and electing the president and vice president of the United States." Yet, when the Commission got into its work, "a somewhat different picture emerged" and it concluded that the "presidential electoral process has, by and large, served the nation well."[23]

Improvement in presidential selection will require measures that are compatible with the political and governmental system already in place, that comport with the values and characteristics of the larger society, and that attract necessary popular support. Even changes that meet these conditions, however, run the risk of producing unanticipated and unwanted consequences. Many current appeals for reform, in fact, are directed at features of the process attributed to past reforms. Any change runs the risk of creating further dissatisfaction, but failure to change can itself be risky. Social architects depressed by the lack of predictability of human reactions may take comfort from Flora Lewis' words that *all* reality—including those envied physical sciences—"is pluralistic, shifting, often contradictory. Order is always decomposing and building up again in other ways."[24]

Excellent, detailed studies of proposed changes in small and large phases of presidential selection have been made. With their aid, it is possible to comprehend presidential selection as one element in the sweeping complex of political arrangements. Analysis of the proposals can provide a basis for determining the most promising avenues to desired goals. The challenge is to view the system as a whole and to comprehend the full direct and indirect results of altering individual components of it. The scale of change is less important than the breadth of perspective from which potential change is assessed.

DISCONTENT AND STABILITY

Some proposals for change are stimulated by the conviction that important inadequacies in America's governance have resulted from deficiencies in presidential leadership. But other proposals locate the deficiencies within the basic design of American government, and a word about those deficiencies and the proffered remedies needs to be said first.

The most dramatic broad proposal has waxed and waned for more than a century: it would remodel American government along the lines of the British parliamentary system. Advocates of an Americanized parliamentary system see the way the American national government's powers are divided among separately structured "branches" to be a source of debilitating deadlock and incoherent policies, and therefore a barrier to governmental effectiveness. The present dispersion of authority among the branches of government—each with its own legitimacy—is said to diminish accountability, and thereby popular control, because voters have trouble assigning credit or blame for what happens. The president can blame Congress, members of Congress can blame the president (or each other), and both can blame the bureaucracy, and sometimes the Supreme Court.

Political parties in parliamentary governments subscribe to more coherent, consistent policies—though successive governments may not—and have greater means of enforcing loyalty to them. They are thus different from the loose constituency parties of the United States. The separate elections of the American president and members of Congress, and the weak party ties throughout the government, all reflect not only structural, institutional differences, but also pronounced disparities in expectations, habits, and political loyalties.

Less sweeping reforms have been proposed, such as giving congressional functions to cabinet members, giving cabinet positions to certain congressional leaders, permitting Congress to call special presidential elections under certain conditions, and correspondingly permitting the president to call a special national election under prescribed conditions. Such proposals aim to reduce the separation between the president and Congress and the likelihood of conflict between the two.

Suggestions are made to alter in other ways the relationship between the president and Congress, usually to enhance presidential power. These include reducing the vote required for treaty ratification from two-thirds of the Senate to a lesser majority; giving the president power to veto individual items in a bill passed by Congress; requiring an extraordinary congressional majority to make increases in the budget proposed by the president; and establishing binding schedules for important congressional roll calls so that major legislation will not be delayed or lost in committee.

Other proposals would draw on the experience of nations that have separate heads of state and government. They would seek to increase presidential capacity by establishing a plural executive to divide present presidential burdens.

Conspicuous during the 1980s was the work of the Committee on the Constitutional System. Spurred by the initiative of Professor Charles M. Hardin,[25] this ad hoc group became active in 1981 and was still in existence as the 1990s began. Some 200 persons have been associated with the Committee, mostly prominent citizens, including many with important experience in the federal government. The Committee has enjoyed the influential bipartisan leadership of Lloyd N. Cutler, former Counsel to President Carter; Douglas Dillon, former Secretary of the Treasury who served in high posts under presidents of both parties; and Republican Senator Nancy Landon Kassebaum of Kansas.

A major Committee focus has been the perception that the executive and legislative branches of the federal government no longer function together in as decisive and timely a fashion as they did in some earlier times when addressing consequential national issues. The budget deficit is prominently mentioned, but over forty unratified treaties since World War II are also cited. The length and cost of presidential campaigns and low voter participation are also deplored by the Committee.[26] In contrast, some participants have noted with envy the perceived traditional ability of victorious British parties to "form a government" that can force adoption of party policies recommended by leadership for addressing such issues—or be held to account for not doing so. The work on this book did not lead to prescriptions as broad as some preferred by some of the Committee's members. But our concern here is more encompassing than that of many journalists, political scientists, and practitioners who have made recommendations for improving the presidential selection process.

Every nation faces a burdensome world regardless of its form of government. It is an uneven world but, in the large, one of increasingly intricate, interlocking technologies; of mounting, mobile populations; of soaring resource consumption; of expanding ambitions for preserving cultural identity and enhancing political self-determination; and it is a world, more so than formerly, of finely differentiated private and public processes through which economic, political, and other relations are conducted.

Despite this environment of dynamic national and international stresses, perhaps in part because of it, most Americans are reluctant to experiment with their basic constitutional structure. There is no widely shared conviction about how to improve it. That is so whether the focus is on "procedural democracy," the manner of conducting the government, or "substantive democracy," the content of public policies. Unlike the founders, present

Americans have no relatively clean slate on which to design a government. Rather, they have two hundred years of experience with generally effective popular government to build upon and a tradition of fits and starts, of ad hoc adaptation that, so far, has proved adequate. And, normally, competitors for political advantage oppose changes they think might reduce their influence, favoring the known present over the uncertain future.[27] In 1987, Columbia University's American Assembly brought together some four dozen diverse and accomplished citizens to address the adequacy of the U.S. Constitution today. They concluded that "the failures of government to meet societal problems are political rather than structural in nature."[28]

We do not recommend in this book radical changes in the fundamental institutional structure of American government, but we do recommend realistic proposals for less basic modification, including some that would require constitutional amendment.

FUNCTIONS OF PRESIDENTIAL SELECTION

Where in this context do the means used to nominate and elect presidents fit, and how important are they? The federal government is more than the presidency—and there is more to the presidency than how the office is filled. With this understood, the framework of this book follows the five functions of presidential selection outlined below that are deemed fundamental to the success of American government. How aspirants seek and achieve office contributes to those functions. Whether and how they could do so better provides the book's substance.

These matters are all addressed in the light of three prior conclusions. First, the way presidents are chosen is important. The means of presidential selection are not a substitute for ultimately addressing adequately the nation's problems, but they are fundamental, essential steps toward doing so. And it is necessary for the stability and continuity of government—qualities needed for successful democracy—that the means of presidential selection enjoy enough confidence for a national consensus to accept the election results. Through the filtering and testing they provide, selection processes influence the personal capacities and political resources a president will bring to this extraordinary job. The preparedness of a president to perform constitutional duties and other obligations of leadership depend on many qualities that are tested (and can be enhanced) on the way to the White House. The process can enlarge the candidate's personal competencies, political alliances, influence, sensitivity to disparate interests, knowledge of the far-flung nation, sense of public tolerances, sustained personal incentives, capacity to inform and educate the electorate, and ability to engender public confidence in the candidate's purposes and achievements. The mode of presidential selection thus affects the resources a president takes into office, including the public's acceptance of its chief executive.

Our second prior conclusion grows from a sober contemplation of American political experience. Throughout American history, the official responsibilities, broad social functions, and operating conditions of the presidency have changed, and consequently so have the skills, experiences, knowledge, and perspectives valuable or necessary for a president, and a candidate, to possess.[29] Dramatic alterations in the presidency came after 1932 and have been evident again since the 1960s. But it is neither realistic nor desirable to contemplate a fundamental reorganization of American government and, by implication, American society.

Presidents fit for their times will not be guaranteed by deliberate, prompt adjustment of electoral procedures and political habits when new circumstances appear. When the need is pressing enough, however, consensus may form for changes in the rules, and candidates with qualities appropriate to their times, as judged by the voters, will inevitably push forward.

Neither abolition of the federal form of government nor a radical restructuring of the division and sharing of powers within the present federal level will occur in the future that we contemplate here. We have chosen as our perspective to look ahead a quarter to a half century. Public acceptance and political feasibility within that span are considerations in framing proposals. The fundamentals of the federal system with its three somewhat coordinate branches must be taken as a given. There will be no cabinet government in the United States on a British model in the reasonably near future. Short of a cataclysmic social upheaval—albeit always a possibility—neither will there be other radical, structural revisions in American government.

Third, ultimately everything is connected to everything else, hence boundaries are needed to keep the analysis manageable. If the existing governmental institutions of the United States are fundamentally unsound, even extensive changes in presidential selection are unlikely to enhance significantly the nation's capacity for effective, popularly controlled government. The process for choosing presidents can be evaluated realistically only in the context of a reasonably fixed institutional structure. The presidential selection process is derivative. A different design of governance for the United States would imply a different selection process, one that would need evaluation by standards appropriate to the specific design.

Our subject is the nomination and election of presidents near the end of the twentieth century. We propose to assay and judge those processes by the contributions they make to five functions of presidential selection we hold to be essential to the success of democratic government in the United States. The scorecard is not easy to keep. The ways presidential selection contributes to the fulfillment of those functions, however, constitute the themes of the analysis, the basis for judging the adequacy of the process, and the rationale for the recommendations made. The five functions, outlined below, stem partly from general characteristics of popular government and partly from the unique governmental structure of the United States.

First, presidential selection should facilitate *a fluid exchange of information* between the governed and those who would govern, providing candidates with the fullest possible understanding of deep public sentiments—not merely fleeting and superficial opinion—and providing the public with the fullest possible understanding of the candidates and the issues they engage.

Information is the lifeblood of democracy. Leaders require it for effectiveness; citizens require it for popular control. If the volume and variety of information exchanged seem to have an atomizing effect on popular consensus and a confusing effect on public officials, that is a reflection of the society, not a fault of communication. Citizens must have sufficient information to assess governmental performance maturely. Without appropriate information, leaders could not long be governed by that "deliberate sense of the community" that Alexander Hamilton declared necessary for fulfillment of the republican principle.[30] The relatively free exchange of information in democratic societies increases their capacity in the long run for effective, responsive action over that of societies in which information is reluctantly exchanged.

Information, to be useful, must be communicated in patterns understandable to those receiving it. The practices of presidential selection affect not only the volume of information exchanged. They also structure it into useful forms, or fail to do so. Nearly a quarter of a billion Americans cannot speak to their national government singly and simultaneously, let alone send much in the way of usable messages about governance. The processes of presidential selection are important determinants of the patterns in which information is communicated. These processes should not only facilitate the transmission of political information, but should help structure it in ways that contribute to effective government.

Second, a vigorous, robust democratic politics is engendered by *citizen participation,* especially when citizens who participate and the information they communicate are broadly representative of the nation and its complexity. Americans deal directly with the institutions of government in record numbers. They write letters, make phone calls, sign petitions, and otherwise lobby for their interests, but such day-to-day self-centered political activity is not necessarily representative of the nation. The presidential selection process should help provide a broadly representative public context for the many individual decisions of government. Only during presidential elections do Americans as a nation speak to their government. Congressional elections every two years engage the entire nation, but in a presidential election the attention of the whole nation is focused on a limited set of national choices as it is at no other time.

Third, the public attention that is focused on government during the selection of a president significantly influences the *setting of the public agenda.* The process ought to help delineate and clarify the important issues facing the nation. It also affords an opportunity for citizens to learn about their government, its possibilities and its limitations. The process ought to contribute to public understanding of the nature of government itself. It should also heighten public understanding of national and international questions and the context in which they arise.

To identify and help create a sense of direction for public policies is an important function of presidential selection. Whatever the deficiencies of 1988, that year's election contributed to that goal. A full program for governance and the details of future decisions cannot be established during the contest for the presidency, but a general attitude toward government and a sense of relative priorities can be encouraged. The process ought ideally to produce an articulation of issues and development of alternatives in public policies sufficient for responsive government, while still leaving enough room for the discretion needed to innovate, negotiate, and adapt.

Although many decisions of government do not directly affect large segments of the public, the unprecedented budget deficits of recent years remind the public of its stake in the cumulative effect of discrete decisions. The "deliberate sense of the community" should lurk near all decisions. The American government must have the capacity to reconcile the nation's many particular interests with the broad general interest. The presidential selection process can contribute to this goal through its part in shaping the public agenda.

Fourth, all democratic nations need *leadership* in public office, individuals who are qualified to govern. To provide such was the main objective of the system developed by the nation's founders. It continues to be the central purpose of the selection process today. The process should bring forth able candidates and provide the public with the information—incomplete though it will always be—and the opportunity to choose well among them.

Finally, the ways of presidential selection should tie the presidency to the rest of government in a manner beneficial for *governance*. The separation of powers ensures that the branches of the federal government will in certain crucial ways be independent of each other. Yet they must also be capable of cooperation. Presidential selection activities should contribute to the capacity for that cooperation. A well-ordered selection process cannot guarantee that effective governance will result. But it can provide valuable resources necessary for effective, popularly controlled government.

The periodic contest for the presidency, with the recurring demonstration of its authenticity, provides—despite all the criticisms of it—an essential element of confidence and continuity in the United States' system of democracy. Neither presidents nor how they are chosen can, however, guarantee the nation's future. Critics sometimes forget that governmental probity and effectiveness, including the quality of presidential leadership, are the products of complex societal and institutional influences. How presidents get to office is only one influence among many.

The nature of the presidency and of the larger political system affects the performance of the occupants of the White House. So do the circumstances of the times. If the presidency itself were fatally flawed by restrictions imposed by the Constitution, or by statutes, or by the constraints of public mood or the excesses of public expectations, how its occupants are chosen would be of secondary importance.[31] If the national government as a whole were so impotent or America's cultural fabric so disintegrated that the nation could not function with necessary unity and effectiveness, how presidents are chosen would again be of secondary importance. What has been called the "environmental and contextual basis for continuation of the American regime" is fundamental to the survival of the formal government.[32]

Thus, to look to changes in the means of choosing presidents as a panacea for the nation's or the government's ills would be to oversimplify American society. We shall propose measures that should be taken to address potential and active difficulties. It is clearly fallacious, however, to regard the improvement of any single sector of the nation's government, or of any one aspect of its common life, as evidence that the United States can cope with the societal, technological, and ecological conditions of an unpredictable and perilous future. Improvement in the way presidents are chosen can, however, contribute to the possibility of a viable American government.

We turn in the next four chapters to the first of the five functions of presidential selection: assuring a fluid exchange of information, the lifeblood of a successful democracy.

CHAPTER TWO

The Lifeblood of Democracy:
Information

☆
☆

The lifeblood of democracy—its essential nutrient—is information. In the twentieth century the characteristics and transmission of political information have changed swiftly and radically. But, always, to be politically effective, information must be communicated in usable form. How it is best communicated depends on the kind of information it is, on who sends it, for what purpose, and for whom it is intended.

The population of each of the fifty states is simple, discrete, and important information used in reapportioning the House of Representatives every decade. It determines, among other things, the number of votes each state has in the electoral college. But other less precise types of information and their communication are also necessary for political democracy. When Franklin Roosevelt advocated passage of the "lend-lease" program to aid Great Britain, he likened the proposal to lending one's garden hose to a neighbor whose house was on fire. He conveyed his conviction of a national interest, which was important political information for the American Congress and public to receive. Third party presidential candidates can also enrich the political discourse. Norman Thomas, six times the Socialist candidate, advocated old-age pensions, public works projects, and unemployment insurance well before they were accepted by the major parties.[1] In its varied forms, information also travels from constituents to leaders, as politicians scrambling to respond to their mail know well. Simply put, political information is that part of a communication that is relevant to political attitudes and actions.

The importance of information to a free society has long been acknowledged. The First Amendment to the U.S. Constitution proclaims it: "Congress shall make no law . . . abridging the freedom of speech, or of the press; or the right of the people peaceably to assemble, and to petition the Government for a redress of grievances."

The freedoms protected by the First Amendment are more than cherished egalitarian guarantees. They were understood to be the very sources of liberty and its protection. The sophisticated governmental structure established by the preceding seven articles would, it was believed, provide a solid foundation for effective government in a free society, but it was accepted from the outset that robust and reliable communication would be required for an electorate's effective political participation, and thus for its ability to direct the attentions of government to whatever agitated the public. But in 1787 when the Constitution was written, and when the First Amendment was ratified shortly thereafter, no one envisioned the radical changes that would occur over the next two centuries in the form, sources, substance, and transmission of information, changes that would test both the fabric of the Constitution and the civic temper of the people.

Free expressions of opinion were not the only sources of information, however, that would influence elected officials. The founders' arguments advocating short terms for public officials showed their understanding of the communications value of elections. James Madison wrote in the *Federalist Papers* that "the genius of republican liberty seems to demand on one side not only that all power should be derived from the people, but that those intrusted with it should be kept in dependence on the people by a short duration of their appointments."[2] It was especially clear that the House of Representatives, whose members were required to stand for election every two years, was expected to provide a reliable channel of communications from the states and their people to the government. Elections are more than devices for deciding winners. They are arrangements for reciprocal learning by constituents and candidates, by voters and officials. One of the major requirements for their efficacy is the efficient exchange of significant political information. The quality of that exchange would be one measure of the process of choosing presidents.

In this chapter, the root role and changing character of information in American presidential politics are examined. In the following two chapters, the significance of information in presidential nominations, and then in presidential elections, is examined. In Chapter Five, the effect of differing institutional arrangements on the kinds of political information generated and transmitted, and their implications for procedures used to choose presidents, are addressed.

INFORMATION: THE HEART OF CITIZEN TRUST AND OFFICIAL RESPONSIBILITY

In the small Athenian democracy of ancient Greece, members of the popular assembly were chosen by lot. Government was close to the daily lives of the people, and all citizens—which did not include women and slaves—were declared equally qualified to make public decisions. Frequent rotation in office assured widespread citizen participation. The governments of modern states, however, are generically different. Their size and remoteness from their citizens make them highly impersonal compared with the relation of Athenians to their government. In the small and intimate life of Athens, citizen interests were more of one piece, and all were concentrated in the city.[3] More sophisticated devices for keeping citizens and government in touch with each other are required in large, heterogeneous, complex modern nations aspiring to democracy, a democracy in which the concept of majority rule is cherished for its own sake without the requirement that it also be deemed most immediately competent or wisest.[4]

Because the government designed for the young American nation was to be representative, information would be as indispensable to competent governance as it would be to freedom. Representatives would bring information from all areas of the country to serve as the basis for lawmaking. In the present day of wizardly processing of information and of instant communications among all sectors of the country and all parts of the world, it is hard to remember the difficulty in the eighteenth and nineteenth centuries of keeping a national government informed and sensitive to the needs and opinions of citizens in an extensive and inexorably changing republic. When a diverse people delegate authority to representatives distant from their daily lives, elections entail more than choosing a fellow citizen to be a spokesman for shared interests and convictions. Such elections elevate a few individuals to positions of authority over other members of the political community. By implication they establish a relationship of trust and responsibility. Without information exchanged between citizens and their officials, such trust and responsibility would not be possible.

Trust and responsibility are two ends of a single relationship. Given the experience of the American colonists with the representatives of King George's government, however, American governmental institutions were designed to limit the need for citizens to trust the competence and good intentions of individual officeholders. Constitutional limits on authority in any system restrain government behavior, but the American separation of powers, which is also a sharing of powers, was designed to curb the independence of both offices and officeholders. But no institutional arrangements can eliminate fully the importance for government of differences among the abilities and virtues of officials, so trust in officials personally, beyond that granted to institutions, is always a requisite for governmental authority. To achieve it, voters require information that gives them a basis for choosing among candidates.

In a democracy, responsibility is a more complicated relationship between citizens and officials than is trust. Responsibility requires, first, that officials operate within boundaries established by a constitution. Second, it requires that officials make decisions they believe serve the public good. Third, responsibility requires that they consider public sentiments in making decisions. Public good and public sentiments may not always be judged by an official to be the same, but the two seldom diverge completely. As with engendering trust, information is also essential to responsibility.

In a democratic political system, voters, candidates, citizens, and officials alike require information. Inevitably, the changing means of assembling and transmitting information have affected presidential selection, even as changes in procedures for selecting presidents have affected the character of information that is relevant and the means of transmitting it. In evaluating the way American presidents reach office, it is useful to start by considering these reciprocal processes.

CHANGING MESSENGERS

The news media cannot stand outside the culture on which they report. Their news is inevitably "a reality constructed within a particular social/political/economic ecology"[5] and, consciously or not, they accept values and assumptions that normally go unspecified. For political reporting, the limitation seems inescapable, but so also is change, and since the mid-1960s newly important originators of political communications have emerged. A national, nonpartisan press has burgeoned along with moods of challenge among all journalists. In addition, the rapid transformation of broadcasting has so intensified the pressures of public opinion on public officials that even a president's influence—nay, power—has become dependent on hourly attention to media demands, satisfying which, one must conclude, diverts attention from other responsibilities and sources of presidential effectiveness. Hence Robert M. Entman concluded that "democracy has gained little from the rise of media power."[6] Swift, radical change rushes ahead, as anyone knows who hopes to maintain state-of-the-science stereo equipment or ponders the political potential of fiber optics. The bearers of political messages change in many ways along with the interests, issues, and organization of politics.

Personal organizations of candidates now contend with political parties as sources of information. And new configurations of voters, notably political action committees (PACs) and single-issue advocacy groups, bypass traditional party channels to vie for the attention of candidates and inform them of their interests and desires. Ben Wattenberg described the "kaleidoscopic pieces" of the new electoral puzzle:

> Since the mid-1960s, we have had an explosion of participatory democracy—more campaign contributors, more political-action committees, more lobbyists, more media freaks, more special interests, more cash, more clout and more players—from left, right and center. These are the new politics.[7]

One dimension of the new politics was vividly illustrated by a listing of sixty-eight media and polling consulting firms that in 1988 had worked in gubernatorial and senatorial campaigns for 173 clients.[8] All these new pieces, sending and receiving political information via new outlets, including cable channels, make the messages conveyed through the communications system of presidential selection difficult to summarize and interpret. The substance and cues are surely less orderly than before—and, some would argue, less adequate as well.

In this new environment of more numerous and varied sources of information and more sophisticated abilities to process it, both quantity and quality are important characteristics of the information. One does not assure the other. Information may be of poor quality—unreliable, superficial, or too abundant to be comprehended. To be useful, information must go from those who have it to those who need it, and must be in an intelligible form. Moreover, information will not be equally available to all. Citizens who do not watch television or listen to the radio, and who do not read a newspaper or news magazine, will have less exposure to political information than those who do. Acquiring information requires time and energy. Education, experience, and past observation of politics make new political information easier to acquire. The more complex a political message, the less likely will a person who is short on these assets be to grasp it and benefit from it.

The way presidents are chosen affects the quality, quantity, and intelligibility of the political information generated. The question is whether changes in that selection process can be designed to improve the information produced. Political parties once provided the dominant means of electoral communication. Party spokesmen, party proclamations, and party candidates dominated the discussion. Voters and candidates have thus been examined for their relationship to parties. The activities of the strong parties of an earlier era provide the standard by which current information-exchange practices are often measured. We shall examine this standard and then address the information currently produced in presidential selections.

DECLINING PARTISAN INFORMATION

Transmitting political information is central to most descriptions of political party functions. Christopher Arterton writes:

> Political organization for electoral competition is a communications process. ... American parties were established to facilitate this communications process. Geographically constructed along residential patterns, they served as vertical, interpersonal links, passing rewards and requests for support downwards, and demands and information upwards.[9]

While political parties have never been the sole channel for transmitting political information, during much of the nation's history they overshadowed all competitors. They served as the primary messenger in presidential elections. They organized alliances, provided linkage between presidential and congressional elections, and encouraged order in the process of governing between elections.

Parties were normally driven by the overriding goal of winning elections. They gathered information about the needs, wants, likes, and dislikes of their partisans and negotiated compromises to keep the loyalty of a maximum number of voters. The consensus emerging constituted the chief information content of the election. Thus, political parties not only spurred participation, but by their role in doing so gave an implied message to the results.[10]

At the same time, parties were the basis on which voters organized *their* political information. The party label provided a cue, based on each party's past performance. It enabled voters to know which candidate was closer to their own political predispositions. This could be done despite the canopy nature of the parties that brought race-conscious southern planters, riding the Democratic donkey, into alliance with northern urban poor, and that put atop the Republican elephant Connecticut Yankee financiers alongside South Dakota plainsmen. The fortunes of the parties fluctuated, but the effort thought necessary to cast an "informed" vote was small.

To the extent that elections operated this way, they were efficient means of communication. The political parties presented understandable, organized information to voters, candidates, and government. Many observers have held such an electoral system to be ideal for a democratic society, some even suggesting that it is the only workable possibility. Whether or not it ever functioned with the effectiveness claimed, the vision does not fit the realities of presidential selection at the end of the twentieth century. Radical changes have occurred.

In the half century following 1940, not only did issues and actors change. So did American communications. The number of magazines increased nearly fivefold and the number of radio stations increased over tenfold. But, much more important politically, television arrived. In 1945, U.S. homes did not have television sets. In 1952, 34 percent did. By 1976, 97 percent had them.[11] The effect of television on viewers far exceeds that ever felt by the audiences of print media and radio. In fact, television soon became the rival of political parties as the dominant source of political information. Viewers' easy access to news is the most important contributor to television's political influence. Television news is presumptively nonpartisan, moreover, and that further undermines the effectiveness of party labels as organizers of political information.

The growing importance of television as a source of political information prompted Pope McCorkle and Joel Fleishman to observe that

> the emerging consensus among political scholars as well as practitioners from various perspectives is that the political parties do not now serve as significant mediators of political information and that the mass media are increasingly taking over the function of organizing and managing the political arena.[12]

Voters are thus no longer dependent on political parties for political information. The media now largely organize and manage the political discourse. Television gives voters more information about more dimensions of political activity than available before, and in a form easier to understand.[13]

The sources candidates have of information about voters have also been changing. Individual candidate campaign organizations, staffed with social scientists, demographers, communications specialists, pollsters, and many others, compose a second new rival to political parties in organizing for electoral competition. A revolution has occurred in the sources candidates use to learn what citizens are thinking and feeling. Political polls were taken intermittently in the 1950s, mostly to assess a candidate's popularity. Since then, continuous national polling has become the norm, with sophisticated analysis of results. This new central source of political intelligence makes national political managers better informed. They can usually gather more information about citizens' views in particular states, and of the best ways to reach them, than local politicians and advisers can provide. The perception that county campaign leaders have of the views in their community has been found to be no better than one would expect by chance, while polls have been improving significantly the politicians' understanding of citizens' think- ing. In consequence, political influence has moved upward to the national level.[14]

Those changes in party rules for nomination of presidential candidates made following 1968 have removed another source of party domination over the exchange of political information. Primaries have largely taken the control of nominations out of the hands of party professionals and given it to the voters. Christopher Arterton notes that "party functionaries used to sit athwart the processes by which information was exchanged between office seekers and voters, and they used that position to dominate the selection of candidates." Party leaders served as brokers, mediators, consensus and coalition builders. But they have lost that power, and "not so much to changes in election and party laws . . . but to the major social, economic, and technological transformations of the 20th century."[15]

Primaries generate a body of political information qualitatively different from that produced by a general election. Party labels are still helpful to voters in distinguishing between general election candidates, but comparable labels are not available in a primary. The triumph of presidential primaries over party-controlled nominations has turned the flow of political informa- tion upside down. The strategies of aspirants have been transformed, as have the options open to the electorate.[16]

The reduced role of political parties in information exchange may be attributable in part, also, to changes in voters themselves. Levels of education have risen. The percent of persons 25 years old and over who finished four years of high school or more rose from 25 in 1940 to 75 in 1986, and the percent of high school graduates (14 to 24 years old) who were enrolled in college, or had completed one or more years, went from 40 in 1960 to 55 in 1986.[17] A higher percentage of college-educated citizens than of the general public considers itself politically independent. Gallup surveys reported that the percentage of college-trained voters who identified themselves as independents rose from 22 in 1944 to 38 percent in 1973.[18] That probably means that later graduates were more likely to be independent than earlier ones. Even so, higher education seems to bring a higher level of information about issues and greater concern for them, and greater self-confidence in reaching political preferences without the aid of a party cachet.[19]

Although self-proclaimed voter independence from political parties has been growing in recent elections, it is not yet rampant. Party labels are still influential.[20] The question is whether parties can change enough, and quickly enough, to accommodate the evolving variety of political interests that many voters have. The mix of interests dear to individual voters may be too heterogeneous and volatile to make such an accommodation possible. If voter preferences do not fall into patterns that permit coherent and *durable* alliances, consistent identification with a party will continue to weaken.[21] A national poll of persons aged 18 to 44 conducted in September 1987 for *Rolling Stone* found considerable evidence that current party labels are poor reflections of voter attitudes:

> [T]his generation's attitudes are vastly more complicated when it enumerates the goals it wants a president to pursue. The list is a mix of liberal and conservative attitudes that would bewilder candidates who are used to simple delineations.... These various goals are not necessarily incompatible—but they don't fit with the standard left-right postures of the two major parties.[22]

If parties are not able to organize information on which voters want to base their voting decisions, the labels will carry little influence.

The forces working to break party control over the content and flow of information in presidential selection are formidable. They produce a jumbled reality at variance with the concept of parties as dominant in organizing opinion and electing officials. In this new condition, what can elections, in fact, say, or mean, given the characteristics of the political information they now produce?

HOW VOTERS DECIDE

What elections "say" is far from a simple message. Within the unique context of each election, anxiety over individual issues, the personal appeal of candidates, and loyalty to a political party can all affect an outcome. Each such influence will differ in importance from one voter to another and their relative importance not only can vary from one election to another but also can evolve over time.

Conflicting interpretations will be given to the meaning of particular election results and therefore to the information they convey to officials and the public. Studies of voting behavior emphasize that no single interpretation of how voters decide how to vote can explain all the decisions they make. Nonetheless, the information and other influences that affect how they vote, and the information that government officials garner from an election campaign and its results, are interrelated. That the influences affecting voter behavior have been changing especially in recent decades requires emphasis. Correspondingly, the meanings elections register have been evolving. The relative importance of parties, current issues, and candidates has changed.

That American voters look backward to make choices for the future—that is, are influenced by loyalty to party—was long the predominant explanation of voting decisions. They leaned more on assessment of past performance than on future promises as a guide to voting decisions.[23] Political parties are essential to this interpretation of voter decisions. It holds that except perhaps for an incumbent president seeking re-election, voters generally evaluate not the candidates, but their parties.

In this perspective, the importance of individual issues is reduced to a minimum. The broad contours of past performance, rather than detailed issues or ideological options for the future, influence the voter.[24] This interpretation does not imply that holding people in power responsible for what has already happened does not sharpen their incentive for the future.[25] For most of U.S. history, winners of presidential elections have been chosen by voters who mostly looked backward. But this has changed.

Morris Fiorina, writing in a 1981 study entitled *Retrospective Voting*, maintained that "future expectations count and count very heavily among contemporary American voters. In analysis after analysis, reported and unreported, future expectations dwarfed the effects of retrospective judgments, simple and mediated."[26] Writing in 1988 on economics and elections in the major western democracies, Michael S. Lewis-Beck asserted that "prospective economic evaluations have an effect at least as strong as that of retrospective evaluations."[27] When voters are preoccupied with issues and the future, glancing only fleetingly at the past, the kinds of information they invoke in their forward-looking decisions are important.

One future-oriented concept of electoral deciding is found in what has become known as the "responsible party" system, one in which voters need only to choose a party. Akin to a European parliamentary system, such an arrangement has been advocated as an alternative to the inherited American electoral arrangements. To realize the benefits envisioned, however, would require changes in U.S. institutions, notably in the separate election of the president and Congress.

In such a hypothetical arrangement, individual voters would not need to make elaborate issue-position calculations. The burden for doing so would fall on the parties as corporate entities. They would advocate divergent programs and the winner would be expected to put its program into effect. At the next election voters could judge the results—looking backward to that extent—and confirm the party in office or dismiss it from power. As Benjamin

Page puts it, in such a system, "the winning party is not simply the one which more nearly agrees with the policy preferences of a majority of voters; it is the one which can convince a majority of voters to agree with its policies.[28]

Another future-oriented concept of electoral decision making is more applicable to contemporary American politics. It is an "economic" one. Voters shop for candidates or parties much as a consumer shops for an automobile. The aim is to buy with the vote as large a share of the voter's preferred positions on issues as possible. Such a voter analyzes issues, examines the positions of the parties, and votes accordingly. Candidates want as many votes as possible and campaign accordingly. Faced by this condition, political parties consciously point their advocacies where voters are concentrated, usually assumed to be near the middle of the political spectrum.[29]

A third future-directed voting orientation has gained importance in recent decades. It focuses on differences among personal characteristics of the candidates. Manifestly, personal attributes have often been consequential in the past. The campaigns of 1928 and 1948 are good examples. But increased recent attention to the personal qualities of candidates—including their "images" as projected through the media—reduces voter concern for policy information. The perceived meaning of election results is thereby considerably altered. Indeed, the emphasis on personal qualities of candidates has prompted worry that those "images" could become—or have already become—overriding influences in presidential elections. Selection on the basis of personal qualities—such as experience, intelligence, personality, fairness, integrity, style, equanimity, and character—has been thought by some to produce elections with little political content.

That is not true, however, whatever else may be said about it. Under the Constitution, U.S. presidents are vested with great autonomy in discharging their responsibility for leadership of the federal administration, for leadership in foreign policy and intelligence activities, for poise and persuasiveness in sustaining citizen morale and national confidence. The personal qualities of presidents, including instinctive political abilities, honesty, and sensitivities, have great importance for the confidence they generate among the citizenry. Jeffrey Smith has argued that concern about trust "is rational, has political content, is of widespread and frequently great importance in vote choice decisions, and provides the basis for a consistent account of recent elections.[30]

Issues debated and positions taken during a presidential campaign provide no guarantee of how an individual will respond to unanticipated crises the nation will surely encounter over the next four years. Voters consequently have a stake in choosing the candidate whose highly personal attributes they find most worthy of their confidence.

Moreover, amid the multitude of modern complex issues that are ill understood—or sometimes not perceived at all by large numbers of voters—information for comparing the personal characteristics of candidates is probably the most accessible and sometimes the best available. Commentators and voters can examine how candidates conducted themselves in previous situations, including the public offices they have held. Past speeches, current interviews, debates, public actions, and appearances of many kinds that are covered by the media can be examined. That a candidate satisfies the minimum requisites for making a serious run at the presidency will itself be information about a candidate that is useful to voters. In fact, the capacity of aspirants to lead a loose, far-flung, highly politicized, crisis-ridden campaign organization is not irrelevant to the demands of the presidency itself. Nor is the intellectual capacity to deal under pressure and public scrutiny with a wide range of complex, controversial, and occasionally unanticipated topics. The physical stamina and emotional resilience required of a president are also given a run in the search for the office.[31]

No prior test can ever assure completely how a president will respond to the unique pressures of the office. But the road to the office at the end of the twentieth century provides both testing and training.

PARTIES VS. ISSUES VS. CANDIDATES

We have examined three kinds of information that influence voting for president: information bearing on party allegiance, on public issues, and on the personal appeal of candidates. None of these elements by itself adequately explains all decisions voters make. Voters are subject to many influences in casting a single vote, and from one election to the next the grounds on which voters make decisions can shift significantly. The scope and variety of factors that influence voting decisions are complex and consequential; not only do they fluctuate from election to election, but their relative importance evolves over longer periods.

Following World War II, the relative influence on voters of identification with a political party declined. It was the one clear-cut change in the influences on voter decisions that John Kessel found in an analysis of voter concerns and candidate characteristics in the elections from 1952 through 1980. Kessel recognized that attitudes toward parties had "never been as salient as those about candidates and issues. But they . . . declined from even this low plateau."[32]

During this period, the electorate as a whole showed an increasing independence from party. The percentage of citizens not identifying with either political party rose from 5 percent in 1952 to 13 percent in 1980. So did those who classified themselves as independents leaning toward Democrats or Republicans, from 17 percent to 21 percent. And voters classified as strong partisans declined from 35 percent to 27 percent.[33] But the drift away from party seems to have moderated in the 1980s when platform and other differences between the parties seemed to become more substantial. In 1984, both the percentage classified as strong partisans and that classified as partisan leaners edged up a bit while the percentage classified as independents fell. In a 1990 poll, the percentage of respondents not identifying or leaning toward either party fell to 11 percent. The fluctuations, up or down, point to the contemporary volatility of partisan loyalties. Close analysts of the 1980 and 1984 elections concluded that "unless issues strongly impelled them otherwise," voters simply voted against an unpopular incumbent in 1980 and for a popular one in 1984.[34]

If American voters sometimes vote for candidates with whom they agree on issues, but do not find personally appealing, perhaps do not wholly trust, and at other times vote for candidates whom they trust, but may depart from on certain issues, what message can elections communicate? Are elections in the United States merely ways to designate a leader, or do they say more than just who shall lead?

RECIPROCAL LEARNING

Shortly after Ronald Reagan's win in 1984, the late Theodore H. White asked in an article for *Time*: "What did it mean?"[35] The answer to this enduring quadrennial question was, for 1984 as always, infinitely deeper than could be found in the election tallies alone. As White pointed out, "A good part of what we need to know of the larger puzzle . . . is buried not just in the size but in the structure and the texture of Tuesday's vote totals."[36] But even the vote, with its structure and texture thoroughly analyzed, is not the sum of all information produced by an election.

Presidential elections accomplish substantially more. The campaigns that culminate in the actions of voters every fourth year must be weighed in any accounting of what elections accomplish. As Marjorie Randon Hershey puts it, "campaigning for any office is a time of learning."[37] All who are involved in campaigns, or are touched by them, including even nonvoters, become more aware of their political surroundings and have their presuppositions and preferences challenged or reinforced. This is especially true of candidates and their activist supporters. The political agenda is enriched by what campaigners learn about the needs and expectations of people as well as by what they themselves advocate.

If political campaigns can be learning experiences for those who take part, the messages communicated by an election will be more complex than the results registered starkly in the vote. Many considerations affect voters' decisions. The means of presidential selection have an influence over the quantity and quality of information that guides those decisions. Candidates need full opportunity to learn and to develop awareness of people's needs and interests. Some current practices may enhance, and some may diminish, voters' and candidates' opportunities to gain and exchange significant information. An end issue is how the capacity of the process for exchanging such information can be enlarged. The matter of what elections "mean" assumes fullest significance in the context of that concern.

CHAPTER THREE

Presidential Nominations and Information

☆
☆

The heated struggles to become a major party candidate in 1988 were a far cry from the elite caucus nominations of the early nineteenth century and the boss dominated convention balloting of the early twentieth. Before the Democratic and Republican national conventions of that year, aspirants for the presidential nomination spent up to twelve months actively canvassing for state primary and convention votes. Some spent as many or more months before *that*, planning and organizing before the first "debate," or forum, which was held on July 1, 1987.

In fact, the strenuous competition stimulated a wider and deeper discussion of issues than did the subsequent general election campaign, issues ranging from global survival and the ascending federal debt to the Seabrook nuclear plant in New Hampshire[1] and foreign textile imports in Georgia.[2] And the Federal Election Commission reported that aggregate expenditures for pre-convention financial activity on behalf of sixteen aspirants for a 1988 presidential nomination had totalled $210.7 million.[3]

The large number of primaries and the often arcane practices of state conventions by which national convention delegates are now chosen are regularly condemned. The huge effort and sums of money called for and the frequent changes made in procedures are deplored. Omnipresent television with its appetite for early and endless "news" is charged with overemphasizing the "horserace" and "character" issues and ultimately with boring its viewers. Campaign finance controls with their limits on donations and expenditures, their stimulus to multiple channels of soliciting and spending, and their debilitating reporting requirements are blamed for undesirably decentralized and independent canvasses. Early caucuses and conventions are perceived to be the products of parochial state vanities with their results exerting unjustified influence.

The new long public nomination contest that developed after 1968 is blamed for sundry other maladies as well, including intensified demands by special political interests, reduced incentives to compromise or moderate demands, and lowered participation in the November balloting. It places such heavy demands on the time and stamina of aspirants that worthy potential candidates are deterred from entering the fray. The system produces a chase for early donors, endorsers, volunteers, and media attention. In turn, state and local parties and interest groups vie with each other and with early informal caucuses and straw polls for the attention of potential candidates. By October 1983 the AFL-CIO had endorsed Walter Mondale for the 1984 Democratic nomination.[4] In 1988 Democratic contenders scrambled for public backing wherever they might find it, including endorsement by three politically potent but reluctant dragons of that year, Senator Sam Nunn of Georgia, Senator Bill Bradley of New Jersey, and Governor Mario Cuomo of New York.

But the new nominating conditions, for all the laments they stirred in some quarters, did not spring from whimsy. They were products of a more segmented, mobile, and agitated electorate, of increased variety in issues, of a new communications environment dominated by television, and of purposeful efforts by newly energized activists. The information developed and transmitted under the new nominating conditions is inevitably incomplete, uneven from state to state, often poorly timed, normally partisan. Yet it is so important to American democracy at the close of the twentieth century that stern assessment is called for.

CHANGE IS CONTINUOUS

The practices used to nominate American presidential candidates have been changing for two centuries as the characteristics of American society and the aspirations of American citizens have evolved. The general election campaign leading to the constitutionally prescribed balloting in the electoral college has also evolved, but the seismic jolts of late years have occurred in presidential nominations.

Recurring change is inevitable because U.S. electoral practices are basically derivative. They were structured originally to serve the eighteenth century government created by the founders for the social context then existing. The nation's essential democratic commitments have expanded since then—notably, in voting, to women, non-whites, the propertyless, and those as young as eighteen years. The ways of politics have necessarily evolved, sometimes by formal action and sometimes by accretion, to accommodate new expectations and conditions in all segments of American society. As citizen hopes and public issues spawned by the expanding and diversifying nation have evolved, so have the contests for presidential nomination and election. Presidents of greatness and presidents of much lesser quality were nominated under former systems. No procedures can guarantee that all candidates nominated will command high acclaim and none will achieve perfection in the eyes of all. But a set of practices must satisfy enough expectations of fairness and competence for its results to be respected and therefore sustained.

With the growth in size and influence of the federal government after 1932, the presidency was transmuted.[5] George E. Reedy observed that "overnight the focus of American attention shifted from city hall to the White House."[6] The titanic changes that came in federal functions and in American society over the following decades had a profound effect on partisan politics and the selection of presidents. The increased diversity in the sources and vehicles of political activism that began to appear in the 1950s contributed to a plural, activist politics that could not be accommodated by the two comprehensive parties in the manner of earlier times. The changes in practice resulted from the new conditions and new aspirations in the society and from the energies they stimulated.

The United States has not been alone, however. All democracies have been experiencing pronounced changes in the functions of their governments, and in their electoral politics, changes that result from general forces at work in Western culture. Anthony Smith, in an examination of electoral processes in twenty-eight democratic nations, found a common effect of television, a medium now widely diffused in advanced democracies. "It is harder than it used to be to mold citizens into some kind of collective national unity; they pursue individual goals and tastes or give their loyalty to participatory subgroups." He saw the age of television as one of declining hierarchy. The interviews, debates, round table discussions, and broadcasts of speeches symbolize the "supplanting of political paternalism by participation at the grass roots."[7]

Not only the channels of political communication, but the substance and characteristics of political discourse have been transformed in advanced democracies. Chief executives have been given increasing importance by voters and their personal qualities have consequently drawn increasing public scrutiny, e.g., "Giscard's imperiousness, Trudeau's temper, Thatcher's iron will, and Carter's indecisiveness."[8] Personal responsibility now, even more than in the past, is fixed on national leaders, not just on political parties or the corporate government. This emphasis on the personal attributes of leaders is especially evident in American nomination politics.

Common trends characterize the electoral processes of all modern democracies. The explosion of easily available political information is one example; longer political agendas stemming from the expanded reach of government are another. But some other developments are, thus far, peculiar to the United States. The rise of candidates and eclipse of parties in the nominating period have altered vividly the ways political information is generated and transmitted in recent competitions for the presidency. Especially did developments after 1968 guarantee that for the nominating period candidates would have ascendancy over parties in the public eye. Voters once waited, largely passively, to be served up nominees by the inner circles of political leaders. Now they take a significant role in selecting candidates through primaries and open party caucuses.

The change increased the useful political information made public, but the nominating phase of presidential selection has received a lion's share of criticism from observers, and the bulk of attention from reformers. We ask in this chapter what the implications are of moving from a quiet to a noisy nominating politics, and from a shorter to a longer season of open political communications.

VOTER INFORMATION AND THE MODERN ELECTORAL CALENDAR

As to their level of information, voters in primary elections, as distinguished from the public-at-large, tend to have much the same characteristics as voters in the general election,[9] and they seem to make their voting decisions in much the same manner.[10] Information tends to be acquired by most individuals as they need it for a specific purpose. Those who decide to vote in a primary or attend a caucus or convention are stimulated to acquire information useful for doing so.

There has always been a division of political labor. In the decades before 1972, nominees were normally selected under the watchful eyes of party leaders who shared keen incentives for their party's success both in winning and in governing. Even though presidential primaries were held in a number of states, the harm that might be caused by unknowledgeable voters seemed minimal. Beginning in 1972, however, the judgment of voters in primaries and of participants in party caucuses largely replaced the peer review previously exercised by experienced politicians. The number of persons active in choosing nominees greatly expanded—from about 13 million in 1968 in primaries and conventions to about 35 million in primaries alone in 1988.[11] This increase has weakened radically what many had viewed as a safety valve in the nominating system. The present widespread popular involvement in nominations gives the quantity and quality of information possessed by voters a new, urgent importance.

Only a few systematic assessments have been made of the kinds of information generated under the new conditions, and what voters learn from it. Some plausible inferences, however, are possible, one being that the public does learn from the long, drawn out process, but not enough. An individual's personal interest seems to some analysts[12]—but not to all[13]—a more reliable predictor of political learning than the richness of the sources of information. The quality of information generated by the nominating process is obviously important, but variety in types and sources may be needed for the public as a whole to become truly informed. Clearly some voters benefit from diversity in the sources of news and data.

Limited "debates" among opponents for a party's nomination began on radio in 1948 and on television in 1956. Their use expanded in the Republican primaries of 1980, dramatically in the 1984 Democratic primaries, and further in the primaries of both parties in 1988. Televised "debates" among aspirants became a source of information not only for primary and caucus participants but also for the general public. This expansion of electoral communication was made possible by new interpretations by the Federal Communications Commission, in 1976 and later, of the long-standing equal time rule as applied to broadcasts of political debates.[14]

In 1983, congressional Democrats arranged for a series of joint encounters among presidential contenders in different parts of the country, to be held before the first round of primaries and caucuses in early 1984.[15] As early as October 13, 1983, seven aspirants met to debate arms control. The discussion was televised to cities containing 25 percent of the nation's households.[16] Seventy debates among Democratic contenders were originally announced leading up to the 1988 convention—to begin even earlier than four years before—but the burden on the candidates led to cancelling some and to partial participation in others.[17] The joint appearances nonetheless assumed greater importance than ever before among Democrats, and were prominent features of the Republican contest, too, until Vice President Bush's emergence in March as the presumed nominee.

The elaborate series of face-to-face encounters became a major component of the candidates' state primary campaigns. They especially presented journalists with new opportunities to assess wins and losses, and, more importantly, other viewers also gained both impressions of the contestants and information about issues.

By contrast, television *news* has been judged of more limited and more mixed effect as a source of prenomination information for voters under post-1968 conditions. One examination of learning by the general public during the 1980 primary season concluded that primary voters did better than the public at large, but were nonetheless "not terribly knowledgeable about the candidates."[18] An examination of the 1976 presidential primaries concluded that the extensive media coverage, especially by television, encouraged voter interest and thus helped determine what voters learn about the campaign.[19] During 1976 the biggest increases in public understanding of Carter's policies were found in the general election campaign, but there were also increases from the nomination contests.[20]

In spite of some gains, the quality of the information voters acquired during the primaries was far from optimum. Contests scattered across the nation among several independent candidates did not produce easily assimilable information.[21] A central criticism is the sparse amount of information about issues versus the large amount about the competitive standings of the candidates: the horserace emphasis. The problem with horserace journalism is not that it determines who wins in the primaries or the general election, but that it uses time that ideally could be devoted to information more useful to voters.[22]

Both print and broadcast media are thus faulted for their information mix during the nominating period. But television is especially targeted. It exhibits a relative inability to treat issues in depth even when it devotes time to them. The inevitable interest in who is "ahead" becomes exaggerated.[23] Even so, voters now get most of their campaign information from television, and it deserves some credit for the increased ability of voters in recent years to identify candidates' stands on issues.[24] Political factors explain the results of primary and general elections—imperfect instruments of democracy that they are—far better than such nonpolitical factors as "the media."

We should not pass too harsh a judgment on the journalists. Alexander Hamilton's notes on the proceedings of the Constitutional Convention for June 6, 1787, include this observation: "One great defect of our Governments are that they do not present objects sufficiently interesting to the human mind."[25] Views differ over the importance to citizen learning of the citizen's own initiative, one view emphasizing that interest is less important than the "information environment,"[26] and another that citizen attentiveness is more important than the richness of the "information source."[27]

One conclusion is certain, however. Variety in the types and sources of information available from the nominating calendar of the 1980s produces an electorate better informed politically than it was under earlier systems. Larry M. Bartels found that primary contests generate "especially plentiful" information, and while he would prefer to have them more widely separated, "actual prospective voters tend to be substantially better informed than the national audience at the same time."[28] That was not the proclaimed aim of those who precipitated the revolutionary changes after 1968—less structured participation in choosing nominees being their goal—but it has been a significant consequence. The more abundant research on voter information in the general election examined in the next chapter points more emphatically to the same conclusion.

CANDIDATE INFORMATION AND THE MODERN ELECTORAL CALENDAR

Assessment of presidential primaries normally centers on the opportunity they offer voters for direct popular participation in choosing nominees. The resulting need for contenders to canvass in a sequence of diverse states produces, however, an important by-product. Time-consuming and expensive though the process is, it forces aspirants to inform themselves about the anxieties and strengths of the extraordinarily diversified nation they seek to lead. Each primary, and each caucus as well, by encouraging face-to-face exposure of aspirants to some of a state's citizens, is a new lesson (and test) in understanding issues of first concern to an individual state and to specific sectors of the population. And, even with the bunching of state selections on and around the same date, as with Super Tuesday, March 8, 1988, the sequence encourages campaigners to adapt the lessons learned in earlier contests to their participation in later ones.[29]

The final vote in any election only shows a preference for one candidate over others. The result is decisive, but not always informative. Even in the day of extensive opinion polling, much is left to conjecture. As Marjorie Randon Hershey puts it, "the election result is a very powerful teacher, but not a very informative one."[30] Learning about the public and its concerns has never been easy. James Wilson, the most vocal enthusiast for democratic electoral arrangements in the Constitutional Convention of 1787, observed the problematic nature of knowing the mind of the public. "With *regard to the sentiments of the people*, he [Wilson] conceived it difficult to know precisely what they are. Those of the particular circle in which one moved, were commonly mistaken for the general voice."[31] Hershey finds that the problem has not changed much. Interpretation of vote totals is found chiefly in the assessment of political reporters and activists. On election day voters speak, but beyond learning who won and who lost, interpretations are inevitably colored by the experiences and predispositions of campaigners and supporters.[32]

To bring together a coalition of supporters is always the politician's task, sometimes by persuasion and sometimes by harmonizing with the views of others. Communication with local supporters and political activists in the diverse primary and caucus states helps in doing these things. But polls play their part, too. They supply a campaigner with a broader spectrum of opinion than supporters alone will provide. Polls help offset the need to trust that one's close associates can report accurately the span of opinions found among the whole group of party identifiers.

A politician seeking a party's nomination needs to put together a nominating "coalition," one that includes individuals and groups with divergent interests. To succeed, the candidate must attract primary votes from the mass of party identifiers and must also win support from party leaders, including those attending the national convention. And party activists must be willing to give money, time, or influence to the party's nominee.[33] Coalitions of support are necessary whatever nominating system obtains. Sequential primaries and caucuses provide a structure in the contemporary climate of expectations within which such coalitions can be built.

Alliances and coalitions developed under post-1968 nominating conditions are significantly different from previous ones. In what Pope McCorkle and Joel L. Fleishman call "the post-World War II [intellectual] synthesis" or, more descriptively, "the semisovereign synthesis,"[34] the substance of electoral politics was the building of a coalition. The party-centered, pre-1972 electoral system provided the framework for building the coalition. The core of the coalition was formed during the nominating convention and then expanded during the general election campaign as much as was thought necessary to win. This electoral coalition became the foundation for a governing coalition, giving the president a base of support for policies and initiatives.

But that has changed. The societal shifts that underlay the stimulus to change, and the work of successive reform commissions, produced the new nomination process and the alterations in the general election campaign. They contributed to the demise of the coalition, a demise symbolized by the decline of political parties. Anthony King, for example, maintains that while

> American politicians continue to try to create majorities.... [T]hey are no longer, or at least not very often, in the business of building *coalitions*. The materials out of which coalitions might be built simply do not exist. Building coalitions in the United States today is like trying to build coalitions out of sand. It cannot be done.[35]

King emphasizes that coalitions are made of pre-existing blocs, each with some semblance of internal structure and often a leader. The ideal bloc to a politician is one whose leader can always deliver its votes or support.[36] What Anthony Smith called an age of declining hierarchy, Anthony King calls an age of the vanishing coalition.

As suggested by the concept of party-dominated information described in the previous chapter, the coalition was for practical purposes the "message" of a presidential election. It was not all the information, but it was crucial, guiding information about the electorate that the winning candidate took into office. With the traditional coalition nearly extinct, any benefits realized by successful candidates from the long, grueling modern campaign that increase their ability to govern are of major importance.

Under the new, lengthy electoral calendar, politicians with active presidential longings early seize what opportunities they can find to ingratiate themselves with fellow professionals. Aspirants have often taken part in mid-term elections on behalf of their party's congressional candidates. John Kennedy in 1958 and Richard Nixon in 1966 did so—before the changes in party rules—as others had before them. So did Jimmy Carter in 1974, Ronald Reagan in 1978, Walter Mondale in 1982, and George Bush in 1986. They were all purposefully engaged in seeking the presidential nomination.[37]

The long, sequential, modern nominating maze now imposes heavy demands on the time and energy of candidates seeking a major-party nomination. Long before the formal primary season begins, candidates must raise funds, begin to assemble a campaign organization, mobilize supporters, and otherwise gear for a long trek. Philip Crane declared himself a candidate for the 1980 Republican nomination twenty-seven months before the election. As early as 1980, eight aspirants for the 1984 Democratic nomination began to ready themselves for the contest. Senator Ted Kennedy in 1982 announced his withdrawal from the 1984 nomination competition.[38] Howard Baker did not seek reelection to the Senate in 1984 to lay the groundwork for a future presidential bid, at least four years away, and President Bush had barely taken office in 1989 before a swarm of aspiring Democrats began addressing political gatherings and paying respects to influential activists from California to New York, inevitably including Iowa and New Hampshire.[39] The public efforts later slackened as several putative presidential aspirants sought reelection to their present office, a fact that itself confirmed that time is an essential political resource.

For a while in the 1980s the suggestion was commonplace that serious contenders for a nomination must be unemployed, or at least not in public office. The candidacies of Jimmy Carter, George Bush, and Ronald Reagan underlay the lore. In fact, however, there has been little change in the matter. John H. Aldrich examined aspiring nominees in four periods of different nomination practices: 1876–1896, 1912–1932, 1952–1968, and 1972–1984. He discovered that "of the serious candidacies, more are in office in the last period than in any other period!"[40] The 1988 nomination campaign was heavily populated by active office holders. The Republican contest included Vice President George Bush, the party Senate leader, Robert Dole, and House member Jack Kemp. Democratic aspirants included Governor Michael Dukakis, Senators Joseph Biden, Albert Gore, Jr., and Paul Simon, as well as Representative Richard Gephardt.

The major perceived new characteristic of presidential selection is "the permanent campaign." Some experienced analysts hold that the greatest significance of the development is neither its financial costs, nor the burden it puts on the stamina of aspirants and the attention span of citizens. Greater anxiety has been stirred by the perceived resulting interference of politics with the good governance of the nation.

Cyrus Vance was secretary of state for more than three years in Jimmy Carter's administration. His book about the experience, *Hard Choices*, carries, in the words of Max Frankel, the "unstated theme ... that Presidential elections can be a menace to national security." Vance "depicts a President who, though earnest, intelligent and often courageous, ended up letting politics make his policy incoherent and, in the all-important Soviet relationship, ineffective."[41] Bert A. Rockman makes the point incisively: "Incessant politicking ... tends to eclipse government.... [Its] sheer length detracts from the business for which politics is waged, the process of policy making."[42]

The complaint stems from a respectable, long-standing distinction in political analysis between politics and government, between the contest for authority (electoral politics) and the exercise of authority (government). Although Rockman attributes the politicking-governance conflict to the U.S. open selection process, analogous developments are found in other advanced democratic systems with very different and considerably less open electoral arrangements. "The Permanent Campaign" is the section of an essay by Michael Pinto-Duschinsky in which he assesses campaigning in Britain as "almost continuous between general elections."[43] Roland Cayrol observed of the 1978 French election that "the unofficial campaign was longer and more intense than ever before. Indeed, it was interminable. It might even be said to have begun as early as May 1974, immediately after the presidential election. . . ."[44] Howard R. Penniman, quoting David B. Truman's claim that American "elections are not likely to be understood until they are studied as a continuous process in which the [official] campaign and balloting are at most climaxes," maintains that this "generalization applies almost equally to other democracies."[45]

In *The Permanent Campaign*, written in 1982, Sidney Blumenthal gives an account of this development in the American system, but it has much wider applicability.

> What I have called the permanent campaign has become the steady-state reality of American politics. In this new politics, issues, polls and media are not neatly separate categories. They are unified by [a] strategic imperative. . . . The elements of the permanent campaign are not tangential to politics; they are the political process itself.

Blumenthal emphasizes that the transformation of American society is only beginning and that the transformation will inevitably alter politics. Knowledge is more than ever a form of capital with technologies revolutionizing work processes and all that goes under the heading of computers joining other innovations in altering politics. *"The permanent campaign, which rests on the new technology, is the political form of the information age."*[46]

MEDIA INFLUENCE AND THE MODERN ELECTORAL CALENDAR

The nominating season clearly offers voters and candidates opportunities to learn from each other through the political information they communicate. Learning does occur. But the sequential structure of the process allows the media to exert powerful influences that are nonpolitical in the sense that they come from outside the political procedures designed for the selection of nominees. In the words of one observer, "the name of the presidential nominating game is perception. . . ."[47]

It is said that early victories—actual or imputed by the media—breed later ones and consequently determine the ultimate results. After going from 1928 to 1948 without a presidential primary, New Hampshire has used one ever since. Every president elected from 1952 through 1988 first won his party's primary in that state. Momentum is often attributed to media interpretation of early victories. George McGovern's surprisingly strong New Hampshire showing in 1972 and Jimmy Carter's early strength in the Iowa caucuses of 1976 are cited as sources of momentum induced by media emphasis on early results.

Bandwagon momentum propelled by early success in any competition is welcomed by its beneficiaries and presumptively strengthens later performance. The media are criticized, however, for what is surely an inevitable and understandable constant emphasis throughout the primary season on the competitive standing of those seeking the nomination. Hear Robert T. Nakamura and Denis G. Sullivan:

> [T]he staggered system is faulted because widespread attention to early, unrepresentative events . . . propels the candidate to the nomination. The core of this criticism is that the sequence of primaries creates its own momentum . . . in which outsiders—the media, campaign consultants, poll takers, issue activists—intervene to formulate choices for relatively uninformed voters.[48]

It is charged that short-run considerations thus come to dominate the long-run institutional needs of the party. But Nakamura and Sullivan doubt that experience wholly supports the conventionally asserted bandwagon results ascribed to the dominance of the primaries resulting from the reforms. They view the bandwagon effect as *"part of a legitimation process in which the various factions in the party learn to adjust to the eventual nominee,"*[49] a process akin to that occurring when multiple ballots were cast at party conventions before the recent changes.

Parallels between nominations by brokered conventions and nomination by sequential primaries and caucuses are, in fact, evident. Before the string of first-ballot nominations began in 1956 in the major party conventions, multiple ballots were often necessary to select a nominee. James A. Garfield was nominated in 1880 on the thirty-sixth ballot, Woodrow Wilson in 1912 on the forty-sixth, James M. Cox in 1920 on the forty-fifth, Warren G. Harding in 1920 on the tenth, and John W. Davis in 1924 on the one hundred and third ballot. Communications before the conventions were slow, the political alliances in the country were evolving, and repeated ballots in convention gave a basis for testing the appeal of candidates.[50] Sequential primaries and caucuses may communicate coalition information much as did multiple convention ballots.

After 1924 and before 1960, in fact, much of the jostling for votes and position that had formerly occurred during the conventions was taking place before the conventions met. With the growing access through the media to information about public preferences within the parties and the intentions of delegates, results became increasingly predictable, and the leverage of losing aspirants was reduced. When public opinion strongly pointed to a majority choice, it prevailed. The bandwagon influence well pre-dated 1960.[51]

It is altogether rational for primary voters to take earlier primary victories into account in deciding how to vote. The ability to attract votes before the convention bears on what an aspirant might do after it. With victory in November the aim, demonstrated ability to attract votes is vital information, and worth a little give on the issues.[52] While party identifiers voting in primaries may well have policy preferences, they also have a stake in winning the general election. Early primary and caucus successes provide useful information for weighing and assessing the trade-offs between the policy positions of candidates and their electability. If, for most party identifiers, the differences between the two major parties are more significant than the differences among potential nominees of their own party, such trade-offs are reasonable.

The race for the 1984 Democratic nomination provided an example. Black voters faced in the Democratic primaries the choice of casting a symbolically important, emotionally gratifying vote for Jesse Jackson, or supporting a candidate with a genuine prospect of getting the nomination and competing seriously against the Republican nominee in the fall. Richard Arrington, the black Mayor of Birmingham—who by 1988 would be in the Jackson camp[53]—reasoned thus to black voters:

> So we come to the point of a tough decision. . . . No matter how strongly we feel about Jesse Jackson, the reality is that this is not a race between Jesse Jackson and Ronald Reagan. . . . We have to avoid illusions, and we can't afford an emotional binge because we aren't going to feel very good if after a good emotional high we wind up with Reagan.[54]

The media are accused of setting up artificial expectations for a candidate's performance in a primary and then interpreting the results by how well the candidate did against those superimposed expectations. If so, the situation is better than it once was. In the nineteenth and early twentieth centuries, before modern polling, reporters drew on the size of crowds and on audience responses to political harangues for signs of a candidate's popularity. Parades and mammoth rallies characterized electioneering in democratic countries, and their size along with reports of political speeches were assessed as evidence of a candidate's appeal.[55] Modern methods of gauging candidate strength are less colorful, but surely more reliable.

John H. Kessel holds that the problem modern candidates face, that of not living up to expectations, is a creature of the media. Performance relative to expectations may be given more importance than actual results. This sometimes leads a hopeful's handlers, always in search of pleasant surprises, to encourage lower prospects than will likely be realized. But reporters normally pursue more objective standards, referring to previous performance in the area, whether the aspirant is a native or a neighbor, what primary polls have shown, the resources of energy and money invested in the area, the effect of current issues, and anything else thought pertinent. Kessel concludes that "in the absence of 'hard' information about the progress of coalition building, the expectations developed by the media probably provide better standards of comparison than the claims of the candidates."[56]

Perceived momentum in gaining political popularity undeniably plays an important part in the current nominating process. Larry M. Bartels has made a searching examination of momentum in *Presidential Primaries and the Dynamics of Public Choice*.[57] The phenomenon may be a less pervasive and determinative factor than critics of the sequential process sometimes claim. A national poll reported by *TV Guide* in January 1988 found that 48 percent of those questioned believed that the television networks attach excessive significance to early primaries and caucuses. Only 30 percent believed them important enough to merit the attention they receive. This suggests that many television viewers do not assume that an event is significant simply because the networks treat it so. Approximately half of the poll respondents attached significance to events on some basis other than the amount of their television coverage.[58] In fact, the nomination races between Ford and Reagan in 1976, between Reagan and Bush in 1980, between Carter and Kennedy in 1980, between Mondale and Hart in 1984, and among the several Democrats in 1988, did not develop immediately into pictures of inevitability. Momentum was variously gained and lost and reasonable doubt persisted until an "inevitable" nominee emerged.

The exact effects of momentum depend on the field of candidates and the conditions obtaining in the sequence of primaries and caucuses. In 1988, Super Tuesday on March 8 gave George Bush a sweep of 16 states, effectively ending the race for the Republican nomination, and reduced the Democratic scramble to three front runners—Michael Dukakis, Jesse Jackson, and Al Gore—who hotly contested subsequent primaries until Dukakis, strong from the beginning, emerged as the winner well before the convention. Although early dominance normally tends to grow to victory, momentum is more important to a contender when several rivals survive well into the primary season than when there are only two serious contenders.

A contentious proposal that California—the state with the largest number of convention delegates—move its presidential primary from June to March passed both houses of the state legislature, in different versions, early in 1990. Later in the spring, an initiative petition toward the same goal was being circulated, in hopes of putting the issue on the fall ballot. Such a change, if made, would alter national nomination dynamics and set aspirants scrambling to accommodate—as they always must—to the financial and other realities of the nomination contest, whatever they might become.[59]

The influence of momentum is affected by specific features of the primary/caucus system, especially by the rules governing the allocation of delegates. Gerald Pomper described the bearing of rules in naming the 1984 Democratic nominee. The 164 "superdelegates" chosen in the House of Representatives were the first delegates named. "Supported by these political professionals, who knew him well and admired his abilities, Mondale led in the count of delegates from the very first moment."[60] The high vote threshold—20 percent—that a candidate had to meet to win delegates in a primary also benefited Mondale. In some states it prevented Jesse Jackson from winning delegates. Mondale also benefited from winner-take-all and winner-take-more allocation schemes in some larger industrial states,[61] as well as from "frontloading," the bunching of state selections early in the season that favors well-known and well-financed candidates.[62]

The success of a contender for nomination will be determined in the end by many factors (aside from such misadventures as Gary Hart's sex scandal in 1987). First and obviously is the candidate's appeal against that of other aspirants in particular primaries and caucuses. But the timing and sequencing of the contests can affect that appeal, as can the effort and other resources the contenders dedicate to capturing delegates in individual states. The attention given by the media and media interpretations of results are of great significance. And particular circumstances—the personalities, the issues, the images, the ideologies, the tactics and strategies adopted—always make every campaign unique.

William A. Crotty and John S. Jackson III correctly emphasize that the rules alone do not select the candidates: "The drama, pathos, and excitement of American politics stem from . . . intersections of time, personalities, and circumstances that are ever changing."[63] The limitless possible political, economic, and social circumstances that condition the temper of the times guarantee that the process is not a simple mechanistic one, nor one easily dominated by a single set of influences. In April 1988, analyst Jeff Greenfield concluded that "1988 has been shaped far less by media images than by political forces far older than television."[64]

Sequential primaries and caucuses may do more to reveal the character of the "party coalition" in the electorate than other proposed nomination methods. A bandwagon effect seems hardly stronger today than in the nomination regimen before 1960. In fact, increased information can neutralize momentum by helping citizens make up or change their minds regardless of the outcomes of the early primaries.[65]

Whatever else may be said of the sequential, drawn out, media-permeated nomination process, it offers both voters and contenders more opportunity to gain political information and insight than would a drastically shortened official nominating season. This is not to say the information is optimum. It will to some extent be incomplete and on occasion erroneous and deceptive, even as is the information with which all democratic processes function.

Be that as it may, nothing suggests that the length of the unofficial campaign, the permanent campaign, will soon be altered.

INFORMATION FUNCTIONS OF NOMINATING CONVENTIONS

National party conventions do much more than nominate presidential and vice-presidential candidates. The convention brings its party together to agree on a platform and to amend or affirm rules for conducting party affairs. And though much of the excitement of earlier conventions has gone, modern televised conventions provide cues, images, views of personality, and hard political knowledge valuable to the public. Many who watch conventions on television gain authentic information. The audience attracted to convention telecasts is irregular, but large. By one estimate, albeit made in 1983, some one-fourth of the nation's eligible voters watch most of one or both national party conventions, with an estimated two-fifths watching at least part of one convention.[66]

Persons most likely to learn about issues from watching the televised conventions are ones least likely to benefit from issue coverage in newspapers. So Thomas E. Patterson concluded in 1980. Because moderate and low-interest voters are inattentive, they gain little information about issues from reading the papers. Patterson found, however, that by watching the conventions, "moderate interest voters ... became moderately better informed from their exposure, and low interest voters became appreciably more aware of the issues if they watched the conventions. ..."[67] High interest voters were already comparatively well informed about the candidates' positions before the conventions and consequently found the information somewhat redundant.[68]

Byron E. Shafer has described recent national conventions as "bifurcated" because they operate under two different conditions—when the television network cameras are on and when they are not.[69] Assuming that the traditional commercial networks together with CNN, C-SPAN, and more limited sources continue to cover important segments of the conventions, the conventions will have significant value for the information they provide to that part of the electorate most in need of it. Their aspect most beneficial to those seeking nomination and the public alike, Patterson avers, is the "extraordinary opportunity for the candidate to present himself on his terms."[70]

Writing in 1984, John H. Kessel stated that in the elections from 1948 to 1980 just over a quarter of the decisions of whom to vote for in November had been made *during* the political conventions. "[T]he Convention stage is both the conclusion of nomination politics and the beginning of electoral politics. ... [W]hile the delegates are listening to speeches and casting votes, citizens are making up their minds about the coming general election."[71] Surely such a conviction motivated George Bush's televised pledge of allegiance to the flag in the 1988 Republican convention. Televised party conventions afford direct exposure of the nominees who will contend in the general election. The conventions may bore many well-informed, high interest viewers, but they give less-informed citizens of moderate and low interest a base of information and perception on which to build during the general election canvass.

IMPLICATIONS OF MORE CHANGE

Many proposals to alter presidential nomination practices would affect their value as sources of political information. A host of proposed minor modifications would influence the process only marginally, but a few proposals promise significant enhancement of its communication value. Some others would transform the logic of a sequential process so substantially, by altering existing patterns of information flow, as to be highly unwise.

One change could make a highly desirable difference. Election campaigns require communication, and communication costs money.[72] The assumption that more money always produces more meaningful communication is not valid, but large sums are normally required for effective campaign communications in the age of television and airplanes. As already noted, the 1988 presidential nomination expenditures for the sixteen aspirants who accepted federal matching funds came to some $210.7 million ($212 million if wind-down expenses through June 30, 1989, are included).[73] This may seem large, but as usual in campaign finance there are no incontrovertible criteria by which to judge, and in 1988 the timing of some prenomination expenditures in fact was handicapped by the ceilings.[74]

Clearly, limits on contributions and expenditures in nomination campaigns can restrict the flow of beneficial political information. The lack of a party label to give guidance in the numerous nomination contests calls for more money than needed in the general election, but present law assumes less.[75] Low limits on nomination expenditures affect the character as well as the quantity of campaign communications, leading to dependence on mass media advertising in preference to other forms of campaigning that could be more instructive for both the candidates and prospective voters.[76] Financial limits, in fact, can also prompt candidates to seek exposure through television news as a substitute for more direct communication with voters.

Existing national limits on nomination spending frequently lead to an uneven campaign effort over the course of the primary season, and consequently to uneven distribution of information. Candidates, to get off to a strong start, spend heavily early in the season. Heavy expenditures may thus be made before the general public becomes attentive. The involved politicians and the journalists assigned to monitor them learn the characteristics of the aspirants and their views, but the public is slower to pay attention, and to learn, and by the time it begins to pay attention, a candidate's resources may be seriously depleted.[77]

The potential to create better informed voters is clear, but Herbert E. Alexander implies that the opportunity for candidates to learn may be enhanced as well: "The expenditure limit makes it difficult for candidates who have spent close to the maximum allowed to alter campaign strategy and tactics to fend off new challenges or to take new developments into account."[78] Low expenditure ceilings reduce their opportunities to treat the nomination process as a sequence of learning experiences.[79] The limits may give them little chance later in the primary season to put that information to use. The rigidity of the limits takes no account of variations from year to year in the intensity of competition and the number and timing of primaries and conventions.

Direct exposure to a vigorously contested campaign has been found to result in better informed voters who were less subject to simple momentum influence.[80] The finding argues for raising limits on individual contributions and on nomination campaign expenditures. To encourage greater exchange of useful political information, we shall recommend in Chapter Eleven raising those limits along with removing state-by-state spending ceilings.

Removing state-by-state limits would free candidates to allocate resources where most needed to reach the voters. These limitations are declared ill-advised by almost everyone associated with campaign finance. They are unenforceable and carry burdensome bookkeeping requirements. They tempt candidates to use "creative accounting" to evade the restrictions. In 1988, for example, automobiles rented in Massachusetts were driven for use into New Hampshire, and candidate Gephardt added appeals for funds to the end of TV ads, allocating half the costs of the ads to fund-raising, which were not counted against limits in New Hampshire.[81] Candidates and their managers also will stimulate independent expenditures in states where they have already reached the limitations. But the most serious criticism against them, in the words of Harvard University's Campaign Finance Study Group, is that they "improperly attempt to dictate campaign strategy, by attempting to legislate what campaigns ought to spend in each state." That decision should be made by the candidates in the immediate context of competition based on their sense of what they must spend to communicate effectively with the voters of a given state.[82]

A different kind of proposal would produce a significantly different nominating system. A mandatory national primary is often urged to replace the current sequential, optional, state-based primaries and caucuses. In fact, some see it as a logical, even inevitable conclusion to the long history of progressive popular participation in nominations.[83] Beginning with a Gallup poll in 1952, U.S. citizens have strongly voiced support for selecting presidential nominees through a national primary—67 percent in 1984.[84] The change would transform the nominating system, with pronounced consequences for its information functions.

The enduring appeal of a single national primary may stem largely from its simplicity. Whatever rules were decided upon for its conduct would surely be more easily understood by voters and candidates than the complex arrangements now in force. And it might shorten the length of the *formal* nominating season, even if there were provision for a runoff election between top contenders.

A national primary would not, however, eliminate any presumed bias in the present process. Bias is ascribed to the disproportionate influence of early primary and caucus results. A national primary would swap such momentum for the bias of inertia. Highly visible candidates, ones well known, well financed, and able to campaign through the mass media, would have an overwhelming advantage. While high prior visibility is an advantage in any nomination scheme, and factors accounting for such may be politically relevant, a national primary would radically increase its importance. The presumed front-runner bias of a national primary would disadvantage lesser known, "outsider" candidates such as Jimmy Carter was in 1976. It would, in Larry M. Bartels' words, "preclude serious consideration of not only shallow, dangerous newcomers but also those who are able, independent, and purposeful."[85] This may well be the hope of some who prefer the pre-1968 nominating system to all alternatives but who, failing its resurrection, would favor a single national primary to the existing sequential state primaries and caucuses.

A field of candidates of uneven prior prominence, who simultaneously bombarded a national electorate, would increase the task of primary voters in receiving, sorting, and assessing information. The heart of competitive campaigning is competition. It can never lead to full, dispassionate delineation of issues and detailed identification of conflicting candidate positions. But while the long nomination season with successive primaries and conventions, as in 1988, is less than fully effective in exposing candidate attitudes and distinctions among them, a shortened, candidate-crowded, nationwide primary would do so much less.

Inevitably, campaigners in a national primary would employ national television. Grass-roots canvassing would necessarily give way in some degree to media politics—as, indeed, it did to a significant extent before the Super Tuesday primaries of March 8, 1988.[86] This would not be a welcome result for those already critical of present media politics. Moreover, voters would surely find themselves with less information about detailed matters of policy.[87] They would also surely welcome a simpler nominating process with more easily understood rules of participation. But any such advantage would be offset by the complexity of competitive campaigns run simultaneously by several aspirants in each party and the inevitably resulting political charges and appeals, often with confusing diagnoses and prescriptions. The net result ironically would thus be a campaign less, not more, informative.

It is argued that a simple, nationwide primary would shorten the formal primary campaign period. This does not mean, however, that it would abbreviate the "permanent campaign." Under the growing conditions of multiple issues and mobile coalitions that have emerged in recent decades—in fact a new citizens' politics—much can be said for long, public nomination campaigns as arenas for testing candidates and informing voters.[88]

In a nationwide primary, candidates would probably lose more significant information than would voters. The national primary would make Anthony King's imagery of politicians who build majorities rather than coalitions all the more applicable. Public opinion polls and the opinions of one's associates would gain added weight in a candidate's efforts to comprehend and appeal to an undifferentiated national constituency in a contracted period of time. There would be less time for candidates to learn from campaigning, to develop and demonstrate political sensitivities and capacities, and to adapt their views and strategies. "The shorter the campaign period," Aldrich asserts, "the less time there will be for a candidate to discuss, say, social security in Florida, agricultural issues in Nebraska, and energy policies in Texas, etc."[89] Moreover, if a national primary were to reduce further the stature of the political party conventions, another source of political information would be diminished—including the public declarations of party figures and the contents of party platforms.

The proposal to hold a convention *before* the nominating primary seeks to strengthen both peer review and the deliberative functions of political parties. The nominee would be chosen in a three-stage process based on a system used in Colorado since 1910. Present state primaries and caucuses would be replaced by a caucus-convention system, uniform in all states, to name delegates to the national party convention where contestants would be chosen to run in a national primary. Finally, national primaries would be held in both parties.[90]

The plan seeks to strengthen the parties by giving activists a chance to make the first cut in the states, the convention the right to deliberate and narrow the field, and the broader party electorate the responsibility for choosing the nominee. Congressional legislation would be necessary and opposition would stem in this as in other cases from deep-rooted preferences for less rather than more national regulation of the political system. In any case, it is unlikely that the length and highly publicized nature of the nomination process would be reduced.

Congressman Charles E. Schumer of New York has proposed that a series of nonbinding primaries and caucuses be held on dates chosen in each state between five and ten months before the election; that a single national nominating primary then be held four months before the election, with a runoff three weeks later if no contestant received over 40 percent of the vote; and that the present convention and delegate system be replaced by a mini-convention two months before the election to write the platform and launch the campaign.[91]

While it is hardly possible to anticipate its full effects, this proposal would, like others for a national primary that abandon the federal principle, lead candidates to cultivate areas with the largest densities of voters at the expense of more remote and less concentrated electorates. How extensively nonbinding primaries and caucuses would be used, and how they would be viewed within the states, are uncertain. The replacement of the national delegate conventions by lesser conclaves for platform writing, however, would assuredly weaken the party's corporate capacities.

Regional presidential primaries have been proposed, a measure intermediate between the current rash of state primaries and a single national primary. A regional primary system would retain a degree of sequencing, but would also have some attributes of a national primary and would increase the relative importance of media campaigning. On Super Tuesday 1988, four states held presidential nominating caucuses and sixteen—fourteen of them southern or border states—held presidential primaries. Democratic contests were held in all twenty of these states and Republican contests in seventeen.

Some southerners believed that their influence in the national Democratic party had declined with the growth of southern Republicanism and that bunching the region's primaries would enhance southern influence in the party. Aspirants in both parties campaigned in the twenty states as best their time and money (and judgment) permitted. As noted, Vice President Bush swept all the Republican primaries, virtually sewing up the nomination. In the Democratic outcome in the South, Governor Dukakis of Massachusetts carried four states, including the two most populous, Texas and Florida; Tennessee's Senator Gore carried five; and the Reverend Jackson, born in South Carolina and living in Chicago, carried five.

The governor of Colorado proposed a 1988 Rocky Mountain regional primary and there were similar noises from other areas. With Democrats in control of the great majority of state legislatures, Republicans had to follow the Democratic lead. Texas State Senator John Traeger, chairman of the Southern Legislative Conference, argued hopefully that both parties would be encouraged to choose truly representative candidates because "the issues of interest to southerners are representative of mainstream America."[92] Whether true or not, regional concerns would presumably take precedence over diversities within the region and over some types of diversity within the nation. And if the notion caught on for future presidential years, the regions might vie for precedence as Iowa and New Hampshire have done, and as California in 1990 threatened to do. Many influences bear on timing of the primaries, including their administrative costs if not held concurrently with other state primaries and the time needed to generate partisan campaign funds.

Actually, the complexity of the current system may be a useful and accurate reflection of the complexity of the nation. Under modern conditions, any nomination scheme that oversimplifies this complexity and reduces its visibility for voters and candidates is likely to reduce important political information and opportunities to learn. Bartels found much merit in a sequential presidential nominating process using primaries—he would have them more sanely spaced—and concluded that "information is especially plentiful in the local political context generated by a primary election" and that prospective voters thus "tend to be substantially better informed than the national audience at the same time."[93]

Nonetheless, an inducement advanced for regionally grouped primaries is to save wear and tear on candidates by reducing travel distances and time. The current system undeniably imposes major stresses on the candidates, but—heartless though the thought may seem—they are not greater than those imposed by four years in the White House. For good or ill, the growing personal expectations of candidates in the selection process in some ways mirror the growing demands of presidential duties.

Although presidential nominations are no longer controlled by state and local party organizations, the parties through their officers and committees contribute to the information available to those who nominate candidates. The party label still directs primary voters and caucus participants to a place of decision, and reminds with emphasis that the *Democratic* and the *Republican* candidates for president are being chosen. A party label reminds voters what rivals for their party's nomination share in common—despite their intense efforts to differentiate themselves from each other. Party labels encourage party identifiers to weigh the electability of contenders as well as to evaluate their policy positions. All this information is relevant to the decisions participants in the nominating process must make, and to the learning they acquire.

Some state party groups still endorse candidates during the nomination season and many party and elected officials at all levels make known their preferences among candidates. While parties no longer tightly control the exchange of political information, they continue to influence it.

Perhaps the gravest criticism of plans to simplify the nomination process—by going to a national or to regional primaries—is the potential for further diminishing political parties as factors in the process. The states and units within them continue to provide the organizational base of the political parties. Systematically broadening the geographic focus of the nomination process to the region, or to the nation, risks additional reduction in the visibility and importance of the parties. Some critics have suggested that a national primary would be tantamount to a nonpartisan election. Some proposals for a national primary have advocated as much.

The presidential nomination procedures that evolved after the 1960s are complex, demanding of both political activists and less involved voters. They grew, however, in response to felt needs, and proposals for simplifying or revising them—or going to a series of regional primaries—should be guided by that reality. With all their diversity and confusing differences, in their information function they offer advantages to voters, candidates, the parties, and in the long run, the nation.

In an age of visible chief executives, declining hierarchy, diminishing coalitions, tidal waves of political information, and the permanent campaign, the current nomination system performs—for the present—the major function of political information exchange about as well as can realistically be hoped. The flow of political information in the nomination process, as well as its quantity, quality, and intelligibility, provide only a single measure, however. We now turn to an assessment of the information produced by the general election.

CHAPTER FOUR

Presidential Elections
and Information

☆
☆

In the fervid intensity of presidential electioneering every four years, battered partisans may well wonder what significant information vital to the success of government is conveyed to anyone. Late in the 1988 campaign 30 percent of those in a national poll did not even know the name of the Democratic vice presidential candidate.[1]

Moreover, public attention is regularly diverted by jaundiced ploys: John Kennedy haranguing about a missile gap and about Quemoy and Matsu in 1960, all quickly forgotten after victory; Barry Goldwater pictured, almost literally, as an atomic baby killer in 1964[2]; George Bush in 1988 talking about a Massachusetts criminal who had escaped while on furlough so much that the name Willie Horton became commonplace.

Overly simplified appeals to bias, ignorance, and credulity have run throughout American presidential campaigns. Andrew Jackson's partisans liberally distributed hickory brooms, canes, and sticks while John Adams' followers asked incredulously, "What have hickory trees to do with republicanism and the great contest?" They proceeded to accuse Jackson of drunkenness, bigamy, theft, and murder.[3] The Cleveland-Blaine campaign of 1884 was called the "vilest" ever waged, with issues submerged and scandal-mongering dominant.[4]

In varying degrees, it was ever thus. Yet, through all the changes that have occurred in the characteristics and qualities of political information and communications, and despite the persistence of distortions and irrelevancies, presidential campaigns do more than test the reputations, poise, and resilience of candidates. In their contest to hold party loyalists and to lure habitual independent voters, as well as potential voters, candidates learn something of the moods, tolerances, and ambitions of the public. And the public, in turn, can observe much about them.

CHANGES IN MEDIA, INFORMATION, AND POLITICS

America's new communications environment shapes the election of presidents just as we have seen it alter the nomination of candidates. Virtually all political information and its interpretation reaching the public travel via the media. The consequences of the much-mentioned evolving technologies and new legal concepts are tangible and often unpredictable. The competition to be heard intensifies constantly, and the struggle to hear intensifies too. In the resulting heated conditions, voters, parties, and candidates have interests in campaign information that overlap but do not fully coincide.

Here, the people's interests are our first concern, and in the constantly altering circumstances of the television age it is important that the content of electoral communications remain sufficiently diverse to satisfy the information wants of a wide variety of citizens—those well informed and not so well informed, those well educated and not so well educated, those interested and not so interested, and those who have grown up less on the written word than on television's "new 'grammar' of images."[5]

No sooner had television become the pervasive mode of communication in American life and politics than it began to change. Cable television, the proliferation of channels, and instantaneous transmission by satellite have multiplied television's capacity to offer targeted, specialized, worldwide information. Those innovations increase the options open to viewers to switch, by remote control no less, from one channel to a choice among many others—from a political discussion to rock music, for example. The emerging "narrowcasting" in television resembles what occurred in radio—development of broadcasters with specialized programming directed to carefully chosen audiences. The role of television networks has already been diminished by such innovations—except, so far, in covering major sports—and Austin Ranney concludes that such "changes in the media are likely to change the nature of politics in the 1990s and beyond."[6]

Just how, and how much, experience will tell, but some consequences can be positive. Cable coverage of proceedings of the House of Representatives and the Senate, for example, has enabled part of the remote public to watch the Congress doing some of its work—with, not incidentally, salutary effects on both the quality and significance of congressional debate.[7]

Technological innovations and their political adaptations will continue indefinitely. Not only are the politically relevant capacities of cable and over-the-air broadcasting enlarging. So also are those of public opinion polling and a host of other capacities that are being developed and applied: direct mail, telemarketing, satellite relays, sophisticated uses of audience-targeting, focus groups for opinion analysis, micro mapping in election canvassing, and other innovations, including the multiple uses of computers that have led Richard Armstrong to speak of a "new era of 'machine politics'."[8] Although experts of sober judgment hold that the full political effect of innovations already in train, much less of others yet to come, will not become evident until the turn of the century or later,[9] the potential is clear for new television and other technologies to serve, in modest degrees, a number of functions.

More opportunities, for example, for direct, two-way communication between candidates and voters could enhance electoral campaigns as learning experiences for both. The technology permitting a candidate to interact with large groups of people, assembled for the purpose, is cost-effective, though less so with individuals in their homes. Perhaps basic cable subscribers, who have traditionally been younger, more affluent, and more urban than the general public,[10] may, as their numbers increase, become more representative of the electorate. Such is desirable, for in a political system that relies on representativeness, better information that reaches only part of a diverse citizenry can interfere with the system's effectiveness unless other sources of information serve other segments of the electorate equally well.

Communications technology including the means and speed of assembling, analyzing, repackaging, and targeting information will continue to change rapidly. Effects on the content, sources, and destinations of political messages, and on the speed, comprehensiveness, and control of information transmission, are inescapable. Although the distant consequences for presidential selection are not predictable with assurance—for example, the significance of the decline in network news coverage of uninterrupted candidate campaign speech from segments averaging 42.3 seconds in 1968 to 9.8 seconds in 1988[11]—but the effect upon politics of broad changes in political information can be assessed.

From its beginning, television has been regarded with an uncomfortable ambivalence over its potential for good and ill. It has become so much the centerpiece of American presidential communications that it has been said Ronald Reagan used it to govern the nation.[12] It may in fact be that public perceptions conveyed by television are unique in their effect on political attitudes and actions.[13] It has clearly become central to American presidential election campaigns, as it has become central to the politics of most democratic nations.

Television is not the only force shaping the flow of electoral information, but its centrality makes it the focus of assessments of communications in contemporary presidential politics. Some observers see adverse consequences for virtually all elements of the American electoral system, even for the substance of politics itself. One criticism charges that television coverage of presidential campaigns produces voters who "are brainwashed, misled and deceived about what the candidates stand for, what they have done in the past and what they intend to do in the future."[14] Critics find that the content of issues, channels of citizen political activity, and the types of people who get elected are all affected.[15] Ronald Reagan's actions and declared attitudes "on issue after issue" were found to be at odds in his overwhelmingly victorious 1984 campaign with positions held by majorities in public opinion polls—a paradox attributed to staged events and other devices of information management spawned by television,[16] and one contributing enormously to a candidate's (and a president's) temptation to indulge in a politics of instant gratification.[17] Other observers acknowledge that the forms of politics have changed, but claim that at bottom the substance is what it has always been.

Television is neither the unqualified blessing nor the thoroughgoing curse it is often said to be. By 1978, Anthony Smith perceived a fall in earlier anxiousness over television's effects. He recalled the argument from the 1960s that "the processes of learning were henceforth befuddled by the experience we absorbed from a contraption which stood between all reality and all comprehension."[18] He was skeptical that this portrayal was ever accurate, but in any event it was beside the point. "If television as such has the power to impose a new cognition upon society, then it has already by now done so; and we are what has resulted; we are what the critics of television warned our parents against."[19] In the same spirit, we can recognize modern campaign politics as, simply, what we have and what, at least for a while, we will continue to have.

Television's effect on political campaigns has been shaped by the structure and rules of the pre-existing electoral system, including its restrictions on campaign broadcasting. While such conditions might be changed and television's role altered, its current characteristics are what now influence the political information available and how the interests of voters, parties, and candidates are represented in the communication of such information. A look at televised political campaigns in Great Britain will put in focus issues of balance among the kinds of information encouraged.

Elihu Katz borrows a metaphor to ask whether campaigns should be understood as "platforms" or as "windows." Campaigns that promote candidate and party interests are viewed as platforms. Those in which voters receive information useful to them in deciding how to vote, but may be detrimental to candidate or party interests, are viewed as windows. British campaign broadcasting has been touted by some American analysts as a model to be emulated, but Katz believes they produce too much platform and too little window.

The virtual monopoly of political broadcasts granted British political parties serves the parties well. It lets them select the information voters receive. But, "the voter, for his part, is less well served. Society—the social system—benefits least of all."[20] Better recognition of the differing interests of candidates and parties on the one hand, and of voters on the other, would enlarge the benefits of the campaigns to British society. Katz looks to American-style candidate debates as a needed corrective. What many see as a shortcoming of the recent American campaign debates—that they are not genuine debates—he sees as a strength. He judges the intervention of journalists as beneficial. They "represent" the voter in trying to make sense of the campaign, forcing attention to issues and information that candidates and parties may prefer to avoid.

In no democratic electoral system can politicians stop soliciting public understanding and approval. But the political discourse between elections can differ sharply. In Great Britain, debate in the House of Commons between Government and opposition spokesmen differs markedly from the speeches in the American Congress, and the cabinet system does not spawn nomination contests like those in the United States. In one important sense, British campaigning never stops, but Britain's formal general election campaign is short and highly structured. It contrasts sharply with the longer, more fluid American election period. The American campaign comprises a variegated pattern of platforms and windows by which electoral information is generated. Adaptation of campaign schedules by candidates and their campaigners to gain television exposure is constant, and while the habits of American television in covering presidential contests are regularly condemned, they nonetheless contribute to diverse information perspectives in American campaigns.

Still, a major criticism of the information mix in presidential campaigns stems from the growing independence from political parties of presidential campaign organizations. American political parties have become, in the eyes of some, the weakest, most poorly represented participants in electoral communications, with a correspondingly weakened later role in the processes of governing.

A bundle of measures has been proposed to improve the quantity, quality, and intelligibility of political information communicated in U.S. presidential campaigns. Typically, the adoption of a particular proposal would produce both gains and losses. To upgrade the quality of campaign broadcasting, for example, some persons advocate mandatory lengthening of paid political advertising. Others, with the same motive, advocate its curtailment. In both cases, any gain would be at heavy cost. Information needs to reach persons with a keen interest in politics, but also others who attend politics less from interest than from a vague sense of duty. Reducing variety in the permissible length of political appeals would create an even larger gap than at present between the information-rich and the information-poor in the electorate. The First Amendment is usually invoked in defense of political advertising, its guarantees viewed as fundamental rights. Those rights also help assure a versatile mix of information essential to democratic vitality.

Elevated political discourse directed to the politically informed contrasts with political communications directed at citizens with presumed less understanding. The condition is inherent in democracy. If electoral communications lack quality, the system suffers; but if they cannot be broadly distributed and understood, the system also suffers. Balance is the only recourse in face of the many antitheses that pervade democracies. The conflict inherent in the distinction between platforms and windows is one of these antitheses. But it is always difficult to know what is proper balance, much less to achieve it.

Such stresses pervade democratic societies. They also pervade our notions of democracy, as those notions have evolved over democracy's long and uneven evolution. When political parties are conceived as the focal points of the electoral process, party platforms become all-important. Democracy then lies in the competition between strong parties with opposing programs and the opportunity for voters to choose by election. Windows for voters become less important, even destructive, if conceived as diminishing the effectiveness of party communications and weakening party loyalties.

Theorists primarily concerned with democratic citizenship, however, argue that windows are an essential communication requirement. They provide voters with an array of information necessary to cast a conscientious, responsible vote. In this view, voting on the basis of party loyalties that may have been developed in childhood falls short of informed, conscientious, responsible voting. Democracy is held to lie in government rooted in the informed consent of its citizens granted periodically through elections, with those citizens accepting corresponding responsibility for the well-being of society.

Other dilemmas in a democracy also rule out simple answers in organizing political processes and structures. Because information is indispensable in the electoral process, efforts to improve its character and communication expose many such dilemmas. When political parties and their valuable contributions to democratic politics are examined singly, or the ideal standards by which voters might perform their citizenship roles are examined separately, many of the tensions can be avoided. But when the electoral process in all its complex interdependence is the focus, and the health of the total political system is the objective, the dilemmas emerge.

In authentic democratic systems, institutional invention and improvement are never simply matters of defining the ideal course and overcoming obstacles that block the path. The task is more intricate—choosing the course closest to the ideal that is most likely to succeed *and* that can be adopted. In the new age of information politics, such a course will be different from that of earlier times. Because television has become the core of communications in general election campaigns for president, we shall start with it in untangling the current pattern of information exchange and its mixture of platforms and windows.

TELEVISION: DIVERSITY IN COVERAGE, DIVERSITY OF EFFECTS

To think of television as a single influence with uniform effect is to oversimplify its informational role. Television influences general elections for president through its coverage of party conventions, of candidate debates, of discussion programs, and of other special events. Its effect is also felt through paid political advertising and through those news reports from which most Americans get the bulk of their daily information, and which are heavily criticized for light treatment of political substance and heavy emphasis on electoral competition. Different types of televised messages reach different types of voters to differing extents and with varying effects on the information level of the general electorate.

Since 1952, television coverage of the national conventions has constituted the effective beginning of the general election campaign. Like the
periodic televised presidential debates—the first of those during a general
election campaign having been held in 1960—convention coverage supplies
voters with information different from that acquired from other sources.

Conventions are declared boring, however, and are lampooned for
conducting no interesting business and for providing only superficial information. They are also censured for accommodating their format to the
convenience of television. But precisely that adaptation permits a substantial
number of voters to gain important campaign information from the televised
conventions. The conventions provide both platforms and windows. The party
and its candidate have a chance to project themselves as they want to be
understood, using the substance and symbols of politics they select. Simultaneously, voters have a window—albeit not fully open—on the dynamics of
the parties and the forces at work in the larger political system. They can thus
be informed and educated, as parties and candidates compete for the voter's
favor on the parties' own terms.

In 1980, the networks spent $10 million apiece to cover each convention.
Forty prime-time hours of exposure were devoted to the conventions, not
counting specials before and after and extra attention on regular news
broadcasts. That was more prime-time coverage of the presidential campaigns than in all the rest of the year taken together.[21] Televised conventions
transmit information about candidates, issues, and the political forces at work
within the parties, about conflict and compromise and the capacity of each
party to overcome division and achieve unity. In the past they have probably
provided the most intensive learning opportunity of the entire campaign, and
those who have benefited most from televised conventions and debates are
those information-needy voters who are least likely to gain information from
newspapers and magazines.

Even well-informed voters have appeared to gain something, even when
much of the content is repetitive for them. Reflecting on television's political
influence in democracies, Anthony Smith concluded that "voters learn to read
the system as well as watch the programs." They can see whether opposition
and minority groups can get air time or whether a dominating elite "is merely
conducting a dialogue with itself."[22] Convention coverage helps viewers
assess the state of each party, including its factionalism and its capacity for
unity.[23]

As noted in the last chapter, television news emphasizes the competitive
performance of individual politicians more than the content of issues, partly
explaining why voters gain more information about issues from televised
conventions—and debates—than from news broadcasts. Moreover, in both
the convention and subsequent general election period of 1976, reading
newspapers was found to lead to significantly greater awareness of both
Carter's and Ford's positions than television news viewing. In contrast,

exposure to the televised debates increased people's knowledge of issues,[24] the effects being, naturally enough, greatest among persons normally less attentive to politics.

Doris A. Graber and her associates have inquired in some detail into the influence and usefulness of the presidential debates. A panel of respondents they used was highly critical: much debate information was redundant; panelists were not interested in some of the intricacies of policy issues; the format was unattractive. It is charged also that "image" politics is encouraged, and journalists' influence increased, whereas exploration, as James David Barber would like, of "what qualifications, demonstrated in their experience, suit them to be President" is ignored.[25] Despite these and other limiting conditions of the debates,[26] it is clear that in the end voters gain significantly from exposure to them. Moreover, the candidates and their parties take them seriously.

The chief deterrent to a consensus about televised debates is the multiple goals sought through them.[27] Still, they have been especially criticized for emphasizing image politics over issue politics, for encouraging voters to respond to debating style rather than issue content. But politicians in every democratic system must project images and have always done so. In fact, the images are rarely divorced from reality. Anthony Smith holds that the images are tied to the foundation upon which a nation's political reality is constructed—its political culture.

> Television viewers watching a politician inquiring the price of an apple in a store understand that the individual wishes to be thought of as concerned about the price and quality of food, familiar with the problems of daily life, and able to get along with storekeepers. We know from a wealth of literature concerning American presidential elections of the enormous expertise that goes into packaging the images of senior politicians in the United States; similar cosmetic attention to the image of leaders takes place elsewhere, though perhaps less frenetically and with less belief in its efficacy. *But everywhere the values with which politicians seek to associate themselves in fashioning their media images reflect the underlying political culture. In portraying acts and projecting images that express those values, television performs its main teaching function.*[28]

Graber found that most of the panelists in her study made their voting choices "by assessing the general trustworthiness of the candidates and weighing their capacity to make intelligent decisions and by looking for evidence that the candidates' past experiences could be brought to bear on the job."[29] She concluded that making choices on the basis of personal qualities makes sense.

> Most people have experience with judging others by their personal at-tributes. Most find it too time-consuming and too difficult to form opinions

about complex issues on the basis of mass media stories, particularly when the experts differ about the merits of conflicting policy recommendations.[30]

She also found that, contrary to political science folklore, the better-educated among her panelists were most likely to stress image qualities. They felt it necessary to determine whether a candidate is honest, experienced, capable, strong, and trustworthy before issue positions or future performance could be assessed. Citing other studies that confirm the tendency of better-educated voters to emphasize personal traits, Graber concluded that persons who respond to political issues are more likely to be those with affected political interests than simply those who are better educated.[31]

Graber drew on analysis of 1984 campaign experience to conclude that in audio-visual presentations a picture was more influential than a verbal message when the two were in conflict.[32] She cited J. David Gopoian's statement that "candidate attributes are the most important variables" involved in candidate choice, and Benjamin Page's that "it may be that, in an age of nuclear weapons, no aspect of electoral outcomes is more important than the personality of the candidate." Graber concluded:

> When television news provides an opportunity to view candidates repeatedly at close range and in many different kinds of situations, it creates ideal conditions for forming images about the character and qualifications of the candidates.[33]

Candidate images, in fact, are not as devoid of content as much written about image politics suggests. What becomes a candidate's image in a voter's mind may begin with specific information, including positions on issues. Stands on issues may lead a voter to judge the candidate as able, compassionate, smart, likable, or otherwise. And the facts that led the voter to draw such a conclusion may be forgotten while the conclusion sticks.[34] Individuals often deal with information by making general interpretations, retaining those interpretations, and discarding the specifics.

Criticism that debates contribute more to imagery than substance is reinforced by the fact that during the days following a debate many viewers change their opinion of who won. Those changes correspond closely to the evaluations of political analysts and reporters that appear on television and in newspapers. This was conspicuous in 1976 when President Ford's gaffe about Soviet domination in eastern Europe was little noted by viewers until subsequent press commentary highlighted it.[35]

Viewers often change their minds about debate results in accord with journalistic analysis. But little evidence suggests that voting decisions are based on such considerations. Patterson investigated whether voters react differently to news stories about the competitive aspects of a campaign than they do to stories about substantive election issues. He found that voters do indeed respond differently. When they receive reports on who's ahead and what tactics or strategy is at work, they react as spectators. Stories about candidate qualifications and the issues at stake stimulate, contrastingly, evaluations of the contestants' personal abilities, attitudes, and political qualifications.[36]

Moreover, Patterson found no evidence that respondents who delay or change their preferences during the general election campaign gravitate toward a candidate solely because they feel that candidate is leading.[37] He concluded that both the debates and the televised conventions increased the importance of the election's substance for viewers.

> People who watched the conventions were more likely, by August, to have formed the judgment that some aspect of policy or leadership was the campaign's most significant feature. Similarly, debate exposure was related to increases in October of people's assessments of the importance of election substance. Indeed, debate and convention viewing was more closely related than either newspaper or evening newscast exposure to a heightened belief in the significance of policy and leadership matters.[38]

No better outcome for voters could be expected.

TELEVISION AND POLITICAL COMMERCIALS

No aspect of television's part in presidential campaigns invites more criticism than the shorthand symbolism of political commercials. Television, however, did not create a politics of symbols. The log cabin as a worthy birthplace for presidents first appeared in 1840 in the canvass of William Henry Harrison, product of a wealthy family. Great processions of torches, banners, and transparencies were familiar in the nineteenth century. Marchers—some volunteers, some paid—shouted slogans and sang campaign songs with slight pretense of discourse and debate. Symbols have been integral to mass political appeals all along. Happy warriors, plumed knights, full dinner pails, bull mooses, and giantkillers are only some of the images that have been invoked in presidential campaigning.[39] A politics of pure fact would not be politics at all.

Important analyses of the effect and significance of political commercials have been made that illustrate their functions.

Thomas E. Patterson and Robert D. McClure, in an innovative study of campaign advertising, acknowledge that "the critics are right . . . in claiming that some presidential advertising does little more than mimic product advertising. But they also are wrong about political imagery. They misjudged its origins. It did not begin with television. It began with politics."[40]

There are limits, however, on the extent that symbols and other forms of shorthand will prevail over straight information, even among poorly informed voters. The real world checks the potential of political advertising to manufacture an alternate reality. Jack W. Germond and Jules Witcover detailed the valiant efforts of Carter's 1980 campaign to overcome its serious political disadvantage and to create a favorable image of him. But "when the voters were focused on the dominating news events of the day rather than on the carefully crafted commercials that ran just before and after the relentlessly bad news, that political diversion was impossible."[41] Robert Strauss, chairman of President Carter's reelection campaign, said it failed because "the real world is all around us."[42]

Gerald Pomper identified the importance of reality as a backdrop to all political communication. He noted that the most frequent explanation of Reagan's popularity and success was his personality and image, but argued that

> Reagan's popularity, while substantial . . . was also substantive. His vaunted communication skills would have done him little good if unemployment had remained at the painful levels of 1982, or if the United States were involved in a Vietnam-like war in Central America, or if the Social Security System had gone bankrupt. To show the limited impact of simple imagery, Amitai Etzioni suggested, "One need simply imagine that instead of talking about God, family and country, the President was extolling Zen Buddhism, unilateral disarmament and sexual license. His rating would of course crash within a week."[43]

Robert MacNeil charges political commercials with cheapening American politics and wishes they could be outlawed.[44] The United States is, in fact, one of a small proportion of democratic nations—about one-fourth—that permits parties to advertise their programs or candidates on radio or television.[45] Critics charge that brief commercial messages are manipulative, misleading, and foster image rather than issue politics. But it would be hard to find competitors who would not claim that their opponents have displayed the same qualities in campaign speeches and in campaign advertisements of whatever length and form. Much criticism is leveled at the thirty-second and sixty-second bursts that have become common in recent years. Other commentators deplore five-minute political commercials as well.[46] Some critics would prefer only formal speeches or "genuine" debates, believing that voters would gain more useful information from more elaborate presentations.

Even if political commercials were as devoid of substance as some claim, it is not clear that they would be the efficient purveyors of duplicity their critics fear. In fact, paid political advertisements are not devoid of substance. An analysis of televised political commercials during the 1972 presidential campaign found 42 percent to be primarily issue communications and 28 percent more to embody substantive issue material. The twelve issues found to be extensively covered in political advertisements received five times more air time through advertising than in the average network's weeknight newscasts.[47]

The elimination of advertising from presidential campaigns might isolate some segments of the public almost entirely from those campaigns. For some citizens, there may be no substitute for the meager but still real information provided by campaign commercials. Political advertising often repeats messages with substantive content that were slighted on the network news. Also, advertisements are far better designed to reach less-interested voters than are other communications via the mass media.[48]

Political interest is not equally distributed throughout the public any more than are education, wealth, and other resources that help citizens relate to politics. Graber assessed the importance of various psychosocial factors on how the panelists she studied selected and processed the news and concluded that lifestyle is the key factor. It influences what topics and information are of interest and the time available to pursue them. Lifestyle is affected by one's sex, age, marital status, whether or not there are children, and other demographic factors—but these are not destiny. "Variations in life-style which run contrary to stereotypes are quite common. When they occur, media behavior corresponds to life-style, rather than to demographic or social characteristics."[49] Higher education when combined with a professional job produced greater interest and need to keep abreast of current information. When not combined with a professional job, higher education lost much of its stimulus.[50]

Just such differences in lifestyle, according to Patterson and McClure, make paid political advertising important for raising the level of political information in the electorate. Advertising is a way of retailing information that narrows the "information gap" between better-informed citizens and those traditionally less knowledgeable about public affairs—the young and old, the poor, the less educated, women.[51]

Only a few countries permit television advertising in segments of less than five minutes, the United States being one of them. The British Broadcasting Corporation has long had a policy of allocating free time to the parties in ten-minute units. Studies of political broadcasts in Europe concluded, in fact, that the most effective length for a political communication is four minutes. Nations that require the longer segments, however, seem to want messages that reach the informed viewer more effectively than the uninformed one,[52] a questionable goal in democratic politics. Brevity may be the single most important factor in the effectiveness of political commercials. Sandwiched as they are between entertainment features, the briefer ads reach a large, if largely inadvertent, audience. To require that advertising be sold only in larger time blocs, eliminating the thirty-second and sixty-second ads and perhaps even the five-minute ads, would diminish the information value of the presidential campaign for important segments of the electorate.

ISSUE POLITICS: LIMITATIONS OF TELEVISION

Many tensions inherent in democratic politics are embodied in criticisms of the sources and the content of presidential campaign information. Proposals for improvement are addressed sometimes to the sources and sometimes to the content.

With most individuals saying they draw on television for most of their news about current events, televised news coverage of presidential campaigns has been a special target of lament. It is accused of addressing issues superficially, with unduly emphasizing competitive features of the contest; with conveying unfair, negative, and fragmentary images of politicians and politics; with ignoring vital matters when they are complex or lack drama; and with contributing to superficial and inconstant viewer preferences. Those who defend its treatment of presidential campaigns cite format constraints, the diverse audience with diverse interests that television serves, the limitations of a visual medium, and the competitive conditions in which television seeks to make a profitable way.

The First Amendment precludes formal government intervention in the content and presentation of television news, although other aspects of broadcasting are less clearly protected. Nonetheless, critics exhort journalists to report the competitive standings of candidates less frenetically, and generally to take a more positive, less cynical attitude in portraying politics, politicians, and government. Longer news programs, fuller treatment of campaign issues, and deeper probing of candidate qualifications are proposed as improvements. The Public Broadcasting System's MacNeil/Lehrer News Hour and Ted Kopple's ABC News Nightline are applauded for offering just those things.

Television newscasting is not regulated directly in most democratic systems, and in the United States broadcasting in general has been far less controlled than in most other societies. Although audience predilections may influence it, it cannot be controlled, certainly not directly, from outside. The privately owned, commercial status of the major American networks contrasts sharply to the direct or indirect government association with broadcasting in European nations. Although changes in broadcast management are occurring in many European countries, broadcasting there has developed within different traditions and structures from those in the United States.

Some Americans view European television with approval, believing it to be more responsible and to have better content. Europeans conversant with their own broadcasting traditions, however, are not always sanguine about its superiority. Native observers of television and political life in six major European countries—each looking at his own country's broadcasting history— often wished for more of what is found in American political journalism. Heavy-handed political regulation of broadcasting is not pictured in most of these nations. Rather, the picture is one of "self-censorship and damaging restraint"[53] imposed by broadcast journalists on themselves in response to subtle pressures bred of broadcasting's lack of institutional independence. Investigative journalism and uninhibited interviewing have tended to be less vigorous than in the United States, and the control that broadcast authorities have over the careers of individual journalists is said to have a restraining influence.[54] While many observers of American television feel it is excessively critical of politicians and unsupportive of the political system, their European counterparts complain of the opposite condition in their own countries.

Television news influences importantly the exchange of electoral information in the United States, but it is only one of many sources of information and persuasion.[55] Austin Ranney examined television news and concluded that "it is not and never will be the only powerful force shaping our society, our politics, and our visions of reality."[56] Newspapers, news magazines, mass mailings, personal experiences, radio, television's more informative special broadcasts, and even campaign advertising supplement television news as sources of information about issues and events. The First Amendment means that deficiencies perceived in news broadcasting will not be addressed directly through public policy. Given constraints imposed upon conscientious journalists by television's very nature, a pluralistic information environment with a variety of information outlets is the best compensation for the perceived shortcomings of television news.

For citizens to have the information they need for self-government, variety is imperative. Shortage of information about issues has been a constant complaint about recent presidential campaigns. Yet government, not election campaigns, is the arena for resolving conflicts. Voters need to know the candidates' general posture and attitudes toward the functions of government and issues current in society, but the information needed for electing is not the same as that needed for governing. Indeed, in the American political system, with its unique institutions of government, "the issues" are raised through the electoral process but are not settled there.[57] American elections specify the combatants.

In a complex, populous nation, the number of active and potential issues that might be posed publicly for consideration is enormous. Some broad categories of issues like national security and the state of the economy are standard fare. They are likely to interest comparatively large portions of the electorate, especially if difficulties are sensed. Within and beyond such broad concerns a vast array of other issues, usually narrower, waits to be activated—by a candidate, interest group, elected official, political party, or other political competitor. We shall address this important aspect of presidential selection—setting the political agenda—more fully in Chapter Eight. It highlights the lack of set topics that constitute "the issues" in a presidential campaign. Beyond the broad enduring problems of national life, and those posed by immediate circumstances, "the issues" are part of what is determined by the presidential selection process itself. In this context, some critics contend that the issue content of presidential selection processes is deficient.

VARIETY IN INFORMATION AND ITS SOURCES

The content of issues raised or illuminated in electing a president is fixed by more than the air waves, cable, newsprint, books, millions of mailings, or by the other means of communication employed by writers, speakers, and agents of the two major political parties. One thinks of Bernard Berelson's comment in the 1940s that "some kinds of communication on some kinds of issues, brought to the attention of some kinds of people under some kinds of conditions, have some kinds of effects."[58]

American third parties, again, have periodically proved to be sources or conduits of significant, novel political intelligence. In fact, the overall structure of the selection process and its attendant procedures, including eccentricities like the electoral college with its pervasive inducement to attend diligently to state interests, influence the information flow and the number and variety of voices heard. Nonetheless, however electoral information is formulated and communicated, and by whatever technology it reaches voters, the content of campaigns remains for many a matter of concern and controversy. It notably anguished Adlai Stevenson, who doggedly hoped, especially as he prepared for 1956, to stimulate a coherent, substantive debate on the great issues besieging the nation, perhaps inspired by the example of his fellow Illinoisan, Abraham Lincoln, a century before. Instead, Stevenson encountered the distractions of local interests and, in Eisenhower, an opponent whose major focus was on electoral appeal through the use of skillfully crafted spot announcements, which he had pioneered in 1952. Stevenson found uncongenial the notion that candidates and presidents should not think alike.[59]

Proposals to lengthen, abolish, or otherwise constrain paid political advertising are, for example, motivated by this concern for campaign content, despite evidence that such changes could reduce the information about issues now available to some segments of the electorate. An example is found in the Clean Campaign Act of 1985, introduced by seven United States senators, to curb negative advertising. The Act calls for any television advertisement that mentions an opponent and is paid for by a candidate or the candidate's authorized committee to bear the face and voice of that candidate. Leaving aside possible first amendment questions, to require candidates to appear in ads that mention opponents seems reasonable enough. But the bill also states that if independent committees or third-party individuals run an ad supporting a candidate, even without mentioning the opponent, the broadcaster would be required to provide free time to the opponent to respond. Under present conditions, this requirement would doubtlessly eliminate such ads altogether. It would thus lessen the volume of political information available to voters, and also threaten to diminish another element important to democratic electoral politics: vigorous competition among aspirants to office.

Incumbents, who are the candidates most likely to be criticized for their voting records and stands on issues, would benefit from such restrictions. Incumbent advantage is already disproportionate in the electoral system. It would be greatly enhanced if independent groups and individuals were seriously handicapped in campaign discourse. Senator John Danforth (R-Mo.) introduced the bill, deploring the effects of "negative political campaigning." He saw a breakdown of senatorial collegiality and growing apprehension "that when we next face reelection, our opponents will use negative tactics against us, and we will have to use such tactics against them to survive."[60] Incumbents are clearly most likely to benefit from the proposed restrictions.

Senator Ernest Hollings (D-S.C.) supported the legislation, remarking that PAC money can seriously upset the balance in a campaign. "In effect, a candidate budgets to fight one well-financed opponent but then ends up fighting many."[61] Balance, achieved by expenditure limits and regulation of information, almost always favors incumbents. Reinforcing the advantage already normally enjoyed by incumbents will not contribute to informed voting. Political debate from all points of view should be encouraged, not suspended, when a campaign for office is underway, and debate on policies (against as well as for) is hardly possible without reference to persons—e.g., "Reaganomics."[62]

Although the fact is often ignored in efforts at campaign regulation, the American presidential electorate is a very mixed bag. It is multiracial, economically uneven, widely scattered geographically, educationally diverse, engaged in highly differentiated occupations. It is generally more heterogeneous than the electorates in European and English-speaking nations, with which it shares a heritage and ambitions for popular government. In such a country, a variety of forms and sources of information is needed to reach the many audiences that compose the electorate. Recommendations affecting presidential campaign information should be judged with this need in mind.

Conflicting attitudes reflect the differing concepts of a campaign. Should the campaign expose differences and clarify alternatives—or blur them in search of consensus?[63] In fact, candidates and their advocates attempt to do both, in whatever ways they judge will contribute most to their advantage. Viewed from the outside, however, clarification of differences is more likely to promote voter understanding, a necessary condition for popular government to be authentic and, in the long run, to survive. But clarification of differences can be sought by a variety of means, and the best among them is seldom unanimously agreed upon. Consider two concepts of televised presidential "debates."

One projects direct confrontation of candidates without a panel of questioners, holding that head-to-head debate would sharpen the issues and the candidates' positions. Skeptics speculate, however, that such a format would permit the candidates to avoid "no win" issues, issues bound to offend significant numbers of voters regardless of the position taken. A panel of questioners is therefore proposed to assure breadth and diversity in the matters addressed. In all democratic nations, both the variety and volume of political information useful to voters have risen sharply. The mode and regulation of campaigning should recognize this fact.

Although under the evolving circumstances in the United States the interests of voters in electoral information do not always coincide with the narrower interests of parties and candidates, the interests of the three do converge at some points. When candidates electioneer through paid advertising, some voters gain information about issues they might otherwise not have had. Although voters vote less often in accord with party labels than they once did, the labels still help them interpret campaign information and improve their understanding of campaign issues. The parties, for their part, benefit from residual partisan predispositions of voters, even when weak.

Political parties in the United States have long functioned differently from those in the British and other parliamentary systems, where the parties have been celebrated for greater policy coherence and member discipline. Even so, the parts played by the formal party organizations in the United States and their officials in presidential selection have declined with the quantum change in the use of presidential primaries, with the public subsidy of primary and general election candidates, with the rising role of political action committees, and with allied developments. Political parties are now widely viewed as the most disadvantaged participants in American electoral communications. When the interests that parties and voters have in information converge, a disadvantage to parties is a disadvantage to voters as well.

Which party nominated a presidential candidate has long been the most important single message communicated about the candidate. The ideal democratic voter is presumed to be interested, informed, attentive, and concerned about the ideological postures of the parties as well as the stands taken by their candidates on contemporary issues.[64] There is, however, a spacious gap between the ideal voter and almost all citizens.[65]

The need to provide food, clothing, and shelter dominates the lives of most adults in the United States, even under modern affluent conditions. A highly specialized, tightly interdependent economy with generally fixed demands for performance in the workplace consumes a large share of the time, energy, and attention of most adults. Some find themselves also responsible for children or aging parents, with social demands from family and friends, and with a limitless array of optional activities both public and personal, many of which they may deem to be obligations of good citizenship.

Presidential selection processes must take this reality into account, and therein lies the importance of party identification as well as campaign advertising. For some citizens to have informed contact with the electoral process, political information must be available to them without costing much in time, energy, and intellectual effort. A candidate's party identification is such important information.

Recent weakening party identification in the United States has not diminished the importance of partisan cues to voters. Many children early in life become aware of a parent's or whole family's predisposition toward, or against, one of the parties. Thus "even weak partisans might acquire many of the cognitive and normative orientations underlying their party's issue positions during childhood and adolescence."[66] They will consequently be influenced, at least to some extent, to accept party positions on contemporary issues.[67] Voters of low or moderate interest are usually not sophisticated politically and are often not exposed regularly to the news. Among them, knowledge of party differences has been found to contribute more to an understanding of the policies of candidates and to heightened issue awareness than it did among high interest voters.[68]

Candidates, officeholders, and voters come and go, but parties must have continuity to perform their information function effectively in the political system. Extreme proposals made to fortify the parties, however—such as providing public subsidies to them rather than to candidates or permitting only parties to buy television and radio time—run against recent deep-running trends in public policy that reflect important changes in the content of issues and in the composition of the electorate. In Chapter Eleven, less radical suggestions are made to enable the parties to become stronger participants in the electoral competition without, however, assuring them an artificial role in the political system.

Diversity is needed in both the sources and substance of political communications. Information should be of a kind and variety to permit informed personal judgments by voters generally. It should also make possible more sophisticated judgments by better informed and more deeply involved segments of the electorate. Many sources enrich the information environment of an election. Political commercials, whatever their length, do so, whether paid for by parties, candidates, independent committees, or persons boosting third parties. Candidate debates do also, whatever the format. A panel of questioners can provide useful probing.

Opportunities for any competitor in the electoral process to be heard, not just the political parties, can produce information helpful to voters. John H. Kessel concluded, in fact, after assessing the information learned by voters in the 1976 general election campaign, that "if campaigns were to end a month earlier, there would be a larger number of uninformed citizens, and they would likely be less at ease with the electoral choice they are advised to make."[69] If the volume of political information available to voters were reduced, or certain types eliminated, the burdens of good citizenship would be increased. Reducing the volume of political speech by changing the channels for its transmission, or the length permitted for individual appeals, would not assure its greater quality or integrity.

Although the words and deeds of candidates and parties as transmitted by the major communications media constitute the crucial information foundation of presidential campaigns, peculiar features of the American electoral system, to which we now turn, contribute additional information to voters, candidates, and political parties.

CHAPTER FIVE

Electoral Systems
and Information

☆
☆

Arthur Schlesinger, Jr., has emphasized that "we will never attain a working political system by concentrating on the revision of party rules and structure. We will attain it only by remembering that politics is the art of solving problems."[1] Lord Bryce wrote that "the student of institutions, as well as the lawyer, is apt to overrate the effect of mechanical contrivances in politics."[2]

Even seasoned Democratic politician Morley Winograd, declaring himself a "leading 'rules freak,' " warned "against overrating the real impact of rules or, for that matter, laws upon the final electoral outcome." He declared that if a rules change is perceived to give some contestants an advantage, a countermove will "neutralize the advantage by changing the rules or laws again . . . . The tinkering may be fun, but its political impact is minimal."[3]

So it may be, but few political competitors can be persuaded that the rules don't matter to them personally and to the causes and values they seek to advance. Defining when and how much they matter, however, and connecting specific provisions to specific consequences, is a slippery business. Beyond claims that they encourage a fairer or more democratic politics, or are easy to administer, or that they promote accountability, procedures and structures influence tangibly who reaches office and the political information, objectives, and limitations they carry with them.

This chapter addresses the significance of electoral procedures for the quality and distribution of political information, and motivations underlying proposals to change them. The likely consequences of several proposals are assayed, including those for approval voting, proportional representation, eliminating or modifying the electoral college, and encouraging "third" parties. Those examinations lead to a discussion of generalist versus specialist politics and the organic significance of information in a democracy.

THE SIGNIFICANCE OF PROCEDURES

Austin Ranney has described two approaches to political reform. One he calls the "virtue is its own reward" attitude and the other the "by their fruits they shall be known" attitude. The first wants politics to be more fair, honest, open, democratic. The second attends results—which groups gain influence, who is nominated and elected, what actions result.[4]

Few advocates of political reforms are not moved primarily by the changes in substance that they envision would flow from changed procedures or structure. Allocating legislative seats by proportional representation, for example, encourages multiparty politics. This in turn affects the types of information and claims generated in the system, and consequently the kinds of issues, conflicts, and settlements likely to surface. The same patterns of interest would not be found in the two-party politics that single-member districts with plurality winners are found to favor.[5] Political analysts like E. E. Schattschneider and James MacGregor Burns, who have advocated more "responsible" parties in the United States in preference to the loose constituency parties the nation has known, have wished to alter political substance as well as political form.[6]

Thus, while political energy will find a way to express itself whenever channels lie open for political action,[7] not all channels are alike or equally open, and different electoral systems breed different information with different political consequences. Some procedures can dilute, distort, or destroy important political content; others can enhance it. How well the political process fosters the communication of political information is not the only measure by which to judge it. But robust communications are necessary for the full success of popular elections—which are the principal instrument of democratic willing—and thus are the base on which other democratic institutions rest.

Citizens, voters, candidates, office-holders, interest groups, political parties, in short, all participants, need to know who expects or demands what, who is willing or unwilling to accept what. These bits of *discrete* information are the staples of campaign communication. But, also, at another level, nominating and electing activities communicate *systemic* information about the nation as a whole. They expose characteristics of the nation's evolving social, economic, and political life, including popular satisfaction with the electoral system itself. Many proposals for altering presidential selection methods would affect its information functions. These functions are so critical to democratic government that the benefits of any change should be both probable enough and large enough to warrant the risk of unanticipated, unacceptable change in the lifeblood of democracy—which is what timely, politically relevant information is.

Democracy is characteristically defined by statements using the vocabulary of "virtue is its own reward." Revered concepts like majority rule, citizen participation, and popular sovereignty dominate the discourse.[8] Concepts like freedom of speech and equal rights bring the discourse closer to issues of substance, but not fully to the concept of "by their fruits they shall be known."

The United States needs electoral conditions that are both acceptably democratic and that produce a government acceptably informed, authoritative, and effective in addressing substantive needs. Opinions differ on how best to ensure these conditions. James Madison was realistic in noting that honorable individuals employing reason are likely to divide in their opinions, while only those possessed of a common passion are likely to arrive at a single conclusion.[9]

VOTING AS COMMUNICATING

Political information influences importantly the composition of political forces. Different electoral systems constitute different communication systems, consequently with different effects on substance. A proposal to introduce what is called approval voting into the United States illustrates the point.

Approval voting enables each voter in a primary or general election to vote for as many candidates as the voter finds acceptable, making no distinctions among those more favored or less favored. Here is a proposal of what could have happened under such a system in 1980:

> If Carter Democrats worrying about Reagan on the right can also vote for Anderson because he is more acceptable than Reagan, and if Reagan Republicans worrying about Carter on the left, can also vote for Anderson because he is more acceptable than Carter, then Anderson would truly be the consensus candidate in the middle. He would be elected and . . . should be elected because this is the expression of popular choice.[10]

The proposed change in process is intended to affect electoral results through the information conveyed in the balloting. Steven J. Brams and his associate, Peter C. Fishburn, urge that changing in this way the definition of what constitutes a democratic choice would improve the outcome of periodic elections. The change would translate "voter preferences, with as little distortion as possible, into consensus choices in multicandidate races."[11]

Approval voting has pragmatic goals, appeal to democratic impulses, and meritorious advocates. Yet, ironically, viewed for the moment solely as a generator of information, it would diminish rather than increase the useful information produced by American presidential selection. The procedure would muffle underlying differences that would benefit more from reconciliation or confrontation. Important political substance would be lost because the proposed procedure would not force every voter to choose her or his most acceptable candidate. In the existing system, the reasons voters vote as they do are hard enough to interpret. Many factors influence them. But under approval voting, the significance of the votes cast and of the outcome would be even more elusive. Conceivably the winning candidate could be everybody's second, or lesser, choice. The resulting consensus would convey less operational meaning than the present system.

Great Britain provides another illustration of the relationship between electoral structure, political information, and governance. In their analysis of the 1983 general election, David Butler and Dennis Kavanagh concluded that "the two main parties were probably less able to represent and aggregate the diversity of interests throughout the United Kingdom than at any period since 1918."[12] This was an important conclusion because the British parliamentary system was long extolled as exceeding other democratic governments in its ability to generate an electoral mandate linking voters to defined policies of government. In recent decades, however, with at least three parties winning seats in the House of Commons, a party drawing less than a majority of votes can capture a majority of parliamentary seats, and with it the power of government. Thus the views of a majority of the electorate may not, by this measure, be represented in the policies of the governing party. Moreover, in these circumstances, even though class has declined in importance in British society, the major British parties have come more and more to represent class-based political programs.[13] Present British practices are consequently perceived as distorting, even destroying, important electoral information.[14]

Recommendations have come forth that Britain abandon its plurality principle in parliamentary elections and adopt a scheme of proportional representation. Advocates of proportional representation argue that placing in Parliament representatives who better reflect voter opinion would largely overcome any present mismatch between what the electorate endorses and what it gets in government.

Theodore J. Lowi, in fact, advocates a full-fledged three-party system for the United States, arguing that "a two-party system simply cannot grapple with complex programmatic alternatives in a manner that is meaningful to large electorates ...."[15] We address third parties later in this chapter but note some of Lowi's views here. He believes the American two-party system is beyond reviving, and in any event believes that change in the form of American political competition to a three-party system would improve the content of information by clarifying policies, programs, and lines of accountability better than two major parties can. Lowi holds that a full-fledged three-party system would reduce the likelihood that any candidate would win a majority in the electoral college; as a result, candidates would not look to the public as their main constituency but to Congress, and presidents would be separated from the public and more closely tied instead to their political parties.[16]

All proposals for procedural and structural change, whatever their abstract merits and however they might be accomplished, need to be concerned with consequences. No democratic system, however pure its form, is desirable if it cannot function effectively enough to sustain itself. Nonetheless, democracy is inherently pledged to realizing "virtue" in addition to earning its own survival. That may be what most distinguishes it from other principles of political organization. In Giovanni Sartori's words, "The *ought* and the *is* of democracy are inextricably intertwined."[17] Societies that would be democratic have sought to wed virtue to prudence through institutions. Ideals and results are almost as difficult to untangle in assessing institutional reform as they are in discussing democracy itself.

THE ELECTORAL COLLEGE AND POLITICAL INFORMATION

The electoral college has influenced decisively the flow and quality of political information in American presidential selection since the nation's birth. It has, moreover, been a fixed, unaltered piece of mechanics since the Twelfth Amendment was ratified in 1804. Although criticisms of it as a leftover from republican elitism are both philosophical and operational, and although serious proposals were made in Congress in the 1960s and 1970s to abolish it by constitutional amendment, no more recent significant move to do so has surfaced.

Fundamentally, critics see the college as obstructing a truly popular election of the nation's chief political officer.[18] In the electoral college each state is given a number of votes equal to the total of its representatives and senators in the Congress. Since every state has two senators regardless of its population, popular votes in some states enjoy arithmetically greater weight than in others. Moreover, except in Maine, the electoral votes of a state are intended to be cast as a unit for one candidate. (In Maine, by state legislation of 1969, the outcome in each congressional district names an elector, and moves were made in 1990 in Connecticut, North Carolina, and elsewhere to adopt a similar system.[19])

The practice can produce a tally in the electoral college significantly more one-sided than the nationwide popular vote—which it usually does— or even at variance with the popular vote, which it did in 1888 when Benjamin Harrison defeated Grover Cleveland. And there are other potential difficulties. A deadlock can develop in the electoral college if no candidate receives a majority of electoral votes, throwing the decision into the House of Representatives, as occurred in 1824. If a faithless elector—one who votes in the electoral college contrary to the plurality in the state—should ever affect the outcome, surely a crisis would result. And hypothetical horrors are invoked. If, in 1976, some 9,000 votes in Hawaii and Ohio had been cast for Gerald Ford instead of Jimmy Carter, Ford would have won the electoral college despite trailing Carter by more than 1,500,000 popular votes.[20] Essentially, critics object to a relic of the original political system that is condemned as not fully democratic.

Advocates of abolishing the electoral college argue that it distorts the popular vote without any offsetting value. Their objections stem from a single strand of democratic doctrine—majority rule determined by one person, one vote. In addition to assuring lack of mathematical equality among voters, the electoral college advantages or disadvantages some categories of citizens and some types of states because of the unequal distribution of population among the states, although who is, in fact, rewarded or penalized at a given time, and how much, is a highly complex calculation.[21] If the system simply distorted the popular vote and diminished citizen equality, it would have no justification beyond the tenacity of tradition, plus such appeals as interests purportedly served by it might construct.

The electoral college, however, strongly influences the way presidential campaigns are conducted, directly and beneficially affecting the distribution of political information in the general election campaign. Geographic considerations are a major focus of current presidential campaigns. They force candidates to heed not only matters of broad national concern—such as social benefits for the elderly, women's employment rights, and relations among nations—but also a wide variety of issues of limited compass that are important in particular states and sections and that would attract little attention if the whole nation were a single election district. Thus, without the electoral college the emphasis would shift even more sharply than at present toward issues of primary significance to very large classes of voters, and candidates could reasonably seek to amass a majority or plurality by appeals principally to such voters, for example to middle-class citizens or dwellers in large urban areas, whose interests are only partly shared by the country as a whole.[22] Such reorientations in strategy would change the substance of national politics, making it less inclusive. The historic incentive to build a coalition widely based among the diverse 50 states would be diluted.[23]

The electoral college consequently encourages important decentralization in the general election campaign. The inducement to presidential candidates and their spokesmen to go where the voters are, in all their scattered habitations and concentrations across a heterogeneous continental nation, has great value. Candidates perforce gain some sensitivity to the nation's diverse downhome issues. Theodore H. White maintained:

> If states are abolished as voting units, TV becomes absolutely dominant. Campaign strategy changes from delicately assembling a winning coalition of States and becomes a media effort to capture the largest share of the national "vote market." ... Issues will be shaped in national TV studios, and the heaviest swat will go to the candidate who raises the most money to buy the best time and most "creative" TV talent.[24]

This may be somewhat overstated, yet absence of the campaign imperatives generated by the electoral college could easily lead to greatly increased centralized, national media campaigning as the preferred use of finite resources. The tendency is already pronounced even with the electoral college in place.

To encourage it would be deleterious, and not justified simply because it would produce technical mathematical equality among votes. True, relatively few voters now encounter a presidential candidate personally. And some present campaign travel is chiefly motivated to create photo opportunities in the provinces. Yet centralizing campaigns even more would remove candidates further from state and local grass-root politics—parties, candidates, activists, and issues. Presidential candidates would have less inducement to learn the nation as a whole than now comes from traveling, campaigning, and studying voters' interests in 50 diverse states. As Max S. Power puts it, "[T]he problem with direct election is that it abstracts presidential elections from the context of American government and politics."[25]

The president has a national constituency, but must work with a Congress composed of members with state-based constituencies. Rather than making a president more responsive to national majorities, abolition of the electoral college would make the president less informed of the nation's complexity and of its inherent limitations and possibilities.

The different constituency bases of the House, Senate, and presidency are principal underpinnings of the separation of powers. Yet the electoral college at least requires presidents to think in terms of state issues and politics, as senators and representatives must, and the inducement for them to do so has increased as one-party dominance of presidential voting within states has declined since World War II. Popular election of the president, meaning full nationalization of the presidential constituency, would make even more pronounced than at present the differences among the presidential and the other two electorates.

Elimination of even a modest potential contribution to cooperation between the two federal branches seems unwise when the principal promised gain is avoidance of minor mathematical inequalities among votes. The linkage between presidential and congressional elections as a basis for political collaboration has become increasingly tenuous without institutionalizing a greater disjunction. Moreover, if the principle of one person, one vote were to be fully implemented, the composition of the Senate would also need change.

The differing constituencies of the House, Senate, and presidency are as important to the system of checks and balances as is the distribution of authority and responsibility specified in the Constitution. Since adoption of the Seventeenth Amendment requiring direct election of senators, the states as corporate entities do not have representation in the federal government. Direct election of senators simply means that in its popular voting the public is subdivided on a different basis than it is in most House constituencies. While the principal checks on government are found in its ultimate control by the public, in the United States further checks (and balances) are encouraged by the electoral independence from each other of the House, Senate, and presidency.

Many influences in presidential selection now increase the leverage of national forces—among them the nationwide orientation of the media, the growing centralization in the conduct of presidential election campaigns, even the recent relative strengthening of national party organizations. The resulting pressures, however, may be no less "particular," no less special or narrowly targeted, than influences originating from more geographically dispersed sources. The general public interest, in competition with special interests, does not necessarily carry greater weight when issues are faced in national forums than when addressed within states.

The flow of information—including data, opinion, argument, claims—from voters to candidates and candidates to voters would seem to suffer, not gain, from direct popular election of the president. National voter opinion is already available to candidates and presidents from the constant stream of public opinion polls. A more sensitive understanding of issues within states would not be gained without the electoral college's strong incentives and its influence on campaign strategy. Whether candidates discuss local issues, national issues in local context, or national issues alone, voters feel the campaign closer to their daily lives when candidates take geographic differences into account in planning their campaigns.

Moreover, local problems are often not local, in the sense that their importance is limited to one or a few locales. Local problems are often national problems with local variations.[26] These variations frequently call for recognition and flexibility in national policy if national policy is to be successful. As American federalism has evolved, solutions to problems have been sought through action in various arenas and levels of the federal system, and, increasingly, especially since 1932, through policies and programs initiated by the national government. To imply that there may be issues, problems, and solutions that are exclusively national, however, as distinct from their state and local implications, is to misunderstand both the issues and problems as well as the nature of the country's federalism. If presidents were elected by direct popular vote, the linkage between national government and politics and their counterparts in states and localities would be weakened, disadvantaging the function of party and government at all levels.

The increased nationalization of political business in recent decades has markedly diminished the independent scope of state and local government action. In large modern nations, strengthening the governmental center has proved inevitable. Nonetheless, in the United States the states serve vital political and governmental purposes. They partition the nation's enormous, complex population into historically accepted subdivisions. Sequential primaries and caucuses for selecting national convention delegates increase state influence in the political information generated through the nomination process. The electoral college does the same thing in the general election campaign.

Genuine regional differences do exist in the United States. Some states produce energy that is consumed in other states. Some states have more homogeneous populations; other states have more heterogeneous populations. Minorities may cluster in some states and not others. Some states are rich, others poor; some are heavily industrial, others heavily agricultural. Inevitably, many disparities divide localities in a continental nation. The presidency functions in a context of public policy complexity borne of deep and myriad disparities. An authentic national perspective requires appreciation of them. The electoral college creates incentive to gain such appreciation. Presidential campaigns offer genuine, though imperfect, opportunities to do so.

In reflecting on the campaign demands imposed by the electoral college, President Carter applauded their educational value.

> I think there is a learning process in going to the liberal centers of the country in Boston and San Francisco, in seeing first hand the devastation in the Bronx, in visiting the midwest farm belt where I had never been, in attending little town meetings where they cross examine you about your policies. In the process you learn. You make mistakes and have to study for better answers. You learn the country in the process.[27]

Unless American government is completely restructured, Congress will continue to reflect and represent regional and local differences. Political partisanship and the factional and party alliances based on it have typically proved unable to eradicate the effects of these diversities. Regional conflicts have become especially evident in Congress as new kinds of issues have emerged. Energy and environmental issues, for example, have produced different patterns of conflict than did older issues.[28] A president innocent of such understanding will be unnecessarily at odds with Congress. A radically rearranged presidential constituency, such as direct popular election of the president would create, could well increase the operative separation of the president from the Congress at a time when the opposite result is needed for more effective collaboration.

When asked how effective the American system of government looks from abroad, a foreign observer and frequent visitor to the United States answered that American government appears effective, in some measure because so much governing goes on at state and local levels. Even when Washington seems stymied, government and the nation go on. Many unitary democracies are, in fact, discussing decentralization, or are already moving toward it, in response to what is seen as overcentralization in government, politics, and society. Thus, the United States ought to examine cautiously any changes likely to centralize its political life further. Some changes that work toward that end, such as strengthening the national party organizations, seem clearly beneficial. But nations with dramatically smaller and less diverse populations show signs of debilitating effects of overcentralization. Richard Rose has emphasized that "the American system in all its variety is often an object of admiration by Europeans who have grown to dislike the centralization of authority in which too many roads seem to lead to Rome, to Paris or London."[29]

Some potential though infrequently encountered difficulties with the electoral college can be eliminated without destroying its present value as a decentralizing influence in presidential campaigns.

The danger of "faithless electors"—ones who do not vote for the winning candidate in their states, of whom there were five in the six elections between 1956 and 1976—can be eliminated by a constitutional amendment awarding a state's electoral votes automatically to the winner of the popular vote in that state. On balance, this is desirable, but at least one thoughtful expert opposes removing the "worthwhile quality of flexibility" afforded by existing arrangements, arguing that third candidates, and referral of the choice of president to the House, could be headed off by major-candidate electors who would switch against their pledge to the other major candidate.[30]

Constitutional amendment is also needed for another matter. At present, if no candidate were to receive a majority of votes in the electoral college, the decision would be thrown into the House of Representatives for choice among the top three candidates. There each of the fifty state delegations has one vote and the majority vote of a state's delegation would determine for whom that vote would be cast. A famous instance of this occurred in 1824. The unitary delegation vote made sense when the states as corporate entities were being represented in the electoral college. Now it is the voters in each state who are being represented. The unit rule could properly be amended to provide that each member of the House cast an individual vote should the selection of a president fall to that body.

How in such a case members of the House would actually vote is not certain. There is evidence that U.S. Representatives, irrespective of party, are influenced in considering president-sponsored legislation by how well the president ran as a candidate in the member's district.[31] Thus, a representative might be disposed to vote for the candidate who led in popular votes among the representative's constituents. To explain not doing so might be a greater burden than a politician, except the most opinionated or courageous, would care to carry. To the extent that representatives followed their constituents' recorded preferences, the House would behave like an electoral college of members from congressional districts rather than states. The candidate who led in the popular vote might well be the likely winner, but not always, as in the very close election of 1960.

Thus, all in all, while the electoral college assures that the weight of each popular vote cast in a state will be slightly different from that cast in every other state, the disparities are insufficient to forego the benefits of the system. If the disparities of influence among voters in different states clearly and consistently operated unfairly in determining the outcome of presidential elections, the continued use of the electoral college would properly be challenged. But present suppositions and likelihood of bias do not suggest a significant distortion of the electorate's will in choosing the president.

The nation has easily accepted presidents in both the last century and the present whose electoral majority was earned with less than a majority of the popular vote—Abraham Lincoln, Woodrow Wilson, Harry Truman, and Richard Nixon among them. The technical possibility always exists that a candidate's popular plurality or majority could be so divided among the states that an opponent could win a majority of the electoral votes and the presidency. This has not happened for a century, and a nationwide popular election is too high a price to pay to avoid the unlikely possibility. If a change were to be made, determining electoral votes by congressional district results would be a far better step to take.

Future changes in national political life may change the value or acceptability of the electoral college. Someday it could become a recognized liability and be, in fact, the antiquated device present critics claim it is. Meanwhile, it increases the political information generated by presidential elections, and the learning inducements of presidential candidates, in ways more beneficial than detrimental to the nation.

AMERICAN "THIRD" PARTIES

The principle of single-member districts with plurality elections used in choosing members of both houses of Congress is a major support of the country's two-party system. So is the practice by which states vote as units in the electoral college as determined by the plurality of votes within each state. Minority parties have often made significant contributions to political debate and evolving public policy, but not since 1856 has a new major party, the present Republican party, emerged and lasted.

Third parties and the divergent, diverse sources of information they provide are hobbled, however, by more than constitutional arrangements. Some analysts propose that third parties have had little electoral success because Americans have a deeply ingrained two-party habit.[32] Although the percentage of Americans claiming independence from party allegiance has grown, a large majority still consider themselves attached to a major party. And the trend toward independence seems to be leveling off, perhaps even declining.[33]

Early in the 1960s V. O. Key, Jr., reported that students of protest movements "seem to agree that the day of the third party, at least in presidential elections, is done."[34] And although since 1968 independent candidates and minor parties have gained greater access to electoral processes, largely as a consequence of the efforts of George Wallace, John Anderson, and federal court decisions,[35] some recent "reforms" have extended third-party handicaps.[36]

The Federal Election Campaign Act favors the major parties in several ways: they get funds before the election, minor parties after; major party candidates for nomination receive matching federal funds, minor parties without primaries do not; contributions up to $20,000 may be made to national party committees, but not to independent candidates.[37] Moreover, political party sponsorship of the presidential debates, as obtained in 1988, is seen as an added detriment to third-party movements.[38] And proposals are made that would hobble third parties further, like basing increased free television time and party subsidies on past electoral performance.

Whatever the motive, any action that severely handicaps third parties reduces an important means of political representation.[39] Pope McCorkle and Joel L. Fleishman warn against proposals they call collectively the "party protectionist solution" to the perceived decline of party influence. Under these schemes, "the two parties would become more analogous to public utilities than to autonomous 'private' political associations."[40] Proposals to subsidize the parties with new measures of public support like more public funds or free television time would weaken further the potential of third parties because eligibility for such funding is usually presumed to depend on past performance.

Frank Sorauf, in a 1967 essay, rejected the tendency to consider political parties as "independent agencies in the political system" and rather saw the political party as "itself a product of the forces of the political system .... The parties cannot step outside of the political system in order to get greater leverage on it."[41] Third parties in the American system have reflected "the forces of the political system" and, as such, have been important agents of adaptation and change. They could not be guaranteed by reform. They are products of intense motivation, enormous work, and a complex of fortuitous circumstances.[42] As such they contribute to the political agenda and consequently are sources of information useful in maintaining governmental flexibility and resilience.

They are important, although the lesser parties taken together attracted only 5.1 percent of the popular vote in the years 1968 through 1980, similar to that of third parties in the periods 1848–60 and 1904–24 and much more than in other periods of American history. In 1984 fourteen minor candidates who received votes in one or more states drew in all only about one-half of one percent of the total, and in 1988 all minor candidates together polled 1 percent.[43]

Third party candidates have at times advocated policies too novel or extreme for the major parties, although the major parties later embraced them. Steven J. Rosenstone, Roy L. Behr, and Edward H. Lazarus, authors of a major modern study of third parties in American politics, conclude that minor parties "are a weapon citizens can use to force the major parties to be more accountable .... They represent the needs and demands of Americans whom the major parties have ignored."[44] Put differently, the components of a party system need to be strong, but they also need to be at risk. Third parties are thus an important source of political information in the electoral process.

GENERALIST POLITICS VS. SPECIALIST POLITICS

Political information expresses the substance of political interests and, as we saw with third parties, the assertion of those interests can affect political structures and processes.

Rising independent groups and their political activities in the United States have affected significantly the content of political communications, but parties and candidates still dominate the electoral process; interests and traditional groups still serve as building blocks of party coalitions. In the United States, as in other western nations, parties with broad programs must function alongside narrow-cast groups concerned about such things as hand-gun control, population growth, refugee quotas, disarmament, and the quality of the environment. A politics of opinions has been growing in the recent years of the Communications Revolution. It contrasts with the interest-based and class-based politics prevalent throughout much of the twentieth century and has been having an important influence on the electoral system.

The dramatic growth of positive government in the United States began with the New Deal, was enlarged by the Great Society, and has had a penetrating effect in nudging American political life away from a generalist politics toward a specialist politics. New alternatives to political party activity have grown rapidly. Special-purpose organizations with sharply defined objectives and concentrated energies appeal to citizens more interested in immediate stakes than in a political party of more diffuse, longer-range ambitions. Persons agitated by specific issues—e.g., equal rights, education, nuclear arms, and the narrow goals and anxieties within them—are attracted to special-purpose organizations led and staffed by dedicated folk, committed to well-defined objectives, who articulate their demands and justify them with abundant data and argument.[45]

Similar developments have been occurring across a broad sweep of advanced democracies. In a large sample of democratic nations in Western Europe, and in the United States, citizen action groups and single issue groups were in evidence almost everywhere in the 1980s, operating partially or wholly outside political parties—with significant effects on the information environment of elections. Although citizen groups have long been active in education and community-level policies, they have recently become active in a much broader and growing group of issues reaching to social services, the morality of policies and regulations, issues of energy, housing, and urbanism, and more. And the number of citizens choosing to become so involved has grown significantly. In several nations, citizen action group membership exceeds formal party membership.[46]

Clearly, change in the subject matter of politics has affected the structure of political action by a shift not only from generalist politics toward specialist politics, but from "class politics to value politics" and from "*social-group* cleavages to *issue-group* cleavages."[47] The messages political parties have been expected to refine and structure have been transformed.

Experts speculate on the future, should present trends continue, of political parties and political systems. A condition could develop in which the party in the electorate had become so diminished that campaigns were almost exclusively issue-oriented and candidate-centered. Voters would consequently not have the information base provided by party identification as a foundation for choice, a situation not unlike the Federalist period in the United States, or earlier times in England with their "currents of opinion."[48]

It was just such political parties, in fact, that M. Ostrogorski, the famed critic of parties, advocated at the beginning of the twentieth century. The parties he envisioned would cease to represent interests, which he saw as already too much represented in political assemblies.[49] Instead of fixed institutions preoccupied with organizational maintenance, political associations would form and re-form "according to the changing problems of life and the play of opinion brought about thereby. Citizens who part company on one question would join forces on another."[50]

The communications of independent groups in presidential campaigns, whether desirable or not, cannot be restricted by direct regulation, and the incentives of activists with issue concerns will not be dampened when given short shrift by the parties. The electoral prominence of such groups is likely to grow.

The influence of independent groups might be curbed by giving more public funds to candidates, thus, possibly, reducing the importance of spending by independent committees,[51] but there can be no guarantee that the activities of the groups themselves would change. Many conditions associated with their growth would remain. In any event, full equality in political communications cannot be achieved as long as the press is free to report and comment as it chooses on issues and candidates. In fact, weakening noncandidate committees would increase the influence of the corporate press.[52]

Independent specialist committees that support candidates have also grown in importance and their activities need diligent monitoring by the Federal Election Commission. Independent expenditures are usually more observable than other activities they pursue. The FEC has become an important potential source of political information about them, but, as in other regulatory matters, much depends on the Commission itself.

The increasingly fluid politics of multiple, particular concerns that transmit and generate information now challenges the older, more stable politics of fewer broad interests. Political parties may ultimately be able to accommodate some aggressive, narrow advocacies within their broad partisan programs, but they will also have to coexist with specialized electoral organizations that cannot be completely tamed. Even if parties continue as the principal sources of partisan political information and shapers of political debate, the number and variety of issues and interests they work with will constitute an information environment of politics more specialized than before.

INFORMATION AND DEMOCRACY

This chapter, so far, and the three preceding ones, have dealt with relationships between political information and the means of nominating and electing candidates for president. What follows now is a coda: reflections on the fundamental dependence of democratic processes on adequate information. Giovanni Sartori concluded that "electoral instruments say just about as much as the voters have to say."[53] The intricacies, ambiguities, and achievements lodged in existing American arrangements are not always readily evident, nor their meanings certain.

To define democracy as a concept, or to describe it in practice, is necessarily to speak with ambiguity and qualification. An absolute monarchy or a governing aristocracy can be characterized more simply, even when such a system needs an elaborate apparatus for collecting information and ensuring discipline. There is little conflict between the theory and practice of monarchy, or of aristocracy. Monarchs and aristocratic councils may need to reckon with the opinions of others in making decisions, and while such concessions may diminish their power, they do not diminish their authority to base their decisions on whatever criteria they choose. But rule by the many—Aristotle's shorthand definition of democracy—is abstruse. It is difficult to comprehend conceptually, and in practice its full range of influences and actions cannot be completely and reliably observed.

Beyond the New England town meeting or Rousseau's assembly under the tree, the democratic will is not manifest at a single site or at a certain time. Nor is the democratic will fully embodied in one leader, or in a restricted number of officials, or even in a set of social roles or governmental actions. We know democracy as a system of institutions, processes, procedures, and structural relationships. But democracy is also an idea that embraces a dazzling array of abstract principles and unrealized aspirations that often are not articulated in the vocabulary of institutions, procedures, processes, and structural relationships. Practice and theory seem at times in harmony, but at other times to have little connection with each other.

Democracy, *democratic willing,* requires a voluminous exchange of information among its diverse participants, including "rulers" and "ruled," voters and candidates, competing interests and cooperating interests. James David Barber has described democracy as "a great conversation, a community defined by the scope and substance of its discourse."[54] The competitive popular election with its boisterous energies and ritualistic exercises is the activity that serves most explicitly the elemental democratic purpose of information exchange. No matter how well actual elections in actual democracies conform to one or more theories of democracy, no better means has yet appeared for stimulating and exchanging the information needed for democratic willing, for democracy, in the modern nation-state.

Samuel P. Huntington, in addressing the relationship of ideas to institutions, has held that Americans genuinely subscribe to their democratic rhetoric in a way that citizens in no other nation fully do. Perhaps it is natural that periodically Americans become preoccupied with discrepancies they discern between that rhetoric and the actualities of their institutions. Moral passions are stirred. A groundswell follows, advocating reform.[55] Electoral procedures have always been a magnet for moral energy. In truth, much purposeful change has resulted in the United States. The goals of change have not always been reached, however, and the soldiers of reform are no strangers to unanticipated results. Inevitably, American electoral processes never achieve a full state of democratic grace. Dissatisfactions with them are always present precisely because they are the central instruments of a democracy.

Spasms of moral passion are not the only source of change in electoral practices. Changes in the context in which established procedures function may alter their outcome even when the procedures themselves remain fixed. New housing patterns, high residential mobility, frequency of employee and tourist travel, growth in group attachments, new diversity and complexity of issues, changes in sources of politically relevant information, changes in media capabilities, ownership, concentration, and diversity, changing educational levels, and many other alterations in personal and community life can affect the adequacy of previously viable procedures. Changes in activities and incentives removed from formal political life expose or create weaknesses in democratic machinery. Reform may then be stimulated less by a drive to achieve a democratic ideal than by a need to cope with decline in the performance of the machinery itself. Incentives can be fired to restore past performance as well as to achieve new goals.

A notion that human institutions never require conscious adaptation is as untenable as one that human institutions need constant change. But the energizing forces of moral passion and pragmatic need are not always readily distinguishable. Advocacy of greater citizen participation in nominating procedures, for example, can stem from both. In both cases, difficult *prescription,* rather than comfortable description, is called for.[56]

Any reform may have implications beyond the principles, data, and analyses summoned to promote it. Reforms assessed only in their own terms will almost certainly be incompletely understood. Prescriptions require standards of evaluation, but whether the standards stem from warm passion or cool reason, hardly ever will they anticipate all the complete, remote, and unplanned results.

Democracy and representative government are inconceivable, cannot be achieved, without a vigorous give-and-take of news, data, opinion, and argument. The requirement is inherent in the concepts of democracy and representative government. It is important, therefore, that proposals to change political organization and procedures preserve or promote the exchange of political information. The degree and ways they do so should also be an essential part of their evaluation.

CHAPTER SIX

Changing Forms of
Political Participation

☆
☆

In his first inaugural in 1885, Grover Cleveland proclaimed that "every voter, as surely as your chief magistrate, exercises a public trust." Voting is certainly the central act of democratic government, and in the last four chapters we have examined the informational base on which that great seminal right—which in the long perspective of history is an immense privilege—is exercised. Americans have exercised the right by directly electing more public officials at all levels of government over a longer period of time than any other people. Yet, whether because of that frequency or not, voting in American presidential elections has often been low compared with voting in other nations, and it fell markedly after 1960.

At the same time, demands have become common in the United States and many other democratic nations for direct citizen influence in societal decisions. Where formal channels to influence prove unyielding, alternatives are often sought. Always a possibility—remember the tea party in Boston harbor and the sit-down strikes in the 1930s—direct political actions then become increasingly frequent. An analysis of electoral change in advanced industrial democracies emphasizes that "as Americans surround Seabrook, [so also] Germans storm Brokdorf, Britons march on Windscale, and Japanese protest Minamata. Citizen action movements are now a common part of the democratic political process,"[1] making the limited act of voting an incomplete index to political participation.

Activities and initiatives in addition to voting are taken to attract the attention of public officials and to induce their action. Individual and group energies separate from voting therefore affect the representativeness, legitimacy, and capability of democratic systems. The concerns that motivate such political participation range from matters of broad public policy to governmental actions of purely local or personal significance.

As political issues agitating the nation have become more diverse, complex, and far-reaching, the United States government's impact on people's lives has correspondingly become more direct and pervasive. Consequently, citizen efforts have grown to exert direct influence on government. From the eighteenth century onward determined Americans have striven to make government serve their personal interests through policies and perquisites. In the last half of the twentieth century, however, changes in the educational, occupational, economic, ethnic and other characteristics of the population, and in the structure, diversity, and dynamism of the economy, have produced citizen initiatives of increasing variety and independence. Traditional party leadership has found it difficult to cope with new expectations, and with the energetic, policy-driven independence of activists.

Changes made after 1968 in party and public regulation of presidential nominations were precipitated by the dammed-up ambitions of the new activists. Vigorous new patterns of politics resulted. As we have seen, the increased use of presidential primaries and open state conventions is the focus of much contemporary assessment of presidential selection. But other forms of political action, ranging from petitions to propaganda to protests to myriad other forms of pressure, are also significant in presidential selection and in their influence on government and its agenda.

Defining political participation conceptually has long divided persons of democratic temperament. The enfranchised citizen's right to vote is accepted by all as the consummate instrument of twentieth-century democracy. But differing concepts and modes of participation beyond the vote complicate and illuminate concepts of democracy, and we turn to them now before addressing voting participation in the next chapter.

EVOLVING NATION, EVOLVING PARTICIPATION

Political participation is both action and symbol. As *action,* it comprises efforts to influence the selection of government personnel and their decisions. In democratic societies, political participation may try to influence the actions of candidates, political parties, officeholders, and ultimately government itself. Such participation may be viewed as a flow of influence upward from the populace, through which national interests ultimately become defined. As *symbol,* political participation is a recurring theme of democratic politics, an ideal and an obligation especially valued in American political history.[2]

In contemporary America, two trends that especially bear on political participation have been underway. Social functions gravitating to government have increased as society has become more tightly integrated. Simultaneously, concepts of citizen participation in societal decision-making outside government have expanded.

The phrase "political participation" immediately evokes images of voting, the most widespread, uniform, and easily measured political activity performed by large numbers of citizens in democratic societies. And the proportion of eligible citizens who vote is deemed a major index of popular control. But types of participation other than voting in general elections are significant and prompt their own set of concerns. The new participatory urge is viewed by some as a public distemper. By others it is seen as a logical stage in the evolution of a new and incomplete blueprint for society. The demands for political participation have broken out of the former confines of democratic theory to become issues of contemporary politics.

Citizen participation influences the messages that flow through the electoral process, supplying information and energy to representative government. It contributes to the formation of the public agenda and thereby can generate increased responsiveness in the system. As the basis of democratic government, political participation in its varied forms ultimately shapes the distribution of political influence in society and determines the incentives operating on elected officials. To the extent that it adequately represents the whole political community, such participation reinforces the logic undergirding representative institutions of government. But when participation, in elections and otherwise, is markedly skewed—if voters or lobbyists or contributors are significantly unrepresentative of the general population, for example—then it complicates the tasks of representative government, such as assuring a representative political agenda. Moreover, when new issues and the protagonists they stimulate appear, time may be needed for those activists to acquire the resources—e.g., money, know-how, alliances—that will facilitate their contest for influence.[3]

Democracies are untidy, and democratic life in the United States has always seemed disheveled. The division of political labor was vague from the beginning, and it has continued to change with the passage of time. The Constitution fixed the institutions of government in a clear pattern, but electoral matters were given only limited attention, and the organization of political forces outside government was given no attention at all. The United States became an independent nation as an adolescent democracy without longstanding traditions of national politics. Swiftly it would become the first adult democracy based on "universal" manhood suffrage, would develop the world's first mass political parties, and eventually would be the first to encroach on the functions of its parties by use of the direct primary.

As symbol, political participation has generally been greeted with enthusiasm; as activity, it has often been viewed with suspicion. Voting is a familiar activity and is normally extolled. Other political actions fashioned to influence government decisions often are not held in such high esteem. Few lobbyists receive good citizenship awards, and the evidence of $2.7 billion spent in all American political campaigns during the 1987–88 election cycle was certain to shock most who knew about it.[4] Direct citizen participation in political decisions is viewed by some as the essence of democracy, and by others as a threat to democracy's very existence.[5] Such mixed attitudes certify the complexity of modern democratic governing and the issues it must address.

POLITICAL PARTIES: AGENTS OR VICTIMS OF PARTICIPATION?

Opportunities for citizens of the United States to take a direct part in presidential selection increased notably in the 1970s with changes in nominating procedures and campaign finance regulations. Ironically, political parties that had long been lauded as the premier vehicles of citizen political action came to be seen as hapless victims of it. The resulting tension between individual voters and the parties is a central strain of democratic electoral life, pitting an ever-changing cast of voters against institutionalized political organizations. To some, the continued viability of democratic government lies in reconciling the two.

In democratic societies, political participation and political parties are not separate, distinct phenomena. They are, rather, a single, indivisible concern. Political parties in some form are requisite to sustained, meaningful citizen action in democratic politics. At the same time, the survival of political parties requires that independent citizen participation be restrained.

E. E. Schattschneider held that "democracy is not to be found *in* the parties but *between* the parties." "The sovereignty of the voter consists in his freedom of choice."[6] Parties are thus seen not as agencies of representation but as creators and vendors of choices. But not all who designate political parties as the cornerstones of democratic life share this view. Jeane J. Kirkpatrick says that

> political parties are not merely or even principally vehicles for enabling or forcing voters to choose among alternative policies. They are agencies of *representation*. The dynamics of competition and the operation of self-interest tend to guarantee parties' responsiveness to voter opinion. The whole edifice of representative, responsible institutions is designed to insure that those who make decisions for the society will remain responsive to the values and preferences of majorities.[7]

To hold that parties should perform functions of representation is understandable; to prescribe how they should organize to do so is more difficult. Representation is a complicated, elusive concept that philosophers have spent much time and language exploring. A society whose government is built upon representation, especially a strikingly pluralistic society such as the United States, must, nonetheless, have a working definition of it.

Both houses of Congress were designed to represent the nation as a whole. But remember that each was intended to capture a different facet of the public interest. The basis of representation in both chambers has evolved somewhat, but the House of Representatives still represents citizens on the principle of one man, one vote, and the Senate reflects the nation's federalism. Although the same individuals now vote for members of both houses, the two principles embody different representations of the public interest.

In the political institutions that have grown up around the presidential selection process, principles of representation have always been far less explicit, far less fixed. An ill-defined but tenacious sense has long prevailed that the two-party system, prodded occasionally by third parties, has been roughly representative of the nation's political forces. The precise mechanisms of that representation have not always been easy to specify, and political parties have looked rather different in different periods.

In some democratic societies, and at times in the United States, the political alternatives represented by parties have been generated more by forces outside the parties than by ones within them. So it was in 1860 as the crisis of secession approached, and at the beginning of the New Deal in 1933. Then the parties were more nearly articulators and advocates than authors of alternatives. When factors such as regionalism or class underlie conflicts, parties have one kind of representative task. When political interests do not fall easily into broad, somewhat durable patterns, parties have a more complex task.

When a party lacks a well-defined programmatic focus, and simultaneously claims to represent its partisans, it must have procedures that generate representativeness when making its decisions. Such procedures need not require widespread, direct, popular participation, but the changes made in Democratic party processes after 1968 aimed at greater representativeness. Direct participation in reaching the party's most significant decisions was broadened. Similar objectives were sought by Congress through the campaign finance legislation of the 1970s.

The changes in Democratic party nomination procedures and in presidential campaign financing were not spontaneous. They came from the demands of claimants who insisted that the distribution of influence in the electoral process be made more equitable, as they viewed it. Abuses attributed to the inner nominating circles of the Democratic party in 1968, and observed in the campaign finance practices of the Republicans' Committee to Reelect the President in 1972, energized efforts for change that previously had not found effective footing.

More diversified public participation was the goal and the result. But many persons feel that gains in *participation* have been more than offset by losses in the *representativeness* of decisions made by the parties.[8] They hold that the participatory mechanisms of presidential nomination and campaign finance emerging from the 1970s have diminished the parties as agents of representation, with loss for the public and the political system. Imbedded in these conflicting interpretations lie complex questions of the need for further change in the manner of presidential selection.

CHANGING CONCEPTS OF REPRESENTATION

Austin Ranney is a student of political parties and was a member of the Democrats' McGovern-Fraser Commission on Party Structure and Delegate Selection that was created after the experiences of 1968. He has considered an aspect of representation that Kirkpatrick addressed. Shortly after the first round of Democratic rules changes, Ranney noted that reformers in all epochs have held that party organizations should, above all, be truly representative. Against this "expressive" vision of the party, he posed the "competitive" view, one preoccupied with winning elections. The urge to win gives the party incentive to choose candidates attractive to voters, and therefore to be representative.[9] The election thus becomes a test of the party's representativeness. The expressive party may be representative in form, but the competitive party is representative in result.

The post-1968 nomination process, with its emphasis on participation, is animated by the expressive vision. The Republican Committee on Delegates and Organization (DO), also formed after 1968, responded to the expressive impulse in a call for more open delegate selection procedures. The Democratic McGovern-Fraser Commission seemed consumed by it, worrying that the newly broadened channels for delegate selection still might not produce delegations sufficiently representative of the popular base of the Democratic party.

The main components of the party as viewed by Democrats for most of the twentieth century had been demographic groups, so the commission assured representation for certain of them. Of the many possible groups, the commission settled on women, youth, and ethnic minorities as needing predetermined representation "in reasonable relationship to their presence in the population of the state." Ranney described the resulting 1972 Democratic National Convention as "a hodgepodge of representative inconsistencies" in which "full representation-by-quotas for blacks, women, and youth" was achieved, alongside significant underrepresentation of "the elderly, the poor, the white ethnics, and labor union members, to say nothing of the party's senators, congressmen, governors, and other notables."[10]

Ranney assigned to the predetermined demographic composition of the delegations important blame for the unrepresentativeness of the 1972 Democratic National Convention. Jeane J. Kirkpatrick, however, dismissed the quotas as inconsequential. She asserted that the characteristics most important for assessing representativeness in the convention were the *political views* of the delegates. She declared that a "new breed," which she dubbed the "symbol specialists," dominated the 1972 Democratic convention. According to Kirkpatrick, symbol specialists are more likely to conceive of the political process "as an arena for setting public agendas and resolving moral problems than as an arena for winning and compromising material interests."

The "new breed" therefore threatened to move the substance of politics away from concern with material benefits and economic self-interest toward more symbolic aspects of politics. This convention composition led Kirkpatrick to conclude that " 'open' participatory politics may turn out (as in 1972) to be less representative of party rank and file (and other voters) than conventions peopled by labor leaders, political 'bosses,' and public officials." She found the "unreformed" Republican convention more representative of the views and values of voters, even though, in 1972, 52.7 percent of Republican delegates were chosen in primaries.[11] Thus the quota system, not the primaries, distorted the quality of representation.

These assessments of the 1972 Democratic National Convention illustrate different concepts of representation. To Ranney, the distortion was found in demographic categories and political roles. To Kirkpatrick, it was found in political orientations and values. Wherever a distortion is declared to exist, it is invoked to challenge decisions made through the changed nomination process and as a call for alternatives. The alternatives proposed, however, range widely, from a single nationwide presidential primary to a system of state party caucuses and conventions with no presidential primaries at all.

The changes in nomination rules and finance regulations brought changes in the characteristics of political competition and participation.[12] Americans who vote in primaries, attend caucuses, serve as convention delegates, and contribute money have always had diverse traits. Simple comparisons of personal characteristics among participants can therefore miss the most important consequences of changes in participation. The gap in representation lies in the altered relationship between political parties and other groups. It is an organizational gap that cannot be understood adequately through demographic comparisons of participants before and after reform.[13]

Traditional groups organized "around the economic or status needs of their clientele" declined in political influence, said Nelson W. Polsby, writing in 1983, and new groups emerged to assume influence.[14] The shift resulted from the loss of state and local party control over nominations, because the traditional groups attached themselves to state and local party organizations.[15] The new groups often attached themselves to candidates and gained their strength from national media attention. Increasingly in the 1980s, a variety of political action committees also gave financial aid to individual candidates, at all political levels, outside party channels.[16] Groups whose influence declined included state political parties, labor unions, farmers' groups, and associations of businessmen. Groups on the rise included, among others, ones that claimed moral rectitude—and were so presented by the media—"such as Common Cause and the Ralph Nader organizations, and those speaking for interests widely perceived as historically disadvantaged such as black, Hispanic-American, and militant women's groups."[17]

Changes in the political influence of certain groups reflect a fundamental restructuring of the nation's economic base. Factory employment declined 24.8 percent between 1970 and 1980 while professional, technical, managerial, and administrative employees increased from 11 percent of the work force to 38.3 percent.[18] Millions of people moved from North and East to South and West. Among women, the percentage in the civilian work force rose from 37.7 percent in 1960 to 54.4 percent in 1985 and was estimated to reach 60.3 by 1995. The percentage in the total work force who were white collar workers rose from 37.0 to 42.6 percent between 1960 and 1984, and was predicted to reach 45.6 by 1995. Union membership fell from 22.2 million in 1975 to 18.3 million in 1984, and by another estimate to 16.9 million in 1987. From 1964 to 1984, workers with college degrees went from 11.2 percent to

20.9 percent and with high school diplomas from 45.1 percent to 59.7 percent. The interest structure within both parties inevitably changed[19] with these and other trends.

Emphasis on demographic representativeness, and the influence of specific groups under the new nomination procedures and campaign finance conditions, does not address all the anxieties stirred by the new practices. The gap in representation resulting from the declining visibility and electoral importance of the political party is a matter of great concern to many. A political party comprises individuals who identify with it and vote for it, groups that ally themselves with it, candidates who run and officeholders who are elected under its banner, along with officers in states and localities and others who regularly promote its interests. Parties were once viewed as embodying a crucially important, continuing, organized community interest in elections, current and future. The implications of the new patterns of participation for the well-being—some would say for the survival—of organized political parties are of prime importance.

Omens of doom for parties and the party system are often seen in candidates' growing independence from their parties during campaigns, weakening party fealty in government, declining party loyalty in the electorate, and unstable party relationships to groups in society. The new nomination practices and campaign finance changes may be viewed as causing these developments, or may be seen as manifestations of accelerating trends that underlie them. In either case, the so-called reforms are widely interpreted as contributing to party decline.

The birth of what has been called the "new" politics may be easily fixed in time—1968 and shortly thereafter—but how long the phenomenon had been gestating is another matter. The changes wrought after 1968 by the McGovern-Fraser Commission and the Federal Election Campaign Act precipitated the new behavior. The extent to which those formal actions were originating causes or intermediary effects with earlier origins may be disputed. There has been reluctance, even among respected critics of the new politics, to use the language of causality in tracing the effects of the reforms. Polsby considers the reforms themselves to be only partly responsible for the changes that followed them.[20] Ranney suggests that one of the consequences of the Federal Election Campaign Act was to accelerate rather than cause the parties' decline in campaign management. The expenditure limits, he says, did not create but accelerated the new emphasis on television campaigning.[21] Kirkpatrick found that the new nomination rules hastened nationalizing trends in American politics and what she called "the circulation of the Democratic presidential elite" that helped bring new people to positions of influence.[22]

The temperate language of facilitation and acceleration used by these careful observers is intrinsically important. It emphasizes the complex social and political matrices of the reforms and their clouding effects on analysis of the results. As long as deliberate change in presidential selection processes is advocated, knowing what causes produce what effects and unanticipated consequences will be a challenge of consummate importance.

CHANGING BASES OF REPRESENTATION

In American electoral politics, the roles of both old and new kinds of groups are changing. Changes are also under way in other democratic political systems, including most western democracies. A new political environment is found that includes the influence of mass media, novel political technologies, the enlargement of government, rising education levels, and independence among voters, in fact, all the factors that affect the functions of political parties.[23]

Contemporary politics in most western democracies is affected by demographic changes. Social groups that once served as the building blocks of party coalitions have become weaker, with consequent erosion of the political foundations on which parties were once built. Parties thus have smaller and less reliable bases of support than formerly, and a more difficult task in gathering votes. As groups lose influence over the political behavior of their members, issues, candidates, and other appeals become more important in determining how people vote. Parties are increasingly separated from the electorate.

Both the new political environment and the changing demographic base of politics characterize virtually all advanced western democracies where parties have increasing tendencies to splinter as social fragmentation increases and old party loyalties weaken.[24] In supporting a formal bill of rights for Britain, Ralf Dahrendorf observed that "individual interests are complex, and situational; but they are real. Parties no longer represent individuals in their entirety, or even all their interests. In an important sense, the individual has become the main actor on the political scene."[25] These trends in established democracies suggest that parallel developments in the United States have been matters of acceleration and facilitation, not creation.

New groups have arisen, bringing new issues that challenge the capacity of political parties to respond. One such issue is participation. In Europe, antiestablishment protest groups often have not found satisfying opportunities for effective political expression within established parties, leading to the charge that the parties needed new structures and methods of communication to remain effective.[26] In the United States also, especially following the 1960s, demands for participatory democracy in all segments of society emerged with new value orientations and political expectations, even when the outcome might not be a visible increase in raw political clout. "America is a vast laboratory of democratic experiments," wrote Henry C. Boyte. "Even as we lament the loss of public life, it reappears in a myriad of forms, with intimations of a citizen politics for the future."[27]

Even when policy results are not dramatically altered by new channels of political agitation, changes in process and structure—such as the effort by

Common Cause to require registration of lobbyists' contacts with congress-men—can increase faith in the fairness of government and trust in its decisions.[28]

More opportunities for political participation, whether in traditional or new forms, will remain an expectation of twentieth-century democratic political life, and beyond. The adequacy of participatory opportunities must therefore concern those who would judge or change how American presidents are chosen. Determining what is satisfactory participation cannot be limited to the relative merits of representative versus direct participatory forms of decision-making. Those questions do not lose their importance, but they must be placed in a larger context than were earlier debates over optimum participation and representation.

Privilege is always suspect in democracies. It has been a political target throughout American history. We know that full political equality is technically unattainable,[29] yet it is a worthy democratic ambition. Money, social position, education, or a family that instills political concerns in its children can generate disparities in political influence among individuals. Organization of kindred political spirits, sufficiently visible to command attention from those seeking elected office, can also magnify political influence. But numbers can be mobilized to offset the effects of education and social position, and money and organization can offset or reinforce the effects of all three. A pragmatic political system will seek to limit the extremes of such influences in its electoral politics, even if it cannot completely eliminate all disparities.

The push and pull of all participants in democratic politics inevitably affect the influence any one of them can exert. As with most systemic problems faced by democracies, a balance among elements is the most positive contribution to the quest for greater political equality in an age of vigorous and versatile political activity.

NEW PARTICIPATION IN NOMINATIONS

When the Democrats' McGovern-Fraser Commission set about its work in 1969, it clearly did not consider that it needed to choose *either* the institutional strength of the party *or* broader public participation in its internal affairs. The commission dwelt on party welfare *and* broader participation, seeming to assume that the combination was possible. The commission intended its recommendations to increase participation of rank-and-file members in all the Democratic party's major decision-making.[30] Republicans, though less pressed to make changes, also saw nothing incompatible between expansion of participation in its nomination procedures and continued strength of the party as an organization. The Republican DO Committee's 1970 report affirmed the spirit of the Democratic commission: "The DO Committee wants to be sure that the door is open in every State for those who wish to participate in the procedures that lead to the selection of an individual for President."[31]

In 1972 the staple nominating procedures of both parties continued to be presidential primaries, state party caucuses and conventions, delegates, and the national party conventions. But the dramatically altered importance of each of these components, described in the discussion of changing political information in Chapter Three, inevitably brought a new dynamic to the selection of nominees. Another result was an altered balance between, on the one hand, voters and delegates identifying themselves with interest groups or issues organizations and, on the other, party loyalists. Voters in the competitive climate of a presidential primary are bound to deliberate less than delegates to caucuses or conventions about who is likely to make the strongest race in the general election. They will respond to the programs advocated by the aspirants as well as their personalities. And so it will also be, at least at the outset, with those delegates who go to conventions and whose primary concern is issues.[32]

The McGovern-Fraser Commission prescribed detailed regulations governing a broad range of state-party activities aimed at greater participation in choosing delegates and presumed greater representativeness among those chosen. As we have seen, the selection of Democratic delegates was heavily regulated to increase the participation of three elements in the party who were viewed as previously underrepresented, i.e., women, youth, and blacks.[33] For their part, the Republicans simply emphasized greater participation and expressed the hope that greater representativeness would result.

More participation and a greater variety of participants resulted from the changes. Between 1968 and 1980, the percentage of adult U.S. citizens taking active part in preconvention politics by voting in a primary or attending a caucus increased from about 10 percent to about 21 percent.[34] Approximately one-half of a party's eligible electorate tend to take part in primaries, one-twentieth in caucuses. In a typical presidential primary state, about one-fourth of the entire voting-age public participates, meaning that primary turnout tends to be about half of general election turnout for presidential elections.[35] Analyses of participation in primaries and caucuses held under different conditions have led to conflicting conclusions about how representative the participants are of either party adherents or voters as a whole. Presumably self-selected participants in primaries and caucuses differ in some ways from other party adherents, and certainly from the larger electorate.

In any event, averages and aggregate statistics often conceal as much as they reveal. One primary season can differ considerably from another. In states that held primaries in both 1980 and 1984, participation in the Democratic primaries went up overall by 3.8 percent in 1984. Thirty Democratic primaries were held in 1984 with nearly 18 million voters. Almost 23 million voted in thirty-seven Democratic presidential primaries in 1988, and nearly 12 million in the Republican primaries of that year. Of the eighteen states that held Democratic primaries in all four years from 1972 through

1984, only California and Nebraska had their lowest turnouts in absolute numbers in 1984. In that year, California had a complicated delegate selection ballot instead of its usual presidential preference ballot, and the candidates did not campaign in Nebraska. Six of the eighteen states had their highest number of primary voters in 1984. In one heavily black district in North Carolina, the Jesse Jackson candidacy coupled with a heavily contested local primary between a white incumbent and a black challenger drew more voters than turned out for the 1982 general election.

Although participation by black voters was up noticeably in 1984, overall participation in southern presidential primaries was down sharply. The mixture of candidates who survived early winnowing accounted for both variations.[36] Differences in the appeal of particular candidates and issues to various categories of potential voters are easily lost in statistical averages.

As both primary and caucus participants became more numerous after 1968, they were sharply different from those who previously chose convention delegates. For most of the century and a half before the rules changes, the national parties were relaxed about who attended their conventions. Party leaders and public officials were the principal participants in choosing delegates, and generally they chose delegates from among themselves, important contributors, and the party faithful of lesser stature.[37] In 1988, despite the automatic seating of "super delegates," nearly two-thirds of Democratic National Convention votes were cast by delegates elected in primaries, while over three-fourths of those voting at the Republican convention were chosen in primaries.[38]

The delegates produced by the earlier and later selection systems contrast interestingly. Frank J. Sorauf portrayed Republican and Democratic convention delegates in the years between 1948 and 1956 as "in no sense a cross-section of the American citizenry." He described them as fully 98 percent white and 90 percent male, well-educated and financially well-off. A very large percentage of them were lawyers and either public officials or high-ranking party officials. "As a group they [appeared] to be representative of activists in the two parties." These delegates to the national party conventions before the changes were "men and women with the time, the money, the knowledge, and the incentives to be politically active."[39]

The changes after 1968 produced increases in the number of persons attending both major national conventions in a delegate capacity—by 1988, up some 60 percent for the Democrats, from 2,622, and 71 percent for the Republicans, from 1,333. And the delegates became more diverse. Because of the quotas adopted, women, blacks, and delegates under thirty increased markedly in Democratic conventions between 1968 and 1972. After 1972, the attendance of younger Democrats declined, but that of women and blacks continued at the new high levels. In 1984, black delegates numbered 18 percent of all delegates at the Democratic convention and the percentage rose to 23 in 1988. The percentage of women was 49 in 1984 and 48 in

1988. Hispanic delegates in 1984 equalled their percentage among all Democrats.

In Republican National Conventions, female participation followed the general pattern of the Democrats, even without provisions mandating increases in women delegates. In 1968, 16 percent of Republican delegates were female; in 1972 the percentage jumped to 29, in 1984 it was 44, and in 1988 it was 33. Black and Hispanic participation also rose a bit, but those groups historically have constituted a smaller share of Republican than of Democratic activists, a fact reflected in convention attendance.[40]

Although by these measures the composition of recent national conventions looks sharply different from Sorauf's 1948–56 description, the delegations continued to enjoy relatively high educational and economic status. Seventy-one percent of the 1984 Democratic delegates and 68 percent of the Republicans were college graduates compared with only 12 percent of all Democrats and 21 percent of all Republicans. In 1988, 88 percent of Democratic delegates had attended college. The median household income for GOP delegates in 1984 was $52,700, for Democratic delegates $43,840, and both were reportedly higher in 1988. The 1984 figures were more than double the U.S. median family income of $20,000 for that year.[41] Although participation of low- and moderate-income party members in the Democratic National Convention did not increase, the changes in delegate selection rules altered the demographic makeup of the national convention in other ways. To some extent, "white, male, upper-middle-class political elites" have been replaced by "black or female upper-middle-class political elites."[42]

CHANGING FINANCIAL PARTICIPATION

Our focus in this section is the financing of nomination and election activities of presidential aspirants and their supporters. In examining that subject, let us recognize that funding practices in elections for most state and local offices largely remain, as one expert put it, the "lost world" of American campaign finance. The attempts made at their regulation—including public subsidies, though in a minority of the states—vary widely, and except in a few cases have not attracted the scrutiny devoted to money in campaigns for federal offices.[43] Conspicuous increases in expenditures in races for the U.S. Senate and House of Representatives since the early 1970s have been reported, however, and in 1990 large donations from outside a senatorial candidate's own state were made in some cases. President Bush and others have advocated measures bearing directly and indirectly on congressional electioneering, and public funding of congressional campaigns has been strongly proposed in some quarters.[44]

A bipartisan panel of experts appointed in 1990 by the Senate Majority and Minority leaders urged, among other recommendations, adoption for Senate races of a new concept of "flexible limits" that would exclude from the count expenditures for certain specified purposes as well as small contributions from within a candidate's state. In mid-1990, however, efforts in both houses toward bipartisan agreement bogged down, chiefly over spending limits that were desired by Democrats but not Republicans.[45]

Not all political inequalities can be eliminated. It is impossible to imagine even a total transformation of society that would equalize the many kinds of resources that are relevant to political competition. Political communicating and organizing cost money, and the wealthy and well-organized gain influence by providing important amounts of that political currency.[46]

The use of that most easily identified and unequally distributed political resource has been rising sharply. Aggregate costs of presidential nomination and election campaigns, adjusted for inflation, rose by a factor of four between 1960 and 1988, and the 1988 expenditure of $500 million was some 55 percent higher in nominal dollars than the $325 million of 1984. There were several causes of the increase, some of them well established and continuing, but 1988 also saw a startling jump in solicitation and distribution of "soft" monies through auxiliary channels. Candidates' finance personnel from the primary season often stayed in place to solicit funds to permit expenditure for presidential candidates at state and local levels from the resources of candidate and party committees, activity permitted by the Federal Election Commission. These expenditures jumped so high as to impinge significantly on the original purpose of public subsidies.[47] The history of recent experience instructs what can and cannot be done.

The increased number and variety of participants in presidential nominating activities that we have noted were initially accompanied by a modest expansion in the number and variety of financial contributors who supported not only nomination efforts but also election campaigns and political activities more generally. Leaving aside the federal tax checkoff program, however, the increase in the percentage of persons who reported making a political contribution rose only modestly between 1952 and 1986, stabilizing between 10 and 15 percent in even-numbered years. This held true despite fund-raising by candidates, parties, and political action committees after the 1974 amendments to the Federal Election Campaign Act (FECA), which limited individual contributors to a maximum donation of $1,000 per candidate. Although returns from television appeals and sophisticated direct-mail solicitation reaped fewer contributions than hoped for from the 1970s onward, these techniques were nonetheless used with special effectiveness by the national Republican party and a number of conservative political action committees (PACs), and they contributed substantially to the aggregate number of political contributions for all levels of political office.[48]

Persons wanting to make *partisan political contributions* can now do so through party organizations, individual candidate committees, and PACs. Between 10 and 13 percent of the total adult population reported making political contributions at some level in the presidential election years from 1956 to 1984. Of those contributing in 1984, according to one survey, 40 percent gave to parties, 36 percent to individual candidates, and 13 percent to other groups supporting candidates. An additional 17 percent gave to groups favoring or opposing ballot propositions.[49] Some political contributors gave through more than one channel, and Republicans raised considerably more money than Democrats.

The *federal tax checkoff* program, first operative in 1973, attracted a new and different breed of financial participant who made contributions qualitatively unlike other political gifts. The contributor could not give to a particular candidate. Those who checked the box on their federal income tax returns designated that a dollar, or two on a joint return, go to a federal subsidy for qualifying presidential candidates. Those who used the checkoff numbered 27.4 percent in 1980, then fell to 23.7 percent in 1984, to 23.0 in 1985, to 21.7 in 1986, and to 21.0 percent in 1987. The dollar total contributed by this means in 1988 was the lowest since 1975. In the twenty-one or so states that provided for a state tax checkoff, it appeared that the rate of taxpayer participation also fell in the mid-1980s.[50]

Public subsidies were intended to reduce the importance of private solicitations and contributions, but success in achieving this goal has been mixed, notably so in 1988. The goal of public disclosure has also been thwarted by adaptations in methods of gathering and reporting donations.

Relatively small givers have often been linked together in recent years through political action committees. But in 1984, persons called *bundlers* became prominent. They collected contributions from a variety of donors and forwarded them to recipients, thereby avoiding committee contribution and expenditure limits, and also often making it difficult to trace contributions to sources.[51] As the players and donations in political finance have grown in variety and volume, so has the complexity of presidential campaigns. These developments magnify the importance of the FECA's disclosure provisions, and of the extent of the Federal Election Commission's perseverance and ability to make public reasonably full, timely, and comprehensible campaign finance information. It should be no surprise that almost every aspect of the Federal Election Campaign Act and its amendments has both partisans and detractors, and that its regulatory provisions have provoked creative adaptations in the fund-raising practices of political activists.

Ruth S. Jones and Warren E. Miller, in a study of 1980 political donors, found that different channels for contributions attracted different types of contributors. Increasing the number and variety of ways to give increased the number and diversity of contributors, including some persons who had not previously given to political campaigns. "The characterization of contributors as a 'contributing elite' belies the social, political, psychological and behavioral heterogeneity of those who gave money to the 1980 campaigns." Jones found that the changes persisted later into the 1980s, but emphasized that they were "modest in degree rather than dramatic in kind."[52]

It is clear that more and different persons now take part in electoral activity. Newly identified issues and interests, in addition to changes in party

rules regulating nomination processes, changes in federal legislation governing campaign finance, and new court decisions, have been stimulants. One
result has been a tendency toward a new separation of electoral constituencies from financial constituencies, with consequences that Sorauf has called
"momentous."[53] Merely citing the new participants and the reasons for them
does not, however, speak to the disquiet of many critics.

Some financial restrictions have a reasonable prospect for technical
enforcement, such as the $1,000 per candidate limit on personal contribu-
tions to aspirants for federal office for each primary, runoff, or general
election, up to an aggregate annual limit of $25,000 to all federal candidates.
But the impossibility of enforcing many limits on campaign finance—for
example, overall spending ceilings—has been demonstrated repeatedly. And
the laws have permitted the parties to raise large amounts of *soft money*—
money raised during and between presidential years that is not formally
intended to benefit the presidential nominees, but which often finds its way
to large states with many electoral votes.

Since the 1979 amendments to the Federal Election Campaign Act
(FECA), state and local party committees can spend unlimited sums of soft
money for volunteer-oriented activities on behalf of party tickets. Soft money
is not subject to federal contribution limits or disclosure requirements and
has repeatedly been called "sewer money" in *New York Times* editorials.
Such funds may be raised by state and local party committees, *and* by the
parties' national committees.

The Republican and Democratic National Committees, in fact, have
solicited and channeled to state organizations contributions from individuals,
corporations, and unions that have already contributed the maximum
amounts permitted by federal law. Herbert E. Alexander declared that in 1988
"the scramble for 'soft' money was as fiercely competitive and conspicuous as
the search for votes," and he called into question the adequacy and integrity
of the system of campaign finance regulation.[54] Interestingly, that year was
marked not only by another jump in total soft-money expenditures—to $45
million, compared with $21.6 million in 1984—but the Democratic candidate
attracted a majority of it, $23 million, whereas in 1984 the party's candidate
drew only $6 million of a total of $21.6 million, and in 1980 only $4 million
of a total of $19.1 million.

In 1988, each of the major party nominees received $46.1 million in
federal subsidies, derived from the income-tax checkoff, to finance his general
election campaign. These funds were controlled by the candidates' organizations, as was the $8.3 million raised and spent by the national parties on
behalf of each candidate. But these sums did not prevent *contributions not
subject to limits* from being made to other campaign organizations, which
found diverse uses for the money. Alexander concluded that at least 267
persons gave at least $100,000 apiece through Republican channels, and at
least 130 persons made similar Democratic contributions.[55] A former am-
bassador to Hungary, Nicolas M. Salgo, gave $503,263 to Republican com-

mittees.[56] According to *The New York Times,* the treasurer of the Democratic National Committee reported shortly after the 1988 election that it raised $68 million for the general election and "we tried to funnel everything into the D.N.C. to have greater control over our electoral strategy." The corresponding Republican total was $69 million, "not counting another $50 million for the party's operational expenses." In October of 1988, both Democratic and Republican officials appealed to independent political action committees to let up in their solicitations because they were interfering with the parties' own fund-raising. The figures presumably were subject to subsequent adjustment, but spokespersons for both fall campaigns said they "made no distinction between the use of public and private funds in their fall campaigns."[57]

Alexander has summarized the sources of funds used in 1988 for major-party presidential candidates in the general election. Extraordinarily, in 1988 the Democratic campaign raised more money, or had more money spent on its behalf, than the Republican: $106.4 million against $93.6 million. In addition to the $46.1 and $8.3 million mentioned above that the law clearly permits each candidate and national committee to spend, funds appeared from state and local party sources ($23.0 million Democratic; $22.0 million Republican), labor groups ($25.0 million Democratic; $5.0 million Republican), independent expenditures ($0.5 million Democratic; $6.7 million Republican), and other sources ($3.5 million Democratic, $5.5 million Republican).[58]

In both the nomination and the election campaigns, conscientious enforcement efforts normally are made only after the campaign is over and the votes are counted. In May 1989, for example, the Federal Election Commission levied fines against Senator Alan Cranston of California for violating spending limits in 1984.[59] Moreover, the FEC fine is only the amount of the overexpenditure, which often is no deterrent in the extremity of campaign combat.[60]

Moreover, unsuccessful aspirants have sometimes been left with large debts. In Gary Hart's conspicuous case, his debt totalled $4.4 million in July 1984, and still stood at $3.4 million in early 1986, which may have influenced his decision not to run for reelection to the Senate that year.[61] In 1988, on the other hand, combined candidate debts were much less. On June 30, 1989, a total of only about $2 million was owed as compared with some $15 million for Democratic aspirants alone following the 1984 prenomination campaign.[62]

The inherent social power of wealth is almost always convertible in one way or another into political activity, and often influence. That is true even though frequently the best-financed candidates do not win. The latent influence of wealth is especially conspicuous in the new, much-criticized multimillion-dollar practice of *independent spending.* The changing technology of politics has combined with the new finance regulations to enlarge the variety of activists in the general election. Candidates and parties now share the stage with a melange of advocates and detractors who campaign largely independently of traditional politicians.

Federal legislation prescribing full public funding of the major candidates' general election campaigns was intended to eliminate an important area of political participation. It prohibited private contributions to such presidential candidates in a general election, although a candidate could decline the subsidy and seek funds elsewhere. The Supreme Court ruled, however, in *Buckley* v. *Valeo* (1976) that money spent by individuals or groups to promote an idea or a candidate in an electoral campaign is a protected form of free speech. The ruling helped to keep open new opportunities for communication in the general election campaign, and in prenomination campaigns as well. The guarantee to independent entrepreneurs of a right, through campaign expenditures, to promote ideas and candidates, or to disfavor them by negative advertising, stimulated a large and dissonant chorus of new voices seeking attention. Use of corporate funds for independent expenditures to promote candidates, however, was barred by many states, and in 1990 the Supreme Court held that funds from a corporate treasury could not properly be spent on a candidate's behalf.[63]

The right of independent entrepreneurs is protected only when neither the candidate nor his organization coordinates or consents to the expenditures. The Court's ruling highlighted a conflict between two contemporary notions of democracy: democracy as competition among political parties, with voters deciding who will govern; and democracy as an open forum for ideas and their advocates competing for public approval. When political parties and their candidates, along with self-selected journalists, held a de facto monopoly of the communication of ideas during electoral campaigns, the potential conflict between the two notions of democracy went largely unrealized. Parties served as the *agora* in which political ideas were bartered. Parties and candidates campaigned, editors opined, and citizens discussed the election freely among themselves. All enjoyed the guarantees of the First Amendment. Changes in technology and law upset the passive relationship between these two concepts of democracy. The structure and substance of electoral communications changed dramatically.

There is no conclusive evidence of the effectiveness of independent expenditures in general elections for president. Nonetheless, such expenditures have been substantial. In 1976, the first year of public funding of the presidential election, $1.6 million was reportedly spent independently of the candidates to promote or defeat a presidential aspirant. In 1980, independent expenditures in the general election were put at $10.6 million (with $2.8 million spent prior to the nomination), and in 1984 at $9.7 million (with $7.7 million spent prenomination). After 1988, an early report by the Federal Election Commission stated that total independent expenditures fell 19 percent below 1984, to a total of $14.1 million; however, expenditures before and after the nomination were not separated.[64]

In 1985, the Supreme Court reinforced its decision in *Buckley* v. *Valeo* (1976) by upholding the protected status of independent expenditures in a 7–2 decision in *FEC* v. *NCPAC*. Justice Rehnquist, writing for the majority, referred to the "marketplace of ideas" concept of democracy in his contention that

> the fact that candidates and elected officials may alter or reaffirm their own positions on issues in response to political messages paid for by the PACs can hardly be called corruption, . . . for one of the essential features of democracy is the presentation to the electorate of varying points of view.[65]

Those who see democracy foremost as competition among ongoing political parties are less inclined to accept the Court's conclusion that spending money for elections is a logical equivalent of free speech as intended in the First Amendment.

Independent expenditures are sometimes seen as symptom, sometimes as disease. As symptom, they are linked to the decline of political parties, the fragmentation of American society, the rise of ideology, the increase in diversity of organized interests and opinions, and the end of pragmatism in the nation's political discourse. As disease, independent expenditures are thought to produce increased political inequality, the substitution of extremism for moderation, and ultimately the triumph of particular interests over general interests. As either symptom or disease, the putative victims of independent expenditures—aside from the principle of public subsidy itself—are political parties, traditional politically oriented groups, the concept of democratic accountability, the electoral process in general, and ultimately candidates, voters, and the less well-financed and less well-organized elements in society.

The increase in the number of groups active in presidential selection is often causally linked to changes in campaign finance regulations and court pronouncements on them. Yet there has been an even more dramatic rise in the number and types of interest groups participating in other phases of the nation's political life.[66] What was once seen as a benevolent politics of groups has become, to many observers, a tumult of frenzied activity that threatens political parties, broader community interests, and even the effectiveness of government itself. Although groups were accepted early in U.S. history as an inherent fixture of the nation's politics, their number has been rising steadily since at least the third quarter of the nineteenth century, and especially since 1960. Like political interests, information, and opinions, they have become far more diverse and unevenly structured than formerly.[67]

Political parties have had a central role in molding democratic discourse into political substance. They consequently are at the center of controversies precipitated by independent expenditures. Although a given political party may be benefitted, damaged, or unaffected by independent expenditures, their growth is seen as weakening the party *system*. Some groups that independently spend money for political purposes may work in parallel with a political party, but others act separately.

The loose fittings of the American electoral process provide a hospitable environment for those making independent expenditures, for PACs, and for other aggregations of politically stimulated individuals, which is a partial explanation of the presence of such groups in contemporary presidential campaigns.[68] To some extent the opportunities have always been there, but the ability to bypass political parties in a presidential campaign has been enlarged by the changes in campaign finance laws and party responses to them. Amplification of political speech by the electronic media has especially encouraged the trend. The weak hold of political parties on candidates and the electorate is inherently hospitable to independent initiatives.

Critics of the new politics argue that participants in the new electoral activities are less representative of the whole citizenry than participants as a group once were. They worry that the increase in independent individual participation undermines the functions of political parties as representative, collective electoral participants. These anxieties go to the heart of the democratic creed and touch long-held convictions about the requisites for a durable democratic politics. But an explanation of the trend for political groups and individuals to act outside the parties does not lie wholly in legal regulations and judicial interpretations. The evolving composition and organization of modern societies with their diversity, fragmentation, and increasing citizen independence are at the bottom of the new politics.

RESHAPING THE NEW PARTICIPATION

Reformers, counter-reformers, almost anyone rallying support for change will simplify reality when prescribing what should be done. Without doing so, little action is likely, but doing so creates a major risk.

Many modifications, largely incremental, have been made in the original "reforms" of the Democrats' McGovern-Fraser Commission. Major and minor changes were made by the Federal Election Campaign Act of 1971. A succession of Democratic party committees added changes to the original changes, and Congress took additional actions on campaign finance in 1974, 1976, and 1979. All the while, calls for more modifications have continued, though none of the new measures has been in place long enough to become institutionalized and seriously tested. No detail of current nomination practices or of the campaign finance system seems acceptable to all. The number and variety of proposed alterations in these major segments of the presidential selection process are so large, and they pull in so many directions, that it is oppressive just to inventory them.

At one extreme are advocates who would ignore political parties altogether. They would pursue more widely participatory arrangements that purport to be more egalitarian. At the other extreme are persons who would return to the more closed parties of earlier years. In campaign finance, some would increase and some would abolish public funding, and some would remove contribution and expenditure limits while others would attempt more stringent ones. More moderate advocates of change seek improvement on the margins of current arrangements. Some would work through state, congressional, or constitutional action; others would have the political parties heal themselves, letting them offset effects attributable to earlier reforms.

Proposals that appear diametrically opposed in their tendencies often turn out, ironically, to be motivated by similar objectives, even to begin from similar premises. The chief source of variety among the large number of extant proposals is not disagreement over open, participatory processes versus strong, controlling parties. The diversity originates mainly in the enormous difficulty of designing means to reach specified goals.[69] Issues of participation and organizational control stimulate much disagreement, but they are not the main sources of variety among proposals for change. Differences over participation as a concept divide the partisans of democracy, but the complex, confounding task of designing means to produce specified ends divides them even more.

Current arrangements for nominating presidential candidates and financing presidential campaigns are criticized at several levels. Structures for electoral participation must take into account several concepts of representativeness if they are to reflect the political forces in society and curb the extremes of attitude and influence found among many political participants and nonparticipants. Here, two concepts of representativeness are important. One is static, the other more dynamic. Desire to maintain the organizational strength of political parties has implications for both static and dynamic dimensions of representativeness. Representativeness measured by socioeconomic and demographic characteristics of individuals is essentially a static concept. A focus on groups captures a more dynamic dimension of representativeness, a dimension not always readily apparent when the characteristics of individuals are the center of analysis. The more dynamic group dimension can be viewed as a tug between old and new political forces.

Arguments favoring closed, professional political parties emphasize the static dimension. They make a credible case that in such parties concern with winning elections encourages representation of the nation's socioeconomic spectrum and its demographic diversity. It is not certain, however, that nonvoters are therefore more advantaged, or less disadvantaged, by closed parties than by more open parties. The fact that the programs of two major parties are somewhat biased toward different ends of the socioeconomic spectrum may help narrow the gap between the interests of voters and nonvoters in a closed party system.

Historically, party realignments and the threat of third parties have stimulated representativeness in the party system. Partisan realignment could correct imbalances between declining and rising viewpoints and the groups holding them. Third parties, pressing claims of neglected groups, could rise and induce incremental adjustments in the positions of one or both major parties. In the middle of the nineteenth century, the new Republican party took part in triggering a general realignment of political forces by becoming, with the demise of the Whigs, one of the two major parties.

But the speed of societal change since World War II may have outpaced the capacity of the traditional processes of party adjustment. The parties may no longer be able to reflect change quickly enough to assure their continuing representativeness. If neither of the major parties is truly responsive to the direction and volume of change, if the choices offered by the parties are inadequate to the times, meaningful party realignment probably will not result. In that context, it is significant that through the twentieth century third parties have proved to be weak stimulants of swift, genuinely basic changes in major party positions. Presently, however, the increasingly open major parties have begun to show a greater capacity to reflect dimensions of social evolution and therefore to improve their representativeness. In an era in which short-term considerations may carry special weight in voter decisions, more open, participatory arrangements may in fact strengthen the role of the parties and of the political system as a whole. Open parties, balanced within by professional party personnel and processes, hold promise that both static and dynamic representativeness can be combined. To say that, however, does not prescribe how such a combination can be achieved.

Proposals have been advanced to improve the balance between the characteristics of open and closed parties when making party nominations. A bicameral convention with one house for elected delegates and the other for ex officio delegates is one example. Analogous recommendations have been offered for changes in campaign finance procedures—to permit, for example, unlimited party expenditures on behalf of candidates, or to provide public campaign funding only through the parties. Such recommendations originate from awareness that broader participation has become unavoidable if the electoral process is to retain legitimacy.

Recent Democratic reform commissions have moved to increase the number of elected officeholders and party officials attending Democratic national conventions, thereby encouraging participation by party "professionals" in the nominating process. Between 1980 and 1984, the number of lawmakers among delegates quadrupled, to 14 percent of the total in 1984.[70] Also by 1984, a minimum of 14 percent of Democratic convention delegates were top party and elected officials. Allocations for the 1988 convention were set even higher, to include all members of the Democratic National Committee (DNC), all Democratic governors, and 80 percent of the Democratic members of Congress.[71] This prescription would produce a convention with almost one delegate in six a party official or elected officeholder.

Measures adopted in 1988 to take effect for 1992 would have reduced that number, largely by eliminating most members of the DNC as ex officio delegates, but that change was revoked in 1989. In another concession won by Jesse Jackson in 1988, the party dropped a previous requirement that to be awarded convention delegates from a state, a candidate must receive 15 percent or more of the votes in the state's presidential caucus or primary. Some worried that this change could lengthen the nomination campaign and adversely affect the party's condition for fighting the general election. In any event, *The New York Times* reported that DNC Chairman Ronald H. Brown said in 1989 that he expected the old rule to be restored in 1990. Possible changes in the modes and timing of Democratic delegate selection were discussed throughout 1989 and seemed unlikely to be resolved until much nearer to 1992.[72]

Open caucuses and presidential primaries continue to be the avenues to nomination in both political parties. Broad participation is consequently assured. In this context, suggestions to enhance the influence of state parties have been made.[73] It is proposed to repeal many national party regulations and thereby decentralize to individual state parties responsibility for specific regulations governing the selection of Democratic National Convention delegates. Republicans have always permitted their state parties great discretion in determining who can vote in their primaries and caucuses, in contrast to the more restrictive rules of the national Democratic party. In 1980, for example, the Democratic party sought to limit participation in presidential primaries, and in caucuses that chose or allocated national convention delegates, to publicly declared and recorded Democrats. The goal was to keep independents and Republicans from interfering in this important party activity.

Although the Supreme Court has ruled that a national party's interest in the presidential nomination contest takes precedence over the interest of the states,[74] crossover voting can occur in states that do not require preregistration for primaries, and the "membership" requirement has been resisted elsewhere. With the growing number of independents in the electorate, proposals are made to leave to the state parties the issue of closed versus open primaries.[75] In 1984, the Democratic party's Fairness Commission again permitted open primaries in Wisconsin and Montana, states with long-standing nonpartisan traditions. In other states, the Democratic party did not allow Republicans to take part in its primaries and caucuses. Both national parties, however, now accept the outcome of primaries in which independents vote.

Future opportunities for independents to participate in state primary elections have been assured by a 1986 Supreme Court decision. In *Tashjian* v. *Republican Party of Connecticut,* the Court ruled that a thirty-one-year-old Connecticut law restricting voting in primaries to people previously enrolled in a party violated the state Republican party's First Amendment right to "freedom of association." The Connecticut Republican party had sought since 1984 to permit independents, who outnumber registered Republicans in the state, to vote in its primary elections. Twenty states in addition to Connecticut prohibit political parties from opening their primaries to unaffiliated voters. The parties in those states may now choose to let independents vote in their primary elections. If they maintain closed primaries in accordance with state law, they may face court challenges by independent voters.[76]

We have noted that, in presidential campaigns, extremes of influence that formerly accrued to persons who gave or solicited campaign money have been modified and in some ways curbed. The representativeness of individuals participating under current finance regulations contrasts sharply with smaller numbers of more affluent participants before the recent changes. Public funding of nomination and general election campaigns has contributed to greater representativeness among donors. In the prenomination period, a candidate must attract a large number of relatively small gifts from a wide geographic area to qualify for federal funds—at least $5,000 in gifts of $250 or less, in each of twenty states. Both the number and variety of individual participants have been dramatically altered. In 1984, in their races for nomination, Walter Mondale attracted over 203,000 contributions and Ronald Reagan over 255,000.[77] When the focus shifts, however, from participation by individuals to participation by groups and by the political parties themselves, many observers find the campaign finance changes detrimental to representativeness.

Some groups have been weakened by changes in the sources of campaign money. The linkage between specific finance constituencies and national campaigns has been loosened, reducing the capacity of group leaders to mediate between candidates and group members.[78] As a result, groups have often lost political influence, with candidates concurrently losing intimacy with such bases of support. Group influence may not always be reduced or eliminated in the nomination campaign, however, but rather may be transformed. A body that can mobilize a network of volunteers from a single-issue constituency, or from a segment of a union or association membership, may win a new importance.[79] Because of contribution limits, groups that give money rather than services to candidates during primary campaigns become relatively less important.

We have emphasized that political parties have been weakened by changes in sources of campaign funding. Public campaign funds are given directly to candidates, not funneled through the parties. Candidates have thereby gained increased independence from the parties, thus weakening the parties. Interest groups bypass the weakened parties, and parties lose their capacity to serve as checks on interest-group influence. Some party-strengthening features are found, nonetheless, when the full array of campaign finance reforms is examined. An important one is the permission given to the national parties to coordinate so-called soft-money fund-raising to support certain presidential campaign activities in the states, the funds solicited being subject to state, not federal, limitations.[80]

Because of the overall disparity between the financial resources easily available to the Republican party, in contrast to those of the Democratic party, it is presumed that proposals to extend public funding of political parties beyond current levels would help the Democrats. Such proposals are usually resisted by Republicans. No less a Republican than Ronald Reagan, who had long opposed public funding, recommended in 1985 that Congress abolish the existing subsidies, even though he had accepted, understandably, a total of some $90 million in subsidies for his 1976, 1980, and 1984 presidential campaigns, a record amount.[81]

The channeling of public funds through the political parties, bypassing the candidates, would surely be resisted by those of whatever party who hold public office and aspire to the presidency, as well as by other potential candidates. Also, officials who do not aspire to other positions presumably would not want public funding of elections for the offices they already hold directed through the parties. They would prefer that such money go directly to their personal campaign coffers. In the short run at least, raising the contribution limits to parties and more concentrated solicitation efforts by the political parties themselves have greater prospects for improving party financial strength than do public subsidies. Placing candidates under the full financial dominance of the political parties is clearly not possible, nor is it desirable.

GRADUAL CHANGE: THE PRUDENT WAY

For the political party system in the United States to continue to serve the nation adequately, it needs freedom from tight external regulation and to maintain flexibility in its own affairs. The parties should be sufficiently open to accommodate to the rapidly changing environment in which they must function. At the same time, they should remain sufficiently stable to cushion society against the effects of excessively abrupt or radical change. That stance may lack precision, but no alternative is more promising. Warren E. Miller and M. Kent Jennings have observed wisely that "party elites can change in outlook and behavior even in the absence of turnover in personnel."[82]

Wide-open parties would structure the nominating process too little; closed parties would do so too much. Dramatic departures from present arrangements are less likely to achieve a desirable balance than gradual adjustments through smaller opportunities. The minor adjustments made by the Democratic Fairness Commission in the party's nominating rules for 1988 were doubly wise. The changes are likely to contribute to the strength of both the national party and the state parties, yet they allowed considerable continuity between the 1984 and 1988 nominating seasons. Contests for influence and power will persist, yet continuity in political processes that need popular understanding and respect has value in its own right.

The new characteristics of campaign finance—substantially more fully reported than under previous conditions—have led to greater and more representative participation in the funding of electoral politics. They may also have weakened the political parties. Some public subsidy to the parties might consequently strengthen the parties in the short run, especially the Democratic party. Larry J. Sabato has urged annual party subsidies from the surpluses that he, at least, sees accumulating in the Federal Election Campaign Fund.[83] However, when Republicans hold a voting majority in either house of Congress, or occupy the White House, increased public funding of the parties is unlikely. The Democratic party will be forced to redress the imbalance in party funds through its own fund-raising efforts, and indeed modest progress toward doing so may have been made between 1984 and 1988. While the receipts of the three major Republican campaign committees—national, senatorial, and congressional—declined 61 percent between those years, receipts of the comparable Democratic committees rose 23 percent. The dollar differential still strongly favored Republicans, though, and significant campaign money was also spent through other channels.[84]

The political system as a whole will benefit more from political parties that adapt to the obstacles imposed upon them, whatever their sources, than from weak parties that have been artificially bolstered by public policy. Whether and in what ways in the years immediately ahead there will be increased "privatization" of political parties, or increased government intervention in their affairs, is uncertain. Probably few or no changes of significance will occur in their legal status.[85] Beyond the law, however, even the much-touted decline in party loyalties may not have the forbidding consequences sometimes seen. The *intensity* of party identification has clearly weakened for many who still think of themselves as party adherents,[86] yet Denise L. Baer and David A. Bositis conclude that

> the politicization of contemporary social movements and Democratic party reforms have indeed resulted in a Democratic party more fully representative of its constituent elements. Yet, at base, we find a strong commitment to party among all cadres of contemporary party elites—and certainly little indication of the loss of party regularity assumed by many political scientists. Judged in this light, the postreform party system is in robust health.[87]

In this chapter we have addressed important varieties of citizen political activity. We now turn to what is ultimately the most important endeavor—voting.

CHAPTER SEVEN

The Decline in
Voter Participation

☆
☆

In 1988, for the first time since 1944 the number of votes cast fell below the number in the previous presidential election—from some 92.7 million votes in 1984 to less than 91.6 million in 1988, or slightly more than half of those potentially eligible.[1] It was the continuation of a long plunge. Even while a radical increase in popular participation in presidential nominations developed after 1968—some 35 million voted in the 1988 primaries[2]—the rate of voting in the general election for president in November fell from 65.4 percent of the nonalien adult population in 1960, to 63.3 in 1964, 62.3 in 1968, 57.1 in 1972, 55.2 in 1976, and 54.3 in 1980. The 1984 election brought an increase, but at 55.2 percent it was still technically less than that of 1976,[3] and participation fell lower still in 1988. Since 1960, education levels have risen and barriers to voter registration have been lowered, so one wonders why the downward plunge.

Voting for president has been coasting downward for over a century, from approximately 81.8 percent of those qualified in 1860 to 73.7 in 1900 and 62.5 in 1940.[4] Newly eligible voters have been added to the population since 1860—former slaves, women, 18–20 year olds—and for different reasons they were slow to begin voting at the same rate as those with longer experience. But the condition has deeper roots. Understanding fully the causes of the long trend, much less reversing it, is a complex analytical exercise. So, also, is discerning the civic significance of nonvoters in presidential elections.

About the United States of the 1830s, Alexis de Tocqueville wrote that "at the present day the principle of the sovereignty of the people has acquired in the United States all the practical development that the imagination can conceive. It is unencumbered by those fictions that are thrown over it in other countries." Tocqueville linked popular sovereignty directly to the expansion of the electoral franchise. It was an inexorable trend of democracy as he saw it, and one fulfilled by the expansion of the American suffrage during the century and a half after he wrote: "There is no more invariable rule in the history of society: the further electoral rights are extended, the greater is the need of extending them; for after each concession the strength of the democracy increases, and its demands increase with its strength."[5]

The right of adult citizens to vote is surely democracy's most distinctive prerogative. Other protections of the Constitution are enjoyed by citizens and noncitizens alike, but only adult citizens may vote. Yet voting has often been treated more as a privilege than as a right. The United States extended the franchise farther and faster than other nations. But in the late decades of the nineteenth century, as cities grew, electoral fraud also grew, and in response state regulations grew, with voter registration systems significant among them. Often both registration and voting were made burdensome.

But electoral procedures are not the only reason why people do not vote. Many factors are at work. Early civic training and a sense of efficacy are important, but also significant are the effectiveness of group influences, the volume of campaign contributions in cash or kind, the success of campaign advertising, the skill and commitment of campaign workers—in fact, the effective use of any resource to send voters to the polls at a particular time. The social circumstances of people, their general views of politics, and their reactions to individual election campaigns also motivate or retard them. Such factors are harder to reach and modify through public policy than changing registration requirements or polling locations. The full causes of nonvoting and the best ways to reduce it are clouded. Does it really matter?

THE CONSEQUENCES OF NONVOTING

A few commentators find comfort in large numbers of nonvoters. They contend that to vote wisely citizens must have both substantial information and high political interest. Nonvoters are viewed as less informed about politics, less interested in its issues, and less committed to the political system. A high level of nonvoting therefore yields an active electorate of better quality than if everyone voted. Moreover, high turnout is often considered a sign of a troubled, conflict-ridden polity. Low turnout has been called "a leading indicator of contentment."[6]

In contrast, declining participation alarms others. If government derives its just powers from the consent of the governed, asks one, where does its authority come from if only half those eligible to vote fail to do so?[7] Editorial pages and election analysts join civic-minded citizens in frequently deploring the failure of citizens to do their duty and exercise their right. Yet, the American government's authority comes not from a level of electoral participation but from the Constitution, and while that in no way diminishes the importance of elections, it does deny that legitimacy rests on the size of the electorate in a single election, or in a discrete series of elections. Seymour Martin Lipset and William Schneider doubt that the decline of confidence in American institutional leadership has diluted the ability of leaders to govern, "except to the degree that, like Carter, our leaders believe it is so and, therefore, make that belief into a self-fulfilling prophecy."

Popularity and authority are not the same. Popularity derives from the public, but the authority of properly elected officials derives from the Constitution. Elected officials may nonetheless experience what Lipset and Schneider call "status insecurity," a condition they say has been common since at least the early nineteenth century.[8] Former representative Richard Bolling, assessing the consequences of low voter turnout, declared that

> it makes a great deal of difference to politicians—or at least some poli-
> ticians—whether they feel that they have a real majority. It's terribly important
> to many politicians when they see the faith of the people dissipated, disappear-
> ing because they don't really think that they have a mandate.[9]

Popularity is clearly important. Submission to general opinion, to use Max Weber's term, has helped keep American government responsive to the electorate.[10] Yet the troublesome consequence of nonparticipation lies not in the diminished authority of leaders, but in the increased potential for distortion in government's responsiveness.

If nonvoters were randomly distributed throughout the voting-age population, there could be small cause for concern over the level of voter turnout. But nonvoting has not been randomly distributed in the population. Moreover, recent declines in participation are disproportionately concentrated in groups that already have low turnout rates: those low in education, income, and socioeconomic status, and the least informed and engaged.[11] Concern over the trend is justified, but clear evidence indicates that the legitimacy of the political system has been left unscathed and that the decline should not be attributed to massive disaffection and discontent.[12]

Although the United States is vitally different now from the group of disparate communities that joined together in 1788 to adopt a Constitution, the voter's role has been elemental all along in the American experiment, a source of both government's legitimacy and its responsiveness. Voting in elections increases the voter's sense of belonging to the community and stimulates civic education and a sense of political responsibility.[13] The importance of achieving high participation in American presidential voting is made vivid by the present differences in levels of voting among persons of different social and economic status.

Despite such differences between voters and nonvoters, they do not differ greatly in their partisan and policy preferences.[14] But an expanded electorate would stimulate a wider agenda of issues than arises within a contracted electorate. Sidney Verba and Norman H. Nie argue that

> it may not be that the *preferences* of the inactive on the issues of the day are
> replaced by the *preferences* of those who are active if political leaders pay
> attention to the activist population. It may be, rather, that the issues of the
> day are *selected* in a way that ignores whatever matters most to the
> inarticulate members of the population.[15]

Absenteeism from voting by lower-income and poorly educated citizens means their unarticulated interests do not reach an active agenda.[16]

Clearly the political health of the United States cannot be judged alone by turnout rates in presidential elections. But political communications from class-biased voting convey incomplete information about the aspirations and priorities of the total population.[17] Although nonvoting can on occasion affect an outcome, it is also important that political leaders inevitably pay heed more to the electoral "messages" of middle-and upper-class citizens than to those of less-advantaged citizens who vote less often and are otherwise politically less active.

Political equality is always at risk when other resources that can be converted into political influence—money or education, for example—are unequally distributed.[18] In fact, universal suffrage is seen, in Ivor Crewe's words, as a "political counterweight to the power of property and wealth."[19] A mid-1970s survey of citizen involvement in politics in the Netherlands, Britain, the United States, Germany, and Austria highlights the several dimensions of participation. Judged by turnout in national elections, the United States had the lowest voting rate among the five nations. But, based on other forms of political participation, such as attending political rallies, discussing politics with friends, signing petitions, and engaging in lawful demonstrations and boycotts, Americans were politically the most active. The United States has been characterized as "a fully developed participant political culture" where "voting is apparently ill-suited as an *overall* indicator of the extent to which citizens are actively involved in the political process."[20] This may be true, but fuller representation of the interests of all the American people should emerge from the selection of presidents; the more who vote, the more responsive and viable will be the resulting government.

The functions of voting participation are of growing importance. The labyrinthian intricacy and unintelligibility of many issues faced by modern governments push the voter away from detailed, confident comprehension of events toward overall, instinctive appraisals of government performance. Those summary evaluations expressed in the voting booth, however informed, intuitive, or habitual they may be, are fundamental contributions to making representative government acceptable to the people who live under it; and to informing that government, no matter how crudely, of citizens' wishes, needs, and tolerances. The more who vote, the better the chance those things will be done adequately.

THE CORRELATES OF NONVOTING

Americans need to reckon with the fact that the number of persons who were eligible to vote but who did not do so exceeded the number of voters for the winner in every presidential election from 1920 to 1988. It has long been true that those who generally voted less often were poorly educated, of low income, blue-collar workers, women, younger citizens, minorities, unemployed, and people who had recently moved.[21] Some of those patterns persist, but not all.

Conditions that correlate with nonvoting fall easily into three categories. From time to time they may be given different labels, but the terms we will use here are psychological orientations, socio-demographic factors, and what we shall call institutional arrangements. Among the *psychological orientations* thought to affect voter turnout are a citizen's sense of civic duty; partisan loyalties; attitudes toward candidates, the political system, and government; and feelings of involvement in political affairs. *Socio-demographic factors* include age, education, occupation, income, geographic mobility, health, the availability of transportation, and group memberships. The third category comprises correlates of nonvoting of a different sort: *institutional arrangements* that embrace the electoral environment and that are potentially or partially amenable to deliberate change, with consequent bearing on voting participation—legal and administrative procedures; mobilization efforts by political parties, unions, religious groups, and racial or ethnic groups; and voter interest stirred by the competitiveness of campaigns, quality of candidates, and nature of issues.

Voting participation has been studied intensively since World War II, largely because it lends itself well to survey research and correlational analysis. Correlates of nonvoting can be identified, but not necessarily its causes.

Psychological Orientations

Jack H. Nagel observes ironically that "in an effective democracy, it is not the futility but the power of electoral participation that weakens the incentive to participate." In two-candidate elections with plurality rule, "elections appear to matter least when they actually are working best—pressuring politicians to perform satisfactorily and inducing them to adopt policy positions that conform to majority desires." Even if true, that does not thwart the advantages gained when groups participate purposefully and intensively for particular interests, and therefore does not minimize the value to democratic government of widespread and representative participation.[22]

Attitudes toward politics—psychological orientations—therefore affect voting participation. These psychological orientations may be called "attitudinal bases of the vote" or "motivational causes" of voting.[23] How voters feel about issues, the political system, the parties, the candidates, and their own civic duties make up their psychological orientations. In scholarly analysis of voting, higher turnout is generally associated with positive attitudes toward each of those subjects, but there is evidence suggesting that some elements of psychological orientation in fact may not correlate tightly with actual voting.[24]

About one-third of those not voting in 1980 abstained because, according to the U.S. Census Bureau, "they lacked sufficient interest in the electoral process or in the candidates to register or, if registered previously, to vote in that specific election."[25] Lack of interest may explain nonvoting in a given election, but not the steady decline in voting in presidential elections between 1960 and 1980. Individuals who reported an interest in politics and public affairs actually increased during that period. The turnout rate of those who stated they are attentive to politics "most of the time" remained stable between 1960 and 1976, in contrast to a steady decline in turnout among those who paid attention to public affairs "only now and then" or "never."[26]

Persons defined as politically alienated lack conviction that what they say or do will have an effect. They participate less in politics.[27] In contrast, citizens with strong feelings of "external" political efficacy believe that, in fact, *government is responsive,* that their votes do make a difference.[28] But such citizens declined dramatically among the white electorate between 1960 and 1980. Decreasing numbers of Americans believed that government would move when pushed by voters. The decline occurred in the presence of race-related issues, Vietnam, Watergate, and government's failure to solve economic and social difficulties that afflicted large numbers of people.[29]

Feelings of *personal political competence,* or "internal" political efficacy, accompany a tendency to vote. By contrast, persons who feel they lack political skills, or adequate political information, or for other reasons are politically ineffective, are more likely to abstain.[30] Overall, levels of "internal" political efficacy, in contrast to lowered feelings of "external" political efficacy, remained stable during the twenty years of decline in voter participation.

A sense of civic duty to vote is one of the most reliable indicators of who actually will vote.[31] Childhood socialization—at home, in school, through the media—instills a "sense of belonging to society and the consequent obligations of that membership."[32] Feelings of moral obligation will draw to the polls persons who would otherwise abstain. Turnout has continued high among citizens with the greatest sense of civic obligation. The new nonvoters have not come from them. Rather, they include the latest generations of persons eighteen to twenty-nine years old, among them rising numbers who express indifference to public affairs.[33]

Partisanship enhances a citizen's psychological involvement in politics. It gives a fast cue to candidates and issues. In presidential elections between 1952 and 1980, strong partisans were more likely than other potential voters to say they voted. Independents with no partisan leaning were least likely to report they voted in presidential elections from 1960 to 1980.[34] Erosion of party loyalties may therefore be a key factor in declining voter turnout. The percentage of whites who strongly identified with either the Republican or Democratic party fell from 36 percent in 1964 to 23 percent in 1980. The percentage of independents with no party leanings, meanwhile, grew from 9 percent in 1964 to 14 percent in 1980. These figures reflect no loss of partisanship among persons who had been party members all along, but rather a lack of party identification among new voters. Party identifiers have increasingly been "more a group of potential supporters than the army of followers that they were thought to be in the past."[35] And such weakened party loyalties may account for 25 to 30 percent of the decline in voter turnout in presidential elections.[36] In this context, strong identification with a racial or ethnic group, like strong party identification, can also motivate citizens to vote.[37]

Thus the psychological orientations that incline a citizen to vote are an interest in politics, feelings of external and internal political efficacy, a sense of citizen duty to vote, and strong political partisanship.

Warren E. Miller emphasizes the importance of accounting for the rise in nonvoting of *new* nonpartisan voters who entered the electorate during the period of decline. He holds that studies conducted between 1952 and 1978 do not indicate that declining turnout grew from a decline among previous voters in "political interest or involvement, or in a decreasing sense of civic duty, feeling of political efficacy or trust in government." Rather, "where patterns of change have coincided, further analysis indicates an absence of possible cause-and-effect relationships."[38] Nonpartisan nonvoters are hard to explain by the psychological orientations we have been examining. But patterns of nonvoting can be found among groups that share certain socio-demographic qualities.

Socio-Demographic Factors

Persons with a college education who work in a white collar occupation and enjoy a family income of $25,000 or more per year (in 1970s dollars) vote more than persons without those attributes. The greatest influence on electoral turnout among these factors is education. More education increases the likelihood a person will have a better job and make more money. Better-educated citizens are also more likely to feel an obligation to vote and to believe their votes count for something. Better-educated citizens show more interest in politics and feel more at ease with the abstract and complicated issues that politics often breeds.[39] Education reduces reluctance to vote by equipping people to understand political information and make political decisions. In addition, schools teach skills needed to cope with registration requirements, e.g., filling out forms and meeting deadlines.

The only rival of education in stimulating voting is life experience; that is, age. Voting participation rises with age, becoming highest between forty-five and sixty-four years. The bulge of new potential voters who entered the electorate in the period of voting decline—newly eligible eighteen-year-olds and the slightly older "baby boomers"—were predictably low participators. More recently, however, the "baby-boom" generation is aging and voting in larger numbers, although in the 1980s persons between eighteen and twenty-four years of age were reported as voting at lower rates than their predecessors. While the rate of increase in voting begins to stabilize as voters reach age fifty-five, turnout continues to rise slowly through the seventies.[40] Voters in the over-sixty-five age group are voting more now than previously. Sickness and family emergencies are the predominant reasons given for nonvoting among persons sixty-five years of age and older.[41]

For the first time since the Bureau of the Census began reporting on registration and voting in 1964, the turnout rate of women equalled that of men in the 1980 presidential election. It exceeded that of men in 1984,[42] and apparently again in 1988.[43] One analysis of participation in the 1972 presidential election found that differences in turnout between men and women were confined to potential voters over forty. Older women were less educated than older men and had grown up when men dominated political matters. Women were not assured the right to vote until the Nineteenth Amendment was ratified on August 18, 1920. Time was needed for voting to increase significantly, for older women to become accustomed to the change, and for younger women who were expecting to vote to move into the electorate.[44] The trend was hastened by the increase in political conscious-ness among women; similarly, blacks have begun to vote at a much increased rate—in fact, higher than their income and education levels would predict—and a 1988 poll found them almost as likely to vote as whites.[45]

Institutional Arrangements

From the viewpoint of public policy, the psychological orientations and socio-demographic factors that correlate with voting participation are societal givens generally beyond the reach of public policies. Institutional arrange-ments that affect voting levels, however, are more amenable to the influence of public policies and electoral procedures. Robert W. Jackson examined average voter turnout in nineteen democracies in the 1960s and 1970s and concluded that legal and institutional differences played a critical role in levels of voting participation. "Where institutions provide citizens with incentives to vote, more people actually participate; where institutions generate disincentives to vote, turnout suffers."[46] In such factors lie the most malleable influences on nonvoting.

In most countries, citizens are permanently registered to vote,[47] but not so in the United States, where registration requirements depress voting rates. In most states, to register to vote is more burdensome than voting itself. In a 1988 poll, 37 percent of nonvoters said they did not vote because they were not registered, and two-thirds of those not registered said they would have voted if they simply could have gone to the polls on election day.[48] Differences in voting rates are closely related to registration rates, and in 1984, 27 percent of the American voting-age population was not registered, and a pre-election estimate for 1988 was 29 percent. In most Western nations, government assumes some or all of the obligation to get citizens registered. Only in the United States does the burden of registering fall almost wholly on the citizen, a practice that accords with a larger American concept of personal responsibility,[49] and which partly, but significantly, accounts for low registra-tion.

Factors that retard registration have included inconvenient registration hours, lack of absentee registration in more than half the states, closing registration twenty-four days or more before the election in thirty states, and election-day registration in only five states.[50] A study of voter registration from 1972 through 1984 confirmed that earlier closing dates contributed generally to decreased turnout, and that later, less restrictive closing dates contributed to increased turnout. The inquiry also found that between 1972 and 1984 states had not adopted significantly later closing dates for voter registration. Five states, in fact, had adopted earlier closing dates.[51]

Yet the scene is not always uniform. The Committee for the Study of the American Electorate concluded that increases in registration were not followed in all cases by increases in voting, "clearly indicating that [in them] political factors rather than registration are more determinative of turnout."[52] And the proportion of registered persons who vote has been falling, by one calculation, from 85.3 percent in 1960 to 80.5 in 1968 and 72.6 in 1984.[53]

In most countries, persons eligible to vote are automatically reregistered when they move from one electoral district to another. Since election regulation in the United States is largely a state matter, citizens who move from one state to another must comply with differing state registration requirements. Approximately one-sixth of Americans change residence each year. Even when the move is within the same city, almost all must reregister in the new location.[54] This residential mobility lowers voting participation. A *New York Times/CBS News Poll* after the 1988 election reported that 16 percent of voters had moved in the last two years versus 35 percent of nonvoters who had done so.[55] The inconvenience of registering anew is high, and getting information needed to frame opinions in a new political setting also calls for initiative. Among persons most adversely affected are middle-aged and better educated citizens who otherwise report the highest rates of voting participation. For persons between the ages of thirty-seven and sixty-nine, a move of residence causes an estimated 31 percent drop in the probability of their voting.[56]

In most states, persons who want to vote must register prior to an election and at a location other than the polling place. Forty-two states require a person to reside in the state ten to thirty days after a move before becoming eligible to vote. Americans in thirty-five states must reregister if they failed to vote in the last election or two.

The importance of the closing date for registration mentioned above deserves emphasis as a prime obstacle to would-be voters. The closer to election day registration is permitted, the more likely are eligibles to register and therefore vote. Curtis Gans, director of the Committee for the Study of the American Electorate, has long concluded that experience in the United States "tends to show that the principal procedural problem in improving turnout is eliminating the two-step process of registration and voting, rather than simply making it easier to register."[57] Easing registration would undoubtedly encourage voting, but, as we have seen, more factors are involved when the proportion of those registered who vote has been declining.[58]

At various times since the 1950s a large number of democracies have penalized nonvoting.[59] Five countries were listed in 1984 as having sanctions for not voting: Australia, Belgium, Greece, Italy, and Spain.[60] Although the penalties are generally negligible, the effect in encouraging law-abiding citizens to vote is considerable. The Netherlands offers an instructive experience. It had compulsory voting between 1948 and 1967 with an average turnout of 94.7 percent. Between 1971 and 1981, after the requirement was abandoned, participation stabilized at about 10 percentage points below its previous level,[61] leading Ivor Crewe, student of voter participation in many nations, to conclude that compulsory voting seems responsible for a minimum turnout gain of 10 percent.[62] The relevance to the United States, where voting has traditionally been viewed as a privilege, is problematic. Failure to use one's influence in self-government is viewed as its own penalty.

Other measures are taken in some democracies to facilitate voting. While they probably make marginal improvements in turnout, the data on their effectiveness are inconclusive, and they are clearly less effective than automatic registration or compulsory voting.[63] The measures, however, offer some perspective on United States practices. Of twenty-seven democratic countries studied by Crewe, five held elections on more than one day, and thirteen held them on Sunday, or made election day a public holiday. Only nine held elections on a work day, one being the United States. In the United States, the polls in most states are open only twelve or thirteen hours, and only a single day, which is less than in many nations. Eight countries provided polling stations in hospitals, old-age homes, ships, barracks, prisons, and embassies abroad. Seven permitted constituency transfer, which allows an elector to vote in a different polling district from the one where he is registered.

Most American states do seek in one way or another to encourage voting. In addition to other provisions for absentee voting, some states permit postage voting by persons in the armed forces and government employees, provided proper application is made, and some states permit proxy voting for the blind and disabled.[64] Moreover, a federal law effective in 1988 permits overseas voters who have applied properly but have not received a general election absentee ballot from their state of official residence to use federal write-in ballots.[65] The effects of such measures on voting participation are desirable but not very significant.

National party systems also influence voter participation. Parties structure the voting choices citizens face. Outside the United States, strong bonds often link parties to particular social and demographic groups—e.g., workers, farmers, Catholics, businessmen—enabling parties to identify issues and choices for their followers. The linkages help the parties know who their supporters are, enabling them to urge their partisans to register and vote.[66]

The absence of a European-style labor party in the United States partly accounts for the skewing of the American electorate toward better educated, more well-to-do, more prestigiously employed citizens. Where workers have binding ties to parties that represent their interests, they are likely to vote as much as their better-educated, more affluent compatriots.[67] American workers, however, have never shared the strong class consciousness found in other nations, and neither major party has been organized along narrow class lines. American blacks, in contrast, have been energized by civil rights controversies to vote well above the level of their socio-economic class.[68] Strong group consciousness and strong Democratic partisanship in recent decades have given blacks incentives to vote not shared by others similarly situated economically and socially.

In 1984, both major American parties worked strenuously to increase voter registration and turnout. The Republicans, better financed, ran a highly sophisticated registration drive. The Republican National Committee and the Reagan-Bush '84 Committee planned to spend eight to ten million dollars to add two million GOP loyalists to the rolls. The Democrats, hoping to add five million, depended on "nonpartisan" activities to promote registration of citizens in categories traditionally deemed Democratic,[69] although some opinion held that registration and mobilization activities conducted by allegedly nonpartisan groups would be less effective than ones conducted by a political party.[70] But such groups demonstrated in 1984 that they could be aggressive mobilizing agents. More than 100 private organizations directed efforts that year at electoral drop-outs. Trade unions, ethnic groups, professional associations, the Chamber of Commerce, the Moral Majority, rock stars on music television (MTV), and others urged citizens across the political spectrum to register and vote, among them blacks, Hispanics, women, students, and poor people.[71]

Although political parties are normally deemed major mobilizers of the electorate,[72] party politicians have sometimes pursued strategies of selective mobilization and demobilization. Paul Kleppner argues that the Republican party has, in fact, pursued a strategy of selective demobilization since the turn of the century. He found that Republicans have repeatedly opposed lowering procedural barriers to voting.[73] Former President Jimmy Carter has said that incumbent office holders of both parties share reluctance to bring in new voters with uncertain preferences.[74]

In 1986, the Republican party undertook a controversial ballot security program designed to keep dead or nonexistent people from voting. Financed by the Republican National Committee (RNC), the program sought to discover whether people actually lived at the addresses shown in the public record and to purge those who did not. Concentrating first on precincts in Louisiana where President Reagan had received 20 percent or less of the vote in the 1984 election, the program was immediately vulnerable to charges that it targeted blacks. The RNC agreed in federal court to stop the program, but rejected charges of intimidation and harassment of black voters and defended the project as a means to protect "ballot integrity." Frank J. Fahrenkopf, Jr., chairman of the RNC, said he would seek the support of the League of Women

Voters, the National Association for the Advancement of Colored People, and the Democratic National Committee in a campaign before the 1988 presidential election to prevent voter registration fraud, and to "cleanse" voting rolls of persons ineligible to vote and people who had died.[75]

Less direct efforts have been made to discourage traditional opponents from voting. Disaffected working-class Democrats and black voters, for example, who envisioned government in New Deal terms, were opposed ideologically by Republican grass-roots elites who grew in strength after the 1960s. Unable to attract those disaffected Democrats to their party, the Republicans instead emphasized life-style and "big government" issues that troubled many such Democrats, hoping to expose them to cross pressures and uncertainties and thereby increase the possibility of their not voting.[76]

When such tactics are employed, discouragement to voting that results is not an argument for giving voters less information. If anything, it is an argument for giving them more. Nonetheless, competitive pressures may be in control. Political consultants at a 1984 conference of voting specialists articulated a demobilizing strategy. John Deardourff, a consultant to moderate and liberal Republican candidates, said that he makes a " 'deliberate attempt to create the maximum amount of cross pressures on the weak [Democratic] Party voter' so that the voter will 'come over to us or not vote at all.' " Democratic consultant Robert Squire confirmed that "some of the tactics we use in political campaigns do very much suppress the vote. We intentionally do that. We call it chloroforming or deep-freezing."[77]

Indeed, competitive factional interests within party organizations can, on occasion, lead party officials to suppress participation by their party's natural supporters. In 1984, Thomas B. Edsall charged in the *Washington Post* that in slums with large numbers of unregistered potential voters, where anti-Reagan sentiment probably was extremely high, local Democratic leaders opposed broad voter registration efforts. "They are intent," he wrote, "on maintaining a small, controlled electorate, guaranteed to cast majorities for endorsed candidates in Democratic primaries. They bitterly oppose letting outside groups add unknown voters to their rolls."[78]

Nevertheless, increased competition between parties normally increases interest generally and leads to more voting.[79] Also, as Tom Wicker observes, participation is stimulated when potential voters "strongly support or passionately oppose" the candidates running, even when the outcome is not in doubt.[80]

The range of factors that can affect voting participation in the laissez faire atmosphere of American politics is indeed wide. Some persons have worried that early projections of results on election night discourage citizens who have not already voted from going to the polls. One study of the 1980 general election, for example, found "the early call to have had a small but measurable impact on presidential and congressional turnout, and a somewhat larger impact on depressing the vote for Democratic candidates at both levels."[81] A 1984 election-night survey of 638 nonvoting registered voters in

Oregon reached a different conclusion: "for better or worse, critics cannot win their war against early projections with proof that election outcomes are reversed or that turnout is suppressed."[82] Surveys after an election, unless meticulously conducted, run great risk of influencing the answers elicited by the nature of the questions asked. There are important reasons not to use polls to predict election results before all polling places are closed, but the effect on the turnout of voters appears not to be as significant in presidential races as it may be in others.[83]

The more general influence of the media on voting participation has been uncertain. No consensus exists. Television coverage may stimulate voter turnout by increasing viewers' knowledge of candidates and interest in issues, or it may depress voter participation by its superficial or negative coverage.[84] Accusing fingers are pointed at the lengthened prenomination campaign as contributing to declining turnout in presidential elections. Former President Gerald Ford has declared that "one presidential primary after another in February through June has certainly contributed to the decline of voter interest in the November finale."[85] The possibility that voters become bored with perennial campaigns that, in Edwin M. Yoder's words, "bid constantly for our notice like spoiled children," may be plausible on the surface,[86] but there are no conclusive data to prove or disprove the thesis. A hot pennant race from April to October never lowered interest in the World Series.

The frequency with which individual American voters are called to the polls may, however, be a different matter. Alexander Hamilton argued in the Constitutional Convention that "frequency of elections tended to make the people listless to them; and to facilitate the success of little cabals. This evil was complained of in all the States."[87] It may also depress turnout in any given election. The United States exceeds other nations in the number and types of elections open to its voters.[88] This surfeit of opportunities may tire the electorate and devalue voting in any single election, especially when races of high interest are run in different years, e.g., for governor and president.[89] Nonetheless, the frequency of elections is rooted in a long heritage deeply skeptical of authority, one confident of the salutary effects on public officials of having to refresh their authority by frequent reference to the people.

The complex determinants of voting participation are difficult to sort out. Much is known about patterns of *group* participation (as we are using the term), but little about the *individual* who chooses or refuses to vote. Changes in public policy that might alter tenacious patterns of nonparticipation are our ultimate concern, and to them we now turn.

TO REDUCE NONVOTING

"[T]he number and percentage of Americans who voluntarily eschew the ballot box is by far greater than those who are blocked by legal, procedural, or administrative impediments." So concluded, in 1987, a study for the Committee for the Study of the American Electorate. Similar conclusions have been reached by others.[90]

The most that rule changes can do is to lessen legal impediments—unless voting were made compulsory, with hefty penalties for failure to vote. Voter mobilization efforts are required, and rule changes are no substitute for them. Candidates, parties, civic groups, schools, the media, any source that can enlarge a citizen's understanding of politics, feelings of trust in it, and sense of efficacy through political activity can raise voting participation. But, also, the easier it is to vote, the more likely it is that a person will do so. The franchise is, by reasonable definition, universal in the United States. Steps to ease its exercise are needed. Recommendations to reduce nonvoting are offered in Chapter Eleven. The discussion here will lay a basis for them, but realism requires awareness that barriers to increased voting are political as well as legal and procedural. As Benjamin Ginsberg and Martin Shefter emphasized in 1990, both political parties would incur "major risks" from significant infusions of new voters of untested loyalties—Republicans particularly in presidential elections and Democrats in local, state, and congressional contests. [91]

To vote requires two steps—establishing the right, and casting the ballot. Some aspects of both steps are regulated by the federal government; others are controlled by state governments. Federal constitutional amendments, for example, preclude states from denying the vote because of race or sex, and federal statutes require states to allow members of the U.S. armed forces and merchant marine, their spouses and dependents, and American citizens residing outside the United States, to register and vote absentee in congressional and presidential elections.[92] On the other hand, states prescribe voter registration systems and regulate polling hours. The ease of becoming and staying registered and the convenience of voting, including absentee voting, vary considerably from state to state.

That tradition is long and deep. Federal intervention has been justified only to assure that the vote will not be denied for reasons the nation has formally declared to be inadmissable. If the goal is maximum *voluntary* voting participation, the question then is how to encourage it—by federal action, state action, or otherwise—within two restraining principles that are bred of American experience and expectations: regulate only when necessary for an essential goal, and regulate as low as possible in the political structure. Four approaches claim our attention, two that are not desirable and two that are.

Holding national initiatives and referenda at the time of presidential elections might stimulate presidential voting, but aside from objections to adopting national legislation in these ways, serious disadvantages to presidential selection would follow. Uniform controversial measures on the ballot in every state would distract from what should be the main national electoral focus of choosing a president. Especially if presidential candidates took opposing positions on initiatives or referenda, the campaign focus could be turned away from them. If the candidates took no stands, the voters' attention to them could still be diluted. Moreover, campaign controversy around one or two highly publicized issues could detract from the larger agenda-setting function now performed by presidential selection.

The burdens of electoral participation are already high. Presidential elections are held in tandem with congressional elections for all voters, plus senatorial and often state and local elections for some voters. In various localities and states, initiatives or referenda already appear on the ballot. To add another national decision, qualitatively different, would increase the electoral burden dramatically.

Shortening the nominating scramble—assuming for argument that it might actually be possible—would, in the opinion of some, increase voting in November. We have seen that former President Gerald Ford believes that the lengthy contests for presidential nominations weary the electorate and contribute to nonvoting. Scheduling regional presidential primaries between April and June of the election year is proposed as a means to shorten the process. So is amending the Federal Election Campaign Act to prevent contributions to a presidential candidate or campaign prior to January 1 of the election year.[93]

But no available data support the assumption that a shorter campaign would induce higher levels of voting. The price of making the suggested changes, however, is certain. It lies, as discussed in Chapter Three, in the loss of information that candidates and voters would suffer from any radical change in the system of sequential state-based primaries and caucuses. To restrict the candidates' capacities to raise early and sufficient funds for the nomination campaign could also affect adversely the political information communicated, as well as the competitiveness of the contest. Some qualified candidates might even find in the limitation a disincentive to entering a race. Uncertain increases in voter participation that a restricted primary season might encourage are not worth the costs.

There are, however, two approaches to increasing voting participation that should be taken: making both registration and voting easier. They can be achieved by feasible administrative and legislative actions.

Easing Registration

Registration requirements are a deterrent to voting. Some proposed remedies would lighten the registration burden; others would eliminate it altogether. Gary R. Orren suggests that Congress mandate for all federal elections four requirements to be met by locally administered voter registration systems: a date close to the election through which registration must be permitted uniformly in all states; day, evening, and weekend hours when registration offices must be kept open; simple, liberal provisions for absentee registration by all citizens of voting age; and automatic transfer of registration for all movers within a state (estimated to be about 83 percent of all movers). Orren judges that a gain of 10 to 15 percent in participation might be realized.[94]

These proposals would not require local officials to adapt to radically unfamiliar procedures, and administrative control of elections would stay in the hands of states and localities. What might be gained in participation would justify federal intervention in local voter registration and also the prospective financial cost.

Proposals for federal legislation have been increasing. In 1986, Rep. John Conyers (D-Mich.) introduced two bills to ease registration in the manner suggested by Orren. HR 1453 called for each state to supply postcard application forms approved by the Federal Election Commission for voter registration by mail for federal elections. Registration for federal elections on regular work days and election-day registration at the polls would have been required by HR 1454. Other proposals for federal intervention have been made, including a plan in preparation in 1989 by Democratic Senators Alan Cranston and Edward M. Kennedy to require federal scrutiny of state voter registration practices. Should the Department of Justice discern discrimination, a state would be forced to adopt one or more of four practices: election-day registration; mail registration; registration in federal, state, and local government agencies; and/or registration when applying for a driver's license.

In early 1990, the House of Representatives approved a bill requiring, among other things, all states to conform to prescribed national voter registration procedures that would allow eligible citizens to register by mail, when they get a driver's license, and at state agency offices. Purging names from voting rolls for not voting would also be prohibited. Many Republicans, including President Reagan, opposed the measure.[95]

One might ask why more severe steps to insure higher voter registration are not desirable. Compulsory registration to vote has been likened to compulsory registration for Social Security or for military service. But the notion has encountered the traditional American concept of voting as a right to be exercised at the citizen's option, not as an obligation enforceable against the citizen's will.

Arrangements other than compulsory registration, however, can relieve the individual voter of initial responsibility and bring practices in the United States closer to those in most other democracies. Canada, for example, has a uniform, federally mandated system of universal voter enrollment that puts on public authority the burden of getting citizens properly registered. Similar plans for the United States suggest dividing the country into districts, with officials conducting door-to-door canvasses to register all eligible and willing citizens. The political obstacles to adopting such a scheme are obviously substantial: loyalty to the states' traditional role in election administration, and corresponding antipathy to centralization and any further federal intrusion. And another matter lurks. The prospect of systematic, affirmative, government-sponsored enumeration of citizens and their whereabouts would alarm many as an unwanted invasion of privacy. A nationally administered registration and election system would be a radical conceptual as well as administrative departure. Moreover, the cost of replacing the 6,500 existing state registration offices is uncertain.[96]

Individual states, however, can study experiences with universal voter enrollment that may be applicable to their own circumstances. Idaho, for example, has a registration system similar to Canada's. County clerks appoint registrars in all precincts who conduct door-to-door canvasses. Turnout rates in Idaho exceeded the national average by 7 to 15 percent after 1960. Other states could implement a plan similar to Idaho's, or a variation of it.[97]

Universal voter enrollment eliminates personal responsibility for registration. Registration on election day would lighten but not eliminate the citizen's burden. Five states—Maine, Minnesota, North Dakota, Oregon, and Wisconsin—have election-day registration. If available nationwide, the practice might, by one estimate, increase voters by six million in four years.[98] In 1977, President Carter sponsored a bill mandating election-day registration. Although it reached the House floor, it was withdrawn without a vote, lacking support from Republicans and conservative Democrats.[99] Because of the wide variety of political conditions in the country—political subcultures, if you will—including greater temptations and opportunities to commit fraud in some jurisdictions than in others, election-day registration is a matter best left to each state.

Clearly, ease of registration encourages voting, but so many variables are at work that fixing a precise effect is difficult.[100] Raymond E. Wolfinger and Steven J. Rosenstone, nonetheless, estimated that in 1972, if the easiest registration requirements had been in effect in all the states, voting in the presidential election would have gone up about 9 percent. Were the United States to adopt a registration system that places on government the burden for establishing valid voter rolls (as found in Europe) voter turnout might increase by considerably more than 9 percent.[101]

Some twenty states and the District of Columbia now permit voters to register by mail as well as in person,[102] providing convenience for the citizen and potential economy in registration administration. With safeguards against fraud, states thus can lighten the task and increase the level of registration. How much the measure would actually contribute to expanded voter turnout is uncertain. From 1972 through 1980, states with provision for voter registration by mail recorded average participation rates that were two points higher than in states without it.[103]

Many other proposals would make registration more convenient and presumably increase voting participation. Qualified high school graduates might be automatically registered when receiving their diplomas. Utility companies might send registration-by-mail forms to customers who terminate, transfer, or initiate service. Because some persons do not register for fear it would expose them to jury call, it has been urged that states deny the use of registration rolls in selecting juries, and publicize the fact.[104] No proposals like these have engendered enthusiasm.

Initial efforts by the Human Service Employees Registration and Voter Education Fund—Human SERVE—were mixed at best. It was organized in 1983 and launched a national campaign to persuade public officials and private agencies to permit registration at facilities easily accessible to citizens, ranging from day care centers to libraries to liquor stores. Advocates have persisted, with positive results in some places, although vigorous and varied opposition in the early stages led analysts Frances Fox Piven and Richard A. Cloward to conclude, in 1985, that "electoral constriction is embedded in contemporary politics, and it is vigorous and pervasive."[105]

Peverill Squire, Raymond E. Wolfinger, and David P. Glass propose a means to stem the loss of voters among Americans who move frequently—nearly one-third of the population moves every two years—and fail to reregister thereafter. Their plan should be implemented by both state and federal governments. They suggest modifying the U.S. Postal Service's change-of-address notices so that when a change of voting address occurs, a copy could be forwarded by the local post office to the chief election official in the state where the move originated. As noted, in approximately 83 percent of moves that would also be the state of destination. Automatic reregistration could be provided. When a person is not already enrolled, an invitation to register could be extended by mail or otherwise. Federal legislation to require the Postal Service to make necessary modifications in postal change-of-address forms has been proposed. If such legislation is adopted, the states should then make the necessary alterations in their voter registration laws to make the plan effective.[106]

Removal from a state's voting list should take place for death, nonresidence, or commission of certain felonies, but never simply for not voting.[107] Several states have a policy that should be emulated. In November 1986, for example, Virginia adopted a constitutional amendment changing its requirement that a person not voting in a four-year period be automatically removed from the registry. A voter now must be notified of the pending cancellation and, if still residing at the same address, remain registered if so requesting in writing.[108] By one estimate, abolishing removal for failure to vote could increase voters by over two million in four years.[109]

Other initiatives to ease registration have been taken in other states. Since 1975, eligible persons in Michigan have been able to register wherever driver licenses are issued, and by 1988 the number of states providing registration at motor vehicle bureaus totalled seventeen.[110] This approach has been declared by the Committee for the Study of the American Electorate to be "the most helpful new development in enhancing registration,"[111] although it should be remembered that persons without drivers licenses are found disproportionately among the poor and minorities.

The partisanship inherent in issues of voter registration was made explicit in 1989 by Representative Newt Gingrich, Republican whip in the

House of Representatives, who in arguing for a bill to ease registration declared that Republicans now stood to gain by increased voter registration, making the legislation not only "good policy" but also "good politics." As a consequence, a bill to ease registration was attracting better than usual bipartisan support in Congress. It embraced several of the measures discussed above. It would require states to permit registration by mail, to accompany applications for drivers' licenses with applications for registration by mail, to make registration forms available at a wide array of public places, and to refrain from removing registrants because they failed to vote. Also, post offices would be required to provide registration authorities with change-of-address information, and election fraud and intimidation of voters would be made federal crimes.[112]

Easing Voting

Voting is easier than registering. Proposals to make it still easier, however, do not assure a larger turnout, and the likely costs of implementation require careful assessment.

Compulsory voting is the most radical option, and there is no significant public support for the concept. It especially would not appeal to persons desiring to stay as mobile, or as obscure, as possible.

Other proposals, often emulating the practices we have noted in other countries, have costs that may outweigh their unpredictable benefits in increased voter turnout. Holding elections on a Sunday is one. Making election day a national holiday is another. Keeping polls open long hours, perhaps as many as twenty-four, is deemed by many, not including this writer, to be too costly.[113] Changing the presidential election day by congressional act to Memorial Day in May is proposed to encourage higher voter turnout. The weather would be better and citizens would be freer to vote if they chose, but the obstacles to adoption and the inertia obstructing such a change would be enormous.[114]

Early projections of election results by broadcasters are an issue. The Uniform Regional Poll Closing bill passed by the House of Representatives in 1986 and subsequently, including 1989, would require that all polls in all states except Alaska and Hawaii close at 9 P.M. Eastern Standard Time in presidential election years.[115] The Senate was initially reluctant, but it was predicted in 1989 that eventually a version of such a bill would pass.[116] Simultaneous poll closings would eliminate reporting of final results from some states while voting is still underway in others. Early projections, some argue, discourage those who have not already voted from doing so. Others, including the author of the 1984 survey of nonvoting registered voters in Oregon cited above, dispute that conclusion. And networks still could make early projections based on exit polling. Given the uncertain effects of early projections on voter participation, federal legislation is not justified.

Liberal absentee voting procedures of the sort in effect in California would increase voter turnout at reasonable costs. Orren reports that use of California's absentee voting rules by the Republican gubernatorial campaign of George Deukmejian in 1982 raised the number of absentee ballots cast to 6.5 percent of the total vote, more than double the 1978 rate.[117]

In recent years, thirty states have had time-off-to-vote legislation, twenty-two providing time off with pay. The evidence is limited, but states where time off is mandated have been found to have a statistically significant higher turnout than states where it is not.[118]

The time may come when political tolerance, the resources of state and local jurisdictions, and computer technology will make possible election-day registration—or, conceivably, despite what was said above, universal voter enrollment. Citizens could then vote on election day wherever it is convenient for them. In most localities at the present time, however, checking registration in several precincts and assuring that a person has not already voted would be cumbersome and costly. In the unlikely event that nationwide political support were marshalled on behalf of radical federal action to increase voting participation, the proposals would have to be measured carefully against their costs, financial and other.

Scenarios for federal action to fix polling hours, polling places, absentee-voting rules, time off from work to vote, and other conditions deemed to affect voting turnout encounter two principal issues. One is the degree of effectiveness in encouraging voting. The other is the extent to which such matters should be left to state determination. The criteria for judgment are not clear-cut. The persistent diversity of conditions throughout the states—not the same differences that characterized the states five or fifteen decades ago, but new differences—argues now as in the past for minimum essential federal intervention in the electoral process. This observer believes the symbolism of a federal requirement to keep the polls open twenty-four hours would be worth the large financial and other costs, but most do not. Actions of the type proposed above to encourage higher registration are the most useful federal steps that can be taken to contribute to a more robust and effective democratic government. For the rest, and for the present, state and local jurisdictions should stimulate larger electoral participation in ways best suited to their individual circumstances.

Even the potentially most effective measures to ease registration and voting do not guarantee increases among those sectors of the population that now vote least—the poor, the less educated, those with low-status jobs.[119] And the discussion often ignores other means for representing the political interests of politically inert citizens—among them, conventional lobbying and legal representation on their behalf, and vigorously disciplined opinion polling.[120]

Nonetheless, diverse efforts to activate nonvoters are needed. Nonvoters should hear that candidates and officeholders respond to the needs and desires of those who vote more than of those who do not. They should comprehend emphatically that voting can make a difference to them over the long haul, even if not always visibly and immediately. Lowering barriers to registration and voting can reinforce other mobilization efforts. Persons of lower socio-economic status are more likely than others to be discouraged by rules and procedures that make registration and voting complicated and inconvenient. Reducing the burdens of participation invites all eligible citizens not only to exercise the franchise, but to contemplate the significance for their own welfare of the political system in the large and the governing decisions it produces.[121]

To complete this discussion, a few words are needed about some recent technological innovations. A major spur to the long evolution of American registration and voting practices has been the effort to reduce fraud. In recent decades, marketers of computer technologies have vied vigorously in electoral jurisdictions across the country to sell equipment for counting votes electronically. In 1988, it was estimated that 55 percent of the votes would be so counted. About a third would be cast on older mechanical-lever equipment—including that in New York City, some two decades old in 1990, which was described then as obsolete and "prone to jamming"[122]—and some 10 percent by paper ballot.[123] Experience with the new electronic procedures in the 1970s and 1980s, however, was flavored with technical mishaps, suspicions of fraud, and contradictory expert opinion on the possibilities and likelihood of inaccurate counting.[124]

The desire of private equipment suppliers to protect their proprietary interests in the public functions they perform has hindered full exploration of the potentials for faulty reporting, including inaccurate reporting sufficient to affect the electoral college outcome. One prudent reporter concluded that "given the crucial role of public confidence in the integrity of the ballot, common sense suggests that the question should be resolved definitively, by the press and, perhaps, by Congress."[125] Given the traditional decentralized control of American elections, however, a considerable national anxiety precipitated by clear probability of fraud, or incompetent counting, would be needed to stir Congress to action. As always, the integrity and adequacy of balloting procedures will rest ultimately with vigorous press scrutiny and attentive citizen concern.

The representativeness of participation in a presidential election is determined by the degree "the structure of popular opinion"[126] expressed in it is complete or partial. The information value of the means by which the nation's leadership is chosen, along with its role in shaping the public agenda, will be enhanced if the citizens who participate, and the information they communicate to government, are broadly representative of the nation in all its scope and complexity. Steps to encourage and ease voting contribute to that end.

CHAPTER EIGHT

Political Agendas and Choosing Presidents

☆
☆

A fundamental goal in writing the Constitution, "that the government should leave the citizen alone," has been transformed. "[T] he problem now is that citizens won't leave government alone. They plunder the State as the State was once thought to plunder them."[1] Thus Senator Daniel Patrick Moynihan describes the revolution in American political agendas. Modern American electorates are offered much the same voting opportunities as electorates in the nineteenth century, but those limited choices now convey a democratic cachet to a massively expanded conglomeration of government undertakings.

The ultimate test of a democratic system is sustained popular acceptance of its processes and their results. The issue is always whether enough procedural and substantive expectations are satisfied for the system to remain viable. In an established, stable democracy that holds the allegiance of most of its population, failure to address even important issues effectively can be sustained for a while, sometimes a long while. But such confidence is not automatic. And expectations change with changes in voters' education, economic status, social mobility, geographic mobility, and other life experiences that affect their knowledge and values. As long as sources of information and opportunities for participation evolve with changing interests in society, the political agenda can set a realistic environment for presidential leadership.

Effective participation in developing a democracy's agenda can be as important to the ultimate stability of the system as electoral participation.[2]

POPULAR INFLUENCE AND GROWING AGENDAS

American presidential elections do not determine policies; they designate the official combatants for policy struggles. The state of the economy is the most important continuing condition influencing presidential popularity, and presidential candidates win or lose more on the basis of general confidence in them than on any detailed policy prescriptions they may offer. The supporters of Richard Nixon in 1968 had no idea they were voting to suspend the convertibility of the dollar into gold, which Nixon did in 1971, or to open relations with the People's Republic of China. Election results are registers of broad policy preferences—the "Reagan realignment" was surely such[3]—but the concrete actions likely to emerge are far from certain.[4] Richard Rose writes that even in British national campaigns, "the speeches of the party leaders are not so much a debate about policy as they are an attempt to resolve a general question of competence."[5] Candidates for Parliament minimize policy debate in their constituencies. Even when a government ignores its commitments, it cannot be forced to honor them. Should voters bring a new party to office, the limits on mandate continue.[6] Regardless of the form of government, the subject of elections is electing.[7]

With the expanded functions of government in the modern state, and government's increased direct impact on personal lives, citizens may properly ask whether their influence over party policies and government actions is now sufficient.[8] Elections do what they have always done in democratic systems, but citizen demands lead the American government to do more and more. Senator Moynihan reflected that, in his early years of government service, health issues seldom intruded on the budget-making process. "Budget examiners never had to choose how many persons with kidney failure they would let live in the next fiscal year. Now they do."[9] In this new day when citizens "plunder" the state, connections between the *electorate* and the agenda of modern policy government are extensive, more so than between *elections* and the agenda.

In some states, municipalities, and other nations, initiatives and referenda give electorates direct influence over policy. Even Britain, traditionally unsympathetic to mechanisms of direct democracy, has had national referenda in the recent past. The American federal electorate, however, does not vote directly on issues. In fact, in the absence of referenda, citizens as a class do not directly determine public policy in any contemporary democracy. The nature of American political parties, however, has always given individual U.S. citizens more chance to influence the nation's public policy agenda—the all-important prelude to legislating public policy—than is found in more tightly structured parliamentary systems. Roger W. Cobb and Charles D. Elder declare that "the importance of popular participation may go well beyond simply voting. . . . It emphasizes the crucial role that various publics may play in shaping the very substance of governmental decisions."[10]

Except in a sudden crisis, political issues gain prominence through purposeful efforts of participants in defining problems and proposing solutions.[11] America's decentralized parties have been hospitable to issue controversies, a condition exacerbated by the increasingly long, loosely structured public presidential selection activities of recent years. The part played by the electoral process in shaping the public agenda has risen correspondingly. The fluid, open structure of American politics is especially hospitable to the political energies stimulated by the profusion of issues that besieges all modern democracies.[12]

Anyone who commands publicity, from journalists to government officials to movie stars, can direct attention to issues and controversies and make them prospects for the public agenda.[13]

THE CHANGING CONTENT OF POLITICAL AGENDAS

National political institutions are continuously tested by new requirements. Foreign events have intruded on politics in the United States since the French Revolution, but the recent increasing internationalization of U.S. political issues, and the Americanization of many internal issues in other nations, stem inexorably from the rising interdependence of nations.

The world scope of many crucial phenomena dilutes the functional sovereignty of all nations and increasingly invades the parochialism of their internal politics. Many influences are at work, including modern multinational corporate activities, population growth and migrations, mounting resource consumption, emerging international banking, credit, and currency systems, and, perforce, national budgetary and fiscal policies. A global community of a newly intense and mounting interdependence is created by issues of space exploration and nuclear contamination, threatened global warming, ozone depletion, sweeping worldwide deforestation, falling water tables, and much else besides. Harlan Cleveland has observed that "the content of international affairs is now mostly the internal affairs of still-sovereign nations. At the White House level, every major issue for policy decision is partly 'domestic' and partly 'international.' "[14] In his study of *The Post-Modern Presidency,* Richard Rose has made it dramatically clear that a president's record increasingly depends on what happens outside the United States.[15]

For years, moreover, advanced industrial societies have experienced increasing heterogeneity. The pace and intensity have differed with national characteristics, but in all such nations, including the United States, political parties have faced difficulty in adjusting to new environments, interests, and issues. It cannot be emphasized too often that new issue-cleavages of great variety and often temporary duration have emerged in Western democracies generally. Political mobilization in contemporary societies is subject to atomizing influences as issues become more complicated, overlapping, and transient, and advocacy organizations more numerous, sharply focused, and egalitarian.

In the United States, we have noted the burgeoning of activist issues that cut across party lines, among them women's, minority, environmental, defense, energy, immigration, trade, and regional concerns. The variety of controversial issues has made it especially difficult for Democrats to cement stable, embracing, national campaign coalitions. Increasing social and geographic mobility and the dilution of earlier organizing controversies have destabilized traditional party loyalties and infused politics with new and changing stakes. Issues are likely to be viewed ad hoc, with allies on one often opposing each other on another. This environment and the increasing volume and importance of members' services to constituents in their relations with the federal government are factors in the diminished turnover in recent decades of membership in the Congress, and consequently in the election of presidents of a different party from the one with a majority in the House or Senate, or both.

Except during a popularly supported war, framing an action agenda has always presented formidable challenges to parties, candidates, and presidents. Since the early 1960s especially, new issues precipitated by the rapidly evolving character of post-industrial society have heightened the actions of interest groups and the mass media. "Cutting across the economic dimension," William Schneider commented in 1983, "are the newer ideological divisions associated with the social, cultural, and foreign-policy conflicts of the past two decades."[16] Issues increasingly have become narrow, require technical solutions, and involve difficult choices among competing values and the means of reaching them. Parties, candidates, and presidents have found it more difficult to develop comprehensive, aggregate approaches to widely diverse problems than they did when the initial focus of most activists was on winning office.[17]

The number of persons in both parties with the interest, time, and education to undertake a continuing politics of issues has grown substantially.[18] Younger voters were reported in 1984 to be more attentive to issues than to party fealty.[19] The results have included a confusing complex of public controversies and diffusion of voter attention, with reward even more than in the past going to presidential aspirants who, like Ronald Reagan, can sweep everything together under a canopy of good will and trust, a trust that rests more on shared predispositions and a search for safe haven than on agreement about detailed policies.

Thus protagonists of contemporary issues do not cluster as easily as they once did under the banner of one of the two major parties. There are now thousands of interest groups. As their goals and alliances have mounted in number and variety, their independence of political factions and parties has risen.[20] The solicitation of citizen views and playback of citizen responses fostered by modern polling have given polling results especially a fixed importance in identifying agenda items and planning political strategies.

Modes of political expression have expanded as electronic media and other means of direct contact with the electorate have become more encompassing and diverse, permitting candidates, officials, and advocates to bypass intermediaries in promoting issues. Moreover, it has become the norm for party platforms to include inventories of disparate political aspirations less confined than earlier to broad stances accompanied by a limited number of proposals for action. All these trends create a changed setting in which agendas are forged and presidents are nominated, elected, and serve.

Inevitably, well-articulated agendas for political action do not emerge from American presidential campaigns. Moreover, one reads in *Campaigns and Elections*, a magazine published seven times a year, that "the manner in which you deliver your message is as important as the message itself."[21] A variety of forces influence, displace, enhance, or otherwise alter issues that arise. The pressures for regulation and deregulation, for empowerment and restriction of government, for authorization and appropriation, stream out of government agencies, affected clienteles, lobbyists, political parties, factional groups, and other sources including the White House. All these proposals for action are stimulated by needs someone thinks government should respond to, including domestic emergencies and foreign threats. Moreover, many hopes and expectations are asserted through sophisticated federal policy and budgetary processes, where substantial technical expertise and professional competence are brought to bear.

In this climate, the information generated in the presidential campaign, and the impulses derived from those who participate, now more than ever inform a newly elected president and influence the victor's aims and initiatives. A presidential election is certainly not the only political contest of importance, but it provides a relatively low-cost opportunity for a broad spectrum of interests in society to influence political competition, catch the attention of future presidents, and affect which issues will ultimately receive attention.

It is also true that political influences on the presidency and Congress are continuous and changing. They bear with relentless tenacity on the objectives selected for emphasis during a presidential term, and success in reaching them. The election of presidents and subsequent presidential decisions are now made in an evolving environment of competitive claims asserted in significantly new ways.

Agendas are influenced in a variety of forums, including party platforms, opinion polls, and the mass media. These forums are not singular, isolated influences on agenda formation. Rather, each modifies or reinforces the effects of the others. An issue highlighted in opinion polls is more likely to receive attention if it is also found in a party platform.[22] News commentaries, testimony by experts, and the appeals of popular presidents, each widely communicated over television, have all been found to move public opinion as measured by the polls.[23]

Relatively open, decentralized political parties have always provided such a forum for the nation, but in recent decades they have become even more open as arenas for the promotional efforts of issue advocates.

PARTY INFLUENCES ON AGENDAS

"When all the rhetorical flourishes are swept away," declared political columnist David Broder, "the Republican and Democratic party platforms of 1984 represent a classic confrontation over the role of government in modern society."[24] As late as 1960 Theodore H. White, famed chronicler of presidential campaigns, had declared that "all platforms are meaningless...."[25] Between the 1960 and 1984 elections, the structure, specificity, and volume of issues, and consequently party politics, were changing. Moreover, White to the contrary notwithstanding, in all the decades after World War II a large proportion of national party platform pledges were actually redeemed within four years. This address to issues within conventions took place despite the priority traditionally given by delegates to immediate party and voter concerns as opposed to issue-oriented goals.[26]

The expanded scope of federal policies and changes in the ways national convention delegations are chosen have led to longer party platforms—from less than three thousand words in 1948 to over ten times that in the 1980s—and to greater issue content. As we saw in Chapter Three, the proportion of delegates selected in primaries grew, the influence of elected officials declined, and the volume and variety of interest-group representatives increased in both major parties after 1968. Almost any issue eligible for government's agenda could provoke controversy in platform negotiations.

The growth of primaries led contenders to reward with convention seats interest-group representatives who could bring them convention votes, votes no longer deliverable by state and local officials. To delegates from interest and issue groups, "the platform is not a document for winning votes in the fall, but a bargaining chip to be used in future policy negotiations." Thus Michael J. Malbin wrote in 1981, "the nomination process and rules affect who becomes a delegate, the nature of the delegates affects the platform process, and the process affects the substance."[27]

The substance of political interests and their advocates are the parents, not the children, of party procedures. New issues, originating in changed societal conditions and altered personal values, are a major source of modern opinions that are held independently of political parties. They have led to breakdown in the constancy of traditional interest-group and class-based alliances. The change burdens party leaders and shapers of opinion. New pressures obstruct the old party unity. The number and importance of newly organized claimants who compete with traditional party authorities have risen, and the new media environment encourages fluctuating and divergent pressures.[28] Platforms after World War II have contained increasingly detailed policy information, and their shaping is part of what Thomas Ferguson and Joel Rogers have called "that complex process through which the basic structures of economic and social life are transformed into political platforms and electoral coalitions"[29]—that is, into political agendas.

Except for declarations of the nominees themselves, the platforms of recent decades have asserted more fully than any other source the issues and philosophical differences at controversy in presidential campaigns.[30] They have been of mounting significance in defining and arbitrating the national political agenda, although few delegates read either platform in full and virtually no voters do so.[31] Presidential coalitions feel intense pressures both to support and to ignore individual planks.[32] Yet, as Gerald A. Pomper has declared, "a campaign is a contest for incremental votes, not for total support, and the platform is one of the means by which marginal voters make decisions."[33]

Pomper's empirical studies reveal that platforms of both the party winning and the one not winning the White House have been a significant guide to subsequent government action. He found that a substantial percentage of platform pledges of the winning and losing parties combined are fulfilled within four years—this being true during the period in which platforms were growing significantly in length and detail—making evident an important degree of nonpartisanship. Nearly three-fourths of all promises were kept following the six presidential elections from 1944 to 1964, and almost two-thirds following the elections from 1968 to 1980. Only one-tenth of the promises in the 1944–64 period were completely ignored, and slightly less than one-third in the 1970–84 period, and a different examiner of the 1984 Republican platform found that about two-thirds of its planks were subsequently adopted in some form.[34] Another assessment of the platforms of parties winning the White House from 1948 through 1984, based on federal spending priorities, found "strong links" between platforms and governmental actions.[35] "If platforms were meaningless," Judson L. James comments, "one would be hard pressed to explain the intense conflicts over alternative wordings that have occurred in national conventions."[36]

The formal procedures of party governance are similar for the two major parties, but their internal constituencies, structures of influence, and party cultures diverge significantly.[37] Because they contest for the same general electorate, however, formal party goals expressed in platforms have often seemed similar. A change appeared in 1980, however, and was repeated in 1984. In those years, sharper differences between the professed values and objectives of the two parties were proclaimed in platforms whose length and specificity had grown significantly since World War II. The Democratic platform of 1948 had 2,800 words, while that of 1984 had 47,800, the longest in U.S. history. The Republican platform had 2,000 words in 1948 and 28,000 in 1984.[38] In 1988, under the leadership of its prospective nominee, Governor Dukakis, the Democratic convention reverted to a platform of more general objectives confined to approximately 3,500 words. The post-war trend continued among the Republicans, however, in a document of approximately 30,000 words that addressed a long list of aims and issues.

Platforms have gone from brief apologies of past actions, joined with attacks on opponents' policies, to extensive advocacy of values, goals, and programs. They have become increasingly comprehensive, detailed, and explicit, inflated by the drive of special interests to insert factional planks. Especially after 1968, various interests seized on platforms to project both narrow aims and broad appeals, often displaying greater concern for platform planks than party victory.[39]

Ever since political scientists started asking convention delegates whether they have an interest in issues, the answer has been yes.[40] Such interest had been evident in convention deliberations all along. It should be no surprise, therefore, that Republican and Democratic platforms have reflected both shared political objectives and persistent differences between the parties. One calculation for the years 1960–76 showed 20 percent of platform pledges to be bipartisan, 7 percent conflicting, and 73 percent offered by one party but not the other. Another analysis on a somewhat different basis for the elections of 1960 through 1980 showed 27 percent of the pledges to be bipartisan, 22 percent conflicting, and 51 percent offered by only one party.[41] By 1984, however, on issue after issue addressing economic, labor, gun control, campaign finance, defense, arms control, and foreign policy issues, the platforms were in conflict by explicit statement or deliberate omission.[42]

Policy differences between the parties have always been mitigated by the pressures to win a majority of the electoral votes and by the historically mixed electoral base of each party. Yet change has been occurring. John H. Kessel concluded in 1984, "Increasingly, Democratic conventions are ending up as contests between left and nonleft coalitions, and Republican conventions as struggles between right and nonright coalitions."[43]

In both parties in both 1980 and 1984, substantive "statements" in the platforms greatly exceeded—in Democratic platforms, more than doubled— their number before 1980. Also evident were increased differences in the scope and substance of party positions on issues. According to Pomper's classification, in both 1980 and 1984, 28 percent of platform pledges of the two parties were conflicting, supporting the interpretation that the Reagan realignment created a significant deepening in party differences.[44] The percentages for the three previous elections had been 7, 5, and 7. Pomper classified platform issues into nine categories. The percentage of pledges in conflict in each category showed a startling jump from the average for the 1944–76 platforms to the percentages in 1980 and 1984. In foreign policy issues, conflicting pledges went from an average of 6 percent in 1944–76 to 19 in 1980 and 34 in 1984; in issues of defense, from 4 to 22 to 25; of economics, 9 to 26 to 16; of labor, 18 to 32 to 23; of agriculture, 7 to 13 to 26; of resources, 9 to 30 to 26; of social welfare, 10 to 36 to 32; of government, 4 to 31 to 37; and of civil rights, 2 to 28 to 27 percent.[45]

The rise in platform conflicts reflects in part the long trudge away from regionally based two-party competition toward a more nationally based issue politics. Trends are not uniform within every category of issues, but changes in the bases of party support and in party positions on policy sharply reveal parties adapting to new political realities. One of the new realities is the changed nomination system since 1968, which has invited challenges to the renomination of serving presidents by rivals who have important policy differences. Contentious public platform contests were fought within the president's own party in 1976 (Republican) and 1980 (Democratic),[46] and in 1984 deliberations on the platforms of both parties were lobbied vigorously and with some effectiveness by diverse interests.[47]

Many factors affect the content of platforms. Presidents in office, but also aspirants for the nomination, as in 1988, seek to influence them. The party less favored to win the White House has usually been inclined to emphasize future pledges and to be more specific about its agenda. The likely winner has traditionally sought to protect its advantage and, by taking comparatively ambiguous stands, to avoid alienating supporters.[48] Whatever length and specificity platforms take in the future, the growth in conflicts over issues signals that American politics is becoming more cognitive and less affective, more substantive and less symbolic. Parties will possess an increasing incentive to seek their electoral fortunes among independent voters, passing over or around organized elites. In shaping formal party doctrines, the national conventions have been adapting to the changing context and agendas of national policy and politics.

Some observers have lamented that the political parties have increasingly become adding machines for wish lists presented by numerous issue advocates on whose support they and their candidates depend, or whom they hope to woo. They no longer serve as gatekeepers of the national agenda, performing traditional mediating functions by filtering, aggregating, and compromising interests in pursuit of consensus. Those who see group influence as the source of overloaded agendas, and ultimately overloaded and unsuccessful government, seek to curb it by strengthening party organization and state party leadership.

Some would seek that goal through increased party control over presidential nominations that could result by shifting from primaries to caucuses. The national Democratic party, acting on the concerns of its 1981–82 Commission on Presidential Nominations (Hunt Commission), exhorted state parties to utilize caucuses rather than primaries as the preferred method of delegate selection in the 1984 presidential contest. Others, like James I. Lengle, hold that diverse state party organizations call for different procedures for delegate selection. In states with strong state and local party organizations, for example, a caucus-convention system can enhance the influence of parties over the nomination process, without losing responsiveness or accountability. On the other hand, in states with weak state and local party organizations, unrepresentative candidate and issue activists can dominate caucuses, producing delegations with candidate and platform preferences—that is, agenda goals—divergent from those of the constituents they are intended to represent. A mixed system permits delegate selection by a method appropriate to the state party's condition.[49]

Among Democrats, advocates of enhanced influence for state party activists—in contrast to special-issue protaganists—both before and at the national convention have turned to candidate right-of-approval (CRA) rules. The rule for 1984 required an aspirant to approve at least three candidates for every delegate slot for which the aspirant competed. This gave the aspirant power to veto any prospective delegate he did not wish running under his banner. According to Rule 11F, an aspirant's delegates at the district level had to be selected by a caucus of persons pledged to that candidate rather than by district party conventions voting as a unit.

Certain groups, however—for example, organized labor—could trade manpower and organizational support in the primary season for aspirant approval of their members as national convention delegates. They exploited the arrangements and concluded that to loosen the candidate-approval provision would weaken their ability to seat delegates of their choice. State party leaders understandably wanted to strengthen their own part in delegate selection in order to favor party workers over candidate partisans.[50]

Groups and issue activists pervade contemporary political life in every democratic nation. The Republican party, without national rules comparable to those of the Democrats, and with a tradition against blatant interest-group politics, has nonetheless experienced similar group pressures in platform deliberations at recent national conventions.[51] The parties are strengthened by the support of activists and their encouragement to address the issues that concern them. Party rules need not assure them dominance at national conventions, but the parties gain when such groups have legitimate opportunities to contribute to the content of party platforms.

POLLING INFLUENCES ON AGENDAS

Daniel Yankelovich has declared that "to think that what the public thinks is what is measured by the polls is totally superficial and misleading."[52] And Bill Kovach, former editor of the *Atlanta Journal-Constitution*, has asserted that the product of much polling is substitution of "ephemeral opinion" for "objective fact in the diet of information the media provide." "Straw Polls" were conducted as early as 1824, and in some states often thereafter, but the modern significance of public opinion polling developed only after 1936, and most significantly during and after the 1950s.[53] Whatever its defects, it has now become dominant in the informational environment of presidential selection—with potent consequences for political agendas.

Polling can have special significance in helping to correct the pronounced "participation bias" in American electoral politics. We have seen that those who take part voluntarily in politics, by voting and otherwise, come disproportionately from advantaged strata in society.[54] Well-run polls can register the transient preferences of large masses who take no part in caucuses, conventions, or primaries, do not volunteer their views, and do not vote or otherwise participate in general elections.[55] Identification of public concerns through private polling has become detailed and trusted, with candidates, campaign managers, and party officials depending increasingly on it.

James R. Beniger and Robert J. Giuffra, Jr., concluded in 1984 that polls "have become virtually the only source of information that candidates, party leaders, and reporters use in making their strategic decisions. . . ." Aspirants consult polls in deciding whether to make a run and, if they do, in identifying voter concerns, campaign appeals, the best deployment of resources, their own and their rivals' strengths and weaknesses, and, if fortunate, a running mate. Other politicians, and journalists too, study survey results when assessing the importance of aspirants to office.[56]

Public opinion has always been central to American society and its politics, Alexis de Tocqueville noted pointedly in 1835.[57] Lord Bryce would declare in 1888 that public opinion "is the central point of the whole American polity."[58] A century after Bryce, sophisticated procedures for measuring and reporting public preferences—procedures commanding the confidence of their users—have radically changed both the means used to identify voter concerns and goals and to comprehend the larger context of information in which presidents are chosen.

Despite charges that polls often reflect opinion, not judgment, competent polling results, properly interpreted, can give politicians a significantly wider understanding of public anxieties and desires than is otherwise available to them. Beniger and Giuffra cite nine campaign stages at which polling is used by presidential aspirants in making important decisions, of which learning voter concerns, targeting opposition weaknesses, and developing advertising themes are three.[59] Polls not only provide information about constituents' concerns, but also about their tolerances, thereby influencing the decisions of politicians and consequently the agendas of candidates and government.

Even polls that are technically flawed because of simplicity, brevity, or inadequate interpretation[60] are used with confidence by politicians in making political judgments. Political consultants, described by Austin Ranney as "just short of being dictators of the modern campaign,"[61] rely heavily on polling data in shaping their strategies and appeals. Polling is a form of direct connection from electorate to politician as broadcasting is a direct channel going the other way.[62] The whole context of political discourse, not simply campaign management, is affected.[63] Polls are more important in helping politicians learn the attitudes of people and the issues important to them than in predicting voting behavior.[64] They are crucially important in identifying and shaping the public agenda, a fact not altered by the deficiencies with which they are charged or their susceptibility to willful manipulation.[65]

The public opinion that has always preoccupied theorists and architects of democratic government is now manifested in new ways that alter the goals, participants, organization, and substance of politics. In a sense, because of polls, we now have "continuing elections"[66]—sources of direct, continuing influence on presidents and others in leadership positions, as observers of the Reagan White House have often noted. And polls influence active agendas when they ask respondents what current issues are important to them, and what matters that are important to them are being neglected.[67] By the same token polls can also, we emphasize, help redress the participation bias of electoral politics, even acknowledging that members of the underclass and some others not likely to vote are more difficult to reach for interviews than others. Less-advantaged citizens will often agree with majority opinion about active issues, but elevating slighted issues of importance to them to an active agenda makes government more responsive.

Polls are sometimes criticized because they reflect public opinion at a specific time. But that is also what a presidential election does. The judgment of the voters on election day is a judgment expressed on that day, but its effects last four years. Polling helps keep democratic politics an ongoing dialogue during an electoral campaign and thereafter.[68] Marjorie Randon Hershey has held that the major challenge to the American electoral process is "to create a learning environment in which the concerns of the quiet citizens can be more effectively understood," while encouraging leaders to act in the long-run interests of the whole nation.[69] Polls, even with their imperfections, help link citizens on a continuing basis to modern government and its policies.

TELEVISION INFLUENCES ON AGENDAS

Although television has been politically significant only a bit more than one-sixth of the Republic's life, it has deeply influenced the structure of political power, the content of political information, the channels for asserting political claims, and the substance of those claims. And, as Tom Wicker said, it "is not something to be repealed."[70]

A shift upward has occurred in the importance of issues that originate outside of party conflict. This was evident especially following 1968. Given the major influence of media in determining what issues command main attention, the media affect deeply the exercise of political power.[71] Changes in the media have altered the traditional functions of political parties and factions within them. Louis Banks, former editorial director of Time Incorporated, observed in 1980:

> The media focus the general interests, juggle the priorities and—in a crisis sense, at least—set the public agenda. . . . [T]he technology and substance of today's newscasting combine in a public impact greater than that of any informational force in the history of democratic societies—redirecting even the traditional processes of politics.[72]

President Reagan's aides reportedly came into office persuaded that media reporting had contributed to the downfall of the four previous presidents. He and his advisers were resolved to prevent the media from determining what constitutes a crisis and the president's responsibility, or, put another way, what should be the president's agenda. The gatekeepers in the news media systems, as they have been called—editors, news directors, some correspondents, and others—decide what subjects to cover, what reports to air or print, where, at what length, and with what "twist." They have much to do with the information reaching the public and the public's awareness of controversies, problems, and promises,[73] and consequently have much to do with activating issues. So, also, it has been reported in Great Britain: "No longer do parties define the agenda of a political campaign. Rather it is the newspaper and the broadcast media that define the political agenda."[74]

In a sophisticated longitudinal study of public opinion, Benjamin I. Page, Robert Y. Shapiro, and Glenn R. Dempsey found that television news commentary has a measurable impact on the movement of public opinion. Experts and popular presidents are also influential, but among the sources of influence examined, "the estimated impact of news commentary is strongest of all, on a per-story basis, though such messages are aired less frequently than those from other sources." Why it has such an impact, however, is far less certain. Page and his colleagues speculate about a variety of possible explanations: "Commentary may be an indicator of broader influences, such as media bias in the selection and presentation of other news, of consensus among the U.S. media or elites generally, or of a perceived public consensus."[75] According to the study's data, television news commentary is clearly related to the movement of public opinion, but its exact status as a cause is not clear. Whether news and commentary are cause or consequence, or partly both, Shanto Iyengar and Donald R. Kinder concluded that "by attending to some problems and ignoring others, television news shapes the American public's political priorities."[76]

Of course, the media helped create as well as report political contests long before television. But television affords direct visual communication to unprecedentedly large audiences, and in the day of specialized cable channels, targeted messages can be sharply honed for specific electoral segments—youth, environmentalists, evangelicals, sports fans, others. Television's effects on the information reaching the public, and therefore on the issues attaining prominence, have been dramatic. In earlier times, information and advocacy were conveyed more directly by partisan participants in terms they chose themselves. But television seems to many to be more authoritative than other sources of influence, especially contributing to judgments by less politically sophisticated viewers.[77]

Clearly, television is more accessible to advocates and audiences alike. In competition with other mass media, it has increasingly influenced what problems receive governmental attention. Politicians and the general public have tended more and more to accept a consensus view conveyed by media commentators of what particular issues need attention, and of what the more general direction of public concerns should be[78]—albeit remembering that such consensus is itself inevitably influenced by the candidates' own selective address to issues.[79]

None of this need imply partisan political motives. Journalists are influenced by commercial imperatives, personal ambitions, their own training and ability, and much else as they respond to media requirements and compulsions. Yet they have a crucial role in promoting specific candidates as well as selected issues. A candidate ignored or treated casually by the media will not be considered important by the public. So it also is with issues.[80] Journalists consequently have become even more important to candidates and their managers than they were before television.[81] Christopher Arterton has noted that journalists may come to be viewed by campaign managers "as an alternative electorate in which they must campaign for the presidency, responding directly to the concerns and values of journalists in addition to, and sometimes in place of, forces in the electorate or the political system."[82]

In this context, a new profession has emerged. It is that of media consultant, declared to be central to post-1968 American party politics. Such consultants discern, measure, analyze, and define public concerns, and therefore help shape agendas. They do not perform many traditional party functions,[83] but they are important additions to the battalions of politics. As the nation stands at what has been called "the beginning of the politics of the electronic age,"[84] they will become increasingly important as sources of information, issues, campaign tactics and strategies, and, ultimately, government action. It is even charged that "the priorities of the media are transferred largely intact onto the public agenda."[85] But that can never be to the exclusion of everything else. A candidate's judgment, personality, record, other political resources, and personal attributes will bear directly on electoral success and the capacity to shape effectively a personal political agenda.[86]

Awareness, however superficial, of divergent world cultures and political conditions, and of international interdependencies affecting Americans, has increased significantly because of television, as well as because of rising education levels, greater travel, and other influences. Worldwide conditions of human rights and other values proclaimed by Americans for themselves are therefore better known than before. Also, the growing prominence of ethnic, youth, women's, environmental, and other issue groups has been abetted to a major extent by media attention. Such groups have learned to catch the camera's eye and to play a different politics from the older organized interests of business, labor, and agriculture.[87] They thus give their pleas sharp-pointed, independent momentum without intermediary interpreters except the media themselves.

Under these conditions, organizations perceived by the public as promoting blatantly selfish interests can be handicapped in shaping public attitudes. Their efforts may even have negative effects, as has proved true of some efforts by labor unions and corporations, and even of organizations of women, blacks, poor people, and Jews when explicitly addressing issues of immediate concern to them. Such experiences may reflect less a disdain for the groups themselves than a preference by the public for policy information from disinterested sources. Indeed, they strongly substantiate the public's preference for neutral sources of policy information. The public prefers information providers to be experts and news commentators rather than interest-group advocates.[88]

Media are thus both transmitters and originators. Agenda items that emerge from the tussle of presidential campaigns and the combative conduct of the presidential office are obviously influenced by the proclaimed goals and pledges of presidents. But abundant information freely circulated in free elections by free media also directs the attention and energies of officials to a wide span of policies and objectives. Some issues that surface in campaigns will result from the initiative of candidates or their parties, some will spring from voters and organized special interests, some will be promoted not only through but also by media personnel, and most will flow from a combination of these sources.[89]

Modern communications media constitute a complex set of systems that are supremely important transmitters of information, the currency of democracy. In their selectivity, emphasis, and investigative and reportorial initiatives, however, the media are also identifiers of issues, analysts of problems, and sometimes aggressive partisans. And, in an important sense, they are also creators of information. They are influential political actors who may be independent of candidates, parties, and other political interests, but who can exercise potent and sometimes decisive initiative in defining issues, positing agendas, and determining outcomes.

THE ELECTORAL PROCESS AND POLITICAL AGENDAS

In a time of concern over the scope of federal government activities, one wonders whether practices in presidential selection contribute to an overloaded government agenda, to what has been described as "an excess of demand, an overburdening of governmental responsibilities, and a withered political capacity to impose short-term costs."[90] In election years myriad interests vigorously press their claims on presidential aspirants through political party platforms and in other ways. Between elections they address government directly. In fact, candidates through their campaigns and officials by their actions often seem to stimulate demands, including ones that cannot be fulfilled. To some watchers, the result is government overload, but not necessarily one caused by new departures in public policies and programs.

In the 1980s government seemed to have an agenda of its own that was born of problems produced by past policies and programs, among them Social Security, Medicare, and Medicaid. New policies and programs addressing new problems were forestalled. Past policy itself is thus a major source of new policy.[91] Preoccupation with a *rationalizing* agenda often makes it appear that policies are incoherent and contradictory and that government is deadlocked on breakthrough issues. Lack of policy coherence has been a major complaint by those who would move the American system toward parliamentary or quasi-parliamentary forms.

But Lawrence D. Brown insists that new conditions obtain, and that institutionalized ambivalence is easily mistaken for illogic and contradiction when in fact it is not. He says,

> the preeminent political fact of the present is that the ideologies that gave order, confidence, and vision to the political thought of attentive elites and average citizens alike ... have faltered badly, transparently unable to offer consistently defensible, comprehensive answers to public problems. . . .
>
> A new reasonableness based on acknowledged ambivalence and a due regard for complexity . . . could be the reward.

A problem remains, of course, for both liberal and conservative policymakers "to explain to their critical ideological brethren outside government why the logical approaches are irresponsible."[92]

Concern that the modern method of choosing presidents leads to an overloaded agenda connects with the anxiety that it also renders presidents excessively vulnerable to public opinion. Political parties are no longer the filters and buffers they once were. Presidents now depend more than ever on direct, personal public support. This dependence can make them overly responsive to public opinion, causing them to alter, abandon, or initiate policies solely in anticipation of the next election, a condition that especially worries those concerned with foreign policy.

Some experienced practitioners hold that the four-year presidential term with eligibility for election to a second term creates serious impediments to objectivity and constancy. Cyrus Vance served in previous administrations before becoming Jimmy Carter's secretary of state in 1977. The preface to his account of working with Carter, *Hard Choices*, opens with a fervent, critical accounting of the results when presidential attention is diverted by the exigencies of reelection—issues ignored, decisions deferred, decisions made badly, and inconsistency and instability in action. He advocates a single six-year term for presidents "in which the president would be free from the pressures of campaigning and would have more time to carry forward the public business." Vance especially emphasizes that the arrangement would afford a context of "continuity and stability for our foreign policy."[93] The Committee for a Single Six-Year Term has invoked endorsements by historic personages such as Andrew Jackson and Grover Cleveland, as well as presidents Eisenhower, Lyndon Johnson, Nixon, Ford, and Carter (all of whom ran for second terms).[94]

As usual, the issue requires estimates of results as well as judgment of values. Clearly a six-year president would function in a heated political environment; it would be inescapable, assuming such a president wanted congressional support for administration policies, and bureaucratic constancy in applying them. Second-term presidents, even in their last two years, are not relieved of partisan and factional pressures in their domestic and foreign policy actions; a six-year president would face the same pressures. Continuity and stability are manifest assets in the execution of all public policies, until it becomes useful to change them. Officials charged with generating and implementing agricultural, environmental, monetary, conservation, immigration, trade, labor, and any other policies welcome stability and predictability. But community living, like personal living, requires choices. Some degree of stability may need to be sacrificed to achieve a more responsive government. Ralf Dahrendorf has proclaimed the need for continuity in foreign policy, yet he declares that in a democracy, "discontinuity and change" are "the life-blood of liberty."[95] In a democratic system there is no way to exempt either foreign or domestic policies from popular influences. Stability and competence in policy must originate in shared values and judgments that command political support.[96]

To hope that changes in presidential selection procedures can remedy all deficiencies in U.S. governance is obviously futile. The national government as a whole, the multilevel federal political system, the whole environment of American life, and structures of international economic and social influence all help fix the qualities of the American government and nation and the issues they must face. A presidential selection system cannot make the United States what it is not. All governmental processes, like most governmental policies, are a trade-off, a choice among values, an effort to maximize what is cherished and minimize what is not. As uncongenial, even naive and credulous, as the notion may seem to battle-weary veterans of the presidency, exposure of the office to a myriad of nagging anxieties, demands, crises, and opportunities—short-, middle-, and long-run—is a critically important source of understanding for a president, and necessary for the public agenda. Such exposure is integral to the sensitivity and responsiveness that, late in the twentieth century, U.S. governmental needs and democratic values require. The agenda of U.S. democracy is always a product of culture, only sometimes a product of logic. And almost every solution is a way station to another problem.

Presidents will by definition of their office attend to public opinions at home. But there are citizens of other countries whose lives are also directly affected by what U.S. presidents do.

Ernest R. May has examined the increased world role of the United States and its implications for our method of choosing presidents. A host of factors make U.S. presidents sensitive to perceived American interests in many nations, including U.S. citizens' family ties abroad, widespread and large-scale international economic ties, mounting education and foreign travel, extensive U.S. worldwide military and diplomatic activities, and all the international linkages spawned by American history and power and the nature of the modern world, with their resulting political urges and expectations. Such conditions also generate the heady notion that much if not all of the planet's affairs are also the United States' affairs, and therefore the president's proper concern. Conversely, foreigners see an immense stake in American policy and actions. Fifteen thousand Americans are said to be employed as foreign affairs lobbyists directly advocating the interests of noncitizens. They often treat Washington as though it were the seat of a worldwide government.

In this context one may well wonder how a government that rests exclusively on American suffrage addresses matters of significant but not always mutual interest to non-Americans. May writes that

> together with coincidence in general selection criteria, the practical means available for foreigners to influence American elections go a long way toward ensuring that the interests of non-Americans are not ignored or even slighted when Americans pick their presidents.[97]

The international agenda that must concern presidential aspirants has mounted in diversity as the immediacy of world issues has mounted. International concerns, usually mixed with domestic and personal ones, must find accommodation in the selection of presidents, as do other requirements of a shifting pluralistic politics. Doing so is complicated by the American tendency to vacillate in foreign affairs between *realpolitik* strategies and ideal, moral goals. Accommodating the needs of world interdependence in a climate of parochial pressures will always call for insight by voters into their personal stakes in long-range national requirements. Voters do not make policy, but through their voices, when they speak up, and their votes, when they cast them, they help determine the active agenda that confronts their national leadership in the modern, fragmented world of interdependent but sovereign nations.

We have examined up to this point how information is generated and transmitted in the course of choosing presidents, the forms of participation in that activity, and how those proceedings bear on the shaping of the public agenda. The main function of the process, however, is to choose the nation's chief leader, and to that subject we now turn.

CHAPTER NINE

Searching for Better Leadership

☆
☆

The view is ascribed to James Madison that the public had only one major role in the Republic: "to select the political leaders who would develop, administer, and adjudicate public policy. Votes were to be cast for men, not for policies."[1] Conversely, in the 1836 presidential campaign the national Democratic party proclaimed, "Principles are everything: men, nothing." Candidate Martin Van Buren's appeal to Democratic voters, concluded one political analyst, "had nothing to do with his personal characteristics but rather derived solely from his nomination by the Democratic party."[2] Whatever the reality was in the early nineteenth century, in the late twentieth the balance between party and person has tipped steadily toward the person.

Unlike most leaders in parliamentary systems, the American president does not emerge from a party in the legislature to lead the government. The president is personally elected to office and has an independent base of authority, one grounded in the Constitution. As much as the founders desired a republican executive who could bring energy and focus to the management of executive affairs,[3] they did not see the president as "the government." Rather, the presidency was conceived as one of three separate institutions sharing powers. In a structure of deliberately divided authority, the president and Congress were each intended to check excesses of the other. The modern prominence of the presidency was unplanned. The fundamental alterations that evolved in American society, and consequently in the functions of government, radically affected the role of president despite the confining restrictions of the constitutional design.

The twentieth-century focus on the president as the source of activist government has produced, in the eyes of some, an institutional monster—"an elective monarchy, an imperial presidency, a plebiscitary chief executive."[4] It thus has led to expectations impossible to fulfill, in one sense dooming all presidents to failure. The American public, however, has always focused on the occupants rather than the office. Seymour Martin Lipset and William Schneider contend that one factor contributing to the sustained legitimacy of the country's institutions is "the public's belief that, since failures of the system are the fault of incompetent power-holders, the situation can be greatly improved by changing the incumbent authorities."[5] They report survey findings that the public believes "we have a good system run by bad or inadequate people." They quote a conclusion of Louis Harris in 1978, a time of great national disquiet:

> ... there has never been much evidence that most people have gone sour on the system itself and have finally concluded that it is unworkable.
>   To the contrary, the constant search over the past years has been precisely to find the kind of leadership that can make the system work. People have not lost faith that somehow they will find that high calibre of public official.[6]

Preoccupation with the performance of individual leaders diverts criticism from the country's executive and legislative institutions. Despite the informed, critical diagnosis by some analysts of perceived deficiencies in the basic structure of American government—Professor James MacGregor Burns notable among them—prevailing attention has vested large expectations in the way in which elective officers are chosen within the existing federal framework, holding that the system is responsible for providing effective leadership, and therefore effective government. Critics speculate that by changing the rules, the contenders would be more impressive, the most qualified of those would be nominated, and the nominee would enjoy a broader political base.

THE CONTENDERS: PERSONS FOR THEIR TIMES

Those who aspire to be president are a source of curiosity and concern in every era. From the tens of millions of Americans legally eligible to become president, a score or two of individuals emerge every four years who will be considered by some consequential individuals or groups to be able to serve as president.[7] Critics worry that the current circle cast up by the process comprises contenders less suited for the office than those who sought the presidency in earlier eras. But that is a dubious conclusion.

John H. Aldrich examined all important candidacies for major party nomination in four politically different historical periods. He concluded that changes in the kinds of candidates flowed more from alterations in the larger political and social environment than from changes in the rules of the nomination system. The first period, 1876–96, was characterized by old-style strong parties, the absence of primaries, and decisive national conventions. The second period, 1912–32, saw increasing use of presidential primaries, which were seized upon by "outsider" candidates, like the Progressive Republicans, to test the strength of the party organization. The third period 1952–68, was characterized by relatively strong parties and the limited use of primaries to demonstrate a candidate's electability. In the last period,

1972–84, there was declining convention control over presidential nominations and the increased use of primaries to win direct nomination.

The first two periods differed sharply from the last two. They preceded, and the last two followed, the Depression, the New Deal, routine air travel, sophisticated public-opinion polling, television, and multiple advances in high-speed communications. In the first and third periods, moreover, party control over presidential nominations was relatively stronger, whereas in the second and fourth periods, public participation in nominations was enhanced through presidential primaries.[8] Aldrich discerned changes in the characteristics of candidates from one period to another, but concluded that the means of nomination was not the explanation.

In 1960, the first Roman Catholic president was elected. In 1964, the first president from a former Confederate state was elected. In 1976, the first modern president from a Deep South state was elected. In 1984, a major party for the first time put a woman on its ticket. In 1984, a black could remain a consequential participant in the Democratic nomination contest to the very end, and in 1988 become a major force in his party. Having been divorced is no longer an impediment. A young Kennedy and an old Reagan—both setting new age records—could be nominated and elected. Woodrow Wilson and his six immediate predecessors all studied law. With George Bush's election, seven of the eight most recently elected presidents were not lawyers.

With all of that, Aldrich nonetheless concluded that the *political* background of candidates for presidential nomination has remained notably stable. That background has included approximately a decade of political experience, the occupancy of a major office while running for or just before nomination, and involvement in partisan politics. When the requisite political credentials are combined with the relatively constant personal background of nominees—mainstream, well-educated, middle-aged males from middle-level backgrounds and with professional or other high-status positions in private life—"there is almost no significant change over time" in the emerging portraits of presidential candidates.[9]

NEW TYPES NEEDED FOR NEW TIMES?

The question nonetheless persists. Will the long, modern, publicly exposed contests for party nominations lead to a new breed of candidate? The argument runs that in the television age media advisers must be able to "package" a candidate for retailing to the television audience. Thus a candidate's ability to project effectively over the "cool" medium has become more important than a capacity to rouse the faithful in halls and stadiums, and than skill in bargaining for leadership support and building coalitions. The reality, however, is more complex. Television skills are surely important in the television age, just as Franklin Roosevelt's persuasive intonation was a major asset over radio and William Jennings Bryan's powerful lungs were highly useful in the era of outdoor speeches. Superior media skills can give a candidate an edge over a competitor, in governing as well as in campaigning. But other qualities are never equal, and good television presence does not by itself make a candidate or a president.

Even politicians who at first seem to owe their careers to a fame birthed by television—among them Bill Bradley (basketball player), John Glenn (astronaut), and S. I. Hayakawa (college president)—assiduously built political bases in their home states. Jeff Greenfield writes that knowing these politicians gained prominence through television "tells us no more than the fact that General Grant was made famous by telegraphic dispatches back to newspapers during the Civil War."[10] They still needed to build political strength by traditional means.

Neither George McGovern nor Jimmy Carter nor Walter Mondale won the Democratic party nomination because he was more talented on television than his competitors. Ronald Reagan won the 1980 Republican nomination not simply because he had been a professional actor and exhibited great skill before the cameras. He had served two terms as governor of California and had been the preeminent spokesman for the conservative wing of the Republican party since the 1960s. His presidential victories in 1980 and 1984 were products more of political substance than media imagery. Jimmy Carter's perceived mishandling of the economy and of the Iranian hostage crisis made a more important contribution to the 1980 outcome than Reagan's superior television personality. The Republican's election appeal in 1984 derived more from declining inflation, economic recovery, and resurgent feelings of national pride than from Reagan's communications skills.

Information is the currency of democracy. Skills in using the prevailing media will always be important assets. But the medium is no substitute for the message. Political experience, performance in office, and the realism of the politician's message remain key influences on electoral success. What government does affects citizens and therefore affects citizen attitudes toward those they hold responsible for government.

The perception that recent contenders for presidential nominations have often been inexperienced and little-known is at variance with Aldrich's findings. Some of the aspirants and one nominee, Carter, may have been nationally less well-known than their predecessors. But length of service in major national offices increased comparatively for candidates in the 1972–84 period. Even Carter's shorter-than-average tenure in high office did not make him demonstrably less qualified than Democrats Alton B. Parker in 1904 and John W. Davis in 1924, who were nominated but did not win the presidency, or Woodrow Wilson in 1912, who did win.[11] Moreover, in all eras aspirants from outside the party establishment have competed with "insider" candidates, and some of them, like Wendell L. Willkie in 1940 and William Jennings Bryan in 1896, have won the nomination.

Declining confidence in the responsiveness and effectiveness of government by Washington-based "insiders" may have accounted for the revival of governors as presidential candidates in 1976 and 1980. Hugh Heclo compared American presidential and British prime ministerial selection and observed that in a time when central governments are charged with lacking vision and effectiveness, experience in the lower reaches of politics may lay a good base for developing and achieving leadership.[12] Such a background may constitute an especially important asset in a federal system that binds together a large nation of rampant diversity.

The lack of experience in foreign affairs of several recent presidents is conspicuous, with George Bush an exception that emphasizes the fact. In a multicultural, interdependent, always potentially dangerous world, exposure to cultures and countries beyond the United States would seem a valuable if not essential experience for a president. No electoral system, however, can assure that there will be nominees of adequate capacity in anything, especially foreign affairs.

State and local leaders who dominated the earlier, less-public nomination system were more interested in a candidate's electability and in the patronage bargains they could strike than in his aptitude for conducting foreign relations. Yet presidents conspicuously internationalist in outlook often emerged—two Roosevelts, Wilson, Eisenhower, Kennedy, and Nixon among them. Those chosen to lead in parliamentary systems do not necessarily bring strong credentials in foreign affairs, although their foreign offices often may have a more continuous grip on foreign policy than is found in the United States. Great Britain's Margaret Thatcher had been secretary of state for education and science before she became prime minister.

One can hope that candidates who get elected will have at least a "correct understanding of the world"[13] combined with "humane values and beliefs."[14] Understanding that we live in a world in which all nations are mutually insecure, Robert C. Tucker argues, should especially encourage American and Soviet leaders to work toward "ordered security" with respect to nuclear arms and relations with third-world countries.[15] No presidential selection system, however, will assure that candidates possess adequate perceptions and understanding of the world any more than it can guarantee their capacity to cope with other issues. If, however, the system is characterized by free-flowing information from many sources, including debates, interviews, and press coverage in all its forms, a candidate's background and understanding of the world can be usefully revealed. In McGeorge Bundy's words, "It is probably true that this ultimate power to make a nuclear attack or counterattack . . . is the most awesome of all presidential responsibilities, and one that voters will take account of when a candidate gives them either affirmative or negative reasons to do so."[16]

ALL BUT THE BEST?

In all eras, persons judged by their fellow citizens to have presidential qualities and to be electable have declined to seek nomination. Many who might win simply may not want to be president, or at least not enough to campaign for it. Those who do seek the office include many who might run well and some who do not expect to do so, but they may not include all or even a representative sample of those who might do so.[17] It is impossible to know empirically whether there have been potential candidates who did not compete because of the burdens of doing so but who would have made more effective presidents than those who ran and won. When individuals declared by others to be fully qualified won't run, the reasons, personal or professional, may be known only imperfectly to the individuals themselves. The important fact is that the incentives and disincentives are more significantly related to the larger political and social context than to technical nomination and election procedures.

This seems true even while admitting that the "permanent campaign" weeds out worthy potentials who are unwilling to campaign publicly for four years. John Glenn, for example, was said to believe that the process had become "so strung out and so expensive that anyone who wasn't an unemployed millionaire might as well forget it." It had become an endurance contest of fifteen- and sixteen-hour days. According to one report, he could not believe that candidates really enjoyed it and suspected that those who claimed they did were "either warped or lying; in either case, they were not to be trusted with the presidency."[18] The dominance of primaries and the requirements to qualify for federal funding may well turn away some potential candidates (as, in fact, any nominating system could). For a time, it was conventional to point to the successful nomination candidacies of Jimmy Carter, Ronald Reagan, and Walter Mondale in declaring that a serious aspirant for presidential nomination must be "gainfully unemployed." Republican Majority Leader Howard Baker did not run for reelection to the Senate in 1984 and Senator Gary Hart did not in 1986. It was widely commented that both would thus be freer to campaign for a presidential nomination in 1988.

Limits on the size of individual contributions do force on aspirants the onerous burden of raising large sums in small amounts before the first primary. Politicians out of office are said to gain advantage thereby. Michael Malbin contends that contribution limits, the large number of primaries, proportional delegate selection, and front-loading have especially handicapped active members of Congress, party leaders, and sitting governors, all of whom lack time to mount a national effort.[19] Indeed, it was no doubt easier under earlier conditions for prominent politicians to accumulate campaign chests than for some of their rivals to do so. Even now, however, established political leaders can benefit by working and travelling under the aegis of privately funded political action committees that raise and spend money to support candidates for other offices.[20]

Rather than working to the disadvantage of prominent, active political leaders, the Federal Election Campaign Act's contribution limits along with federal matching funds have given eligible but lesser known aspirants a better opportunity to compete in a nomination campaign. Rosalynn Carter wrote that "the new campaign financing law was a great advantage to us; in fact, if it had not been for the 1974 Federal Elections Act, Jimmy would not have been able to run for President at all."[21]

The result has been a more robust contingent of active aspirants in nomination races, except within the party of an incumbent president running to succeed himself. Most active aspirants, however, are not unemployed. Of the serious contenders in the nomination races between 1972 and 1984, Aldrich found that more were in office than in any of the three earlier periods he surveyed.[22] And in 1988, the nominees of both parties for president and vice-president held high elective office, as did three of the four leaders in each party's balloting on March's Super Tuesday.

The current delegate selection and campaign finance systems do make it difficult, however, for plausible candidates to do as they once could: jump *publicly* into the nomination contest at a late date. Late-starting candidates, such as Robert Kennedy in 1968, are no longer able to gather large sums of money quickly from a few contributors. Taken together, present conditions favor aspirants who make a fast start in the early primaries and caucuses.

THE PUBLIC MARATHON

The long prenomination campaign is accused of discouraging able candidates. But the new characteristic of preconvention activity is not its length. Since the beginning of the Republic, aspirants for the presidency have nursed ambitions and cultivated support over many long years in their efforts to become president. The novel feature of the modern presidential nomination campaign is its structured public nature.

On August 5, 1986, Michigan Republicans elected precinct delegates to county party conventions that in 1987 and 1988 would choose delegates to the state convention. It, in turn, would choose Michigan's delegates to the Republican National Convention of 1988. Expensive, well-staffed campaigns were active across Michigan several months in advance of the 1986 voting, as they would be in early activities in other states as well. Political action committees were vigorous, one founded by supporters of Representative Jack F. Kemp of New York and another with Vice-President George Bush as honorary chairman. A tax-exempt foundation organized by the Reverend Marion G. (Pat) Robertson was said to be spending on candidate recruitment as much as both those two committees combined.[23] The course of this early contest was fully reported by the media.

Before the post-1968 reforms, candidates not favored by party leaders also had to campaign early to gain serious consideration.[24] John F. Kennedy launched his nomination campaign well before 1960, the year he won the nomination, as did Barry Goldwater well before the year he was nominated, 1964. In fact, Goldwater's efforts to draw to his support, or to replace, the political elite that governed the nomination system—precinct committee members, county chairpersons, and state party leaders—began six years before 1964.[25] Elaine Ciulla Kamarck emphasizes that the record of earlier campaigns refutes the claim that changes in the nomination system have forced presidential candidates to launch ever-earlier campaigns. Rather, the changes have made actions before election year more public.[26]

"Front-loading" is also not unique to the post-1968 period. The train of first-ballot presidential nominations goes back to 1956 in both parties. By March of 1964 almost one-fourth of the Republican National Convention delegates or their electors had been chosen. One-third of the Democratic party's 1968 convention delegates had also been selected by March. This prereform front-loading, however, was not easily covered by the press. The main significance of front-loading in the existing system, Kamarck observes, is its public character, its increased visibility in primaries and caucuses. Not only were the presidential preferences of 40 percent or more of Democratic national convention delegates determined by the end of March in 1980, 1984, and 1988, but the media could easily record a candidate's progress in assembling support from the earliest contests onward. The distinguishing characteristic of the new system is not so much the numbers of delegates selected early in the season but the high visibility of the process and of the contestants.[27]

That visibility obviously is significant to individuals aspiring to be president. Whether it means that fewer or less-qualified candidates contend for the presidency is a different matter. Clearly the hurdles have changed, but there is no dearth of runners. Announced contenders for the Democratic presidential nomination in 1984 numbered eight, including four sitting United States senators, and in 1988 another eight, including two senators, one United States representative, and one governor. Six Republican aspirants in 1988 included, in addition to the vice-president, a senator, and a representative. The contest for a party's presidential nomination requires more highly publicized full-time work and more money than it once did, but the consequences of that fact will differ among individual aspirants. Whether the results are disadvantageous to the Republic is a different matter. Any system will have features more agreeable to some persons than others. As yet there is no evidence that the number of serious contenders has been reduced.

THE POSSIBILITIES AND LIMITATIONS OF CHANGE

The centrality of the presidency in the U.S. governmental system and the public's perennial desire for "better," more competent leaders foster the urge to change the system we use to search for a leader. Yet a person's desire to run for the nomination is determined less by rules of the nomination system than by forces in the political environment. Changing the rules is unlikely to inspire aspirants with significantly different social and political backgrounds to seek nomination. Candidate backgrounds have remained relatively constant over the years under several selection systems. If or as they change in the future, the explanation will be found in cultural evolution, not changes in procedures. New rules might affect the enthusiasm of a potential candidate now and then, but the hope that new rules will produce a whole new cast of characters of significantly superior qualifications is vain.

We have seen in earlier chapters the significant roles political finance plays in information exchange and as a form of political participation. And we shall find recommendations in Chapter Eleven for improving the supply, control, and reporting of money in nominations and elections. Changes in some existing campaign finance controls and party rules would undoubtedly make the environment more hospitable to aspiring leaders and more comfortable for elected officials, but they could not assure more capable officeholders. For example, federal funding regulations could make adequate sums more easily available for nomination campaigns. At a minimum, the present limit of $1,000 on permissible individual contributions per candidate should be raised, the overall limit of $25,000 per person to all federal campaigns should be raised or eliminated, and federal matching funds should be increased.

Further, the total of federal funding should keep pace with inflation. An increase from one dollar to two dollars per person in the contributions made by checkoff on federal income tax returns would be salutary. The tax credit an individual could claim for contributions to a candidate or party should have been raised rather than eliminated by the 1986 tax reform act.[28] The limits on total expenditures should be repealed, or at least raised significantly, and the required reports simplified. Such proposals point out the direction that modifications of campaign finance regulations should take to make the political environment more hospitable to potential leadership.

In addition to the need to attract funds, other nominating conditions have been conducive to early campaigning. The Republicans have had few national rules governing delegate selection and no national requirement for proportional representation. The Democrats have had requirements for proportional representation but have revised them for every convention from 1972 to 1988. Proportional representation places a premium on campaigning well in advance of election year. Given the wide differences among states in their social, economic, geographic, and political characteristics, and in their traditions, the party would do better to let each state decide for itself how to award its delegates to candidates for the presidential nomination. The Democrats should encourage a mixture ranging from strictly proportional allocation of delegates to winner-take-all systems by district or state.[29]

The tendency toward "front-loading" might be diluted if states could schedule their primaries whenever they wished during the year of the national convention. This would require the Democratic party to abandon or modify its "window rule" that aspires to restrict nomination contests to a period between early March and early June. But we have seen the recent move toward bunching primaries on Super Tuesday. It is uncertain whether large states, if again able to adopt a winner-take-all rule, would schedule their contests at the end of the nomination season, confident that the large number of delegates to be won would attract candidates to them. Such a development could enable a candidate who gathers momentum later in the season to compete better against early winners. Such changes would not be fundamental or disruptive and might lead to competition for the nomination among a wider range of experienced and qualified aspirants.

Presidential nominations constitute a critically important aspect of self-government in the United States, perhaps the most important in the judgment of some.[30] It is thus worth repeating that in both major parties the important contenders for the nomination in the present system, as in those that came before, continue to be politically experienced, well-educated, energetic, not incapacitated by scandal, and at the outset show prospects of making a serious contest of the general election.

DELIBERATION: KEY TO COALITION BUILDING

A more deliberative process in searching for a nominee is the aim of a spate of proposals to alter delegate selection. Democratic experience, more than Republican, has stimulated concern over lack of deliberation and its effect on the candidate nominated and the political base the candidate builds—that is, on the capacity for leadership. Yet similar anxieties intrude in both parties and, in any event, how one party does its business normally affects the other, especially when legal regulation results.

Several convictions underlie a number of recent proposals to strengthen the search for leadership: that convention delegates should represent their party constituents, not candidates; that the party would be strengthened by such delegates; that voters in primaries and caucuses presently choose among candidates without sufficient information; that this is particularly true early in the nominating season; that convention delegates, especially when they include a large number of party and public officials, will be better informed than primary voters about the candidates' ability to win election and govern effectively; that thinking delegates, unlike primary elections, can take into account not only their constituents' first choice, but their second and third and other choices as well, making it possible to decide which candidate would be most acceptable to the party as a whole.

There are doubts that a national convention of delegates who are pledged to or leaning toward candidates, whether chosen in primaries or conventions, can have any significant deliberative quality. Binding primaries and, especially in the Democratic party, candidate control over the choice of individual delegates have led to the near extinction of uncommitted delegates. Terry Sanford, former governor of North Carolina who was elected to the U.S. Senate in 1986, has asserted that the candidates, not the constituents, now pick the delegates. In the process, the likelihood that delegates will revise their preferences on the basis of new information has been forfeited.

Senator Sanford has offered one of several remedies proposed. He would have "thinking delegates" chosen by election or caucus from the smallest possible district. They would attend the national conventions "uninstructed or, at least, not irrevocably bound."[31] Candidates for delegate could run completely uncommitted, inclining toward a candidate but subject to change, or permanently committed to a candidate. Considering those positions and other qualifications of the candidate for delegate, voters in small districts would make their choices. Sanford also urged that delegates be chosen two months before the national convention. Candidates would thus have time to electioneer among delegates, delegates would be able to investigate candidates, and constituents could communicate with delegates. A "contemplative convention," it is argued, could result from such consultations. Citizens could inform and shape the nominating process without dominating it. States wishing to do so could hold a single, statewide primary within time limits established by the parties, but such primaries would be preferential and would not elect delegates.[32]

Sanford has been president of Duke, and that university's Forum on Presidential Nominations reflected his concerns and those of others. It recommended that "all delegates be permitted to decide their votes at the time of national convention balloting." It urged that delegates should be freed from the control of candidates. Although the delegates' candidate preferences would probably be known at the time of their selection, and would in most cases govern convention voting, the possibility of switching preferences should exist. Such a possibility, the forum argued, would prompt candidates to try to persuade the delegates of their abilities and electability. The motivating hope was contained in the statement that "these changes could go far to transform a system characterized by sloganeering, media hype, and a slavish dependence on polls of the candidate organizations, into a system emphasizing persuasion, conversation, and deliberation of delegates and their constituencies."[33]

A Commission on the Presidential Nominating Process at the University of Virginia also recommended that "no change is more important than to return to the delegates and the conventions the practical possibility of making an independent judgment." To reinstate the discretionary role of the delegates as well as to ensure their competence, the commission recommended that state laws and party rules be changed so that all delegates "would retain the option of exercising independent judgment in their convention vote"; that ex-officio delegates—members of Congress, governors, and high party officials—who are not bound by the outcome of state delegate selection contests be included; and that a percentage of delegates in primary states be chosen outside the primary process and not be bound by its results.[34]

The Democratic party included uncommitted party leaders and elected officials among its 1984 and 1988 national convention delegates, a response to the concerns underlying such proposals. Experience revealed, however, that politicians are political. Most of the uncommitted superdelegates did not withhold their judgment of candidates until after the nomination season. Their early commitments indicated that delegates, however chosen, are vulnerable to candidate lobbying, and that they seek to satisfy personal, policy, and patronage interests as well as to assess the candidates' credentials, character, and electability.

If candidates were chosen in the present social and political milieu by delegates declared to be free and thinking, they would not be likely to differ greatly by objective standards from those chosen in primaries. The pre-science of such delegates in picking the candidate with greatest appeal to the electorate may be no greater than that of rank-and-file partisans voting in primaries. Formation of a broad winning coalition would be fostered by campaigns of aspirants among uncommitted or unbound delegates, but probably not significantly more than in the existing nomination system.

In any event, in the present political culture the public will continue to insist that it participate directly in nominating presidential candidates. Proposals for nomination by party officers and elected officials that exclude widespread popular participation simply will not fly.[35] Moreover, it is not clear that the electorate will vote more wisely for a local delegate than for a presidential contender. In fact, even in the smallest possible districts advo-cated by Sanford, voters in most places would often have more politically relevant information about candidates for a party nomination than about local candidates for convention delegate. David E. Price writes that the known presidential preferences of delegates "are the most critical bits of information about them for many of those doing the selecting, and the party risks illegitimacy and voter alienation if it does not provide such information."[36]

NEW CONTEXT, NEW CONTEST

In the new American politics, a national convention's choice will be limited to contenders who have survived the primary-caucus season. The nomination system is now deeply rooted in the logic and expectation of public participation. When a clear consensus candidate emerges from the primaries and caucuses, a convention decision that disregarded that expres-sion of popular will would be considered illegitimate. Absent sudden illness, scandal, or other unforeseen disabling of a prospective nominee, delegates will not soon again be free, as they once were, to nominate a candidate who fared poorly in the primaries and caucuses, or did not contest in them at all.

An Adlai Stevenson or Charles Evans Hughes can no longer be plucked from the wings. There may be losses in that limitation. But in an age of voter independence and declining party identification, candidates must be able to test the nation's political waters and demonstrate mass electoral appeal. Moreover, as argued in Chapter Three, coalitions are now built as candidates compete for the nomination in a series of sequential primaries and caucuses rather than through multiple ballots in a brokered convention. Deliberation occurs, but in different ways and at different stages. Society and its institutions have changed.

Parties in the old sense of groups that knew their constituents and what they wanted, and could deliver their votes, no longer exist. Candidates at all levels campaign independently and win. The national committees raise money, call conventions, and provide services. The forms of party politics have accommodated to new realities. Writes historian Richard Wade, "as in other periods of American history our politics reflect the society that floats it."[37]

The structure of competition differs, however, within the two parties. It also changes every four years as the lack in 1990 of the customary hubbub over the next Democratic presidential nomination illustrated. Also, once the process begins, a clear-cut winner does not invariably emerge from the primary season. So it was for the Democrats in 1972 and 1984, and the Republicans in 1976. On such occasions, the opportunity arises for convention delegates to influence the results.[38] Party and convention rules ideally should recognize this possibility, and delegates should be free to reconsider their candidate commitments, if they have made any, and to help decide which of the contenders would make the party's ablest standard-bearer.

For national convention delegates to commit themselves to a candidate, to be elected as a delegate on that basis, and to keep that commitment in the absence of radical political change, seems to many a reasonable arrangement, or at least an unavoidable one given present expectations. The urge to limit delegate discretion has especially marked the Democratic party. Democratic rules have given an aspirant for nomination the right to approve or disapprove persons running for delegate under his or her banner, or to hold a candidate caucus to choose delegates. Some states, moreover, have a statutory requirement that delegates must vote for the aspirant to whom they were originally committed, at least on the first ballot. The Democratic Winograd Commission's much noted Rule 11 had eight provisions, most of them lengthy, and all of them detailed and intrusive into state party affairs. One requirement was desirable, however: that candidates for national delegate should state either their preference for a nominee, or their preference to go uncommitted. State parties could then decide whether to retain candidate right of approval, or to continue to select delegates in candidate caucuses.[39]

A SURROGATE FOR BARGAINING

In the absence of national conventions with delegates generally free to use judgment, alternative voting schemes are proposed to give flexibility in primary-election choices. Much mentioned is the proposal for "approval voting." Its utility in information exchange was discussed in Chapter Five, with the conclusion that it would diminish rather than enhance the value of political information generated in a general election. Nonetheless, the contention that the plan would produce a winner acceptable to the largest number of voters in a multicandidate primary election deserves a look. Its foremost proponents, Steven J. Brams and Peter C. Fishburn, state:

> In an election among three or more candidates for a single office, voters are not restricted to voting for just one candidate. Instead, each voter can vote for, or "approve of," as many candidates as [he or she] wishes .... Each candidate gets a full vote from each voter who votes for him. The candidate with the most votes, and presumably acceptable to the most voters, wins the election.[40]

Proponents of approval voting in multicandidate elections contend that it elects the candidate with the greatest *overall* support. Under plurality voting, in contrast, voters are forced to designate only one acceptable candidate and the victor is the individual with the largest following even if that is less than a majority. The advocates of approval voting believe it would enhance legitimacy by demonstrating a broader popular mandate than plurality voting does. It offers voters greater flexibility and fewer dilemmas and might therefore increase voter turnout. Approval voting accurately reflects the strength of minority candidates, and any number of candidates can be accommodated without distorting anyone's electoral strength. It could, moreover, be easily implemented. Statutory change would suffice in most jurisdictions, and existing voting machines could be used.

Dissenters question approval voting on several grounds, in addition to its potential for obscuring further the already elusive information communicated by voting, as discussed in Chapter Five. The effect of approval voting on the quality of candidates elected concerns some critics. They argue that because approval voting does not permit the ranking of candidates it can promote mediocrity by advancing candidates who are merely the least offensive to large constituencies. Nelson Polsby suspects it would not guarantee the election of centrists or moderates: "[I]f centrist voters, being moderate, find a wide range of alternatives acceptable and ideological voters meanwhile bullet-vote, an extremist candidate could end up the winner."[41]

Approval voting has only rarely and recently been used in a political unit. It is not known with certainty what its consequences would truly be in presidential nominations, and how it would affect the quality of victorious candidates or the character of electoral coalitions. Conventional American plurality elections are deeply rooted, and wholesale change to a voting system whose full consequences are not predictable is unlikely. But trial usage in multicandidate state primaries with full assessment of the experiences is desirable and would be instructive.[42]

THE LIMITS OF INSTITUTIONS

Neither party professionals nor rank-and-file members have a thoroughly reliable means of unambiguously assessing contenders for the presidential nomination—nor do general election voters as they choose between major-party candidates.

Defining the qualities needed to be an effective president has intrigued political pundits and kibitzers almost as much as ranking the "greatest" presidents. Richard Neustadt's notable book, *Presidential Power—the politics of leadership,* which first appeared in 1960, emphasized the significance of a president's capacity to make the powers of his office "work for *him,*"[43] a capacity inevitably dependent on a president's understanding and using effectively the sources of his influence, as well as on elements outside his control. The mobile intersection of personal, institutional, societal, and public policy variables in a presidency is so complex that defining all the qualities desired is not a matter of easy enumeration.

The ability to harness the presidency's full potential for leadership requires a wide range of qualities (not necessarily including, however, the dishonesty that Louis McHenry Howe declared to be inevitable in a politician[44]). Hedley Donovan, formerly editor in chief of Time Incorporated, who watched presidents for half a century and worked for twelve months in 1979–80 as senior adviser to President Carter, wrote that "we have no up-to-date working standard to measure presidential candidates against."[45] Others have argued that it is impossible to compile an objective list of presidential qualifications or to define criteria for predicting successful leaders. Ultimately, it is asserted, presidential qualifications can be assessed only arbitrarily and retrospectively.[46]

This does not mean that processes that sift individuals as possible worthy candidates are irrelevant to assessments of their potential performance. In fact, political insiders as well as the public are keenly sensitive to the qualities potential candidates exhibit—their experience, education, knowledge of the nation, exposure to the world, sense of history; their capacity to communicate and negotiate; their humor, compassion, intelligence, adaptability; to say nothing of bearing, appearance, general manner, and an instinct for command, along with a syndrome of qualities that James David Barber celebrates, which includes character, style, worldview, and self-esteem.[47]

How fully these and other characteristics are found in aspirants, nominees, and presidents will differ from one time to another. Donovan finds over thirty good qualities desirable—but usually only in moderation—in a president: stamina, drive, dignity, humor, pragmatism, curiosity, optimism, presidential bearing, sense of priorities, knowledge of history, integrity, and more.[48] But there is no way to program an electoral system to test for these and other qualities, except as they are judged by activists and perceived by voters to be important, and then to be present or absent. No formal procedure can

program quality control in presidential selection. Even constitutional requirements are minimal: a person must be a native-born citizen, thirty-five years
old, and a resident for fourteen years within the United States.

The changing circumstances of presidential nominations and elections
have affected the willingness of eligibles to contend, and the qualities others
have considered necessary for a person to be deemed eligible. Ronald
Reagan's effectiveness on television, like Theodore Roosevelt's bully-pulpit
oratory, proved an asset in both campaigning and governing, reinforcing
Samuel Kernell's thesis that these two phases "draw upon the same concep-
tions of politics."[49] The stump oratory of Stephen A. Douglas and James G.
Blaine was a major political resource in their time. That neither of the latter
two won the presidency simply means electoral success is a child of many
parents. Herbert Hoover, with a public personality as monotonous as a
metronome, was twice nominated and once elected. Alf Landon, with a voice
that seemed to his critics flat as a Kansas prairie, won the Republican
nomination in 1936, and Adlai Stevenson, of immense dignity and stirring
eloquence, lost the general election in both 1952 and 1956.

Requisite qualities of political organization and communication have
altered in fundamental ways. Those required in a specific period may
inconvenience or eliminate from effective competition individual aspirants to
the presidency who might have done well under other conditions. But there
is no significant and controllable method of eliminating aspirants based on
personal qualities. Presidents must win and serve the nation as it is. The
corporate chairman, university president, or military commander who dis-
plays character, effectiveness, and appeal in a chosen career may well lack the
institutional knowledge, personal attributes, and electoral experience, to say
nothing of the political base and allegiances, necessary for effective presidential leadership. But this is not always the case, as the political acumen,
leadership experience, sober perspective, and winsome personality of
Dwight D. Eisenhower demonstrated.[50]

A presidency is an establishment as well as a person. The most important
qualification for a president is the capacity to function effectively on behalf of
chosen objectives in the extant political environment, which always includes
a separately chosen U.S. Congress. Functioning effectively calls for instincts
and understanding in selecting and pursuing objectives. A well-chosen
president will know when to get out front and when to hold back. Such a
leader will know how to harness the latent talents and active energies of men
and women at all levels of politics in fashioning and implementing policy.[51]
And a president ought to be able to cope when powerful forces in the
political environment prevail over whatever influences he or she can
marshal.[52] The prevailing choice among candidates always flows from
multiple conflicting impressions and assessments of their suitability for the
job, as well as from conflicts over values and issues.

In each presidential selection, it is ultimately the voters who decide which qualifications are most important to them. Whether and how the citizen votes will depend on the net impact of a wide and varied combination of subjective factors and more objective considerations. Issues and policy stances are more important in some years than in others. The durability of Ronald Reagan's personal popularity as candidate and president was rooted significantly in the values he persuasively espoused—family, neighborhood, freedom, peace, work.[53] Tom Wicker has emphasized that a candidate who focuses "on issues and nothing but issues . . . is a loser."[54] The average voter, veteran analyst Doris Graber concludes, will be looking for "a good man, capable and experienced." Given the uncertainty at the time of the election of what tests a candidate will face as president, "it may be best to concentrate on general leadership qualities and characteristics of integrity and trustworthiness, rather than dwelling on specialized competence in a variety of areas."[55]

The impossibility of institutionalizing standards to guarantee the choice of a "good" leader explains the varying quality of candidates who emerge from every selection process. Lincoln won his first nomination under the same system that selected Buchanan, and Franklin Roosevelt won his under the same system that produced Warren Harding. And no matter who is doing the nominating—partisans or the general public, professionals or rank-and-file party members—universally acceptable candidates will not emerge. To some, it will often even seem that the candidates who do emerge present a choice of the lesser of inferiors.[56]

Changes in the setting and means of gaining nomination have affected how ambitious politicians organize their political careers, how they build their political base, and what they do to seek the nomination. Those changes, however, have had less effect, if any, on the quality of those who run. The important element is that nomination is a required stage on the road to the general election. The decision to run for president remains an individual, voluntary decision restricted to a rather large group of ambitious politicians who possess the credentials called for at the time.

The contributions of party professionals, of the more numerous party identifiers in the electorate, and of interested independent voters, both organized and not, are all important in the contemporary nominating process. None of these categories of participants has displayed a monopoly of good judgment or unerring instinct in picking winners and discerning qualities that make for presidential success. Rather, the political perspectives of each, registered in different ways in a mixed nominating system of sequential primaries, caucuses, and national conventions, seem to inform the others and strengthen the legitimacy of the process. Broad participation permits candidates, party leaders, elected officials, rank-and-file party members, interest-group leaders, and the general public to know and be responsive to one another. A coalition of members of these groups is required for the nomination of acceptable candidates as well as for electoral success and effectiveness in governing. Presidential candidates and presidents seize opportunities to forge coalitions when they have the chance, regardless of the means of presidential selection. Present selection practices are well-suited to that task.[57]

A public president involved in a permanent campaign must build ties with diverse particular constituencies as well as with the more general public. Whether or not the potential for a grand coalition exists, support from both narrow and wide constituencies will be needed throughout a presidential term. Under existing conditions, a nominating process that stimulates the involvement of a wide array of participants will facilitate the selection of qualified presidential candidates and the construction of a broad coalition that can help in the continuing search for better government.

CHAPTER TEN

Searching for Better Government

☆
☆

In drafting their constitutions early in the nineteenth century, some of the newly independent nations of Latin America looked north and drew heavily on the Constitution of the United States. From the perspective of a century and a half later, we should not be surprised that the transplanted systems failed to produce the political stability and popular confidence achieved by their northern neighbor.

It was misguided to expect that organizational mechanics and legal formulations would be enough. The successful experiment in the United States required the cultural and material conditions that underlay its democratic political institutions, including the political unity, inherited common values, indigenous habits, pragmatic restraints, and continental wealth that characterized its polity. Political institutions must fit and adapt to the circumstances in which they serve. Efforts to sustain and increase effective democratic government in the United States must proceed in a context defined by the nation's condition—the traditions, expectations, tolerances, frailties, abilities, visions, and dilemmas found in the country as it is and as it is likely to become.

Numerous proposals offered in one quarter or another to improve the selection of U.S. presidents are identified in previous chapters, and their merits and feasibility assessed. The next chapter records the recommendations to which our excursion has led. The present chapter addresses the broad characteristics of American government that affect proposals for making it better.

NEW POLITICS AND OLD GOVERNMENT

Henry Brandon, after over three decades in Washington as chief American correspondent of *The Sunday Times* of London, concluded that "operating the American government . . . is the greatest political gambling casino in the world, where not even the president . . . can ever take anything for granted or count his winnings in advance." In such a milieu, the ultimate question becomes how government as a whole performs.[1]

The presidency is but one segment of American politics and government. Some observers and activists who are dismayed by what they see as the results of current presidential selection, and who dislike the new characteristics of electoral politics generally, look to governmental institutions as the source of remedy. Many such proposals predate the recent changes that have occurred in the selection process, but because of them have been advocated with new urgency. This view holds that a significantly different relationship between politics and government cannot come from changes in the manner of choosing presidents, but only from changes in government itself. As Bert A. Rockman has put it, "governance is aided by a more coherent politics, but it also requires more than that. A better organized politics ... does not necessarily translate into more effective governance."[2]

Looking over the full course of America's history, however, Samuel P. Huntington has found occasions when he sees the old government adjusting itself to fit a "new politics." The adjustment came not as a result of reform, but rather as a consequence of the flexibility inherent in the nation's odd and complicated governmental structure. He labels as political earthquakes "the profound upheaval in the overall relations between social forces and political institutions" during the Revolutionary period, in the Jacksonian and Progressive eras, and in the 1960s-1970s. These adjustments, especially those beginning in 1828 and 1896, involved more than a simple partisan realignment. Party realignment occurred, but as part of a broader mutation that embraced changes in the functioning of governmental institutions, including their structure and power. In the most recent period, the political parties were less significant in the political system; consequently, changes in constituencies and power did not affect the parties as severely as in earlier times.[3]

Huntington finds this pattern of readjustment among institutions unique to the United States. In other systems, governmental institutions and political parties tend to be firmly attached to specific social forces, and they decline when those forces decline.[4] Such a change occurred in Great Britain with the decline in power of the Crown and the House of Lords and the corresponding rise of the House of Commons.[5]

In the United States, however, institutional *appearances* remain steady even when significant shifts occur in their functions, constituencies, and the relationships among them. Huntington accounts for this "peculiar genius of the American system"[6] with the observation that "the framers of the Constitution created a system of government that was responsible to society yet also autonomous from it."[7] Particular institutional forms did not necessarily derive from one or more social forces. Rather, they showed an inherent facility to adapt to new constituencies that reflected changes in the influence and power of different social forces.[8] The old government of the United States remains old only in its broad, general framework. Within that old framework, "new governments" have formed periodically to fit the several "new politics" that have arisen in American society over the course of the nation's history.

In the same spirit, Richard Rose has argued that "the structure of a nation's politics is not solely a matter of institutions. It is also determined by how well politicians adapt institutions at hand to the problems that confront the country."[9] Flexible institutions do not self-adjust, but they may allow those who control them to respond to shifts in political forces.

There is often difficulty distinguishing between adaptation and decline.[10] For a century and a half, competitiveness in contests for the House of Representatives has been declining. Presidents lacking a party majority in one or both houses of Congress have become familiar. Divided partisan control of state governments has risen in recent years also.[11] But when a dynamic reality is interpreted through static models, and inevitably diverges from those models, decline may become a more tempting explanation of the departure than adaptation.

The electoral process and the institutions of government are interdependent, yet separate, as they function in the nation's political life. Change in one always affects the other, but there are close limits on the extent that modifications in the electoral process can alter the nation's subtle, complex, and encompassing system of government. The logic of the fundamental American governmental arrangements is embedded in the written Constitution. In spite of its many ambiguities, the Constitution will yield only so much to interpretation. Radical, dramatic alterations in the governmental system can occur only when the logic itself—that is, the Constitution—is directly and formally altered. The electoral process, including how presidents are chosen, occurs within these larger, separately established institutional arrangements.

Most critics of the method by which U.S. presidents reach office are complaining, knowingly or not, about the general functioning of the government. Appeals for changes in the processes of presidential selection that claim extensive consequences for the governmental system as a whole should therefore give pause. That is especially so when the changes proposed are borrowed from other political systems that, first, have a different structure of government and, second, serve a nation with different patterns of social organization. Notably, efforts to use the electoral process to unify offices that are given independent bases of authority in the Constitution cannot produce the results of a unitary parliamentary system. The American governmental system has displayed a critically important capacity to accommodate to changing external circumstances, but it also has shown an inherent and durable capacity to sustain its fundamental institutional character even in the face of major changes in the environment in which it functions.

The American political system is complex in a way not often acknowledged. It has both an electoral process and a government. The loosely coupled relationship between the two permits the nation to enjoy a variety of values that are sometimes contradictory—for example, loyalty by a senator or representative to party in elections alongside loyalty in Congress to constituency. The electoral process should be judged by standards specific to it. So should government. The two are interdependent, but a government grounded in a written constitution has an autonomy that cannot easily be mastered by electoral changes. Effective collaboration between president and Congress depends heavily, for example, on the committee systems and other internal organization that the two houses set for themselves. While electoral processes affect the political forces inside government at a particular time, other elements in the larger political system deny them the sole role. Despite his substantial personal victories at the polls, President Reagan was unable to get congressional approval for much that he wanted.

It may be that leadership for an adequately coherent government under future changing conditions will be found best through the loose, adaptable conditions that have traditionally characterized the selection of political leadership in the United States. Contemporary organizational environments, including those of government itself, continue to change and constantly call for new skills, abilities, strategies, and vision.[12] The means of choosing presidents has responded in the past to the changing context with modified procedures and altered opportunities for participation. That may be the inevitable course for the future. The qualities relevant to getting elected are also relevant to presidential leadership; relevant, but not by themselves sufficient in the sometimes libertine and always self-centered environment of American politics, as any critique of presidential performance makes clear.

The present way of presidential selection has unique benefits for the unique United States government. If it is changed in an effort to produce dramatic results in government's performance, its present capacities are put at risk without reasonable assurance of realizing comparable gains in the quality or success of government. Moreover, there are limits to what can be achieved by governmental institutions. After a detailed study of British economic policy under each of the major political parties over several years, Rose concluded that neither political party, nor by implication Britain's parliamentary system, has been adequate to improve economic conditions in Britain. The most intractable problem successive governments have faced has been the control of public expenditures. In principle, Britain's two major parties favor very different approaches to public expenditure, but

> in practice, the growth of public expenditure has shown a steady secular trend upwards through the years, varying little with the complexion of the party in office. Once in office, parties do not reverse the pattern of their predecessor. Public expenditure has risen in constant price terms during the life of every government from 1957 to 1982.

Rose concludes that the condition results from forces outside government and well beyond the control of government.[13] Neither party doctrines nor institutional arrangements have been able to bring economic improvement to Britain over the course of several successive "party governments." There is more in determining public policies and a nation's civic health than electoral procedures.

LIMITS OF REFORM

To ask, then, whether and how the selection of American presidents can be improved leads directly to the American system of government. For over a century, important critics have yearned for more coherence in United States governmental actions and greater consistency in its policies. Believing some parliamentary systems have offered both—Great Britain being most often cited—they have urged institutional modifications to gain for American government some of the desirable features perceived in parliamentary models. The present inquiry began explicitly hospitable to such proposals for improving presidential performance and the success of American governance. It ended with six conclusions:

First, there is no single perfect way, not even a single right way, to perform any large and complex political function, such as choosing the American president.

Second, the complex system we use in the United States to nominate and elect presidents is but one component in the complicated multi-tier political-governmental system through which the country is governed to some satisfactory degree or another, and by which it lives.

Third, two hundred years of the competitive evolution of political interests and institutions have generated connections, vested interests, habits, confidences, momentum, and what is generally perceived to be successful governance. The pragmatic effect of this evolutionary process is to remove any real possibility of a planned, deliberate, fundamental restructuring of the American system, or of a disruptive tampering with its historic basic components. To take the most important examples, the American public will not accept fundamental changes in the separation of powers, the federal system, or the Bill of Rights.

Fourth, a sobering law of unintended consequences has operated throughout the nation's history—beginning with the way the electoral college originally prescribed in the Constitution actually functioned. The difficulty of producing intended results—and *only* the intended results—in competitive political processes through adoption of party or public regulation has repeatedly proved difficult, as illustrated by recent experience with the nominating process and political finance. That fact should sober all reformers.

Fifth, for a system to function most productively, whatever its characteristics, the people it serves, from passive citizens to vigorous activists, need to understand it well enough to be able to function in it and to have general confidence in it. At least they should not find themselves bewildered by it. For such a condition to obtain, there must be some deliberate continuity in regulations and practices. Therefore the volume, variety, and speed of changes in the conditions of presidential nomination and election should be paced so that citizens in general as well as political practitioners can become accustomed to them, and so that critics can better assess their effects.

Sixth, and finally, it is solemn fact that changes made in a complex subject of high stakes such as the means of presidential selection seldom follow a comprehensive scheme, a model, if you will. Rather, changes normally flow from fragmentary approaches and compromised solutions of individual elements.

These conclusions leave us searching for improvements in presidential selection practices within the main contours of the existing governmental system.

SEEKING BETTER GOVERNMENT THROUGH BETTER PARTY POLITICS

Despite the confines of the above six conclusions, there is still much to contemplate in the search for better government through better politics, a search that leads to the recommendations in the next chapter.

The business of choosing the next president never really stops.[14] Overt campaigning ends when the votes have been cast, but electoral politics continues and government is not easily separated from it. Whether or not a recognized presidential campaign is under way, any official act can be either an act of governing or an electoral ploy, or both.[15] Free, competitive elections sustain the ambiguity. They assure that concerns of the electorate, or some portion of it, press persistently on the minds of elected officials. More open and visible government, especially with the easy availability of information about its activities in recent decades, makes all the words and deeds of elected officeholders and their aides seem like electoral politics.[16] That intimacy between government and politics has led to proposals to change presidential selection in hopes of bringing greater separation between the two and thereby improving the possibilities of organizing a strong governing coalition.

The majority of proposals to improve government by improving politics grow from a now-familiar aphorism: the skills needed to win a presidential nomination are not the skills needed to govern; and from its analogue, that an electoral coalition for winning the presidency is inadequate as a coalition for governing. Some persons view the pre-1968 nominating process as superior to subsequent arrangements as a base for effective government. Others have always viewed it as inadequate.

Plans have been advanced that seek to alter the performance of government by altering the politics that precedes the exercise of government power. To bind elected officials closer to their parties by changes in campaign practices is a recurring suggestion. At a minimum, doing so could entail little more than an increased role of formal party organizations in campaigns of presidential and congressional candidates.

An oft-heard recommendation would revise campaign finance laws to reroute public funding for presidential campaigns away from candidates and to the political parties. If candidates felt more dependent upon party organizations for campaign resources, including money, it is presumed they would act more cohesively, or at least more cooperatively, once in government. As a consequence the president might gain greater leverage over his party in Congress. Correspondingly, in some circumstances the congressional party might gain a new source of influence over the president. Additional or unlimited fund-raising by the parties might also increase their clout in congressional campaigns.[17] Some who advocate public funding for congressional campaigns would also have those funds channeled to the parties instead of to individual candidates.[18] The prospect is not appetizing to most in Congress who would have to vote for it, but were such a system in effect it might produce a more collegial spirit among elected officials of the same party.

Ingenious adaptation of existing campaign finance regulations by presidential hopefuls and their supporters can produce the collegial party spirit sought by these proposals. Presidential political action committees (PACs) created by prospective but undeclared presidential candidates permit them to travel widely, gain public exposure, and seek support for their candidacies from federal, state, and local candidates and party organizations to whom they make direct and in-kind contributions. The money raised and spent through presidential PACs does not count against the spending limits that apply to presidential contenders who have announced their candidacies and accepted federal matching funds.[19] Critics accuse candidates of adapting this vehicle, which is sanctioned and regulated by the Federal Election Commission (FEC), to circumvent the intent of the law. They are, in effect, using presidential PACs to keep themselves in the political spotlight and finance activities that advance their political objectives. In the process, however, they are establishing useful ties with the party leaders and elected officials with whom they may one day form a governing coalition.

The most extreme vision of a party role in campaigns is slate, or team-ticket, voting. This alternative would link a party's presidential candidate, Senate candidates, and House candidates on a single ballot—with terms of office adjusted to make this possible—requiring the voter to vote for the slate of one party for all national government offices.[20] The requirement would go far toward excluding all the bases of constituency except the political party. It would alter the geographic constituency base that has characterized Congress and been integral to the concept of representation in the American system. Not surprisingly, the idea has stirred little enthusiasm, and some opinion surveys have revealed a popular preference for the restraints inherent in divided government, restraints rooted ultimately in the country's pluralistic political culture. In any event, executive-legislative cooperation reached high points, and notably important lawmaking occurred under present arrangements during Woodrow Wilson's and Franklin Roosevelt's first terms, Lyndon Johnson's early years, and Ronald Reagan's first year. Even so, excesses in those cases, especially in the last two, have been attributed to inadequate legislative opposition.[21]

Changing the terms of office alone is advocated as a step that would encourage more coherent government by strengthening the bond between the president and his party in Congress. Off-year elections would be eliminated and all representatives and senators would stand for election in the year a president is being elected. Several combinations of terms are possible; one prominent proposal would extend the term for representatives to four years and for senators to eight.[22] As a result, presidential influence in House and Senate elections might increase. It would also eliminate the possibility that a president's party in Congress would suffer losses in midterm elections.

However, the degree of change in *government performance* that might be induced by changes in styles and forms of *electoral politics* cannot be easily predicted.

RESTRAINING AND ENHANCING PRESIDENTIAL LEADERSHIP

Some schemes of change start from the premise that the presidency has become excessively autonomous and powerful. It is argued that presidents have accumulated sufficient power to affect independently the nation's well-being, especially with the coming of the activist welfare state. True, limits are imposed on presidential discretion by deeply held national habits, by specialized bureaucracies and decentralized administration, by international constraints, by the size of government, and by hosts of political pressures. Nonetheless, American presidents have extraordinary opportunities to be wise or foolish, strong or weak. The absence of a corporate cabinet—unique among established democracies[23]—enhances those opportunities. Also, the evolution of the presidential selection process, notably since 1968, has contributed to increased presidential independence. The inherently weak collective responsibility of the American government, with its separation of powers, has been further diminished.

Theodore J. Lowi and Robert A. Dahl have made suggestions that help illuminate quandaries of contemporary political leadership in the United States. Even as they endorse what can be thought of as "un-American" remedies, they more nearly share the vision of the presidency held by the founders than do most contemporary advocates of reform.

Lowi offers a number of discrete proposals to reduce what he deems the excessive power of the existing personal presidency. The linchpin of his scheme is a multiparty system. If Congress were composed of three or more parties, he argues, instead of the two internally divided parties of recent Congresses, the president would not only become more dependent upon his own party in Congress, but would be forced to negotiate coalitions with one or more other parties to acquire a legislative majority. The two effects in combination, Lowi argues, would rupture the present illusion that the president is the whole of government. They would have the possible allied benefit of reducing the public's unrealistically high expectations of what any president can or should accomplish.[24]

Dahl likewise intimates his preference for a multiparty system in the context of arguments that the president needs further systematic restraint, and that the nation needs more political and social equality and more effective citizen participation in public life (including, he believes, in the workplace).[25]

It is not certain that a formal multiparty politics in the United States would produce the desired results. In many respects, weak party discipline in loose coalitional parties has caused the American system to function as if there were several parties in Congress.[26] But the implicit multiparty politics of American government, past and present, lacks the elements of formal responsibility present in explicit multiparty politics. The pattern of collective party decision-making that Lowi seeks would, it is hoped, make the terms of negotiation for each party clear to the electorate. In the American context and tradition, it is problematic whether such would be the case.

Sometimes expressly, but often unwittingly, proposals to strengthen the parties would expand presidential power. A system of two "responsible" parties invariably implies presidential enhancement, intended or not. The concept of responsible party government does not require increases in presidential power. But changes proposed for party reform, and ones that look toward more responsible party government—for instance, election of United States senators and representatives only in presidential election years—would usually enhance presidential leadership.[27]

In fact, Donald L. Robinson, who would change House terms to four years and Senate terms to eight years, has proposed that federal elections for president, representatives, and half the senators be made subject to call by either executive proclamation (with the consent of one-third of either the House or Senate), or by congressional joint resolution. The election would be held within sixty days. Perhaps party structures would be strengthened by the need to maintain a state of readiness.[28] Even if such a plan were adopted, however, the parochial constituencies of the country might well confirm the stalemate rather than resolve it.

Proposals to restore seemingly diminished cohesion among the traditional American parties might enhance presidential leadership. Modest suggestions for strengthening the parties, such as increasing the financial leverage of the national party organizations, could do so. If unlimited national party spending were permitted, presidential influence over Congress—party discipline—could well increase.[29] The separation of powers is dependent on the different constituency bases of the separate branches. But if national parties could control significant campaign resources in congressional elections, greater influence would be concentrated in the presidency and the separation of powers diminished, a result that would be heartily welcomed by some, but only by some.

Proposals to alter the nomination process often have less obvious implications for the presidency, and for governance. They, too, however, stem from visions of the best relationship between the president and Congress. An explicit aim of the bicameral nominating convention advocated by Lloyd N. Cutler is to bring the president and his party's members in Congress closer together toward the goal of more coherent government.[30]

One chamber of Cutler's proposed convention would be composed of public delegates chosen in primaries and caucuses, like the majority in present national conventions. A second chamber would seat the party's holdover senators, and candidates for the House of Representatives and the Senate, "as selected in the state primaries and caucuses up to the date of the presidential nominating convention."[31] A nominee would be chosen if one candidate obtained majority support in both chambers; or, failing that, a majority in both chambers' runoff ballots; or, if the two houses still did not agree, by calculating the winner of the highest percentage of votes in both chambers added together.

The proposal seeks peer review without altering public involvement through primaries and caucuses. The convention would be constrained, however, by the outcome of the primary-caucus season. The influence of delegates to the congressional chamber would be greatest when no consensus candidate emerged from the primaries and conventions. Whether the nominees produced would differ significantly from recent candidates and whether a more cooperative relationship between the president and Congress would result could be determined only by experience, but the built-in biases of the present system will impede the proposal's adoption.

In contrast, advocates of restoring a substantial role in nominations to decentralized parties are more likely to view Congress as a desirable check on presidential power. Strong state and local parties are themselves thought at times to temper presidential power. There are limits, however, on the constraints on the presidency that will result, as illustrated by the experiences of Lyndon Johnson before the system was changed. Rockman wrote that in the case of Johnson's Viet Nam policy, "as in Nixon's case, there is no evidence that he was opposed in any significant way by party leaders until sharp declines in public confidence set in."[32]

The hope that an electoral coalition resulting from a brokered convention will check excesses in the presidency is only that—a hope, and one not always realized in the past. The independent constitutional base of the presidency, combined with statutory authority legislated by Congress over the years, gives the presidency a strength difficult to check, especially in the many areas of policy and action where legislative consent is not required. Indeed, presidential influence over a more cohesive political party in government might have the effect of enhancing, rather than checking, presidential influence. But as long as separate votes are cast for three federal offices, there can be no guarantee that a president's party will command a majority in both houses of Congress. And how political reform can guarantee more effective checks on the presidency seems even more problematic.

THE MATRIX OF ADVOCACY

Obviously, the United States is now, as always, in a time of change. The founders worked in a time of change. America in the late eighteenth century was suffused by challenges to political allegiances, to societal structure, and, underneath it all, to philosophical convictions. Those political and intellectual pioneers rarely thought in dichotomous terms, believing that many remedies are worse than the maladies they are meant to cure. They usually approached the difficulties of political and social organization as a matter of treating clinical symptoms rather than eliminating causes—causes they readily ascribed to human nature, or at least to the nature of humans-in-society. And they consciously balanced conflicting concepts of government, and competing forces in politics, through the great compromises embodied in the sharing of powers among the branches of the national government, and in the division of powers between the levels of the federal structure.

Most of the controversies in American history over the organization of politics and government have taken place within the framework established at the founding. The debate leading to the Civil War, acknowledging its economic and moral origins, took the form of a core dispute over the place of states in the federal union. But rarely is the validity of constitutional fundamentals at issue. The most persistent debates have been about the degrees of emphasis to be accorded to some principles in contrast to others.

The standards of judgment effectively applied in the United States are ultimately set by the majority. The final criterion of governmental effectiveness is the public's long-term satisfaction with government's performance. Two kinds of popular judgments are made: short-range responses to immediate governmental actions, and long-range evaluations of the governmental system compared with envisioned alternatives.

Despite well-articulated anxieties by a small number of able and experienced persons, there are no widely supported challenges to the fundamentals of the present electoral system. As one observer put it when reflecting on the patterns of change stemming from attitudes and behaviors in the 1960s, there "is a rejection of some of the rules but not enough to design a new game."[33] Or, as another concluded, accommodation rather than reaction is more likely in the "largely unalterable circumstances."[34]

The "circumstances" so described do not, however, assure the system's permanence. In Peter Drucker's words, we are facing a world that is "totally new and dynamic" and for which we are quite unprepared.[35] Adlai Stevenson once remarked that "tyranny is the normal pattern of government."[36] American democracy may still be "the world's best hope" to some, as it was to Thomas Jefferson, but in the gray light of reality popular government in any setting will last only as long as it satisfies enough people with its performance—its processes and achievements—to be preferred over imagined alternatives, and resistant to subversive challenges. The ultimate purpose of enhancing confidence in the way American presidents are chosen is to continue justifying confidence in the country's system of democratic self-government.

Critics of presidential selection are understandably tempted to make judgments based on the personal attributes of recent presidents or by their perceived effectiveness in office. Following the Nixon and Carter administrations, public and private criticisms of the means of presidential selection were bipartisan and rampant. But critics sometimes forget that governmental effectiveness, and even probity, including the quality of presidential leadership, are products of dynamic societal and institutional influences. The means of choosing the president is only a part, and on occasion may not even be an important part, of those influences. Citizen tolerance of humbug, along with societal myopia, have deeper roots than electoral procedures. So do cable television and the First Amendment and the education of the electorate. The quality of political messages won't be improved by changing electoral mechanics.

Realistically assessing the performance of individual presidents is a sophisticated undertaking. The conditions of the times, including transient presidential circumstances and the nature of the larger political system, affect the performance of presidents. John W. Gardner observes that "leaders cannot be thought of apart from the historic context in which they arise, the setting in which they function . . . and the system over which they preside. . . . They are integral parts of the system, subject to the forces that affect the system."[37] Clearly, public perceptions of Lincoln, Wilson, and Franklin Roosevelt as leaders would be different had they served only in peacetime.

If the presidency itself were fatally flawed by the restrictions imposed by the Constitution, or by statutes, or by tradition, how its occupants are chosen would be of secondary importance. Similarly, if the federal government as a whole were so impotent, or America's cultural fabric so disintegrated, that the nation could not function with necessary unity and effectiveness, how presidents are chosen again would be of secondary importance. And there are challenges to a society's welfare that reach beyond the capacities of any political structures and transcend in significance its social organization. The ultimate test may become society's intellectual capacities, moral vision, and will to survive. Issues such as ozone depletion, acid rain, the world's population-resource ratio, ocean pollution, and the consequences of Arctic warming require, but also transcend, the competence of political institutions. To look to changes in the means of choosing presidents as a remedy for all the nation's or its government's limitations oversimplifies the human condition.

In making recommendations, two limits are inescapably present. First, few proposals to alter public processes are adopted as first presented. They are normally changed in the turmoil of advocacy and opposition, even when approval is the outcome. Second, the results that will actually flow from changes in political institutions are perplexingly difficult to predict. Politicians and political interests display extraordinary ingenuity in coping with new conditions. The rapid growth of political action committees, for example, was importantly a response to changed attempts to regulate campaign finance. Moreover, changing one part of an electoral system may unintentionally alter another part. The goal of revision in Democratic party rules after 1968 was diversity among convention delegates, not the enormous rise in use of presidential primaries that actually resulted. In fact, in recent years, candidate selection practices have been changed so often and swiftly that candidates, parties, and voters—much less scholars—have been hard pressed to assimilate them, much less assess them.

In the next chapter, some precise proposals for legislative or other action are made, some more general objectives are advanced, and some alternatives not favored are discussed. Objectives are sometimes more important to identify than detailed prescriptions for reaching them; often means to ends must be fashioned in competitive controversy that requires their adaptation.

CHAPTER ELEVEN

The Continuing Quest

☆
☆

On July 9, 1788, Benjamin Rush of Pennsylvania wrote: "'Tis Done. We have become a nation."[1] In ten months enough states had ratified the Constitution for the new nation to begin the task of creating itself. The United States has been at it ever since, but the slate has never been as clean nor the options as open as they were at the end of the eighteenth century. We cannot now reinvent the United States. All appraisals of American government and attempts to improve it begin where we are now.

No experience, starting with the writing of the Constitution, suggests that Americans can design logically and adopt dispassionately a set of procedures for choosing their presidents that will work strictly as intended and with constant results. Some unmeant consequences have resulted in the past, even from relatively simple arrangements such as the early voting in the electoral college. Attempting to predict results continues to be an uncertain exercise as new expectations of government appear, as the social environment of government evolves and becomes more complex, and as human ingenuity in twisting rules and circumstances endures. The issue is whether in the face of this pervasive reality we can plot changes in the means of selecting U.S. presidents that, with reasonable assurance, will benefit the country. We must respect the reality of George F. Will's conclusion that "much of the drama of the American political experience is the combination of cultural dynamism and institutional stability."[2]

In the end, a future fully worthy of the American heritage lies beyond the probabilities and guarantees of institutional design and regulatory tinkering. Such a future will require presidents with the vision, courage, ingenuity, and talent to inspire their fellow citizens to share a faith in their own capacities. Such leadership, however, is ultimately rooted in the heritage, values, and ever changing circumstances of those citizens. It is expressed through electoral procedures but does not originate in them. Electoral structures and processes can facilitate or retard the emergence of particular leaders, or types of leadership, without constituting the ultimate determinants of the nation's destiny.

We have noted that elections are always, first and foremost, about getting elected and that the way our presidents get elected should contribute to the five functions of presidential selection set forth in Chapter One and addressed in subsequent chapters: (1) to facilitate the vital exchange of information and opinion among citizens and their government that is at the heart of effective democracy; (2) to encourage citizen participation in government that is broadly representative of the nation; (3) to delineate and clarify the important issues facing the nation, thereby helping to establish the public agenda; (4) to secure able leadership for the nation; and (5) to help prepare the nation's leaders to work together institutionally and personally for effective governance.

Each of the individual processes or practices that, taken together, make up the presidential selection process does not contribute exclusively to only one of the five functions. Many practices, such as use of television, are relevant to all five. Some others are especially relevant to two or more, such as participation in campaign finance with its impact on political agendas. It consequently would be awkward in this concluding chapter to organize recommendations by the five identified functions. Recommendations can best be grouped by their relevance to the *principal political activities* through which the five functions are performed when presidents are chosen. The proposals thus are directed at improving the political parties (including their nominating function), campaign finance (pertaining to nominations and elections), the general election, and governance. A bare-bones summary of proposals will appear near the beginning of each of the sections addressing those subjects.

The proposals vary greatly in scope and character and the actions needed to achieve them. Some desirable changes would require constitutional amendment, some federal or state statutory action, some national or state party action, some a change in popular attitudes. Also, a recommendation to do nothing can be as important as one to do something. Moreover, the goals sought differ greatly in scope, significance, and popular appeal. The steps advocated to reach them may also differ sharply from each other in their specificity and complexity as well as in other ways. Most changes advocated to improve government and politics assume that other parts of the system will remain unchanged, or at least will not change in a way that distorts the results of a particular proposal if it were adopted. Such assumptions are often unwarranted.

IMPROVING POLITICAL PARTIES

Political parties are integral to general election campaigning and campaign finance, but most importantly they are instruments of democracy. Their justification lies in their usefulness in governing. Like any human combination, they may at times house undesirable behavior, but they are not inherently evil. Nor are they unqualifiedly good. Their value is neither symbolic nor absolute, but practical and variable. They serve many masters, from voters to office holders and others in between. A democratic party system organizes electoral competition around options, options that in the United States offer a general basis for choosing between broad stances toward the role of government in society and the characteristics of public policies.

The conclusions and recommendations for improving the usefulness of political parties are as follows:

Patterns for party improvement should uphold the constitutionally based principle of geographic constituencies for the popular election of the president and members of Congress.

Public policies should not artificially weaken or bolster existing political parties, nor should they contribute to more highly centralized parties. The goal should be to strengthen the party system, not the existing parties.

Public policy by its restraint should therefore induce the parties through their own energy and imagination to adapt to the evolving conditions under which they must function, and thereby to assume the chief responsibility for their own viability.

Public policies that influence campaign funding and party strength should enhance party effectiveness in stimulating electoral participation, in contributing to presidential-congressional cooperation within the constitutional division of powers, in holding their own in competition with volunteer campaign organizations and interest groups, and in developing a strong and balanced federalism within each party. The goal is to make the parties more effective in their corporate partisan activities while still leaving them open to challenge from within and without.

The relationship between television and party strength argues that the federal government should reclaim broadcast time from the networks, or appropriate funds to purchase it, and assign it to political parties for use as they see fit, allowing provision for potential new parties.

The relationship between presidential nominations and party strength makes clear that Congress should not adopt a national nominating primary, abolish primaries, or legislate the composition of national nominating conventions. American political parties should bear the responsibility for their own continuing adaptation to evolving circumstances.

The relationship between party procedures and party strength presents parties with opportunities. In their structure, the major parties will continue much like parties of the past, but national party regulations ought to allow state parties substantial autonomy in determining how and when national convention delegates are named, how their votes shall be cast, whether to experiment with new procedures such as approval voting, and generally how state parties adapt to particular circumstances within individual states. The parties should vigorously pursue opportunities for technical and administrative innovation to increase their own effectiveness.

In contemplating the role political parties play in selecting presidents, remember that the loose, decentralized political parties of the United States have always been keenly sensitive to their environment. No human institution—not even the family and the church, and especially not government—can insulate itself from social change. As the context in which political parties function has evolved, so have the parties, sometimes subtly, sometimes dramatically. Political parties have become less dominant in contemporary politics, as families and churches have become less dominant in the lives of contemporary individuals. Whether altered by social fragmentation or by increased pluralism, these institutions nonetheless continue to be vitally important to individuals and society.

Patterns for Party Improvement

The American political parties best suited to serve in a world of steady evolution will be open, flexible, and entrepreneurial, capable of adjusting to a swiftly changing environment. Much public policy is inevitably biased toward the status quo, but public policy, whether purposefully directed at political parties or inadvertently affecting them, should neither weaken nor bolster them artificially.

Especially, attempts to strengthen parties should not challenge the principle of geographic constituencies with officials elected individually. That principle is central to the concept of representation set forth in the Constitution. It leads to candidate rather than party orientation in the system. The potential hazards inherent in altering that founding tenet should weld our loyalty to the American system of constituency-based representation.

It is important, moreover, that public policy not artificially increase the dominance of the two parties that currently are the most influential. Third parties have made important contributions to American public policy and to the efficacy of the political system. The goal should be to strengthen the *party system,* not the two extant parties. Public policies, therefore, ought not unnecessarily penalize third parties, nor capriciously deny them a share of public benefits available to the two major parties.

Nor should public policy contribute to excessive nationalization of the political parties at the expense of state and local parties. Local and state parties continue to provide a link, however tenuous, between voters and the national parties, and among candidates and officials at the several levels of public office. As long as the nation is divided into small constituencies, each electing officials to public office, federal parties are essential.

Public policy toward the parties is important, but it is not the only influence affecting their future well-being. Their own rules and practices affect their vitality. Changes made by the Democratic party in its internal nominating practices precipitated the preoccupation with electoral reform following 1968. Subsequent public actions, especially campaign finance regulation with its ramifications for political finance generally, added to the effects, but changed party rules and practices led the way.

If state and local parties are to survive, and certainly if they are to prosper, they must adapt to changes in their immediate environments. Party rules should therefore permit substantial decentralization in organization and electoral activities. On some issues, especially in the Democratic party, a degree of national regulation would be hard to turn back. Even so, unless issues of equity in participation were to arise, increased nationalization should be resisted by both parties in all areas of party life, including the mode of choosing delegates to the nominating conventions. Excessive central control would rob state and local party organizations of both vitality and capacity to adapt.

Many changes occurring in the political environment in recent decades have brought opportunities as well as threats to the parties. Party leaders can convert threats into opportunities. They should exploit the evolving potentials of polling, computers, personal and media communications, new sources of information, and other innovations to strengthen their parties.

The parties' roles in electoral campaigns need not be diminished by the new technologies and the new professionals who can master them. The parties can modernize themselves and increase their capacity to serve candidates who run under their banners at all levels. Communications consultants can work for party victory even as precinct captains once did. Such help would encourage candidates to identify with their party. The new political specialists have become potent actors in the processes of politics. Lee Atwater at age thirty-eight became the chairman of the Republican National Committee, the first professional campaign consultant to head a major party national committee.[3] Shrewd leaders will strive for balance in party affairs between the new technicians and the traditionally important party activists, both of whom have contributions to make to the modern political party.

When national legislation is directed at altering the rules of the political game, or otherwise affecting the distribution of political power, those who make the laws usually want to ensure that they themselves are protected. Proposals for change are often advanced as being best for the political system as a whole—with minimal proclaimed regard for how a party, group, or individual might gain or lose—but legislators and presidents will inevitably dwell on the personal effects. Recommendations to rearrange aspects of electoral competition should be scrutinized especially for undesirable benefits to incumbents. Increasing incumbent advantage and entrenching the two extant parties, by sheltering them and the benefits they enjoy from otherwise viable competition, will benefit neither the party system nor the political system.

Campaign Funding and Party Strength

The American political system would benefit if its political parties were more effective as partisan political organizations—notably in stimulating voting participation, contributing to presidential-congressional cooperation, and competing with volunteer candidate organizations and interest groups.

Public policies are often charged with reducing the importance of parties. Campaign finance regulations are especially criticized. Measures to increase the parties' financial role and to encourage more representative financial participation are desirable, but they are also hard to design to gain adoption and still have any prospect of achieving the intended results.

A retreat from some provisions of the federal campaign finance legislation of the 1970s would ameliorate its party-weakening effects. The bill of particulars is long. Public reporting requirements of the Federal Election Campaign Act (FECA) of 1971 made federal candidacies into independent operations for the purpose of reporting financial receipts and expenditures, thereby diluting their already weak ties to party. What is more, the income tax checkoff and tax deduction/tax credit provisions of the 1971 Revenue Act, and the public funding provisions of the FECA amendments of 1974, had a companion effect on presidential candidates. These developments weakened the already loose ties between candidates and their parties. Limitations on amounts that state and national party organizations could contribute to federal election campaigns, imposed by the 1974 amendments but eased somewhat in 1979, added further to the weakening of party ties.

Proposals to strengthen political parties, however, need to be designed specifically for the kind of parties it is desired to strengthen. Any one of the following proposals, chosen from a much larger array, and offered here as illustrations, not recommendations, could bolster the political parties, but some of them might also give an advantage to one of the major parties over the other: remove limits on the sums a party committee may spend to support a candidate; allow national as well as state and local party groups to spend unlimited amounts for buttons, bumper stickers, support of voluntary activities, and get-out-the-vote drives; eliminate limits on contributions to political parties; eliminate restrictions on party contributions to candidate campaign committees; require that uses of "soft money" be reported; direct public funds for presidential campaigns to the parties instead of the candidates.

Herbert E. Alexander envisions a desirable direction in party develop-ment. He proposes that political parties ought again to serve as mediators between policymakers and the individuals and organized groups that help them achieve office through financial support. He does not seek a return to smoke-filled rooms. He hopes, rather, that further changes in campaign finance can build up "modern parties based on democratic principles, open and welcoming, interested in issues, but seeking to accommodate conflicting interests."[4] In regulating campaign finance, the structure of the political parties, and their relative advantages over other organizations in electoral politics, are important considerations.

Campaign finance controls can encourage centralized or decentralized parties. A balanced federalism should be the goal. A viable federal structure within American political parties is highly desirable, and to that end the parties at state and local levels could be strengthened by extending to congressional candidates the provisions of the 1979 FECA amendments. These would permit party committees in localities and states to spend unlimited sums on volunteer activities for congressional candidates. This might encourage the parties to set up volunteer structures every two instead of every four years.[5]

Many proposals for change, however, are primarily oriented toward the goal of strengthening the national parties. They include permitting unlimited party expenditures on behalf of candidates, elimination of limits on the size of individual contributions and on total contributions to political parties, and channeling public funding for presidential campaigns through the parties. Only if such parties were balanced by strong state and local party organiza-tions, however, would they fit the logic of a division of powers between state and national levels of government. Moreover, proposals to channel public funds exclusively through the national parties would have small chance of adoption.

Public policies designed to strengthen the parties without regard to the kinds of parties likely to result carry unpredictable risks and should be resisted. Proposals that would make individual congressional candidates dependent upon a political party for campaign funding—were such a situation actually attainable—would lessen the degree of responsiveness to constituency that Americans have come to expect and demand.

Political parties contribute significantly to the capacity of government to make collective decisions, and they therefore can facilitate the functioning of governmental institutions. But constituency remains an essential presence in the design of American government arrangements and has significant influence on them. Also, the United States is a far-flung and diversified nation with an increasingly heterogeneous population. Constitutional limitations, including shared powers with checks and balances, are the principal sources of restraint in the system against an excessive centralization and uniformity that would ultimately prove unacceptable to the nation. Proposals for highly centralized and disciplined parties able to override constituency influences would leave the system with inadequate restraints and, ultimately, insufficient legitimacy.

Some public actions intended to strengthen presidential leadership through stronger political parties could also have undesired consequences. Policies that resulted, for example, in new constraints on third parties and independent candidacies for federal offices would contribute to unwanted rigidity. Increased incumbent advantage in any form would be undesirable. Incumbents already have dramatic advantages in electoral competition in several ways, including greater access to the media and the perquisites of federal office. Incumbents would gain further advantage through any influence they could command over the distribution of additional funds through party channels.[6]

Disproportionate incumbent advantage benefits neither the political parties nor the political system. Joseph A. Schlesinger found that party influence in Congress is strongest when electoral politics are genuinely competitive, and weakest when they are not.[7] Incumbent advantage can insulate officeholders from political parties as well as from voters. Improving the party system's chances for survival is one thing; guaranteeing the survival of two particular parties in a particular form is quite another. Measures to strengthen individual parties in the short term ought not weaken the party system in the longer term.

Strengthening the parties vis-a-vis other organizations, especially political action committees (PACs), is a major goal of many who want to nourish the parties by means of public policy. Some advocates would improve the parties' competitive position by circumscribing the activities of PACs. Others would leave PACs to their own devices within the existing law. But nothing can be accomplished with a strategy of limitations that does not recognize that the fundamental source of interest-group power—human self-interest—has little to do with campaign finance. Interest groups in the United States get their incentives and take their shape from the environment in which they function—political, governmental, technological, societal.[8]

Television and Party Strength

Television has replaced the political parties as the chief supplier of political information. In doing so it has signally weakened the parties. Consequently, one asks whether television can be used to strengthen parties by building new party links to the electorate.

The most widely advocated proposal, and a highly desirable one, would have government reclaim broadcast time from the networks and assign it to the political parties to use as they see fit. A party could promote itself as a whole or allocate time to its nominees. Free television time for candidates as well as the major parties has been urged by the chairman of both the Republican and Democratic National Committees. Alternatively—and more realistically, given network influence—Congress should appropriate funds to the parties to purchase television time for any use they wish. In either case, the institutional parties would be put before the public more frequently than at present, and by the medium currently most favored. That would temper the pressure on voters to focus on candidates individually and encourage them to view the election in broader context. Such broadcasts under party control would permit the parties to present themselves as they wish rather than as interpreted by television newscasters.[9]

In recent years, the Republican party, with its abundant resources, has purchased television time to promote itself as a party. Traditionally less affluent, the Democratic party has done less as a party to communicate with the public over television.[10] In the short run at least, free television time for the parties, however achieved, would benefit Democrats more than Republicans. Free time carefully provided, however, would be good for the party system as a whole.

The number of American television channels has grown so much in recent years that small risk exists that the kind of political party dominance of broadcast time found in Great Britain, which has concerned some, will develop in the United States. Individual candidates, groups spending independently for campaign communication, and the television press all contribute to the campaign discourse. The First Amendment and the pervasive habit of Americans to organize to influence the social agenda make unlikely a system of campaign communications like that found in Great Britain.[11]

If political parties have too great an advantage in their hold on electoral communications in Great Britain due to lack of competition from other sources, they have been at too much of a disadvantage in recent years in the United States. Not only are the parties and the party system likely to benefit from greater institutional communication by each of the parties, but voters and other citizens would also gain from the resulting enriched information. Political parties ought not displace other sources of campaign information, but campaign information can be improved by strengthening the voices of the political parties without diminishing other voices.

Any guarantee of television time to political parties, whether reclaimed free from the networks or purchased by public funds, would need to assure reasonable access for third parties—at least for those that demonstrate a specified degree of public interest—without squandering limited national television time on frivolous claimants. Wise policy may not require that minor parties receive time equal to that given the major parties, at least at the outset; but some provision for them is essential to achieve the goal of strengthening the party system, as opposed to fortifying the positions of the current major parties.

Presidential Nominations and Party Strength

There are regulatory measures that should not be taken. Some persons, to strengthen the political parties, have focused on the rules, procedures, and traditions followed in nominating candidates for president and have advocated congressional intervention in matters that historically have been left largely to the parties.

Some urge that Congress adopt a national primary plan, as discussed in Chapter Three, although the several schemes offered vary in particulars. Others would abolish primaries and have Congress legislate that the nominating convention of each party consist of its elected public officials and party leaders.[12] These two proposals seem starkly different, but they share potential consequences. By removing control of this uniquely important activity from the parties, and putting it with Congress and the president, they would fix in law practices that previously could be modified with ease by the parties as changing circumstances made desirable. Such uniform rules would disregard state differences, robbing individual state parties of the ability to adapt general practices to their own circumstances.

Pope McCorkle and Joel Fleishman observe that those who seek congressional regulation of presidential nominations hope to "prolong the political existence of the two major parties" and "ensure a formal institutional status for the two major parties in the presidential nominating process." They maintain that this type of "protectionist" solution would render the parties more akin to public utilities than to autonomous "private" political associations.[13] Evidence that the political parties will disappear is insufficient to warrant statutory measures to preserve them. If sustained only in that way, they would be hollow shells with little influence over their own activities and destinies.

Party Procedures and Party Strength

The rules political parties adopt to govern their own affairs often affect their functioning more than regulations imposed from without. The parties are obviously constrained generally by the environment in which they function, but within limits parties can establish the organizational structures and procedures they judge will best serve their own purposes, the political system, and the nation. Growth in the independent importance of the Republican and Democratic National Committees was fostered by the new political environment that developed after 1968. The previous dominance by state and local party organizations was eroded by the revolution in nominating practices and the growth of competing political activists. At the same time, the national party organizations gained in significance through increasingly effective central fund-raising and increasingly sophisticated modern campaign procedures. In the future as in the past, political parties in the United States will respond to the new conditions in which they find themselves.

In their structures, procedures, and powers of adaptation, it should be hoped that they will be much like those of America's past. This conclusion does not flow from frustration, nor from reverence for tradition. As the parties have evolved over the decades, they have served the nation extraordinarily well. The parties, with their loose and malleable structures, can continue to accommodate the nation's diverse habits and expectations as well as the narrower requirements of the political-governmental order. Parties must be suited to the society and the government they serve.

Continuing adaptation of America's parties to evolving circumstances is required, but modernization does not mean transformation. We have witnessed much recent change. And the process continues,[14] although not at the same pace within both major parties. Recently, the national Democratic party has devoted less time and energy than it did in the years immediately after 1968 to changing nominating rules and procedures. Rules changes after 1984 and 1988 were significant but few in number. They were important less for their immediate effects than for the directions they signaled.

Recognition by the Democratic National Committee of the validity of open primaries in states that had resisted national party dictates against them was important. It signalled awareness by the national party of state differences that strain the principle of uniform national rules and procedures. The Democratic party would gain from expansion of that recognition.

State parties ought to decide whether and how primaries should be used to select national convention delegates. They can decide not to use primaries at all, or to confine them to "beauty contests" that report voter preferences but do not name delegates. In the absence of primaries, delegates are chosen in caucuses or conventions. For purposes of "representation, accountability and responsiveness to party membership," strong state parties may be best served by caucuses and weak state parties by primaries.[15] Such a mixed system permits state parties to choose procedures that will most enhance their influence in nominations. Moreover, a mixed nominating system can contribute more to an aspirant's political education in the widespread and diversified United States than a more uniform system would.[16]

If some states that hold primaries experimented with approval voting, the effects of this controversial proposal could be assessed. Presently, in primary elections a voter votes for only one candidate. The ballotting thus registers only the first preference of each voter. The results may not reveal the candidate most widely acceptable to all factions. In approval voting, we have seen, the voter shows his approval of all candidates he finds acceptable. Advocates of approval voting contend that the candidate with the greatest overall support would thus be elected under their system. Many observers disagree, but experimental use of approval voting in selected multi-candidate state primaries, with careful assessment of the results, would be instructive.[17]

The influence of state Democratic parties would be enhanced desirably if many national party regulations were eliminated and individual states were given greater responsibility for the way national convention delegates are named. Deep opposition from some quarters to moves in that direction would be certain. Nonetheless, the criteria and conditions of delegate selection have gone through such an important metamorphosis that suitable modifications warrant consideration. One proposal would repeal all of the Winograd Commission's complex Rule 11, except for the stipulation that a person wishing to become a national delegate must declare a presidential preference or the desire to go uncommitted. Beyond that stipulation, state parties could decide whether to keep the candidate right-of-approval requirement, and whether to continue to use caucuses for selecting delegates.[18] They should also be permitted to decide whether to allocate their state's delegates by proportional representation, or on a winner-take-all or winner-take-more basis.[19]

A national convention composed entirely of unbound or uncommitted delegates is no longer desirable, much less feasible. But the presence of some uncommitted delegates, which is now encouraged by Democratic provisions for attendance of party leaders and elected officials, is desirable. Preferably, however, uncommitted delegates should be selected late in the primary-caucus season. Ideally, if improbably, they should remain uncommitted until chosen, or even until the national convention meets. As Democratic rules now stipulate, delegates committed to a candidate and selected on that basis should be free to reconsider their commitments if political circumstances change significantly in the course of the preconvention season.

The role of state and local political parties in a nomination system of sequential state-based primaries and caucuses is stronger than if a series of regional primaries, or a single national primary, were to be held. Disadvantages of regional primaries or a single national primary were discussed in Chapter Three. State and local party organizations in all their varying strengths and weaknesses continue to be the structural base of political parties. Their potential to contribute to well informed state-based nominating contests remains great. Were the geographic focus of the nomination process expanded to regions, or to the entire nation, state parties would suffer a loss of visibility and importance.

A mixed nominating system of sequential state presidential primaries and caucuses usefully exposes candidates to the complexity of the nation. Such a system reflects the composition of the "party coalition" in the electorate, and offers voters and candidates constructive time to learn about each other. Flexible, adaptable state parties are likely to be stronger parties, and stronger state parties are indispensable to a stronger national party system.

The Democratic party continues to struggle with a confounding problem that arose in the wake of changes after 1968. The Democratic National Convention suddenly became more a convention of political amateurs than ever in the past. Energetic newcomers worked to wrest control of the party, and especially of presidential nominations, from, as they saw it, the death grip of "professional" politicians. The effort succeeded to a flaw. There had always been a hefty turnover in delegates from one quadrennial convention to the next, but the number of old-style party followers in evidence at Democratic National Conventions beginning in 1972 declined precipitously. Incremental adjustments in party rules have increased their numbers in more recent conventions.

While all elements of a party can be important to its strength and development, public officials who blend state and local viewpoints with a national outlook can reinforce the federal character of the party and enrich the convention's perspective on platforms and candidates. If the national Democratic party were to assign to the state parties the bulk of responsibility for deciding, within legal limits, how to select delegates to the national convention, and otherwise to conduct their affairs, it would still have major contributions to make to a well-ordered federal party strong at both national and lower levels.

The different experience of the Republican national party is telling. It did not spend its energies prescribing in detail what its state parties should and should not do. Rather, it set out to modernize and professionalize its own capacities to serve as an effective partner in Republican electoral campaigns at all levels of government. Increased prowess in fund-raising, polling, the production of campaign advertisements, and other processes central to modern campaigning has made the national party a resource of mounting value to Republican candidates. The Republican party as an institution has been skillfully promoted. Clearly evident has been a desire to find the means best suited to the new times for establishing links between the party and the voters.

The measures mentioned above illustrate activities that a national party can take to strengthen the leadership it offers the nation. Divisions of responsibility, labor, and expertise can embrace the best of both centralization and decentralization, providing a foundation for strong, truly federal political parties with much to offer candidates and party organizations at all levels of the system.

Amid the welter of concerns Americans have felt or heard about their presidential nominating procedures, a voice from across the Atlantic came in 1988. *The Economist* headed an editorial comment with: "A system that works—For all their flaws, America's primaries and caucuses have produced two decent candidates with distinctive views."[20]

IMPROVING CAMPAIGN FINANCE

The relation of campaign funding to party strength was addressed above in the recommendations for improving political parties. In Chapter Three the importance of money to political communication was emphasized. The conclusions and recommendations here pertain to money as an agent of political participation, a matter treated in detail in Chapter Six.

Money has attracted special notice in politics because of its easy conversion to diverse political uses, and because some people have a lot more of it than others. The history of legislative efforts to regulate campaign finance has been long and frustrating for its advocates. Changes made by congressional actions in the 1970s, however, produced what many deemed significant improvements. But in 1988, startling increases in "soft money" and permissive rulings of the Federal Election Commission raised questions about the ultimate effectiveness and fate of the efforts at control. Some improvement, nonetheless, is possible. The conclusions and recommendations proposed to better the practices of presidential campaign finance are these:

Do not attempt to restrict the volume of campaign spending by candidates and parties for authorized purposes.

Do not purposefully and unnecessarily handicap third parties and independent candidates by finance regulations. In fact, changes in political finance should help rather than hinder such parties and candidates.

Encourage multiple opportunities for financial participation, including restoring the income tax credit for small political contributions.

Raise the limit on individual contributions to nomination campaigns and the amount matchable by federal funds, and repeal the aggregate annual limitation and the state-by-state spending limits in nomination contests.

At least double the amount taxpayers may earmark on their federal income tax returns for the Presidential Election Campaign Fund.

Retain and increase public funding of major presidential nominees in the general election.

The Federal Election Commission (FEC) should monitor carefully and publicize effectively the activities of independent electoral groups, but not attempt to restrict contributions to noncandidate committees.

Fundamental, radical improvement in the clarity of purpose, operating conditions, and quality and comprehensiveness of the reporting functions of the FEC is essential. The commission's address to "soft money" especially needs revision, toward the goal of authentic, prompt, and comprehensible public disclosure as the cornerstone of campaign finance regulation.

Guides for the Future

Although there are no accepted standards, the sums now spent for political campaigning may not be excessive when viewed as the cost of trying to educate and stimulate the electorate of a large, heterogeneous nation of a quarter of a billion people. Howard R. Penniman calculated that expenditures per eligible voter in federal primary and general election campaigns in the United States in 1980 were substantially less than comparable expenditures in the same year in the Federal Republic of Germany, Ireland, Israel, Venezuela, and—including the value of free television and radio time—Canada as well.[21]

In a democracy, effective political education of both voters and candidates is essential. It is also time-consuming and expensive. The large, innovative changes in campaign finance regulation adopted in 1971 and since have not eliminated all the concerns they addressed. As we saw in Chapter Six, the ingenuity of political interests in mastering their environment is capacious. It suggests several guides for future regulation.

While the view that campaign expenditures should be restricted is easily understood,[22] there is little American experience to suggest the feasibility of doing so on any significant scale with the desired results. Consequently, attempts should not be made to restrict campaign expenditures by candidates and parties for authorized purposes. It is in the public interest for politically significant aspirants to be able to raise and spend money in nomination and election campaigns sufficient to inform themselves and potential voters adequately about both issues and personalities.

Fund-raising requirements can weed out nuisance candidates, but they ought not be so burdensome that by themselves they dissuade tested, eligible political leaders from running for president. It should be feasible for such leaders to field a viable nomination campaign while holding another political office.

Nor should third parties and independent candidates be purposefully handicapped by campaign finance regulations. The temptation to those in power is both great and understandable, but proposals for new campaign finance changes should avoid adverse effects on third parties.

Because private contributions can best come from a large number and variety of sources, multiple opportunities for financial participation should be encouraged. Abundant small and moderate contributions by individuals expand the base of financial participation and especially should be fostered.

Finally, the quality of the system and confidence in it will be fortified when the origins and uses of political contributions are reliably reported and publicized.

Nominations

Beginning in 1972, and until new tax legislation in 1986, an income tax credit could be claimed for *50 percent* of political contributions to qualified political candidates or committees—national, state, and local—up to a total credit of $50 per contributor or $100 on a joint return. The 1986 legislation eliminated the credit. The credit had been designed to encourage individuals to broaden their financial participation in electoral politics by means of small contributions. In 1982, Harvard University's Campaign Finance Study Group had recommended that the tax credit be *raised from 50 to 100 percent* of individual contributions to candidates and political parties—but not to PACs—up to a maximum contribution of $50 per person, or $100 on a joint return.[23] Tax credits for political contributions to political parties and candidates should be restored.

The limits on contributions to nomination campaigns should be raised. Increasing the amount individuals may give to support aspirants to a presidential nomination would acknowledge the effects of inflation on campaign costs, as well as the candidate's need for early seed money. Several recommendations are offered to facilitate direct contributions to presidential campaigns to reduce the incentives to make independent expenditures. Each of several proposals to raise limits on contributions has merits and any combination of them, provided the raises were large enough, would be desirable: increase the limit on individual contributions from $1,000 to $5,000 per candidate; apply to the contribution limit the automatic cost-of-living increases from the base year of 1974 that now apply to the prenomination campaign spending limit;[24] index to inflation both the contribution limit to a single campaign and the $25,000 annual limit on the total an individual may contribute to all federal election campaigns;[25] better still, repeal the $25,000 aggregate annual limit to permit individuals to contribute to more federal election campaigns, and directly to political parties;[26] round new limits to the nearest $100 to ease compliance.

If there were an increase in the amount of each individual's contribution in presidential nomination campaigns that can be matched with federal funds, the fund-raising burden on candidates would be eased. Since the inception of public funding in 1976, federal funds have matched the first $250 of all individual contributions up to a maximum of half of the prenomination campaign spending limit, which is $10 million plus a cost-of-living increase from the base year 1974. In 1984, the maximum federal subsidy any one candidate could receive was $10.1 million, half of the $20.2 million prenomination campaign spending limit. In 1988 the limit rose to $23.1 million and the subsidy to $11.5 million.[27] Proposals have been made to increase the amount that can be matched, while retaining the existing dollar-for-dollar ratio of matching funds to individual contributions.[28] A sensible alternative suggested by Michael S. Berman, treasurer of Walter Mondale's presidential campaign, would index the $250 matchable amount to inflation so that it is increased automatically on the same basis as the expenditure limits. He also recommended extending the period during which contributions can be matched. It might, he argues, usefully begin as early as two or three years before the election year and extend to at least one full calendar year beyond it.[29]

Eliminating an aspirant's national expenditure limit in the nomination campaign would encourage a more even distribution of expenditures during the primary season. If not eliminated, the limit should be raised substantially. Candidates now spend heavily in the early stages of the campaign—it is called front-loading—running the risk that they will not be able to spend sufficiently in the later contests when the general public has become more attentive. This was the case with Ronald Reagan in 1980 and Walter Mondale in 1984.

Repeal of state-by-state spending limits in presidential prenomination contests would also rationalize the flow of political information by permitting candidates to spend adequate sums to reach the voters in a given state. Serious accounting and enforcement problems are generated by the existing state-by-state restrictions. Moreover, they prevent candidates from spending what they consider necessary to communicate effectively with a state's voters.

The proposal to increase the amount that taxpayers may earmark for the Presidential Election Campaign Fund from $1 to $2 on individual income tax returns and from $2 to $4 on joint returns, or higher, would help insure adequate public funding in the future, which would be especially needed if the prenomination spending limit were raised or repealed.[30] The staff of the FEC estimated in early 1990 that at present levels of subsidy the fund's balance might well be exhausted by the end of 1992, even with no increased rate of inflation.[31]

The General Election

Public funding of major-party presidential nominees in the general election campaign should also be retained. The public treasury grants are $20 million plus a cost-of-living adjustment from the base year 1974. Each major party candidate received a grant of $40.4 million in 1984 and $46.1 million in 1988. In addition, the national parties may raise a sum to be spent by them on behalf of the ticket, the maximum being $8.3 million in 1988. Only political parties can legally make direct expenditures that are coordinated with the candidate's campaign in a publicly funded general election. That has not, however, freed the candidates from making time-consuming appeals for contributions to party committees.

In recent years, legislation has been proposed to increase the general election expenditure limit, and accordingly the public funds within the candidate's control, as well as the amount a political party can spend on behalf of its presidential nominee.[32] If more public funds were given to the candidates, the comparative value of independent expenditures on their behalf would be diminished. If additional money is necessary for candidates and parties to communicate effectively with the electorate, increasing public and party funds for that purpose is wholly appropriate. The extent to which those extra resources would curb the growth of electoral activity by independent groups, however, is doubtful, as suggested by the large independent funds raised in 1988.

The electoral activities of independent groups are healthiest when visible. They merit careful monitoring by the FEC. Otherwise, attempts to regulate or restrict contributions to noncandidate committees should be avoided. This view does not appeal to many who would direct political energies as much as possible to within the political parties, yet major societal shifts that bear on the matter have occurred.

In all democratic societies, groups express a growing politics of opinions, as opposed to a traditional politics of interests, with corresponding effects on political agendas. Groups have arisen in response to many new societal conditions, including the increased diversity of interests, the consequent increased issue orientation of the electorate, the growth of positive government, and media coverage of issues, especially by television. Computerized mailing lists facilitate the ability of special-interest groups to communicate directly with individuals. The contributions of independent groups to the political debate in a presidential campaign, even when the appeals are negative, are not avoidable; in fact, they enrich the exchange of information and help balance the agenda-setting power of the press.

Changes in political finance should help rather than hinder third parties and independent candidates. Federal subsidies to qualifying presidential candidates, for example, are needed during the heat of the general election campaign, not retroactively. A provision enabling a qualifying minor party to receive such subsidies in a timely fashion would enhance its capacity to compete effectively.

Administering the Federal Election Campaign Act

Early in 1988, a writer in *Time* reporting on the financing of the nominating contests declared that "cynicism is rampant because enforcement by the Federal Election Commission is belated and haphazard."[33] That same year Brooks Jackson, who had searchingly examined money in congressional politics, declared that Congress had designed the commission to fail and concluded that "the Federal Election Commission doesn't do its job, and any serious reform plan must overhaul it or replace it."[34]

The lenient stance of the FEC toward campaign practices, including reporting expectations and the solicitation and uses of soft money, has often been criticized, but also frequently welcomed. Improvement in the assigned functions and operating conditions of the FEC, and in public understanding of them, is essential to bettering presidential campaign finance practices. Making public to the fullest extent feasible the sources and uses of electoral money should be the steady goal. Required reports should be simplified. To relieve candidates, their campaign staffs, and the FEC of tasks that have become unproductively onerous, the size of contributions to be reported with their source should be increased from $200 to at least $500.[35]

On the other hand, requiring disclosure of carefully defined soft-money contributors, contributions, and expenditures would give the attentive public an informed sense of the sources and uses of the mounting sums of such money. It is given to state and local parties for volunteer-oriented, "party-building" functions on behalf of the presidential ticket, and it is not presently subject to federal contribution limits or disclosure requirements. Early in the 1988 campaign, the Democrats pledged to raise some $42 million in soft money and the Republicans spoke of $30 million to $50 million.[36] One estimate near the end of the campaign was $50 million each, about five times the 1984 total, although later estimates were half or less than that. Herbert E. Alexander reported *national* soft-money totals for 1988 as $22 million for Republicans and $23 million for Democrats.[37]

Critics of contemporary campaign finance worry about devices that enable candidates, parties, and PACs to bypass federal contribution and expenditure limits. Many vehicles are used to channel unregulated funds into presidential races, including committees backing persons who aspire to go as delegates to the national conventions, presidential PACs, state-level PACs, and—in their ultimate effects—some tax-exempt research, educational, and civic foundations. Rather than seeking to amend federal election law to close such loopholes, assuming such were possible, it would be preferable to ensure disclosure by the FEC in a clear and timely manner of the source, amount, and recipient of contributions, and the amount and purpose of expenditures. Political campaigns need money. When donated and spent in the sunshine, the potential for mischief, misunderstanding, and corruption is less than when it passes in the shadows.

The FECA's disclosure provisions should be the cornerstone of campaign finance regulation, even when restrictions are attempted to prevent the commercial exploitation of contributor lists. A conference of presidential finance officers recommended in both 1984 and 1988 that a centralized process at the national level be developed to report gifts and uses of soft monies by analyzing their distribution to state and local levels in support of presidential campaigns. These professionals also proposed that the FEC improve its usefulness by emphasizing trends and new developments in campaign finance, by using more graphics in data dissemination, and by making computerized finance data available. All these moves would enhance the value of information the FEC makes available to the public.[38]

To perform its missions more effectively, the FEC needs to be freed from several current constraints. Its internal processes should be more independent of congressional control. The scope of its jurisdiction and responsibility, as well as the roles of its staff director and general counsel, should be more clearly defined by Congress. The commission's budget should be increased to enable it to discharge its responsibilities more effectively.[39] Most importantly, only persons of deep commitment to those responsibilities should be appointed to the commission. It would doubtless help, for reaching decisions, if the commission were composed of an odd number of members instead of an even six.

All actions that encourage widespread, publicized, popular financial participation in politics enhance the prospects for more nearly representative participation and political agendas.

IMPROVING THE GENERAL ELECTION

The basic function of a general election for president is to choose by acceptable means a national chief executive, but it also does much more that is essential for the success of democracy in the United States.

One challenge is to enhance the election's function in generating information in forms that will be most useful to parties, candidates, and voters at many levels of political interest and sophistication. Another is to encourage electoral participation. And proposals for improving the general election campaign should not run so contrary to deeply held American expectations and values as to give them small chance of success.

Following are conclusions and recommendations to improve the general election:

Retain the electoral college.

Amend the Twelfth Amendment to the Constitution to require that members of the electoral college must vote in accord with their state's popular vote.

Amend the Twelfth Amendment to require that when an election of a president is thrown into the House of Representatives, the members will vote individually, not by state delegations.

Amend the Twenty-second Amendment to permit presidents to succeed themselves without limit.

By state action, make voter registration as easy as possible compatible with protection of ballot integrity, including universal voter enrollment, election-day registration, mail registration, and notification to registration officials by the U.S. Postal Service of change-of-address requests.

By federal legislation, require states to permit registration through a uniform date close to the election, to keep registration offices open long hours, to assure liberal provision for absentee voting, and to implement automatic transfer of registration of all movers within a state.

By federal legislation, require all states to keep all polls open twenty-four hours—the same twenty-four hours in real time—or, absent that, require all states except Alaska and Hawaii to keep them open the same hours in real time.

By state action, make voting as easy as possible by liberal absentee voting procedures, convenient location of polling places, and guarantees of time off to vote.

By action of political parties, candidates, civic groups, schools, and the media, mobilize voter participation.

Avoid public policies that limit the amount, variety, form, and quality of political information available to the public, including that in radio and television political commercials and public affairs programming.

Extend the value of presidential debates among contestants in primaries and the general election through experimentation and modification in format, frequency, sponsorship, and participants.

The Electoral College

The oft-maligned electoral college should be retained even though it does slightly magnify the presidential votes of citizens in smaller states. Each state's electoral votes are determined by the number of its representatives plus its senators, and the latter number two for every state regardless of population. Also, presently in every state except Maine, all of a state's electoral votes go to the winner of popular votes in the state. Votes cast for another candidate are therefore said to be "lost." And Gallup polls report that many citizens, when asked cold, say they would prefer direct popular election of president and vice president. So do some political analysts,[40] and it is always possible that one year an incongruous result could precipitate widespread loss of confidence in the electoral college system.

The notion of direct popular election has a down-to-earth appeal, but it is the complicated truth that the electoral college as it now functions serves the unique American system in valuable ways. It compels presidential candidates to seek to understand the heterogeneous continental nation they would lead because it forces them to conduct more decentralized, state-focused canvasses than they otherwise would, especially under contemporary pressures toward national media appeals. And the incentive for a presidential candidate to attend to the concerns of state-based constituencies also helps a president in office understand constituency pressures on members of Congress.

It is argued, nonetheless, that the unit rule is not well-suited to a time when loyalty to the two traditional major parties is declining, although some defenders of two-party politics would advocate it for that very reason. In the early nineteenth century, some states chose some electors by districts, and states could choose to do so now, as in fact Maine did by legislation adopted in 1969 and as Democratic partisans were advocating in some other states in 1990.[41] Choosing electors by districts would be much preferable to direct popular election. So would award of bonus votes in the electoral college to the popular vote leader, as proposed by a task force of the Twentieth Century Fund in 1978.[42]

As recommended in Chapter Five, two changes should be made in the electoral college by amending the Twelfth Amendment to the Constitution. The Constitution should stipulate that a state's electoral votes go automatically to the winner of the popular vote in that state, eliminating the possibility, albeit remote, that an elector could vote contrary to the plurality in his state to affect a close outcome. In five instances in presidential elections from 1956 to 1976, an "errant" elector voted in the electoral college for a candidate other than the one who carried his state. In 1988, in a declared protest against the system, a West Virginia Democratic elector voted for Lloyd Bentsen for president and Michael Dukakis for vice-president.[43]

It has been argued, as also noted in Chapter Five, that such flexibility is desirable to permit major-candidate electors in a possible multicandidate race to switch to the other major candidate to avoid throwing the election into the House of Representatives.[44] The electoral college already operates to bolster two-party dominance, however, and if American politics were to change so radically that a third or fourth party might threaten the present two-party supremacy, it would be better for the system to register that development than to depress it further. For that reason, the proposal to award bonus votes in the electoral college to the candidate receiving a plurality of popular votes is not desirable, although it would be much preferable to the direct election of president.

Another constitutional change could be more consequential. Presently, if no candidate receives a majority of votes in the electoral college, the choice goes to the House of Representatives where *each state has one vote* in making the decision. No presidential choice has been thrown into the House of Representatives since 1824, but with the present and possibly growing fluidity in party loyalties, leading to the contingency, remote though it may seem, of significant third or fourth candidates, the House may be called on again. Representatives now directly represent their constituents in a way different from the original concept of representing their constituents' state. The unit rule should be dropped. Each representative should be required to vote individually in a House election of the president.

Also, the Twenty-second Amendment to the Constitution should be repealed. It says that no one shall be elected president more than twice, and in some cases not more than once. It was adopted in 1951 in reaction to

Franklin Roosevelt's four terms. And many a Democrat was relieved in 1988 when it removed the possibility that Ronald Reagan could run again. Proposals for repeal are controversial and seldom command serious support.

The character of the presidency has changed mightily in the decades following World War II. So has the system for nominating presidential candidates. The filter formerly provided by party leaders in the states (and in Congress) has lost much of its effectiveness, being largely supplanted by polls, primaries, mass media, and open conventions as sources of influence and delegate support. Nonetheless, more basic restraints affect a president's tenure, as Lyndon Johnson demonstrated in 1968 and Richard Nixon discovered in 1974. And Jimmy Carter, in the White House, was challenged for his party's nomination in 1980. The country is still capable of protecting itself against undesired candidates, in office or out. A president ought to benefit from whatever leadership influence the possibility of running again might give him.[45] Moreover, the nation should have the option of commissioning a president for further service. By the same token, any move toward a single six-year term should be resisted.

Registration and Voting

The discussion in Chapter Seven underlies the recommendations made here to increase registration and voting and covers other procedures that may be appealing to some jurisdictions. Unlike some phases of presidential selection, effective legal and administrative actions can be taken to affect those two matters.

The requirement in most states that a person must register in advance in order to vote seriously impedes higher voter turnout. Thus proposals are advocated to make registration easier. At the extreme are plans for universal enrollment that would remove the citizen's personal responsibility to register. Most other democracies, including Canada, have programs of voter enrollment that place the registration burden on the national government rather than the individual.

In the United States, however, the states have always controlled election administration, and the desire to avoid federal regulation of registration and election administration traditionally has run deep. Many citizens, out of varied motives, have devoutly opposed any government-sponsored enumeration that would make their names and addresses easily accessible. Any plan that departs significantly from existing practices and their conceptual underpinnings must overcome strong opposition.[46] Individual states, however, should examine experience elsewhere with universal voter enrollment—in Idaho, for example—for its applicability to their own circumstances.

Making it possible to register on election day would ease registration for all, but especially for persons who travel regularly or move frequently. The *New York Times* asked editorially after the 1988 election, "Why not allow voters to establish their identities on Election Day with Social Security cards or driver's licenses?"[47] Maine, Minnesota, North Dakota, Oregon, and Wisconsin have had instructive experience with election-day registration.[48] Citizens whose interest is stirred only close to election day, or who are perplexed by procedures and deterred by deadlines, would find registration on voting day easier. National legislation mandating election-day registration has been proposed, but not adopted. The dangers of fraud vary greatly from state to state, but all states should consider election-day registration appropriate to their own circumstances, and when adequate protections against fraud can be assured, should adopt it.

Some twenty states and the District of Columbia permit voters to register by mail. With safeguards, states can thus facilitate citizen qualification to vote.[49] Among a variety of proposals to make registration more convenient, a promising one is described in Chapter Seven. If a change of voting address occurs, a copy of the U. S. Postal Service change-of-address notice could be sent to the chief election official in the state where the move originated. Since approximately 83 percent of all changes of residence in the United States are made within a state, this would help registrars keep their rolls current. More importantly, automatic reregistration could be provided. And if the person were not already enrolled, an invitation to register by mail or otherwise could be sent.[50] With adequate means of personal identification, opportunities for fraud could be minimized.

Gary R. Orren endorses such automatic transfer and, as we saw in Chapter Seven, has proposed to ease registration further by a federal mandate requiring states to permit registration through a date, uniform in all states, close to the election; to keep registration offices open longer hours than now customary; and to assure liberal provisions for absentee registration.[51] States should take these steps whether federal legislation is enacted or not. Citizens of all states should have a reasonably equivalent opportunity to register and vote, though a technically identical one does not seem necessary, leaving detailed administrative arrangements to each state.

Once registration requirements are met, voting itself is relatively simple. Proposals are made, nonetheless, to facilitate voting. Keeping the polls open for twenty-four hours—the same twenty-four hours in real time in every state—strikes this observer as a worthwhile symbolic and practical federal measure, albeit expensive, but few agree. Costs would be substantial and in some areas extra steps would be needed to protect the integrity of the balloting. Nonetheless, a salutary influence on voting participation ought to result. In any event, projections of election results should not be made until all polls in all states—or at least in the lower forty-eight—have closed at the same hour in real time, whatever that hour may be. Voters ought not be embittered or frustrated by feeling that their votes for president won't count, even if whether and how they vote were not significantly affected by projections. The Uniform Regional Poll Closing bill referred to in Chapter Seven has passed the House of Representatives several times in recent years and has seemed to have a possibility in the Senate as well.

The chance to vote near one's place of work, rather than in the precinct where one lives and is registered, would facilitate voting in urban areas where people work some distance from their designated polling places. Stringent safeguards against fraud would be needed. In the absence of targeted research, it is difficult to predict the likely increases in voter turnout. In states where it does not now exist, time-off-to-vote legislation that permits employees to leave the job to vote—two hours often being suggested—with or without compensation, might increase voter turnout somewhat. Thirty states now have such legislation, and those that do not should adopt it. All states should also enact liberal absentee voting rules, with procedural protections against fraud.[52] And the mounting use of electronic voting procedures calls for constant alertness by election officials at all levels to insure that the integrity of vote casting and counting under new as well as old conditions is assured, and that it is perceived to be so.

As long as registration and voting are viewed as an individual's personal responsibility, procedural measures can facilitate but not ensure larger and more representative voter participation. Changes such as those proposed need always to be supplemented by mobilizing efforts of political parties, candidates, civic groups, schools, and the media. Citizens are most likely to vote when they perceive a clear personal stake in an election result.

Information Exchange

Former president Gerald R. Ford has observed that "our process of nominating and selecting presidents . . . forces candidates to take positions on issues in an unrealistic atmosphere."[53] His statement poses a dilemma of elective politics. It is accurate, yet the practice cannot be avoided if voters are to have a fair crack at assessing the candidates and their claims. A presidential election campaign should generate the optimum volume of political information that would be useful in the campaign and later to voters, candidates, parties, and their government. As discussed in Chapter Four, public policy should minimize conditions that limit the amount or quality of relevant information, restrict its variety, or make it confusing to the citizens of many degrees of political interest and sophistication to whom it would be useful in forming opinions.

Education for informed, effective participation is essential to democratic politics and can take many forms. Citizens vary greatly in their political knowledge, experience, interest, and ability to comprehend and assess political messages reaching them. Low voting participation already renders the voting public unrepresentative of the nation. Instructive political advertising therefore has great importance as a potential stimulant to political interest, understanding, and participation.

Television commercials, even the much-criticized thirty-second spots— even the shorter "sound bites" of traditional political advocacy—are not wholly devoid of substance. In fact, they are often a highly significant source of information not only for less-interested, less-attentive, less-informed voters, but for all to whom a phrase can symbolize a goal (a "new deal" for the American people) or a pledge ("no new taxes").[54] And for those worried about demagoguery, it can be found in long speeches as easily as in short quips. To eliminate paid political advertising or, as often suggested, to restrict it to lengthier commercials would diminish the diverse information mix useful in a democracy of heterogeneous constituencies. To do so would handicap those potential voters who are least effectively exposed to other political information. With political commercials of differing lengths and characteristics, political messages can reach an electorate of many degrees of political interest and sophistication.[55]

Pluralism among the sources of political commercials also enriches the information environment. To restrict those sources would normally favor incumbent officeholders. Political advertising by candidates, political parties, independent groups, third-party individuals, and others invigorates and informs political competition. It would be reasonable to require that ads mentioning an opponent and paid for by a candidate or his committee bear the face or voice of the candidate. But in any event, strengthening the voices of political actors in comparison with the interpretations of press and broadcasters is highly desirable. Strong, competitive political parties and well-organized diverse groups, in addition to candidate organizations, contribute to a valuable exposition of attitudes and positions, to some extent offsetting the influences of the audience-counting media.

Television coverage of campaign activities, beginning with the conventions, along with political commercials on behalf of candidates provide political information useful to voters during a general election campaign. Television coverage of conventions offers viewers information about issues as well as perceptions of candidates and parties—an interesting condition, because television news, unlike newspaper articles, does not seem to convey meaningful information to voters about issues. The televised presidential debates, however, do increase viewer's awareness and knowledge of issues, and debates held close to the election refresh voters' recollections of information already acquired but forgotten. The limitations of the televised presidential and vice-presidential debates that have been held since 1960 during the general election campaign are much noted. (Limited radio debates among aspirants for party nomination were held as early as 1948.[56]) The televised debates at least have given voters opportunities to observe the candidates under a special kind of stress, a glimpse of their personalities and character, and insight into their ability to handle situations they cannot fully control.[57]

Proposals for presidential debates during the general election campaign usually address their sponsorship, frequency, and format, but the differing expectations held for them lead to divergent plans. Representative Lee Hamilton, Democrat of Indiana, has proposed that in each of six or eight weeks before the election each candidate should address a major issue and then submit to questioning by a panel of experts.[58] The *New York Times* proposed editorially after the 1988 election that participation in a specified number of debates of specified kinds be made a condition of qualifying for federal campaign funds.[59] Democratic Representative Edward J. Markey and Republican Senator Bob Graham in 1989 advocated that to qualify for public funding presidential candidates be required to participate in four debates (and their vice-presidential running mates in one) under nonpartisan sponsorship.[60] John B. Anderson proposed for 1992 a scheme of nineteen meetings, conferences, and debates, with differing participation by candidates, supporters, interlocutors, and inquisitors, with twelve of the sessions to be broadcast.[61] Kathleen Hall Jamieson and David S. Birdsell in 1988 reviewed political debating in interesting detail from before the American Revolution onward. They framed a comprehensive set of recommendations, among them a call for the candidates, press, and public to view the campaign "as a series of distinct but equally important communicative events."[62]

In April 1986, the bipartisan Commission on National Elections recommended that between Labor Day and the election three debates should be scheduled for major presidential candidates (because of Republican insistence, only two were held in 1988) and one for vice-presidential candidates, and that the debates should follow a format congenial to the candidates.[63]

The commission also recommended that the 1988 presidential debates be sponsored by the two major parties instead of, as previously, the nonpartisan League of Women Voters. The change seemed self-serving and if adhered to could further handicap third-party movements.[64] Nonpartisan sponsorship should be restored, perhaps even sponsorship by a federally funded commission, if that proved necessary. Over the nation's life, third parties have rendered authentic, salutary services as political interests and issues have evolved. They are already placed at an excessive disadvantage in U.S. presidential politics by measures designed to prevent harrassment by frivolous and insignificant movements. Sponsors of the debates, whoever they may be, ought not deny reasonable participation to a third-party or independent candidate who gives evidence of attracting as large a following as John B. Anderson did in 1980.

Suggestions to vary the format offer an opportunity to enhance the value of future debates. A report from Canada in October 1988 reported that "an angry, finger-pointing confrontation on national television ... brought new life to Canada's [national] election campaign." With leaders of the three main political parties participating and arguing directly with each other, and with no time limit on responses, the debate lasted for three hours.[65] In the United States, a panel customarily has questioned the candidates. Head-to-head conflict between the candidates could lead to a sharper exchange of views and presumably greater clarity of issues. A conversational format, however arranged, would be less stressful.[66] In fact, varying the debate format could be beneficial.

At least some of the debates ought to include a panel of questioners. Elihu Katz, a critical observer of the more party-dominated exchange of political information in Great Britain, argues that the questions of journalists who serve as interrogators in American campaign debates do in fact represent the voters' interests. They raise the uncomfortable "no-win" issues that the candidates themselves might be inclined to avoid.[67] Ideally, experimenting with formats would permit comparisons of candidates' strengths and weaknesses—recognizing that no candidates, except under extreme public pressure, are likely to agree to any arrangement they deem at the outset to be uncongenial to themselves.

Television news coverage of presidential campaigns is persistently criticized, yet proposals to force changes in media practices run afoul of First Amendment protections. Journalists can be exhorted to focus less on "horse-race" aspects of campaigns—hard to do with poll results arriving almost daily—and more on candidate qualifications and issues. But discretion remains with them. As A. M. Rosenthal has said, in such matters "the law cannot give us an answer."[68] The people get what they demand, or tolerate. Manifestly, greater depth in news programs and more sensitive treatment of politics, politicians, and government would contribute to better understanding of the nation's self-government, and thereby contribute to its eventual improvement.

Those who need not be predominantly preoccupied with audience ratings envision many unrealized opportunities through which television programming could advance public understanding of live controversies and latent issues. Republican chairman Lee Atwater—no slouch in exploiting the competitive vulnerabilities offered by television—has urged that giving each candidate five minutes of free television time every night during the last weeks of the race "would change the entire nature of the campaign," forcing the candidates "to campaign on substance and issues." In 1990, the Public Broadcasting Service announced hopes to offer 1992 presidential candidates regular opportunities to speak over television, for several minutes each time, without interruption.[69] Surely more imaginative formats that hold viewer interest could illuminate issues for a wider circle of voters. Special programs during prime time in October could especially afford candidates and other party speakers—including representatives of third parties—the chance to advocate their stands on major issues. Topics of moment such as nuclear weapons and budget deficits, but also lesser and more parochial concerns, could be the foci of longer and deeper discussions than now reach the public.

Candidates, and especially their managers, do not often hanker for such hazardous opportunities. Even so, public funds could properly be used to subsidize such autumn specials if suitable provisions could be made for significant third parties and independent candidates. And Congress has the power, as urged by Martin Schram, to require stations and networks to offer qualifying candidates personal free airtime during both the nomination and election periods, with the requirement in the nomination phase being similar to that needed to qualify for matching federal funds during the pre-convention season.[70]

IMPROVING GOVERNANCE

In recent decades, critics searching for greater coherence and continuity in federal government policies, and greater consistency in their administration, have looked beyond issues of nomination and election to urge institutional adaptations that would bend the American system toward a type of parliamentary government, toward some variation of the kinds found in the British Commonwealth and much of Europe. Concern has been accelerated by the diminished role of political parties in the new media environment of the United States, and by the frequency since 1968 with which neither party simultaneously controls both the presidency and Congress. Such critics acknowledge that the separation and sharing of powers within the federal government, and the division and sharing of responsibilities between it and the states, were knowingly designed to restrain the power of government. They argue, however, that the characteristics of the nation and the issues it must resolve have changed so much over two centuries that fundamental institutional modifications are needed.

The grave importance of maintaining coherence in economic and foreign policy, and more recently the failure to restrain growth in the federal debt, are advanced as reasons to modify the allocation of powers among the branches of the federal government. It is not clear, however, that important substantive issues would be addressed better by Americans and their government if radical changes were made in the established institutional arrangements of the national government.[71]

Two fundamental conclusions emerged from the explorations reported in this book into the means of filling the presidency:

Radical changes in the basic constitutional structure of the federal government are not feasible and ought not be attempted.

Conscious modifications of lesser magnitude ought to combine with natural evolution to adapt the American system to the rapid and radical changes that are inevitable in the technological and social environment.

James Q. Wilson has emphasized that the comparable national deficits in 1984 of eight European parliamentary democracies plus Canada, measured as a percentage of gross national product, were greater than that of the United States. In some instances the deficits, at least in that year, were *several times* greater. Decisiveness and continuity in economic policies in parliamentary systems has limits, too. After World War II, Great Britain nationalized several of its important industries, then denationalized them, then nationalized and denationalized them again.

Concern for continuity and coherence in U.S. foreign policy underlies anxieties expressed by some over the ability of the present American structure to function adequately in our newly dangerous world. In the conduct of foreign policy, however, presidents already are weighted with exceptional independence, and, for many observers, U.S. experience since 1960 with both Democratic and Republican presidents does not argue for greater independent presidential power.[72] Nonetheless, a sense of peril grips many serious observers. James David Barber wrote, albeit long before Gorbachev came to power in the Soviet Union, that we do not "seem to see the looming international civil war which threatens . . . once and for all, the fragile fabric of the human community."[73]

Mankind may now live in a protracted state of emergency, but it is not clear that Americans would live more safely if the separation of powers or the federal system were changed to give greater independence of action to the president, or greater and swifter curbs on executive initiative to Congress.[74] Such changes in the basic tenets of the constitutional system are unlikely in any event. Presidents will need to do in the future what they have had to do in the past, that is, function largely within the opportunities and limitations of the system as it exists. They will have to do that in foreign policy no matter how heavy they feel their responsibilities to be, nor how heady they envision their opportunities are to make a new world.[75]

Even if some of the structural revisions that have been proposed could be achieved, it is not likely that present realities would be significantly altered. The nation-state continues to be the primary unit of the international order. More and more nations seek to have their material and symbolic interests respected by the foreign policies of other nations. And with the growing importance of the Third World, symbolic politics has become significant in international affairs alongside traditional interest politics, thereby increasing the difficulty of maintaining formal continuity and coherence in a nation's policies.

Few would argue that government in the United States should not be strengthened to become more capable—if you will, more rational, consistent, decisive, and authoritative. But any kind of government in the United States, however outfitted for effective action, must function amidst noisy, assertive, competitive demands—often expressed via faulty media[76]—bearing on both goals and the means of reaching them. If "government" and "politics" are viewed for a moment as separate processes, efforts to make the former more rational and authoritative must be balanced by the heterogeneous needs of a complicated, dynamic, far-flung, decentralized, diverse society.

A politics of parties is a valuable supplement to a politics of groups, minorities, geographic units, and other interests, but typical American voters will not accept a strong, dominating political party as a substitute for their own representative, senators, and president. Americans speak of a government of laws, not men, but American politics—indeed all democratic politics—is highly personal. American politics is often highly emotional, too, with the humor, style, intellect, tastes, instincts, and personality of politicians frequently determining governmental outcomes. Franklin Roosevelt's power to lead derived from his own vision, personality, political instincts, campaign skills, and intelligence, not from his party's or the government's structure. Perhaps this helps to explain Hedley Donovan's observation that it is "incongruous that our presidents, created in an electoral process increasingly separate from the realities of governing, usually represent us well."[77] To be effective, a president's formal authority for national leadership must be augmented by sources of influence outside the official powers of his office.[78] "Personal political authority," writes Judith N. Shklar, "is based on something close to love which is unstable and incalculable, and it has made the liberal state far less procedural and far less predictable than its first designers had hoped."[79]

If some envision strong government for the United States that is dependent for its strength on a dominant political party, it is likely to be a vision unfulfilled.[80] Government must function in the context of the nation's traditional, enduring bases of representation. Those foundations of American representative government are largely hostile to sustained political-party dominance. This context may be a function of the nation's size, of its diversity, of a political culture conditioned by the evolving institutions created in 1787, or all of those plus additional pressures. It is highly unlikely to change readily to altered processes bent on improving governmental efficiency through the grand illusion of disciplining politics. Americans, divided and subdivided into diverse societal, governmental, and political units, will continue to press to get their interests on the nation's agenda, and to have issues decided favorably to themselves. The blessings of democracy are seldom easy pleasures.

Modest as well as dramatic changes in American electoral processes are urged by persons who sense national peril. They argue that if presidential selection can be arranged to assure the nomination of competent candidates, who are able to build comprehensive political bases as they seek nomination and election, the likelihood is high that an effective presidency will ensue. The conviction is appealing, but changes in the electoral process are limited in their power to shape the workings of government. Congress sets its own processes and determines its own leadership. Leadership is exercised by people, but no system can guarantee effective leaders, which should make Americans grateful that the presidency is not the whole of their government.

The electoral process and the institutions of government obviously are interdependent, yet they are separate in their influence on political outcomes. Change in either to some extent affects the other, but alterations in the electoral process have necessarily limited influence on the totality of government. To alter substantially the operations of the nation's subtle and complex system of government would require changing the basic institutional structure. The presidential selection process and organized government must by assayed by standards appropriate to each. Unique benefits of the existing electoral process should not be risked in a vain hope that changes in it could dramatically improve governmental performance.

The way the people of the United States choose their presidents is quintessentially American. The process was made in America. Like the government to which it is prelude, the process lacks the formal consistency of the sort read into arrangements in many other democracies. Its complicated and awkward appearance is the product of the pragmatic compromises embodied in founding precepts, of the evolutionary adaptations to changes in its environment over many decades, and of conscious reform stimulated by changes in prevailing national values.

The system works, albeit to no one's full satisfaction, and to the continuing dismay of some. It accomplishes the selection of a chief executive and keeps the citizenry loosely but surely linked to its government. The present arrangements can be improved, as the proposals made in this book have hoped to demonstrate. Existing practices are but another way station on the long and—Americans can hope—unending road toward a self-government that both consciously and involuntarily adapts to history's most rapidly changing technological, social, and cultural environment.

REFERENCE NOTES

☆
☆

The notes are confined to citations of sources and references. Within each chapter, the first citation is given in full in the note. Subsequent abbreviated citations give the note number of the first citation, unless it is in the immediately preceding note.

Notes for pages vii–3

Foreword

1. Plato, *The Republic,* Book VII.
2. Robert Penn Warren, *New and Selected Essays* (New York: Random House, 1989), 46.

Chapter One. What's the Problem?

1. Laurence I. Barrett, "Oh, What a Screwy System," *Time,* January 25, 1988, 20.
2. *Time,* October 3, 1988, 18–25; Jeffrey K. Tullis, *The Rhetorical Presidency* (Princeton, N.J.: Princeton University Press, 1987), 137–44.
3. Jack W. Germond and Jules Witcover, "Campaign No Test of U.S. Political Direction," *National Journal* 20 (November 5, 1988): 2808.
4. Stephen Hess, "Why Great Men Still Are Not Chosen President," *Brookings Review* 5, no. 3 (Summer 1987): 35; Michael Oreskes, "America's Politics Loses Way As Its Vision Changes World," *New York Times,* March 18, 1990, p. Y16.
5. "Marinated in America," *New York Times,* February 8, 1988, p. 16.
6. *Gallup,* Report No. 230, November 1984, 18.
7. George F. Will, "Two Cheers for Iowa," *Newsweek,* February 1, 1988, 64.
8. William Crotty, *Party Reform* (New York: Longman, 1983), 136.
9. Austin Ranney, ed., *The American Elections of 1980* (Washington: American Enterprise Institute, 1981), 369.
10. David E. Price, *Bringing Back the Parties* (Washington, D.C.: CQ Press, 1984), 209; *Elections '88* (Washington, D.C.: Congressional Quarterly, Inc., 1988), 31.

11. Barrett, "Screwy System" (see n. 1), 22; also, Warren E. Miller, *Without Consent: Mass-Elite Linkages in Presidential Politics* (Lexington: University Press of Kentucky, 1988), 139.

12. Kirkpatrick Sale, *Human Scale* (New York: G.P. Putnam's Sons, 1980), 25.

13. Seymour Martin Lipset and William Schneider, *The Confidence Gap: Business, Labor, and Government in the Public Mind* (New York: Free Press, 1983), 159.

14. Ibid., 408–9; see also Barbara Kellerman, *The Political Presidency—Practice of Leadership* (New York: Oxford University Press, 1984), 3–11.

15. Gordon S. Wood, "The Fundamentalists and the Constitution," *The New York Review of Books,* February 18, 1988, 40.

16. Gordon S. Wood, *The Creation of the American Republic, 1776–1787* (Chapel Hill: University of North Carolina Press, 1969), viii.

17. Ibid., 7–9.

18. See, for example, Fred I. Greenstein, "Nine Presidents in Search of a Modern Presidency," in *Leadership in the Modern Presidency,* ed. Fred I. Greenstein (Cambridge: Harvard University Press, 1988), 347–52.

19. John Naisbitt, *Megatrends: Ten New Directions Transforming Our Lives* (New York: Warner Books, 1982), 159–88.

20. Douglas W. Jaenicke, "The Jacksonian Integration of Parties into the Constitutional System," *Political Science Quarterly* 101 (1986): 85.

21. Kenneth S. Davis, "FDR As a Biographer's Problem," *The Key Reporter* 50 (Autumn 1984): 2.

22. An extensive inventory of proposals to alter presidential selection and the institution of the presidency appears in Marcia Lynn Whicker and Raymond A. Moore, *When Presidents Are Great* (Englewood Cliffs, N.J.: Prentice Hall, 1988), 202–13.

23. Robert E. Hunter, ed., *Electing the President: A Program for Reform* (Washington, D.C.: The Center for Strategic and International Studies, Georgetown University, April 1986), 1.

24. Flora Lewis, "The Quantum Mechanics of Politics," *New York Times Magazine,* November 6, 1983, p. 99.

25. Charles M. Hardin, *Constitutional Reform in America—Essays on the Separation of Powers* (Ames: Iowa State University Press, 1989), ix–xiii.

26. Committee on the Constitutional System, *A Bicentennial Analysis of the American Political Structure* (Washington, D.C.: January 1987), 3; see also Hardin, *Constitutional Reform,* 99–101, 173–76.

27. Miller, *Without Consent,* (see n. 11), 76.

28. *The U.S. Constitution Today* (New York: The American Assembly, Columbia University, 1987), 6. Much analysis accepts divided responsibility between president and Congress in foreign policy and looks for improvement elsewhere, e.g., Cecil V. Crabb, Jr., and Pat M. Holt, *Invitation to Struggle—Congress, the President, and Foreign Policy* (Washington, D.C.: CQ Press, 1989), 250–55.

29. Ryan J. Barilleaux, *The Post-Modern Presidency—The Office after Ronald Reagan* (New York: Praeger, 1988), 154–57.

30. Alexander Hamilton, James Madison, and John Jay, *The Federalist Papers,* ed. Clinton Rossiter (New York: New American Library, 1961), no. 71, 432.

31. Richard Ellis and Aaron Wildavsky, *Dilemmas of Presidential Leadership—From Washington through Lincoln* (New Brunswick, N.J.: Transaction Publications, 1989), 216–17.

32. Fred W. Riggs, "The Survival of Presidentialism in America: Para-constitutional Practices," *International Political Science Review* 9 (October 1988): 272.

Chapter Two. The Lifeblood of Democracy: Information

1. Richard M. Ketchum, *The Borrowed Years—1938–1941* (New York: Random House, 1989), 572-73; National Portrait Gallery, *'If Elected . . . '—Unsuccessful Candidates for the Presidency 1776–1968* (Washington, D.C.: Smithsonian Institution Press, 1972), 363–64.
2. Alexander Hamilton, James Madison, and John Jay, *The Federalist Papers,* ed. Clinton Rossiter (New York: New American Library, 1961), no. 37, 227.
3. George H. Sabine, *A History of Political Theory* (New York: Henry Holt, 1937), 13.
4. Giovanni Sartori, *The Theory of Democracy Revisited* (Chatham, N.J.: Chatham House Publishers, Inc., 1987), 137–38.
5. Allan Rachlin, *News as Hegemonic Reality—American Political Culture and the Framing of News* (Praeger Publishers: New York, 1988), 127.
6. Robert M. Entman, *Democracy Without Citizens—Media and the Decay of American Politics* (New York: Oxford University Press, 1989), 126–27, 129.
7. Ben Wattenberg, "The Reborn Political Center," *New York Times,* August 26, 1984, p. E21.
8. "Consultant Scorecard," *Campaigns and Elections* 9 (December 1988): 22–23. "More than 4,000" political consulting firms of all types are referred to in Carol Matlock, "In Person," *National Journal* 21 (September 30, 1989): 2416.
9. Christopher Arterton, "Presidential Campaigns and the News Media" (Paper prepared for the Study of the U.S. Presidential Selection Process sponsored by the Alfred P. Sloan Foundation, Alexander Heard, Director, 1984), 10.
10. Gary R. Orren, "The Changing Styles of American Party Politics," in *The Future of American Political Parties: The Challenge of Governance,* ed. Joel L. Fleishman (Englewood Cliffs, N.J.: Prentice Hall, 1982), 5.
11. *New York Times,* April 1, 1990, sec. 4, p. 18; John H. Kessel, *Presidential Parties* (Homewood, Ill.: Dorsey, 1984), 571.
12. Pope McCorkle and Joel L. Fleishman, "Political Parties and Presidential Nominations," in Fleishman, *Future of American Political Parties* (see n. 10), 157 .
13. Ivor Crewe, "Electoral Participation," in *Democracy at the Polls: A Comparative Study of Competitive National Elections,* ed. David Butler, Howard R. Penniman, and Austin Ranney (Washington, D.C.: American Enterprise Institute, 1981), 217; also see Brian Lamb and the staff of C-SPAN, *C-SPAN: America's Town Hall* (Washington, D.C.: Acropolis Books Limited, 1988), xiv–xvii.
14. Kessel, *Presidential Parties* (see n. 11), 569, footnote 15.
15. Christopher Arterton, "Political Money and Party Strength," in Fleishman, *Future of American Political Parties* (see n. 10), 134–35.
16. Richard L. Rubin, *Press, Party, and Presidency* (New York: Norton, 1981), 210.
17. U.S. Bureau of the Census, *Statistical Abstract of the United States, 1988* (Washington, D.C., 1987), 125, 140.
18. Everett C. Ladd, Jr., with Charles D. Hadley, *Transformations of the American Party System: Political Coalitions from the New Deal to the 1970s* (New York: Norton, 1975), 292–93.

19. Ibid., 300.
20. Austin Ranney, *Channels of Power: The Impact of Television on American Politics* (New York: Basic Books, 1983), 93.
21. Jeffrey Smith, *American Presidential Elections* (New York: Praeger, 1980), 184.
22. William Greider, "The Rolling Stone Survey: Tuned Out, Turned Off," *Rolling Stone* 523 (April 7, 1988): 53–54. The survey was conducted by Peter D. Hart Research Associates.
23. V. O. Key, Jr., *The Responsible Electorate: Rationality in Presidential Voting, 1936–1960* (Cambridge: Harvard University Press, 1966), 61.
24. Orren, "Changing Styles" (see n. 10), 29.
25. Benjamin I. Page, *Choices and Echoes in Presidential Elections: Rational Man and Electoral Democracy* (Chicago: University of Chicago Press, 1978), 222.
26. Morris P. Fiorina, *Retrospective Voting in American National Politics* (New Haven: Yale University Press, 1981), 197.
27. Michael S. Lewis-Beck, *Economics and Elections—The Major Western Democracies* (Ann Arbor: The University of Michigan Press, 1988), 133.
28. Page, *Choices and Echoes* (see n. 25), 22.
29. See ibid., chap. 2, for a fuller account of these arguments.
30. Smith, *American Presidential Elections* (see n. 21), 181.
31. Page, *Choices and Echoes* (see n. 25), 263.
32. Kessel, *Presidential Parties* (see n. 11), 493.
33. Ibid., 521.
34. Paul R. Abramson, John H. Aldrich, and David W. Rohde, *Change and Continuity in the 1984 Elections* (Washington, D.C.: CQ Press, 1986), 183, 210, 300; Michael Oreskes, "Republicans Show Gains in Loyalty," *New York Times,* January 21, 1990, p. 15.
35. Theodore H. White, "The Shaping of the Presidency, 1984," *Time,* November 19, 1984, 70.
36. Ibid., 83.
37. Marjorie Randon Hershey, *Running for Office: The Political Education of Campaigners* (Chatham, N.J.: Chatham House, 1984), 1.

Chapter Three. Presidential Nominations and Information

1. Andrew Rosenthal, "Simon Takes Gephardt to TV," *New York Times,* February 11, 1988, p. 11.
2. *Time,* March 7, 1988, 19.
3. Richard L. Berke, "1988 Candidates Spent $210 Million," *New York Times,* August 27, 1989, p. 14.
4. Rob Gurwitt, "Unions Hope Endorsement of Mondale ... Will Advance Labor's Legislative Goals," *Congressional Quarterly* 41 (October 8, 1983): 2080.
5. Fred I. Greenstein, "Change and Continuity in the Modern Presidency," in *The New American Political System,* ed. Anthony King (Washington, D.C.: American Enterprise Institute, 1978), 45.
6. George E. Reedy, "Discovering the Presidency," *New York Times Book Review,* January 20, 1985, p. 1.

7. Anthony Smith, "Mass Communications," in *Democracy at the Polls: A Comparative Study of Competitive National Elections,* ed. David Butler, Howard R. Penniman, and Austin Ranney (Washington, D.C.: American Enterprise Institute, 1981), 182.

8. Bert A. Rockman, *The Leadership Question: The Presidency and the American System* (New York: Praeger, 1984), 177.

9. William A. Crotty and John S. Jackson III, *Presidential Primaries and Nominations* (Washington, D.C.: Congressional Quarterly, 1985), 145.

10. Mark J. Wattier, "The Simple Act of Voting in 1980 Democratic Presidential Primaries," *American Politics Quarterly* 11 (July 1983): 284.

11. Crotty and Jackson, *Presidential Primaries* (see n. 9), 83; 1988 primary data from the Associated Press, reported in *New York Times,* June 9, 1988.

12. John H. Kessel, *Presidential Parties* (Homewood, Ill.: Dorsey, 1984), 486.

13. Scott Keeter and Cliff Zukin, *Uninformed Choice: The Failure of the New Presidential Nominating System* (New York: Praeger, 1983), 188.

14. Kathleen Hall Jamieson and David S. Birdsell, *Presidential Debates—The Challenge of Creating an Informed Electorate* (New York: Oxford University Press, 1988), 222–27; Herbert E. Alexander, *Financing the 1976 Election* (Washington, D.C.: Congressional Quarterly Press, 1979), 470–71.

15. "6 Democratic Candidates Agree on Debates," *New York Times,* August 23, 1983, p. 9.

16. Robert Pear, "Democratic '84 Candidates Debate Arms Control," *New York Times,* October 14, 1983, p. 9.

17. *The 1988 World Book Year Book* (Chicago: World Book, Inc., 1988), 295.

18. Keeter and Zukin, *Uninformed Choice* (see n. 13), 112, emphasis added.

19. Thomas E. Patterson, *The Mass Media Election: How Americans Choose Their Presidents* (New York: Praeger, 1980), 75.

20. Ibid., 155.

21. Keeter and Zukin, *Uninformed Choice* (see n. 13), 199.

22. Jeff Greenfield, *The Real Campaign: How the Media Missed the Story of the 1980 Campaign* (New York: Summit Books, 1982), 273.

23. Patterson, *Mass Media Election* (see n. 19), 99.

24. Michael Robinson, reported in *Television and the Presidential Elections: Self-Interest and the Public Interest,* ed. Martin Linsky (Lexington, Mass.: Lexington Books, 1983), 33.

25. Max Farrand, ed., *The Records of the Federal Convention of 1787,* vol. 1 (New Haven: Yale University Press, 1966), 146.

26. Keeter and Zukin, *Uninformed Choice* (see n. 13), 188.

27. Kessel, *Presidential Parties* (see n. 12), 486.

28. Larry M. Bartels, *Presidential Primaries and the Dynamics of Public Choice* (Princeton, New Jersey: Princeton University Press, 1988), 289, 291.

29. Marjorie Randon Hershey, *Running for Office: The Political Education of Campaigners* (Chatham, N.J.: Chatham House, 1984), 99; see also Charles Brereton, *First in the Nation—New Hampshire and the Premier Presidential Primary* (Portsmouth, N.H.: Peter E. Randall Publisher, 1987), xvi.

30. Hershey, *Running for Office* (see n. 29), 94.

31. Farrand, *Records of the Federal Convention* (see n. 25), 253.

32. Hershey, *Running for Office* (see n. 29), 103.

33. John H. Aldrich, *Before the Convention: Strategies and Choices in Presidential Nomination Campaigns* (Chicago: University of Chicago Press, 1980), 196.

34. Pope McCorkle and Joel L. Fleishman, "Political Parties and Presidential Nominations," in *The Future of American Political Parties: The Challenge of Governance,* ed. Joel L. Fleishman (Englewood Cliffs, N.J.: Prentice Hall, 1982), 148–49.

35. Anthony King, "The American Polity in the Late 1970s: Building Coalitions in the Sand," in King, *New American Political System* (see n. 5), 391.

36. Ibid., 390.

37. Roger G. Brown, "Presidents as Midterm Campaigners," in *Presidents and Their Parties: Leadership or Neglect?* ed. Robert Harmel (New York: Praeger, 1984), 145–46.

38. Crotty and Jackson, *Presidential Primaries* (see n. 9), 152–53.

39. Rhodes Cook, "Home-State Political Trouble Can Hit White House Seekers After Their National Plans Fail," *Congressional Quarterly* 43 (July 27, 1985): 1489; Jack W. Germond and Jules Witcover, "It's Never Too Early to Test the Political Waters," *National Journal* 21 (October 7, 1989): 2478.

40. John H. Aldrich, "On the Relationship between Methods of Presidential Nomination and Candidates Who Seek Nomination" (Paper prepared for the Study of the U.S. Presidential Selection Process sponsored by the Alfred P. Sloan Foundation, Alexander Heard, Director, October 1983), 33.

41. Max Frankel, review of Cyrus Vance's *Hard Choices: Four Critical Years In America's Foreign Policy* (New York: Simon and Schuster, 1983), *New York Times Book Review,* May 29, 1983, p. 3.

42. Rockman, *Leadership Question* (see n. 8), 167.

43. Michael Pinto-Duschinsky, "The Conservative Campaign: New Techniques versus Old," in *Britain at the Polls: The Parliamentary Elections of 1974,* ed. Howard R. Penniman (Washington, D.C.: American Enterprise Institute, 1975), 89.

44. Roland Cayrol, "The Mass Media and the Electoral Campaign," in *The French National Assembly Elections of 1978,* ed. Howard R. Penniman (Washington, D.C.: American Enterprise Institute, 1980), 144–45.

45. Howard R. Penniman, "Campaign Styles and Methods," in Butler, Penniman, and Ranney, *Democracy at the Polls* (see n. 7), 114.

46. Sidney Blumenthal, *The Permanent Campaign,* rev. ed. (New York: Simon and Schuster, 1982), 10; emphasis added.

47. Hugh Winebrenner, *The Iowa Precinct Caucuses—The Making of a Media Event* (Ames: Iowa State University Press, 1987), 165.

48. Robert T. Nakamura and Denis G. Sullivan, "Neo-Conservatism and Presidential Nomination Reforms: A Critique," *Congress and the Presidency* 9 (Autumn 1982): 87.

49. Ibid.

50. Kessel, *Presidential Parties* (see n. 12), 564, footnote 13.

51. Paul T. David, Ralph M. Goldman, and Richard C. Bain, *The Politics of National Party Conventions,* rev. ed. (New York: Lanham, 1964), 324–25.

52. Aldrich, *Before the Convention* (see n. 33), 84.

53. Jack W. Germond and Jules Witcover, *Whose Broad Stripes and Bright Stars?—The Trivial Pursuit of the Presidency 1988* (New York: Warner Books, 1989), 280–81.

54. Ronald Smothers, "Black Leaders Who Back Mondale in Alabama Arguing for Pragmatism," *New York Times,* March 12, 1984, p. 13.

55. Penniman, "Campaign Styles" (see n. 45), 129.

56. Kessel, *Presidential Parties* (see n. 12), 254.

57. Bartels, *Presidential Primaries* (see n. 28); see also Nelson W. Polsby, ed., *The New Hampshire Primary* (Chatham, N.J.: Chatham House, 1987).

58. Michael A. Lipton, "Exclusive TV Guide Poll: Campaign '88 and TV," *TV Guide,* 36, 4 (January 23, 1988): 5.

59. Thomas R. Marshall, *Presidential Nominations in a Reform Age* (New York: Praeger, 1981), 108–11; 1988 Super Tuesday results taken from Rhodes Cook, "One Side Is Clearer, The Other Still Murky," *Congressional Quarterly* 46 (March 12, 1988): 638-39; Daniel M. Weintraub and Richard C. Paddock, "Assembly Votes to Move Up State Primary to March," *Los Angeles Times,* July 1, 1989; Virginia Ellis, "Senate Spurns Early Presidential Primary," *Los Angeles Times,* September 15, 1989; *Los Angeles Times,* September 16, 1989; Richard L. Berke, "2 Major Parties Back California On an Early Presidential Primary," *New York Times,* February 15, 1990, p. 1; *New York Times,* February 23, 1990, p. A7; *Election Administration Reports* 20 (March 19, 1990): 7.

60. Gerald M. Pomper et al., *The Election of 1984: Reports and Interpretations,* ed. Marlene Michels Pomper (Chatham, N.J.: Chatham House, 1985), 12.

61. Ibid., 13.

62. Ibid., 10.

63. Crotty and Jackson, *Presidential Primaries* (see n. 9), 156.

64. Quoted in S. Robert Lichter, Daniel Amundson, and Richard Noyes, *The Video Campaign—Network Coverage of the 1988 Primaries* (Washington, D.C.: American Enterprise Institute for Policy Research, 1988), 109.

65. Keeter and Zukin, *Uninformed Choice* (see n. 13), 167, 173.

66. Thomas E. Patterson, "Television and Presidential Selection: A Proposal for Restructuring Television Communication in Presidential Election Campaigns" (Paper prepared for the Study of the U.S. Presidential Selection Process sponsored by the Alfred P. Sloan Foundation, Alexander Heard, Director, December 1983), 55.

67. Patterson, *Mass Media Election* (see n. 19), 163, 165.

68. Ibid., 165.

69. Byron E. Shafer, *Bifurcated Politics—Evolution and Reform in the National Party Convention* (Cambridge: Harvard University Press, 1988), 330–31.

70. Patterson, "Television and Presidential Selection" (see n. 66), 54.

71. Kessel, *Presidential Parties* (see n. 12), 257–58. Allen D. Hertzke comments on the "several important political purposes" modern conventions perform in "National Party Conventions: The Enduring American Spectacle," *extensions* (The Carl Albert Congressional Research and Studies Center, Winter 1989): 6–7.

72. Judith S. Trent and Robert V. Friedenberg, *Political Campaign Communication: Principles and Practices* (New York: Praeger, 1983), 15.

73. Richard L. Berke, "1988 Candidates Spent $210 Million," *New York Times,* August 27, 1989, p. 14. See also Herbert E. Alexander, "Financing the Presidential Elections, 1988" (Paper delivered to the International Political Science Association Mid-term Roundtable, Tokyo, Japan, September 8–10, 1989), 3, 44.

74. Alexander, "Financing the Presidential Elections, 1988," 8.

75. Michael J. Malbin, "Financing Presidential Nomination Campaigns" (Paper prepared for the Conference on Presidential Primaries, Gerald R. Ford Library, Ann Arbor, Mich., April 24–26, 1985), 28.

76. Herbert E. Alexander, "American Presidential Elections Since Public Funding, 1976–1984" (Paper prepared for the International Political Science Association 12th World Congress, Paris, France, July 15–20, 1985), 39.

77. Malbin, "Financing Presidential Nomination Campaigns" (see n. 75), 16.

78. Alexander, "American Presidential Elections" (see n. 76), 38.

79. Hershey, *Running for Office* (see n. 29), 99.

80. Keeter and Zukin, *Uninformed Choice* (see n. 13), 161–64.

81. Herbert E. Alexander, "The Price We Pay for Our Presidents," *Public Opinion* (March/April 1989): 46.

82. "Financing Presidential Campaigns: An Examination of the Ongoing Effects of the Federal Election Campaign Laws upon the Conduct of Presidential Campaigns" (Research report by the Campaign Finance Study Group to the Committee on Rules and Administration of the United States Senate, Institute of Politics, John F. Kennedy School of Government, Harvard University, January 1982), sec. 1, 24.

83. Shafer, *Bifurcated Politics* (see n. 69), 343.

84. "Many Americans Call for Changes in Electoral Process," *Gallup Report,* no. 230 (November 1984), 18.

85. Bartels, *Presidential Primaries* (see n. 28), 288.

86. Germond and Witcover, *Whose Broad Stripes and Bright Stars?* (see n. 53), 278–92.

87. Crotty and Jackson, *Presidential Primaries* (see n. 9), 222.

88. Aldrich, *Before the Convention* (see n. 33), 208.

89. Ibid.

90. Letter by Susan Furniss to Terry Sanford, May 12, 1980, cited in Terry Sanford, *A Danger of Democracy—The Presidential Nominating Process* (Boulder, Colo.: Westview Press, 1981), 130; also, Thomas Cronin and Robert Loevy, "The Case for a National Pre-primary Convention Plan," *Public Opinion* 5 (December/January 1983): 50–53; Thomas E. Cronin and Robert D. Loevy, "Putting the Party As Well As the People Back in President Picking," in *The Presidential Nominating Process,* vol. 1, ed. Kenneth W. Thompson, The George Gund Lectures (Lanham, Md.: University Press of America, 1983), 49–64; and William Schneider, "How to Choose a Presidential Nominee," *National Journal* 21 (September 9, 1989): 2238.

91. Charles E. Schumer, "The Primary System Is Broken, and It's Time to Fix It," *New York Times,* August 15, 1986, p. 23.

92. William Schneider, "Democrats' Cure for a Primary Problem," *Los Angeles Times,* March 2, 1986, sec. 4, p. 3.

93. Bartels, *Presidential Primaries* (see n. 28), 289.

Chapter Four. Presidential Elections and Information

1. Michael Oreskes, "Study Finds 'Astonishing' Indifference to Elections," *New York Times,* May 6, 1990, p. Y16

2. Theodore H. White, *America in Search of Itself* (New York: Harper and Row, 1982), 175–76.

3. Paul F. Boller, Jr., *Presidential Campaigns* (New York: Oxford University Press, 1984), 44–45.

4. Ibid., 146.

5. Robert W. Pittman, "We're Talking the Wrong Language to 'TV Babies,' " *New York Times,* January 24, 1990, p. A15.

6. Austin Ranney, "Broadcasting, Narrowcasting, and Politics," in *The New American Political System—Second Version,* ed. Anthony King (Washington, D.C.: AEI Press, 1990), 190.

7. Andy Plattner, "The Lure of the Senate: Influence and Prestige," *Congressional Quarterly* 43 (May 25, 1985): 994–95; "Inside Congress," *Congressional Quarterly* 44 (March 15, 1986): 635; "Senate TV," *Washington Post National Weekly Edition,* August 11, 1986, p. 15.

8. Richard Armstrong, *The Next Hurrah—The Communications Revolution in American Politics* (New York: William Morrow, 1988), 27.

9. Jeffrey B. Abramson, F. Christopher Arterton, and Gary R. Orren, *The Electronic Commonwealth—The Impact of New Media Technologies on Democratic Politics* (New York: Basic Books, 1988), 108. See the concerned analysis of Jeffrey Abramson, "The New Media and the New Politics," *AQ—The Aspen Institute Quarterly* 2 (Spring 1990): 18-49. A condition of "multiple uncertainty" that also obtains in western Europe is examined in *New Media Politics—Comparative Perspectives in Western Europe,* ed. Denis McQuail and Karen Siune (London: SAGE Publications Ltd., 1986). See also Larry Sabato and David Beiler, "Magic … Or Blue Smoke and Mirrors?—Reflections on New Technologies and Trends in the Political Consultant Trade," in *Media Technology and the Vote—A Source Book,* ed. Joel L. Swerdlow (Boulder, Colo.: Westview Press, 1988), 3–17. More generally, with respect to federal regulation, see Edwin Diamond and Norman Sandler, and Milton Mueller, *Telecommunications in Crisis: The First Amendment, Technology, and Deregulation* (Washington, D.C.: Cato Institute, 1983).

10. Richard Matthew Pious and Susan Delancey Weil, "New Communications Technologies: Emerging Political Applications" (Paper prepared for the Study of the U.S. Presidential Selection Process sponsored by the Alfred P. Sloan Foundation, Alexander Heard, Director, September 1983), 45–50.

11. Robert G. Meadow, ed., *New Communication Technologies in Politics* (Washington: Annenberg School of Communications, 1985), 108; also, Andrew Rosenthal, "Cable TV Playing Key Role in 1988," *New York Times,* January 16, 1988, p. 8; Rosenthal, "Modern Science Allows Old-Fashioned Politicking," *New York Times,* January 25, 1988, p. 14; "Special Technology Section" in *Campaigns and Elections* 9 (March-April 1989): 23–38; and Kiku Adatto, *Sound Bite Democracy: Network Evening News Presidential Campaign Coverage, 1968 and 1988* (Cambridge: Joan Shorenstein Barone Center, John F. Kennedy School of Government, Harvard University, June 1990), 4, Research Paper R-2.

12. Robert E. Denton, Jr., *The Primetime Presidency of Ronald Reagan—The Era of the Television Presidency* (New York: Praeger, 1988), 69.

13. Dean Alger, "Television, Perceptions of Reality and the Presidential Election of '84," *PS* 20 (Winter 1987): 49.

14. Jack W. Germond and Jules Witcover, *Wake Us When It's Over: Presidential Politics of 1984* (New York: Macmillan, 1985), xix.

15. Denton, *Primetime Presidency* (see n. 12), 59. Keith Blume issues a severe indictment and challenge in *The Presidential Election Show—Campaign '84*

and Beyond on the Nightly News (South Hadley, Mass.: Bergin and Garvey Publishers, Inc., 1985).

16. Alger, "Television '84" (see n. 13), 49–50.

17. Michael F. Bennet, "U.S. Leaders: No Vision, All Expediency," *New York Times,* October 1, 1989, p. 21.

18. Anthony Smith, "Just a Pleasant Way to Spend an Evening—The Softening Embrace of American Television," *Daedalus* 107 (Winter 1978): 211.

19. Ibid., 212. Douglas Davis has written on "Zapping the Myth of TV's Power," *New York Times,* May 20, 1988, p. 25.

20. Elihu Katz, "Platforms and Windows: Broadcasting's Role in Election Campaigns," in *Sociology of Mass Communications,* ed. Denis McQuail (New York: Penguin, 1972), 364, drawing on work of Jay G. Blumler and Denis McQuail.

21. Jeff Greenfield, *The Real Campaign: How the Media Missed the Story of the 1980 Campaign* (New York: Summit Books, 1982), 154.

22. Anthony Smith, "Mass Communications," in *Democracy at the Polls: A Comparative Study of Competitive National Elections,* ed. David Butler, Howard R. Penniman, and Austin Ranney (Washington, D.C.: American Enterprise Institute, 1981), 184.

23. Greenfield, *The Real Campaign* (see n. 21), 177.

24. Thomas E. Patterson, *The Mass Media Election: How Americans Choose Their President* (New York: Praeger, 1980), 157.

25. James David Barber, *Politics by Humans—Research on American Leadership* (Durham, N.C.: Duke University Press, 1988), 469; see also 25, 156, 430.

26. Doris A. Graber, *Processing the News: How People Tame the Information Tide* (New York: Longman, 1984), 103, 105, 210.

27. Kathleen Hall Jamieson and David S. Birdsell, *Presidential Debates—The Challenge of Creating an Informed Electorate* (New York: Oxford University Press, 1988), 219. See also Sidney Kraus, *Televised Presidential Debates and Public Policy* (Hillsdale, New Jersey: Lawrence Erlbaum Associates, 1988); Joel L. Swerdlow, ed., *Presidential Debates 1988 and Beyond* (Washington, D.C.: Congressional Quarterly Inc., 1987); and Newton N. Minow and Clifford M. Sloan, *For Great Debates—A New Plan for Future Presidential TV Debates* (New York: Priority Press Publications, 1987).

28. Smith, "Mass Communications" (see n. 22), 184–85, emphasis added.

29. Graber, *Processing the News* (see n. 26), 68.

30. Ibid., 69. A similar general conclusion was reluctantly reached by veteran TV journalist Sig Mickelson in *From Whistle Stop to Sound Bite—Four Decades of Politics and Television* (New York: Praeger, 1989), 176.

31. Ibid., 70.

32. Doris A. Graber, "Candidate Images: An Audio-Visual Analysis" (Paper prepared for delivery at the 1985 Annual Meeting of the American Political Science Association, New Orleans, La., August 29–September 1, 1985), 11.

33. Ibid., 1. A more constricted, less benign interpretation of television's impact on presidential selection is found in Martin Schram, *The Great American Video Game—Presidential Politics in the Television Age* (New York: William Morrow and Company, Inc., 1987), 23–36, 307–16.

34. Graber, *Processing the News* (see n. 26), 165.

35. Patterson, *Mass Media Election* (see n. 24), 123.

36. Ibid., 89–90.

37. Ibid., 132.

38. Ibid., 103.

39. Kathleen Hall Jamieson, "The Evolution of Political Advertising in America," in *New Perspectives on Political Advertising,* ed. Lynda Lee Kaid, Dan Nimmo, and Keith R. Sanders (Carbondale and Edwardsville: Southern Illinois University Press, 1986), 1–12. See also Jeff Greenfield, *Playing to Win: An Insider's Guide to Politics* (New York: Simon and Schuster, 1980), 153–54.

40. Thomas E. Patterson and Robert D. McClure, *The Unseeing Eye: The Myth of Television Power in National Politics* (New York: G. P. Putnam's Sons, 1976), 102.

41. Jack W. Germond and Jules Witcover, *Blue Smoke and Mirrors: How Reagan Won and Why Carter Lost the Election of 1980* (New York: Viking, 1981), 318.

42. Ibid., 319.

43. Gerald M. Pomper, "The Presidential Election," in *The Election of 1984: Reports and Interpretations,* Gerald Pomper et al., ed. Marlene Michels Pomper (Chatham, N.J.: Chatham House, 1985), 79–80.

44. Martin Linsky, ed., *Television and the Presidential Elections: Self-Interest and the Public Interest* (Lexington, Mass.: Lexington Books, 1983), 51–52.

45. Howard R. Penniman, "Campaign Styles and Methods," in Butler, Penniman, and Ranney, *Democracy at the Polls* (see n. 22), 132.

46. Linsky, *Television and the Presidential Elections* (see n. 44), 125; Richard Joslyn, "Political Advertising and the Meaning of Elections," in Kaid, Nimmo, and Sanders, *New Perspectives* (see n. 39), 183.

47. Patterson and McClure, *The Unseeing Eye* (see n. 40), 103–4.

48. Thomas E. Patterson and Robert D. McClure, "Television and the Less-Interested Voter: The Costs of An Informed Electorate," *Annals of the American Academy of Political and Social Science* 425 (May 1976): 95.

49. Graber, *Processing the News* (see n. 26), 36.

50. Ibid., 37.

51. Patterson and McClure, *The Unseeing Eye* (see n. 40), 128.

52. Penniman, "Campaign Styles" (see n. 45), 132–33.

53. Anthony Smith, "Some Conclusions," in *Television and Political Life,* ed. Anthony Smith (New York: St. Martin's Press, 1979), 237.

54. Ibid.

55. Douglas Davis makes the point vigorously in "Zapping the Myth of TV's Power" (see n. 19).

56. Austin Ranney, *Channels of Power: The Impact of Television on American Politics* (New York: Basic Books, 1983), 182.

57. Linsky, *Television and the Presidential Elections* (see n. 44), 122–24.

58. Quoted in Edwin Diamond and Stephen Bates, *THE SPOT—The Rise of Political Advertising on Television,* rev. ed. (Cambridge, Mass.: The MIT Press, 1988), 351.

59. Porter McKeever, *Adlai Stevenson—His Life and Legacy* (New York: William Morrow and Company, Inc., 1989), 356–88, and Stephen C. Wood, "Television's First Political Spot Ad Campaign: Eisenhower Answers America," *Presidential Studies Quarterly* XX (Spring 1990): 265-83.

60. *Congressional Record,* 99th Cong., 1st sess., 1985, 131, no. 80, S8267.

61. Ibid., S8268.

62. Richard Smolka, "The Campaign Law in the Courts," in *Money and Politics in the United States: Financing Elections in the 1980s,* ed. Michael J. Malbin (Chatham, N.J.: Chatham House Publishers, Inc., 1984), 228.
63. The Twentieth Century Fund, *With the Nation Watching: Report of the Twentieth Century Fund Task Force on Televised Presidential Debates* (Lexington, Mass.: Lexington Books, 1979), 93–94.
64. Stanley Kelley, Jr., *Interpreting Elections* (Princeton: Princeton University Press, 1983), 148–49.
65. Graber, *Processing the News* (see n. 26), 209.
66. Ibid., 197.
67. Ibid.
68. Patterson, *Mass Media Election* (see n. 24), 167.
69. John H. Kessel, *Presidential Parties* (Homewood, Ill.: Dorsey, 1984), 488.

Chapter Five. Electoral Systems and Information

1. Arthur Schlesinger, Jr., "Can The System Be Saved?" *Encounter,* January 1983, 22.
2. Lord Bryce, quoted by Arthur Schlesinger, Jr., in "Leave the Constitution Alone," in *Reforming American Government—The Bicentennial Papers of the Committee on the Constitutional System,* ed. Donald L. Robinson (Boulder, Colo.: Westview Press, 1985), 54.
3. Michael J. Malbin, ed., *Parties, Interest Groups, and Campaign Finance Laws* (Washington, D.C.: American Enterprise Institute, 1980), 308.
4. Ibid., 324.
5. Maurice Duverger, *Political Parties* (New York: John Wiley and Sons, 1954), 207–28.
6. E. E. Schattschneider, *Party Government* (New York: Rinehart, 1942), 206–10; also, James MacGregor Burns, "The Deadlock of Democracy Revisited," *The Center Magazine,* July/August 1986, 2–19.
7. Samuel H. Barnes and Max Kaase, "In Conclusion: The Future of Political Protest in Western Democracies," in *Political Action: Mass Participation in Five Western Democracies,* ed. Samuel H. Barnes, Max Kaase, et al. (Beverly Hills: Sage Publications, 1979), chap. 17.
8. David B. Truman, *The Governmental Process* (New York: Knopf, 1951), 129.
9. Alexander Hamilton, James Madison, and John Jay, *The Federalist Papers,* ed. Clinton Rossiter (New York: New American Library, 1961), no. 50, 319.
10. Robert S. Hirschfield, ed., *Selection/Election: A Forum on the American Presidency* (New York: Aldine, 1982), 195.
11. Steven J. Brams and Peter C. Fishburn, *Approval Voting* (Boston: Birkhauser, 1983), 172.
12. David Butler and Dennis Kavanagh, *The British General Election of 1983* (New York: St. Martin's Press, 1984), 9.
13. Ralf Dahrendorf, *On Britain* (Chicago: University of Chicago Press, 1982), 88–91; also, Vernon Bogdanor, *The People and the Party System: The Referendum and Electoral Reform in British Politics* (Cambridge: Cambridge University Press, 1981), 144–46.
14. Bogdanor, *The People and the Party System,* 177–93; Dahrendorf, *On Britain,* 115–20.

15. Theodore J. Lowi, *The Personal President: Power Invested, Promise Unfulfilled* (Ithaca, N.Y.: Cornell University Press, 1985), 203.

16. Ibid., 204, 207, 209.

17. Giovanni Sartori, "Democracy," *International Encyclopedia of the Social Sciences,* vol. 4, 1968: 117.

18. Neal R. Peirce and Lawrence D. Longley, *The People's President: The Electoral College in American History and the Direct Vote Alternative,* rev. ed. (New Haven: Yale University Press, 1981), 342.

19. Allan P. Sindler, "Alternative Modes of Presidential Election" (Paper prepared for the Study of the U.S. Presidential Selection Process sponsored by the Alfred P. Sloan Foundation, Alexander Heard, Director, November 8, 1983), 30–35. See George F. Will, "The Electoral College's Campus Radical," *Washington Post National Weekly Edition,* June 11-17, 1990.

20. A. James Reichley, "The Electoral System," in *Elections American Style,* ed. A. James Reichley (Washington, D.C.: Brookings Institution, 1987), 17. For other examples, see Richard A. Watson and Norman C. Thomas, *The Politics of the Presidency,* 2d ed. (Washington, D.C.: CQ Press, 1988), 490–91.

21. John H. Yunker and Lawrence D. Longley, "The Biases of the Electoral College: Who Is Really Advantaged?" in *Perspectives on Presidential Selection,* ed. Donald R. Matthews (Washington, D.C.: Brookings Institution, 1973), 172–203; and George Rabinowitz and Stuart Elaine MacDonald, "The Power of States in U.S. Presidential Elections," *American Political Science Review* 80 (March 1986): 65–87.

22. John H. Kessel, *Presidential Parties* (Homewood, Ill.: Dorsey, 1984), 357–58.

23. Nelson W. Polsby, *Consequences of Party Reform* (Oxford: Oxford University Press, 1983), 83.

24. Theodore H. White, quoted in Benjamin I. Page and Mark P. Petracca, *The American Presidency* (New York: McGraw-Hill, 1983), 106.

25. Max S. Power, "Logic and Legitimacy: On Understanding the Electoral College Controversy," in Matthews, *Perspectives* (see n. 21), 231.

26. Robert D. Thomas, "Cities as Partners in the Federal System," *Political Science Quarterly* 1 (1986): 63.

27. Alexander Heard interview with President Jimmy Carter, September 22, 1983, Atlanta, Georgia.

28. Barbara Sinclair, "Coping with Uncertainty: Building Coalitions in the House and the Senate," in *The New Congress,* ed. Thomas E. Mann and Norman J. Ornstein (Washington, D.C.: American Enterprise Institute, 1981), 184.

29. Richard Rose, *The Capacity of the President: A Comparative Analysis* (Glasgow: Centre for the Study of Public Policy, University of Strathclyde, 1984), 80.

30. Reichley, "Electoral System," in Reichley, *Elections American Style* (see n. 20), 20.

31. George C. Edwards III, *Presidential Influence in Congress* (San Francisco: W. H. Freeman, 1980), 100–110.

32. Steven J. Rosenstone, Roy L. Behr, and Edward H. Lazarus, *Third Parties in America: Citizen Response to Major Party Failure* (Princeton: Princeton University Press, 1984), 40–41.

33. Thomas E. Cavanagh and James L. Sundquist, "The New Two-Party System," in *The New Direction in American Politics,* ed. John E. Chubb and Paul E. Peterson (Washington, D.C.: Brookings Institution, 1985), 47.

34. V. O. Key, Jr., *Politics, Parties, and Pressure Groups,* 5th ed. (New York: Thomas Y. Crowell, 1964), 281.

35. James W. Ceasar, *Reforming the Reforms: A Critical Analysis of the Presidential Selection Process* (Cambridge, Mass.: Ballinger Publishing, 1982), 102–3; also, Richard P. Roberts, "Ballot Access for Third Party and Independent Candidates after *Anderson v. Celebrezze," Journal of Law and Politics* 3 (Winter 1986): 174–76; and Rosenstone, Behr, and Lazarus, *Third Parties* (see n. 32), 19–25.

36. Rosenstone, Behr, and Lazarus, *Third Parties,* 25–33; also, Leon D. Epstein, *Political Parties in the American Mold* (Madison: University of Wisconsin Press, 1986), 198.

37. Ibid., 26–27.

38. Phil Gailey, "2 Parties to Run Political Debates; League of Women Voters Sees Threat to Minor Candidates," *New York Times,* November 27, 1985, p. Al; and Rosenstone, Behr, and Lazarus, *Third Parties* (see n. 32), 35.

39. Rosenstone, Behr, and Lazarus, *Third Parties,* 224.

40. Pope McCorkle and Joel L. Fleishman, "Political Parties and Presidential Nominations: The Intellectual Ironies of Reform and Change in the Mass Media Age," in *The Future of American Political Parties: The Challenge of Governance,* ed. Joel L. Fleishman (Englewood Cliffs, N.J.: Prentice Hall, 1982), 161–63.

41. Frank J. Sorauf, "Political Parties and Political Analysis," in *The American Party Systems,* ed. William Nisbet Chambers and Walter Dean Burnham (New York: Oxford University Press, 1967), 50.

42. Rosenstone, Behr, and Lazarus, *Third Parties* (see n. 32), 203.

43. Ibid., 6; and *Congressional Quarterly* 47 (January 21, 1989): 139.

44. Rosenstone, Behr, and Lazarus, *Third Parties* (see n. 32), 222.

45. Lawrence D. Brown, *New Policies, New Politics: Government's Response to Government's Growth* (Washington, D.C.: Brookings Institution, 1983), 51–52.

46. Russell J. Dalton, Scott C. Flanagan, and Paul Allen Beck, *Electoral Change in Advanced Industrial Democracies: Realignment or Dealignment?* (Princeton: Princeton University Press, 1984), 471. See also David P. Conradt, "Changing German Political Culture," in *The Civic Culture Revisited,* ed. Gabriel A. Almond and Sidney Verba (Boston: Little, Brown, 1980), 249.

47. Ibid., 474.

48. Ibid., 462.

49. Moisei Ostrogorski, *Democracy and the Organization of Political Parties,* vol. 2 (New York: Macmillan, 1902), 698.

50. Ibid., 658.

51. Richard Bergholz, "Campaign Financing Expert Sees a Need to Ease Up on Public Funding Limitations," *Los Angeles Times,* May 21, 1983, sec. 2, p. 8.

52. Richard G. Smolka, "The Campaign Law in the Courts," in *Money and Politics in the United States—Financing Elections in the 1980s,* ed. Michael J. Malbin (Chatham, N.J.: Chatham House Publishers, Inc., 1984), 227.

53. Giovanni Sartori, *The Theory of Democracy Revisited* (Chatham, N.J.: Chatham House Publishers, Inc., 1987), 105.

54. James David Barber, "And Now, Mr. Lincoln, You Have 15 Seconds," *New York Times Book Review,* October 30, 1988, p. 36. Michael G. Gartner argues for greater freedom of "commercial speech" than now afforded by federal and state regulation, e.g., prohibitions against cigarette ads on radio and television, in *Advertising and the First Amendment* (New York: Priority Press Publications, 1989).

55. Samuel P. Huntington, *American Politics: The Promise of Disharmony* (Cambridge, Mass.: Belknap Press, 1981), 85–129.
56. For distinctions between descriptive and rationalist approaches to democracy, see Jeane J. Kirkpatrick, "Democratic Elections, Democratic Government, and Democratic Theory," in *Democracy at the Polls—A Comparative Study of Competitive National Elections,* ed. David Butler, Howard R. Penniman, and Austin Ranney (Washington, D.C.: American Enterprise Institute, 1981), 325–48.

Chapter Six. Changing Forms of Political Participation

1. Russell J. Dalton, Scott C. Flanagan, and Paul Allen Beck, eds., *Electoral Change in Advanced Industrial Democracies: Realignment or Dealignment?* (Princeton: Princeton University Press, 1984), 452. See also Russell J. Dalton, *Citizen Politics in Western Democracies—Public Opinion and Political Parties in the United States, Great Britain, West Germany, and France* (Chatham, N.J.: Chatham House Publishers, Inc., 1988), 35–36.
2. Sidney Verba and Norman H. Nie, *Participation in America: Political Democracy and Social Equality* (New York: Harper and Row, 1972), 3. On the growth, purposes, and forms of political action in addition to voting, see Jack H. Nagel, *Participation* (Englewood Cliffs, N.J.: Prentice-Hall, Inc., 1987), especially chaps. 9, "Pressure," and 10, "Administration."
3. Max Kaase and Alan Marsh, "Political Action: A Theoretical Perspective," in *Political Action: Mass Participation in Five Western Democracies,* ed. Samuel H. Barnes, Max Kaase, et al. (Beverly Hills: Sage Publications, 1979), 38.
4. Herbert E. Alexander, "Financing the Presidential Elections, 1988" (Paper delivered at the International Political Science Association Mid-Term Roundtable, Tokyo, Japan, 1989), 3.
5. Samuel P. Huntington, "Post-Industrial Politics: How Benign Will It Be?" *Comparative Politics* 6 (1974): 163–91.
6. E. E. Schattschneider, *Party Government* (New York: Rinehart, 1942), 60.
7. Jeane J. Kirkpatrick, *The New Presidential Elite* (New York: Russell Sage Foundation, 1976), 368–69.
8. James W. Ceaser, *Reforming the Reforms: A Critical Analysis of the Presidential Selection Process* (Cambridge, Mass.: Ballinger, 1982), 1–10, and Byron E. Shafer, *Quiet Revolution* (New York: Russell Sage, 1983), 125–32.
9. Austin Ranney, *Curing the Mischiefs of Faction: Party Reform in America* (Berkeley: University of California Press, 1975), 119, 134.
10. Ibid., 108, 196.
11. Kirkpatrick, *New Presidential Elite* (see n. 7), 3, 246, 72, 330, 331.
12. Shafer, *Quiet Revolution* (see n. 8), 525.
13. This analysis is offered by a number of commentators. See especially, Shafer, *Quiet Revolution* and Nelson W. Polsby, *Consequences of Party Reform* (Oxford: Oxford University Press, 1983).
14. Polsby, *Consequences,* 133.
15. Ibid., 139.
16. Theodore J. Eismeier and Philip H. Pollock III, *Business, Money and the Rise of Corporate PACS in American Elections* (Westport, Conn.: Quorum Books, 1988), 34, 94–104.

17. Polsby, *Consequences* (see n. 13), 133.
18. *U.S. News and World Report,* September 2, 1985, 46–47, and John W. Wright, ed. *The Universal Almanac* (Kansas City: Andrews and McMeel, 1989), 298.
19. William Crotty and John S. Jackson III, *Presidential Primaries and Nominations* (Washington, D.C.: Congressional Quarterly, 1985), 69–73; also, Thad A. Brown, *Migration and Politics—The Impact of Population Mobility on American Voting Behavior* (Chapel Hill: University of North Carolina Press, 1988), 145–55.
20. Polsby, *Consequences* (see n. 13), 4.
21. Austin Ranney, "The Political Parties: Reform and Decline," in *The New American Political System,* ed. Anthony King (Washington, D.C.: American Enterprise Institute, 1978), 242, 243.
22. Kirkpatrick, *New Presidential Elite* (see n. 7), 45, 48.
23. Dalton, Flanagan, and Beck, *Electoral Change* (see n. 1), 460–2.
24. Ibid., 473, 451.
25. Ralf Dahrendorf, *On Britain* (Chicago: University of Chicago Press, 1982), 123; see also Dalton, *Citizen Politics* (see n. 1), 13–73.
26. Risto Sankiaho, "Political Remobilization in Welfare States," in Dalton, Flanagan, and Beck, *Electoral Change* (see n. 1), 91.
27. Harry C. Boyte, *CommonWealth—A Return to Citizen Politics* (New York: The Free Press, 1989), 157. See also Samuel H. Beer, "In Search of A New Public Philosophy," in King, *New American Political System* (see n. 21), 28.
28. Andrew S. McFarland, *Common Cause: Lobbying in the Public Interest* (Chatham, N.J.: Chatham House Publishers, Inc., 1984), 151.
29. See Robert A. Dahl, *Dilemmas of Pluralist Democracy: Autonomy vs. Control* (New Haven and London: Yale University Press, 1982), 81–107.
30. Commission on Party Structure and Delegate Selection (McGovern-Fraser Commission), *Mandate for Reform* (Washington, D.C.: Democratic National Committee, 1970), 10.
31. Delegates and Organizations Committee, *Progress Report,* pt. 2., "The Delegate Selection Procedures for the Republican Party" (Washington, D.C.: Republican National Committee, 1971), 2.
32. Alan I. Abramowitz and Walter J. Stone, *Nomination Politics—Party Activists and Presidential Choice* (New York: Praeger, 1984), 136; also, Byron E. Shafer, *Bifurcated Politics—Evolution and Reform in the National Party Convention* (Cambridge: Harvard University Press, 1988), 108–47.
33. Ranney, *Curing Mischiefs* (see n. 9), 108.
34. Thomas R. Marshall, *Presidential Nominations in a Reform Age* (New York: Praeger, 1981), 48.
35. Crotty and Jackson, *Primaries and Nominations* (see n. 19), 83–84.
36. "Turnout Up Outside the South: Democratic Primaries Shaped by Small Share of Electorate," *Congressional Quarterly* 42 (July 7, 1984): 1618–20. Data for 1988 from the Associated Press, reported in the *New York Times,* June 9, 1988, p. A1.
37. Warran J. Mitofsky and Martin Plissner, "The Making of the Delegates, 1968–1980," *Public Opinion* 3 (October–November 1980): 37.
38. *Elections '88* (Washington, D.C.: Congressional Quarterly, Inc., 1988), 31.
39. Frank J. Sorauf, *Party Politics in America* (Boston: Little, Brown, 1968), 280.
40. Martin Plissner and Warren J. Mitofsky, "The Making of the Delegates, 1968–1988," *Public Opinion* 11 (September/October 1988): 47.

41. George Skelton, "Delegates Strikingly Unified on Issues," *Los Angeles Times,* July 15, 1984, p. 11. Also, Plissner and Mitofsky, "Making of the Delegates, 1968-1988," 46–47.

42. Crotty and Jackson, *Presidential Primaries* (see n. 19), 113.

43. Frank J. Sorauf, *Money in American Elections* (Glenview, Ill.: Scott, Foresman and Company, 1988), 294–95, 7. More recently, Richard L. Berke has written, "Campaign-Fund Limits: Congress Blushes, States Act," *New York Times,* June 24, 1990, p. E4.

44. Hays Gorey, "For the Love of Money," *Time,* May 7, 1990, 32. See Richard L. Berke, "Most of Senators Go Out of State for Contributions," *New York Times,* April 16, 1990, pp. 1, A10; Maureen Dowd, "Bush Urges Campaign Fund Curbs And Limits on Fees for Congress," *New York Times,* June 30, 1989, pp. 1, 9; Alan I. Abramowitz, "Finance House Campaigns," *New York Times,* June 27, 1989, p. 23; and Richard L. Berke, "Candidates Reach Fund-Raising Peak," *New York Times,* May 8, 1990, p. A10.

45. Campaign Finance Reform Panel (Herbert E. Alexander et. al.), "Campaign Finance Reform—A Report to the Majority Leader & Minority Leader, United States Senate," March 6, 1990; also Richard L. Berke, "Campaign Reform Stalls in Senate," *New York Times,* June 17, 1990, p. Y17.

46. Benjamin I. Page, *Choices and Echoes in Presidential Elections: Rational Man and Electoral Democracy* (Chicago: University of Chicago Press, 1978), 287.

47. Alexander, "Financing the Presidential Elections, 1988" (see n. 4), 3, 26–33. For a recent historical survey of the evolution of federal campaign finance regulation, see Robert E. Mutch, *Campaigns, Congress, and Courts—The Making of Federal Campaign Finance Law* (New York: Praeger, 1988). The continuing concern of Common Cause was reemphasized in a review of soliciting and contributing behavior in 1988 by Jean Cobb, Jeff Denny, Vicki Kemper, and Viveca Novak, "All the President's Donors," *Common Cause Magazine,* March/April 1990, 21-27, 38-39.

48. Herbert E. Alexander and Brian A. Haggerty, *Financing the 1984 Election* (Lexington, Mass.: Lexington Books, 1987), 98–102; also, Peter Kerr, "Campaign Donations Overwhelm Monitoring Agencies in the States," *New York Times,* December 27, 1988, p. 1. The considerable differences among PAC purposes and vigor are addressed by Ann B. Matasar, *Corporate PACs and Federal Campaign Financing Laws—Use or Abuse of Power* (New York: Quorum Books, 1986). See also Ruth S. Jones, "Contributing as Participation: Mass or Elite Control?" (Paper presented at the Conference on Campaign Finance Reform and Representative Democracy, The Bradley Institute for Democracy and Public Values, Marquette University, Milwaukee, Wis., February 24–25, 1989), 7.

49. Ruth S. Jones, "Campaign Contributions and Campaign Solicitations: 1984" (Paper presented at the meeting of the Southern Political Science Association, Nashville, Tenn., November 6–9, 1985), citing the Center for Political Studies.

50. Alexander and Haggerty, *Financing the 1984 Election* (see n. 48), 89. Also, Federal Election Commission, "Presidential Fund—Income Tax Check-Off Status," March 1989; and Ann McColl Bryan, "An Analysis of the Public Financing of State Political Campaigns" (Paper prepared for the North Carolina Center for Public Policy Research, Raleigh, N.C., 1989), 39.

51. Michael Wines, " 'Bundlers' Aid Campaigns in Evading Spending Laws," *Los Angeles Times,* October 1, 1984, sec. 1, p. 1.

52. Ruth S. Jones and Warren E. Miller, "Financing Campaigns: Macro Level Innovation and Micro Level Response," *Western Political Quarterly* 38 (June 1985): 207. See also Jones, "Contributing as Participation" (see n. 48).

53. Sorauf, *Money in Elections* (see n. 43), 4.

54. Herbert E. Alexander, "The Price We Pay for Our Presidents," *Public Opinion* 11 (March/April 1989): 46–47; and Alexander, *Financing the 1980 Election* (Lexington, Mass.: Lexington Books, 1983), 297–98. See also Xandra Kayden, "The Relationship Between the Presidential Selection Process and Campaign Finance and the Federal Election Commission" (Paper prepared for the Study of the U.S. Presidential Selection Process sponsored by the Alfred P. Sloan Foundation, Alexander Heard, Director, 1983), 64–65; and Thomas B. Edsall, "Loophole Lets Parties Raise Millions From Firms, Unions," *Washington Post,* April 17, 1984, p. A9.

55. Alexander, "Financing the Presidential Elections, 1988" (see n. 4), 27.

56. Richard L. Berke, "Big Donors Give G.O.P. $10 Million," *New York Times,* September 27, 1988, p. 9; Berke, "Democrats Disclose List of Some of Wealthy Donors in the Campaign Year," *New York Times,* November 16, 1988, p. 13; Berke, "Big Donors Aided G.O.P. Near End of Campaign," *New York Times,* November 17, 1988, p. 11; Berke, "Prodded by Lobby, G.O.P. Reveals $100,000 Donors," *New York Times,* January 24, 1989, p. 13.

57. Richard L. Berke, "True Tales of Spending in the Presidential Race," *New York Times,* December 11, 1988, p. 23; Berke, "Parties Ask Outside Groups to Stop Raising Ad Money," *New York Times,* October 8, 1988, p. 1.

58. Alexander, "Financing the Presidential Elections, 1988" (see n. 4), 33.

59. *New York Times,* June 30, 1989, p. 6.

60. Alexander, "Financing the Presidential Elections 1988" (see n. 4), 9.

61. Alexander and Haggerty, *Financing the 1984 Election* (see n. 48), 230–31.

62. Alexander, "Financing the Presidential Elections, 1988" (see n. 4), 40.

63. Linda Greenhouse, "Justices Restrict Corporate Gifts to Political Drives," *New York Times,* March 28, 1990, pp. 1, A10.

64. "Court Strikes Down Limits On Independent PAC Outlays," *Congressional Quarterly* 43 (March 23, 1985): 532–34; also, Herbert E. Alexander, *Financing the 1980 Election* (see n. 54), 111; Alexander and Haggerty, *Financing the 1984 Election* (see n. 48), 85; and Federal Election Commission release, May 19, 1989.

65. "Court Strikes Down Limits" (see n. 64), 532–34.

66. Jack L. Walker, "The Mobilization of Political Interests" (Paper prepared for the Annual Meeting of the American Political Science Association, Chicago, Ill., September 1–4, 1983).

67. Jack L. Walker, "The Origins and Maintenance of Interest Groups in America," *American Political Science Review* 77 (June 1983): 390–406.

68. See especially Eismeier and Pollock, *Corporate PACs* (see n. 16).

69. For a clear and interesting example, see Jeane J. Kirkpatrick et al., *The Presidential Nominating Process: Can It be Improved?* (Washington, D.C.: American Enterprise Institute, 1980).

70. Steven B. Roberts, "Rules of Party Playing Desired Role, Poll Finds," *New York Times,* July 15, 1984, p. 26.

71. Rhodes Cook, "Party and Elected Officials Get More Clout: Democrats Alter Rules Slightly in Effort to Broaden Party Base," *Congressional Quarterly* 43 (October 26, 1985): 2158–59.

72. *New York Times,* September 29, 1989, p. 8. See also E. J. Dionne, Jr., "Democrats Agree on Rules To Select Nominee in 1992," *New York Times,* June 26, 1988, p. 12; Thomas B. Edsall, "Playing By the Rules—The Democrats decide to go along with the Dukakis-Jackson deal on delegate selection," *Washington Post National Weekly Edition,* June 26–July 2, 1989, p. 13; Fred Barnes, "Jackson Rules," *The New Republic* (May 1, 1989), 14, 16; E. J. Dionne, Jr., "Democrats Clash Over Party Rules for the Primaries," *New York Times,* May 15, 1989, p. A12; Rhodes Cook, "For Democrats in '92, New Hurdles Loom," *Congressional Quarterly* 21 (October 21, 1989): 2834; R. W. Apple, Jr., "California Has Dream of Making Presidents," *New York Times,* November 2, 1989, p. A26; and Rhodes Cook, "Democratic Party Rules Changes Readied for '92 Campaign," *CQ,* March 17, 1990, 847-49.

73. See, for example, Elaine Ciulla Kamarck, "Democrats: Deregulate The Delegates," *Washington Post,* June 23, 1985, p. B1. Also, Ronald Brownstein, "DNC Weighs 'Deregulating' Nominating Rules," *National Journal* 17 (July 6, 1985): 1555.

74. *Cousins* v. *Wigoda,* 419 U.S. 477 (1975); and *Democratic Party of the U.S.* v. *La Follette,* 450 U.S. 107 (1981).

75. David E. Price, *Bringing Back the Parties* (Washington, D.C.: Congressional Quarterly, 1984), 127–32; Kamarck, "Democrats: Deregulate the Delegates" (see n. 73); and Brownstein, "DNC Weighs 'Deregulating' Nominating Rules" (see n. 73).

76. Lena Williams, "2 Parties Doubtful About Opening Primaries," *New York Times,* December 12, 1986, p. A27; also, "Closed Primary Laws Barred by 5–4 Supreme Court Ruling," *Congressional Quarterly* 44 (December 13, 1986): 3064–65.

77. Alexander and Haggerty, *Financing the 1984 Election* (see n. 48), 150.

78. Byron E. Shafer, "Reform and Alienation: The Decline of Intermediation in the Politics of Presidential Selection," *Journal of Law and Politics* 1 (Fall 1983): 93–132.

79. Michael J. Malbin, "Looking Back at the Future of Campaign Finance Reform," in *Money and Politics in the United States: Financing Elections in the 1980s,* ed. Michael J. Malbin (Chatham, N.J.: Chatham House, 1984), 255. See also Kayden, "The Relationship Between the Presidential Selection Process and Campaign Finance" (see n. 54), 88.

80. David Adamany, "Political Parties in the 1980s," in Malbin, *Money and Politics* (see n. 79), 70–121; and Herb Asher, "The Three Campaigns for President" (Paper prepared for the Study of the U.S. Presidential Selection Process sponsored by the Alfred P. Sloan Foundation, Alexander Heard, Director, 1984), 13–15.

81. Sorauf, *Money in Elections* (see n. 43), 221.

82. Warren E. Miller and M. Kent Jennings, *Parties in Transition—A Longitudinal Study of Party Elites and Party Supporters* (New York: Russell Sage Foundation, 1986), 241.

83. Larry J. Sabato, *Paying for Elections—The Campaign Finance Thicket* (New York: Priority Press Publications, 1989), 56, 72.

84. "Financing Congressional Campaigns: Contributors, PACs and Parties—An Analysis of Congressional Campaign Financing Trends" (Paper prepared for a conference sponsored by the Citizen's Research Foundation, Washington, D.C., May 11–12, 1989), 12.

85. Leon D. Epstein, "Will American Political Parties Be Privatized?" *The Journal of Law and Politics* 5 (Winter 1989): 239–74.

86. Leon D. Epstein, *Political Parties in the American Mold* (Madison: University of Wisconsin Press, 1986), 271.

87. Denise L. Baer and David A. Bositis, *Elite Cadres and Party Coalitions— Representing the Public in Party Politics* (Westport, Conn.: Greenwood Press, 1988), 183.

Chapter Seven. The Decline of Voter Participation

1. Rhodes Cook, "Turnout Hits 64-Year Low in Presidential Race," *Congressional Quarterly* 47 (January 21, 1989): 135–39.

2. *New York Times,* June 9, 1988, p. A1.

3. Walter Dean Burnham, "The Turnout Problem," in *Elections American Style*, ed. A. James Reichley (Washington, D.C.: The Brookings Institution, 1987), 113–14.

4. Ibid.

5. Alexis de Tocqueville, *Democracy in America,* vol. 1 (1835; reprint, New York: Knopf, 1948), 57.

6. Charles Krauthammer, "In Praise of Low Voter Turnout," *Time,* May 21, 1990, 88.

7. Harvard/ABC Symposium, *Voting for Democracy* (Booklet prepared by Austin Ranney at the conclusion of "Voting for Democracy," a symposium sponsored by the John F. Kennedy School of Government of Harvard University and the American Broadcasting Companies, Washington, D.C., September 30–October 1, 1983, published 1984), 37.

8. Seymour Martin Lipset and William Schneider, *The Confidence Gap: Business, Labor, and Government in the Public Mind* (New York: Free Press, 1983), 340, 376-77.

9. Harvard/ABC Symposium, *Voting for Democracy* (see n. 7), 37.

10. H. H. Gerth and C. Wright Mills, eds., *From Max Weber: Essays in Sociology* (New York: Oxford University Press, 1946), 188.

11. Warren E. Miller, "Disinterest, Disaffection, and Participation in Presidential Politics," *Political Behavior* 1 (1980): 24.

12. Lipset and Schneider, *The Confidence Gap* (see n. 8), 411–12. See also Ruy A. Teixeira, *Why Americans Don't Vote: Turnout Decline in the United States 1960–1984* (New York: Greenwood Press, 1987), 113.

13. Gary R. Orren, "The Linkage of Policy to Participation," in *Presidential Selection,* ed. Alexander Heard and Michael Nelson (Durham, N.C.: Duke University Press, 1987), 78.

14. Raymond E. Wolfinger and Steven J. Rosenstone, *Who Votes?* (New Haven: Yale University Press, 1980), 108–14; also, Stephen D. Shaffer, "Policy Differences between Voters and Non-voters in American Elections," *Western Political Quarterly* 35 (December 1982): 496–509; and Teixeira, *Why Americans Don't Vote* (see n. 12), 116.

15. Sidney Verba and Norman H. Nie, *Participation in America: Political Democracy and Social Equality* (New York: Harper and Row, 1972), 271.

16. Paul Kleppner, *Who Voted? The Dynamics of Electoral Turnout, 1870–1980* (New York: Praeger, 1982), 161–62; also Roger W. Cobb and Charles D. Elder, *Participation in American Politics: The Dynamics of Agenda-Building,* 2d ed. (Baltimore: Johns Hopkins University Press, 1983), 180.

17. James D. Wright, *The Dissent of the Governed: Alienation and Democracy in America* (New York: Academic Press, 1976), 279.

18. See Robert A. Dahl, *Dilemmas of Pluralist Democracy: Autonomy vs. Control* (New Haven: Yale University Press, 1982).

19. Ivor Crewe, "Electoral Participation," in *Democracy at the Polls: A Comparative Study of National Elections,* ed. David Butler, Howard R. Penniman, and Austin Ranney (Washington, D.C.: American Enterprise Institute, 1981), 262.

20. Max Kaase and Alan Marsh, "Distribution of Political Action," in *Political Action: Mass Participation in Five Western Democracies,* ed. Samuel H. Barnes, Max Kaase, et al. (Beverly Hills: Sage Publications, 1979), 168–69, 198.

21. For 1920–76, see Charles E. Johnson, Jr., "Nonvoting Americans," *Current Population Reports, Special Studies,* series P-23, no. 102 (April 1980): 1–27. Carol A. Cassel and Robert C. Luskin warn against "Simple Explanations of Turnout Decline," *American Political Science Review* 82 (December 1988): 1321–30.

22. Jack H. Nagel, *Participation* (Englewood Cliffs, N.J.: Prentice-Hall, Inc., 1987), 114.

23. Bruce A. Campbell, *The American Electorate: Attitudes and Action* (New York: Holt, Rinehart, and Winston, 1979), 232–58; and Harvard/ABC Symposium, *Voting for Democracy* (see n. 7), 10.

24. Miller, "Participation in Presidential Politics" (see n. 11), 24.

25. U.S. Bureau of the Census, "Voting and Registration in the Election of November 1980," *Current Population Reports, Population Characteristics,* series P-20, no. 370 (April 1982): 6.

26. Miller, "Participation in Presidential Politics" (see n. 11), 13, 16, 20.

27. Wright, *Dissent of the Governed* (see n. 17). Other studies report similar findings: Morris Rosenberg, "Some Determinants of Political Apathy," *Public Opinion Quarterly* 18 (Winter 1954): 349–66; Robert S. Gilmour and Robert L. Lamb, *Political Alienation in Contemporary America* (New York: St. Martin's Press, 1975); and Howard L. Reiter, "Why Is Turnout Down?" *Public Opinion Quarterly* 43 (Fall 1979): 297–311. On the effect on political participation of loss of trust in the political system, see the comments of Sissela Bok, *School for Scandal* (Cambridge: Joan Shorenstein Barone Center, John F. Kennedy School of Government, Harvard University, April 1990), 1–4, Discussion Paper D–4.

28. Angus Campbell, Gerald Gurin, and Warren Miller, *The Voter Decides* (Evanston, Ill.: Row, Peterson, 1954), 187; and George I. Balch, "Multiple Indicators in Survey Research: The Concept 'Sense of Political Efficacy'," *Political Methodology* 1 (Spring 1974): 1–43, esp. 24.

29. Paul R. Abramson, John H. Aldrich, and David W. Rohde, *Change and Continuity in the 1980 Elections* (Washington, D.C.: Congressional Quarterly, 1982), 87. See also Philip E. Converse, "Change in the American Electorate," in *The Human Meaning of Social Change,* ed. Angus Campbell and Philip E. Converse (New York: Russell Sage Foundation, 1972), 311–37; James S.

House and William M. Mason, "Political Alienation in America, 1952–1968," *American Sociological Review* 40 (April 1975): 123–47; and Wright, *Dissent of the Governed* (see n. 17), 168–200.

30. Balch, "Multiple Indicators in Survey Research" (see n. 28), 24.

31. Comment of pollster Richard Wirthlin at Harvard/ABC Symposium, *Voting for Democracy* (see n. 7), 16.

32. Campbell, *American Electorate* (see n. 23), 238.

33. Miller, "Participation in Presidential Politics" (see n. 11), 18–20; see also Warren E. Miller, Arthur H. Miller, and Edward J. Schneider, *American National Election Studies Data Sourcebook, 1952–1978* (Cambridge: Harvard University Press, 1980), 288; also, Michael Oreskes, "Profiles of Today's Youths: Many Just Don't Seem to Care," *New York Times,* June 28, 1990, pp. 1, A11, citing reports from the Times Mirror Center for the People and the Press and from the American Way.

34. Abramson, Aldrich, and Rohde, *Change and Continuity* (see n. 29), 86.

35. Leon D. Epstein, *Political Parties in the American Mold* (Madison: University of Wisconsin Press, 1986), 271.

36. Paul R. Abramson and John H. Aldrich, "The Decline of Electoral Participation in America," *American Political Science Review* 76 (September 1982): 505, 510. See also Stephen D. Shaffer, "A Multivariate Explanation of Decreasing Turnout in Presidential Elections, 1960–1976," *American Journal of Political Science* 25 (February 1981): 90.

37. Verba and Nie, *Participation in America* (see n. 15), chap. 10.

38. Miller, "Participation in Presidential Politics" (see n. 11), 7.

39. Wolfinger and Rosenstone, *Who Votes?* (see n. 14), 35–36, 102.

40. Ibid., 47, and Oreskes, "Profiles" (see n. 33), p. A11.

41. U.S. Bureau of the Census, "Voting and Registration in the Election of November 1980" (see n. 25): 7.

42. U.S. Bureau of the Census, "Voting and Registration in the Election of November 1984," *Current Population Reports, Population Characteristics,* series P-20, no. 397 (January 1985): 1–2.

43. New York Times/CBS Poll, "Portrait of the Electorate," *New York Times,* November 10, 1988, p. 18.

44. Wolfinger and Rosenstone, *Who Votes?* (see n. 14), 43.

45. Poll, "Portrait" (see n. 43), p. 18.

46. Robert W. Jackman, "Political Institutions and Voter Turnout in the Industrial Democracies," *American Political Science Review* 81 (June 1987): 419.

47. Harvard/ABC Symposium, *Voting for Democracy* (see n. 7), 12–13. See also the report of the Clearinghouse on Voter Education, "How Voter Registration is Maintained in the U.S.," cited in "Outdated Voting Rules Deplored in U.S. Survey," *New York Times,* September 21, 1984, p. 16; also, the Committee for the Study of the American Electorate, in "Non-Voter Study '83–'84," Washington, D.C., December 20, 1983, accompanying news release, 4; and G. Bingham Powell, Jr., "American Voter Turnout in Comparative Perspective," *American Political Science Review* 80 (March 1986): 17–37.

48. E. J. Dionne, Jr., "If Nonvoters Had Voted: Same Winner, but Bigger," *New York Times,* November 21, 1988, p. 10.

49. Walter Dean Burnham, *The Current Crisis in American Politics* (New York: Oxford University Press, 1982), 128; and Richard L. Berke, "Study Finds Marked Drop in Voter Registration Since '84," *New York Times,* November 4, 1988, p. 12.

50. Orren, "Linkage" (see n. 13), 107.

51. John R. Bauer and Neftali G. Garcia, "Voter Registration Reform since 1972: An Update," *State Government* 59 (September/October 1986): 108.

52. The Committee for the Study of the American Electorate, *Creating the Opportunity—How Changes in Registration and Voting Law Can Enhance Voter Participation* (Washington, D.C.: 1987), 13.

53. Berke, "Study Finds Marked Drop" (see n. 49), and "Government of (Half) the People," *New York Times,* November 6, 1988, p. 24.

54. David Glass, Peverill Squire, and Raymond Wolfinger, "Voter Turnout: An International Comparison," *Public Opinion* 6 (December–January 1984): 52–53.

55. Poll, "Portrait" (see n. 43), p. 18.

56. Wolfinger and Rosenstone, *Who Votes?* (see n. 14), 54.

57. Committee, "Non-Voter Study '83–'84" (see n. 47), news release, 4.

58. Committee for the Study of the American Electorate, "Non-Voter Study '84–'85," news release dated November 9, 1984, 1.

59. G. Bingham Powell, Jr., *Contemporary Democracies: Participation, Stability, and Violence* (Cambridge: Harvard University Press, 1982), 113.

60. Glass, Squire, and Wolfinger, "Voter Turnout" (see n. 54), 52–53.

61. Orren, "Linkage" (see n. 13), 91.

62. Crewe, "Electoral Participation" (see n. 19), 240.

63. Powell, *Contemporary Democracies* (see n. 59), 115.

64. Crewe, "Electoral Participation" (see n. 19), 241–48.

65. Herbert E. Alexander and Brian A. Haggerty, *Financing the 1984 Election* (Lexington, Mass.: Lexington Books, 1987), 26.

66. Powell, *Contemporary Democracies* (see n. 59), 116.

67. Sidney Verba, Norman H. Nie, and Jae-On Kim, *Participation and Political Equality: A Seven-Nation Comparison* (Cambridge: Cambridge University Press, 1978), 119–21; and Robert R. Alford, *Party and Society: The Anglo-American Democracies* (Chicago: Rand McNally, 1963), 302.

68. Verba and Nie, *Participation in America* (see n. 15), 157; and Wolfinger and Rosenstone, *Who Votes?* (see n. 14), 90–91.

69. Thomas B. Edsall, "Money, Technology Revive GOP Force," *Washington Post,* June 17, 1984, p. A1.

70. Thomas E. Cavanagh of the Joint Center for Political Studies was quoted to that effect in Thomas B. Edsall, "Elections Can Hinge on Persuading Likely Opponents Not to Vote," *Washington Post,* April 29, 1984, p. A2.

71. For examples, see Richard Harrington, "Vote, Yeah, Yeah, Yeah—On MTV, Rock Stars Try to Raise the Electorate," *Washington Post,* September 25, 1984, p. C1; Susan Rasky, "Indians Begin to Weigh Their Political Potential," *New York Times,* September 16, 1984, p. E8; Kathlene Teltsch, "Philanthropic Groups Spur Drives for Registering Voters," *New York Times,* July 28, 1984, p. 7; Bill Cutler, "Planting Seeds—The Voter Education Project," *Southern Exposure* XII (February 1984): 41-45; Gary Delgado, "An Alternative View— Will it build the power of low-income people, or deliver them to the Democratic Party?" *Southern Exposure* XII (February 1984): 53-54; "Plan to Register Hispanic Voters Is Announced," *Washington Post,* September 16, 1983, p. A2; Willie Velasquez, "542 Campaigns—The Southwest Voter Registration and Education Project," *Southern Exposure* XII (February 1984), 46-48; and Thomas B. Edsall, "New Voter Sign-Ups May Favor the GOP," *Washington Post,* November 2, 1984, p. A1.

72. Abramson, Aldrich, and Rohde, *Change and Continuity* (see n. 29), 87.

73. Kleppner, *Who Voted?* (see n. 16), 158–59.

74. Harvard/ABC Symposium, *Voting for Democracy* (see n. 7), 27.

75. Phil Gailey, "G.O.P. Aide to Seek Wider Vote Fraud Drive," *New York Times,* October 24, 1986, p. 13; and Paul Taylor, "GOP Drops Its Ballot-Security Program," *Washington Post National Weekly Edition,* November 3, 1986, p. 11.

76. Kleppner, *Who Voted?* (see n. 16), 158–59.

77. Edsall, "Elections Can Hinge" (see n. 70).

78. Thomas B. Edsall, "More Bad News for Mondale: Party Bosses and Feuding Factions Sabotaged the Drive for New Voters," *Washington Post,* October 21, 1984, p. C1.

79. John H. Aldrich, "Some Problems in Testing Two Rational Models of Participation," *American Journal of Political Science* 20 (November 1976): 713–33.

80. Tom Wicker, "Big Voter Turnout Benefits Whom?" *Tennessean* (Nashville), September 5, 1984, p. A10.

81. Michael X. Delli Carpini, "Scooping the Voters? The Consequences of the Networks' Early Call of the 1980 Presidential Race," *Journal of Politics* 46 (August 1984): 866. See also Orren, "Linkage" (see n. 13), 102–6.

82. William C. Adams, "Early TV Calls in 1984: How Western Voters Deplored but Ignored Them" (Unpublished paper, George Washington University, Spring 1985), 19.

83. For another interpretation of certain polling results, see Curtis B. Gans, Testimony before the United States House of Representatives Committee on Administration, August 1, 1985. Alex S. Jones reported that economic incentives might induce network collaboration in a single election day poll, "Television Networks Reported Ready to Form Group to Poll Voters," *New York Times,* February 24, 1990, p. 8.

84. Shaffer, "Multivariate Explanation" (see n. 36), 70; and Michael J. Robinson and Margaret A. Sheehan, *Over the Wire and on TV: CBS and UPI in Campaign '80* (New York: Russell Sage Foundation, 1983).

85. Harvard/ABC Symposium, *Voting for Democracy* (see n. 7), 30.

86. Edwin M. Yoder, Jr., "Why Don't We Vote?" *Washington Post,* October 11, 1983, p. A15.

87. Max Farrand, ed., *The Records of the Federal Convention of 1787,* vol. 1 (New Haven: Yale University Press, 1966), 362.

88. Crewe, "Electoral Participation" (see n. 19), 232.

89. Richard W. Boyd, "Decline of U.S. Voter Turnout: Structural Explanations," *American Politics Quarterly* 9 (April 1981): 141–46; and Boyd, "The Effects of Primaries and Statewide Races on Voter Turnout," *Journal of Politics* 51 (August 1989): 730–39.

90. Committee, *Opportunity* (see n. 52), 6; see also Martin P. Wattenberg, "From a Partisan to a Candidate-centered Electorate," in *The New American Political System—Second Version,* ed. Anthony King (Washington, D.C.: AEI Press, 1990), 155.

91. Benjamin Ginsberg and Martin Shefter, *Politics by Other Means—The Declining Importance of Elections in America* (New York: Basic Books, 1990), 192-94.

92. *Voting Assistance Guide '86–'87* (Washington, D.C.: Voting Assistance Program, Office of the Secretary of Defense, 1986), 3.

93. Harvard/ABC Symposium, *Voting for Democracy* (see n. 7), 30–31.

94. Orren, "Linkage" (see n. 13), 114–16; see also Wolfinger and Rosenstone, *Who Votes?* (see n. 14), 72–78.

95. Alexander and Haggerty, *Financing the 1984 Election* (see n. 65), 26. See also James A. Barnes, "Eyeing Federal Voter Registration Rules," *National Journal* 21 (February 25, 1989): 480; and Michael Oreskes, "Easy Voter Registration Approved by the House," *New York Times,* February 6, 1990, p. A13.

96. For a discussion of universal voter enrollment, see Kevin P. Phillips and Paul H. Blackman, *Electoral Reform and Voter Participation: Federal Registration—A False Remedy for Voter Apathy* (Washington, D.C.: American Enterprise Institute, 1975), 23–34; William Crotty, "The Franchise: Registration Changes and Voter Representation," in *Paths to Political Reform,* ed. William Crotty (Lexington, Mass.: Lexington Books, 1980), 102–4; and Orren, "Linkage" (see n. 13), 112–13.

97. Orren, "Linkage," 113.

98. Committee, *Opportunity,* (see n. 52), 11.

99. Richard G. Smolka, *Election Day Registration: The Minnesota and Wisconsin Experience in 1976* (Washington, D.C.: American Enterprise Institute, 1977); and Orren, "Linkage" (see n. 13), 111.

100. Orren, "Linkage," 111–12.

101. Wolfinger and Rosenstone, *Who Votes?* (see n. 14), 88.

102. Orren, "Linkage" (see n. 13), 110; and Richard G. Smolka, *Registering Voters by Mail: The Maryland and New Jersey Experience* (Washington, D.C.: American Enterprise Institute, 1975).

103. *Election Administration Reports* 7 (January 5, 1977), cited in Orren, "Linkage" (see n. 13), 376.

104. Glass, Squire, and Wolfinger, "Voter Turnout" (see n. 54), 55.

105. Frances Fox Piven and Richard A. Cloward, "Prospects for Voter Registration Reform: A Report on the Experiences of the Human SERVE Campaign," *PS* 18 (Summer 1985): 592. For a full report and analysis, see Piven and Cloward, *Why Americans Don't Vote* (New York: Pantheon Books, 1988), 209–47.

106. Peverill Squire, Raymond E. Wolfinger, and David P. Glass, "Residential Mobility and Voter Turnout," *American Political Science Review* 81 (March 1987): 57.

107. Committee, "Non-Voter Study '83–'84" (see n. 47), summary, 6. Raymond E. Wolfinger discusses this and some other provisions of the National Voter Registration Act, approved by the U.S. House of Representatives in 1990, in "How to Raise Voter Turnout," *New York Times,* June 6, 1990, p. A15.

108. *Election Administration Reports* 16 (November 10, 1986): 6.

109. Committee, *Opportunity* (see n. 52), 11.

110. Richard H. Austin, *A New Approach to Voter Registration* (Lansing: Department of State of Michigan, c. 1985), 1–24; also, Frances Fox Piven and Richard A. Cloward, "National Voter Registration Reform: How It Might Be Won," *PS* 21 (Fall 1988): 872.

111. Committee, *Opportunity* (see n. 52), 14.

112. E. J. Dionne, Jr., "Bill to Ease Registration of Voters Makes Gains," *New York Times,* May 7, 1989, p. 17.

113. For a fuller discussion of these measures, see Orren, "Linkage" (see n. 13), 101–2; Richard G. Smolka, "Can Sunday Voting Make a Difference?" (Paper prepared for "Voting for Democracy" symposium; see n. 7); Kevin C. Gottlieb, "Twenty-four Hour Voting" (Paper prepared for "Voting for Democracy" symposium); letter of Patrick J. Cleary, "Uniform Poll Closing Gives the Voter a Break," *New York Times,* December 20, 1988, p. 30; and Orren, "Linkage," 101.

114. Stephen Hess, "Proposal: A New Presidential Selection Timetable," in *The Presidency in Transition,* ed. James P. Pfiffner and Gordon Hoxie (New York: Center for the Study of the Presidency, 1989), 99–104.

115. Peter Bragdon, "House Approves Bill Setting a Uniform Poll Closing Time," *Congressional Quarterly* 44 (February 1, 1986): 200.

116. Dave Kaplan, "House Again Asks to Close Polls Uniformly," *Congressional Quarterly* 45 (November 14, 1987): 2826; and *Tennessean* (Nashville), April 6, 1989, p. 1.

117. Orren, "Linkage" (see n. 13), 101.

118. James E. Zinser and Paul A. Dawson, "Encouraging Voter Participation," in *Political Finance,* ed. Herbert E. Alexander (Beverly Hills: Sage Publications, 1979), 232–36.

119. Stephen Earl Bennett, *Apathy in America, 1960–1984: Causes and Consequences of Citizen Political Indifference* (Dobbs Ferry, N.Y.: Transnational Publishers, Inc., 1986), 163–72. See also Bennett, "The Uses and Abuses of Registration and Turnout Data: An Analysis of Piven and Cloward's Studies of Nonvoting in America," *PS* 23 (June 1990): 166-71.

120. Herbert J. Gans, *Middle American Individualism—The Future of Liberal Democracy* (New York: Free Press, 1988), 123–33.

121. See Gerald John Fresia, *There Comes A Time—A Challenge to the Two Party System* (New York: Praeger, 1986).

122. Dean Baquet, "Feuds and Favoritism Keep Old Voting Machines in New York," *New York Times,* June 5, 1990, p. B12.

123. Ronnie Dugger, "Annals of Democracy—Counting Votes," *The New Yorker,* November 7, 1988, 43.

124. Ibid., 56.

125. Ibid., 104.

126. Kleppner, *Who Voted?* (see n. 16), 160.

Chapter Eight. Political Agendas and Choosing Presidents

1. Daniel Patrick Moynihan, "The 'New Science of Politics' and the Old Art of Government," *Public Interest* 86 (Winter 1987): 27–28, 33.

2. Roger W. Cobb and Charles D. Elder, *Participation in American Politics: The Dynamics of Agenda-Building,* 2d ed. (Baltimore: Johns Hopkins University Press, 1983), 164.

3. Jeffrey K. Tulis, *The Rhetorical Presidency* (Princeton, N.J.: Princeton University Press, 1987), 189.

4. Theodore J. Lowi, "Party, Policy, and Constitution in America," in *The American Party Systems,* ed. William Nisbet Chambers and Walter Dean Burnham

(New York: Oxford University Press, 1967), 263–64; and Vernon Bogdanor, *The People and the Party System: The Referendum and Electoral Reform in British Politics* (Cambridge: Cambridge University Press, 1981), 13.

5. Richard Rose, *Do Parties Make a Difference?* 2d ed. (Chatham, N.J.: Chatham House Publishers, Inc., 1984), 48.

6. Ibid., 53–54.

7. Anthony King, "What Do Elections Decide?" in *Democracy at the Polls: A Comparative Study of Competitive National Elections,* ed. David Butler, Howard R. Penniman, and Austin Ranney (Washington, D.C.: American Enterprise Institute, 1981), 293–322.

8. Russell J. Dalton, Scott C. Flanagan, and Paul Allen Beck, "Political Forces and Partisan Change," in *Electoral Change in Advanced Industrial Democracies: Realignment or Dealignment?* ed. Dalton, Flanagan, and Beck (Princeton, N.J.: Princeton University Press, 1984), 461–62; and King, "What Do Elections Decide?" (see n. 7), 296.

9. Moynihan, "New Science of Politics" (see n. 1), 32–33.

10. Cobb and Elder, *Participation* (see n. 2), 163.

11. Ibid., 175.

12. Bert A. Rockman, *The Leadership Question: The Presidency and the American System* (New York: Praeger, 1984), 5.

13. William M. Lunch, *The Nationalization of American Politics* (Berkeley and Los Angeles: University of California Press, 1987), 251–52.

14. Harlan Cleveland, "Foreign Policy and Presidential Selection" (Paper prepared for the Study of the U.S. Presidential Selection Process sponsored by the Alfred P. Sloan Foundation, Alexander Heard, Director, 1984), 19. Peter Drucker identifies four current economies: of the nation; of the region; of the world network of money, credit, and investment flows; and of transnational enterprises, viewing the world as one market. See "The Post-Business Society," *New Perspectives Quarterly* 6 (Fall 1989): 24.

15. Richard Rose describes deep-rooted changes in the structure of American political interests in *The Post-Modern President—The White House Meets the World* (Chatham, N.J.: Chatham House Publishers, Inc., 1988).

16. William Schneider, " 'Old Politics' Yield to New U.S. Ideologies," *Los Angeles Times,* March 13, 1983, sec. 4, p. 3.

17. See Robert Harmel and Kenneth Janda, *Parties and Their Environments: Limits to Reform?* (New York: Longman, 1982), 121–25; and Sylvia Tesh, "In Support of Single-Issue Politics," *Political Science Quarterly* 99 (Spring 1984): 27–44.

18. Everett Carll Ladd, Jr., with Charles D. Hadley, *Transformations of the American Party System: Political Coalitions from the New Deal to the 1970s* (New York: Norton, 1975), 327–28.

19. Rhodes Cook and Tom Watson, "New Generation Poised to Tip Voting Scales," *Congressional Quarterly* 43 (November 23, 1985): 2421–28.

20. Harmel and Janda, *Parties and Their Environments* (see n. 17), 121.

21. James M. Dwinell, "Master of the Media," *Campaigns and Elections,* May/June 1988, 4.

22. Alan D. Monroe, "American Party Platforms and Public Opinion," *American Journal of Political Science* 27 (February 1983): 39.

23. Benjamin I. Page, Robert Y. Shapiro, and Glenn R. Dempsey, "What Moves Public Opinion?" *American Political Science Review* 81 (March 1987): 23–43.

24. David S. Broder, "Parties Resharpen Decades-Old Ideological Clash," *Washington Post,* August 18, 1984, p. A1.

25. Theodore H. White, *The Making of the President 1960* (New York: Atheneum, 1961), 193.

26. Warren E. Miller, *Without Consent: Mass-Elite Linkages in Presidential Politics* (Lexington: University Press of Kentucky, 1988), 77.

27. Michael J. Malbin, "The Conventions, Platforms, and Issue Activists," in *The American Elections of 1980,* ed. Austin Ranney (Washington, D.C.: American Enterprise Institute, 1981), 134–35.

28. Richard L. Rubin, *Party Dynamics: The Democratic Coalition and the Politics of Change* (New York: Oxford University Press, 1976), 181.

29. Thomas Ferguson and Joel Rogers, eds., *The Hidden Election: Politics and Economics in the 1980 Presidential Campaign* (New York: Pantheon Books, 1981), ix.

30. William Crotty and John S. Jackson III, *Presidential Primaries and Nominations* (Washington, D.C.: Congressional Quarterly, 1985), 137.

31. For example, see Denis G. Sullivan et al., *The Politics of Representation: The Democratic Convention 1972* (New York: St. Martin's Press, 1974), 71–78.

32. Jeff Fishel, *Presidents and Promises: From Campaign Pledge to Presidential Performance* (Washington, D.C.: Congressional Quarterly, 1985), 28.

33. Gerald M. Pomper, *Voters, Elections, and Parties—The Practice of Democratic Theory* (New Brunswick, N.J.: Transaction Books, 1988), 164.

34. Gerald M. Pomper with Susan S. Lederman, *Elections in America: Control and Influence in Democratic Politics,* 2d ed. (New York: Longman, 1980), 161–65; data for 1980, letter from Gerald Pomper to Alexander Heard, September 11, 1985. Using a somewhat different method, Alan D. Monroe reached a similar finding for 1980 in "American Party Platforms" (see n. 22), 38–39. See also John Machacek, "Politicians run under—and away from—party platforms," *The Sun* (San Bernardino, California), July 17, 1988, pp. 20–21.

35. Ian Budge and Richard I. Hofferbert, "Mandates and Policy Outputs: U.S. Party Platforms and Federal Expenditures," *American Political Science Review* 84 (March 1990): 111-31.

36. Judson L. James, "Conventions and Coalition Building," in *Politics in America: Studies in Policy Analysis,* ed. Michael P. Smith (Washington, D.C.: University Press of America, 1981), 39.

37. Jo Freeman, "The Political Culture of the Republican and Democratic Parties," *Political Science Quarterly* 101 (Centennial Year 1886–1986): 327–56.

38. Fishel, *Presidents and Promises* (see n. 32), 28. Totals are rounded to nearest hundredth word.

39. Anne N. Costain, "Changes in the Role of Ideology in American National Nominating Conventions and Among Party Identifiers," *Western Political Quarterly* 33 (March 1980): 85–86.

40. John H. Kessel, *Presidential Parties* (Homewood, Ill.: Dorsey, 1984), 562–63.

41. Monroe, "American Party Platforms" (see n. 22), 30.

42. Broder, "Parties Resharpen Decades-Old Ideological Clash" (see n. 24).

43. John H. Kessel, *Presidential Campaign Politics: Coalition Strategies and Citizen Response,* 2d ed. (Homewood, Ill.: Dorsey, 1984), 52; also, John H. Kessel, "A Consideration of Some Party Functions" (Paper prepared for the Study of the U.S. Presidential Selection Process sponsored by the Alfred P. Sloan Foundation, Alexander Heard, Director, 1984), 46–47.

44. Tulis, *Rhetorical Presidency* (see n. 3), 189.

45. Pomper, *Elections in America* (see n. 34), 134–35. The treatment of platform contents here and elsewhere has drawn on generous letters from Gerald M. Pomper of July 23, August 16, and September 11, 1985, and from researcher John R. Martin of August 16 and September 11, 1985.

46. James W. Davis, *National Conventions in an Age of Party Reform* (Westport, Conn.: Greenwood Press, 1983), 113–14; and David E. Price, *Bringing Back the Parties* (Washington, D.C.: Congressional Quarterly, 1984), 284–88.

47. Paul Laxalt, quoted by Nadine Cohodas in "Solidly Conservative Platform Ready for Adoption by GOP," *Congressional Quarterly* 42 (August 18, 1984): 2023; also, Helen Dewar and James R. Dickenson, "Laxalt Terms GOP Platform Non-Binding," *Washington Post,* August 19, 1984, p. A14; and T. R. Reid, "Democrats' Platform Built to Support Weight of Three Candidates," *Washington Post,* July 18, 1984, p. A11.

48. Pomper, *Elections in America* (see n. 34), 145–46.

49. James I. Lengle, "Changing the Rules Changes the Game: An Assessment of Three Nomination Reforms for 1984," *Commonsense,* 1982, no. 2:18.

50. Price, *Bringing Back the Parties* (see n. 46), 174.

51. Jeffrey L. Pressman, "Groups and Group Caucuses," *Political Science Quarterly* 92 (Winter 1977–78): 673–82; and Malbin, "Conventions, Platforms, and Issue Activists" (see n. 27), 99.

52. Daniel Yankelovich, "How the Public Learns the Public's Business," *Kettering Review* (Winter 1985): 8.

53. Bill Kovach, "Too Much Opinion, at the Expense of Fact," *New York Times,* September 13, 1989, p. 23; and Kathleen A. Frankovic, "Media Polls: Monitoring Changes in Public Opinion," *ICPSR Bulletin* (February 1990): 1–2.

54. Sidney Verba and Norman H. Nie, *Participation in America: Political Democracy and Social Equality* (New York: Harper and Row, 1972), 268.

55. Thomas R. Marshall, *Presidential Nominations in a Reform Age* (New York: Praeger, 1981), 142; and Verba and Nie, *Participation in America,* 268.

56. James R. Beniger and Robert J. Giuffra, Jr., "The Role of Public Opinion Polls in Presidential Selection" (Paper prepared for the Study of the U.S. Presidential Selection Process sponsored by the Alfred P. Sloan Foundation, Alexander Heard, Director, 1984), 61; also Beniger and Giuffra, "Public Opinion Polling: Command and Control in Presidential Campaigns," in *Presidential Selection,* ed. Alexander Heard and Michael Nelson (Durham, N.C.: Duke University Press, 1987), 189–215.

57. Alexis de Tocqueville, *Democracy in America,* vol. 2 (1835; reprint, New York: Knopf, 1948), 10–11.

58. James Bryce, *The American Commonwealth,* vol. 1 (New York: Macmillian, 1888; New York: AMS Press, 1973), 8.

59. Beniger and Giuffra, "Command and Control" (see n. 56), 190.

60. Albert H. Cantril, "The Press and the Pollster," *Annals of the American Academy of Political and Social Science* 427 (September 1976): 45–52.

61. Austin Ranney, quoted by Ron Suskind in "The Power of Political Consultants," *New York Times Magazine,* August 12, 1984, p. 32.

62. Theodore J. Lowi, *The Personal President: Power Invested, Promise Unfulfilled* (Ithaca, N.Y.: Cornell University Press, 1985), 116.

63. Michael Wheeler, *Lies, Damn Lies, and Statistics: The Manipulation of Public Opinion in America* (New York: Liveright, 1976), xiii; also, Richard L.

Henshel, "The Emergence of Bandwagon Effects: A Theory," *The Sociological Quarterly* 28 (1987): 493–511.

64. Dennis Kavanagh, "Public Opinion Polls," in Butler, Penniman, and Ranney, *Democracy at the Polls* (see n. 7), 213.

65. Wheeler, *Lies* (see n. 63), xiv–xvi. Many journalists questioned polling results during the 1984 nomination and election campaigns, e.g., Robert Reinhold, "Polls' Divergence Puzzles Experts," *New York Times*, August 15, 1984, p. 1; Everett Carll Ladd, "Polls Apart: A Primer on Wayward Surveys," *Wall Street Journal*, August 16, 1984, p. 22; Richard Harwood, "Conflicting Campaign Polls Point to One Certainty: Some Are Wrong," *Washington Post*, October 31, 1984, p. A6; Adam Clymer, "Polls and Hunches on Impact of Female Candidate," *New York Times*, July 9, 1984, p. 11; and Michael Barone, "The Polls and Central America," *Washington Post*, August 25, 1983, p. A21. David E. Rosenbaum, however, wrote on November 8, 1984, in the *New York Times* (p. 11) under the heading: "A Good Election for Poll Takers: Major Companies Predicted the Winner and Most Were Close on Final Results."

66. Harold Mendelsohn and Irving Crespi, *Polls, Television, and New Politics* (Scranton, Pa.: Chandler Publishing, 1970), 43–49.

67. Kavanagh, "Public Opinion Polls" (see n. 64), 213.

68. Richard Rose, "Toward Normality: Public Opinion Polls in the 1979 Election," in *Britain at the Polls, 1979: A Study of the General Election,* ed. Howard R. Penniman (Washington, D.C.: American Enterprise Institute, 1979), 209.

69. Marjorie Randon Hershey, *Running for Office: The Political Education of Campaigners* (Chatham, N.J.: Chatham House Publishers, Inc., 1984), 273.

70. Tom Wicker in *The Press and Public Policy,* moderated by John Charles Daly (Washington, D.C.: American Enterprise Institute, 1979), 17.

71. Maxwell E. McCombs and Donald L. Shaw, "The Agenda-Setting Function of the Press," in *The Emergence of American Political Issues: The Agenda-Setting Function of the Press,* ed. Shaw and McCombs (St. Paul: West Publishing, 1977), 13–14; and McCombs and Shaw, "Agenda-Setting and the Political Process," in ibid., 150.

72. Louis Banks, "Living in a Newsocracy: All the News All the Time" (Working paper, Alfred P. Sloan School of Management, Massachusetts Institute of Technology, August 1980), 4.

73. McCombs and Shaw, "Agenda-Setting Function," in Shaw and McCombs, *Emergence of American Political Issues* (see n. 71), 11.

74. Karen S. Johnson and Camille Elebash, "The Contagion from the Right—The Americanization of British Political Advertising," in *New Perspectives on Political Advertising,* ed. Lynda Lee Kaid, Dan Nimmo, and Keith R. Sanders (Carbondale and Edwardsville: Southern Illinois University Press, 1986), 296–97.

75. Page, Shapiro, and Dempsey, "What Moves Public Opinion?" (see n. 23), 39.

76. Shanto Iyengar and Donald R. Kinder, *News that Matters* (Chicago: University of Chicago Press, 1987), 33.

77. Ibid., 60.

78. Doris A. Graber, *Mass Media and American Politics,* 3d ed. (Washington, D.C.: CQ Press, 1989), 287, 300. See also David L. Paletz, ed., *Political Communication Research: Approaches, Studies, Assessments* (Norwood, N.J.: Ablex Publishing Corporation, 1987), 176–77; and Shanto Iyengar and Donald R. Kinder, "Psychological Accounts of Agenda-Setting," in *Mass Media and*

Political Thought, ed. Sidney Kraus and Richard M. Perloff (Beverly Hills: Sage Publications, 1985), 177, 133–36.

79. Denis McQuail, "The Influence and Effects of Mass Media," in *Media Power in Politics,* ed. Doris A. Graber (Washington, D.C.: Congressional Quarterly, 1984), 49; and S. Robert Lichter, Daniel Amundson, and Richard Noyes, *The Video Campaign—Network Coverage of the 1988 Primaries* (Washington, D.C.: American Enterprise Institute for Public Policy Research, 1988), 104–6.

80. Shanto Iyengar, Mark D. Peters, and Donald R. Kinder, "Experimental Demonstrations of the 'Not-So-Minimal' Consequences of Television News Programs," in Graber, *Media Power in Politics* (see n. 79), 58–59.

81. Christopher Arterton, "Presidential Campaigns and the News Media" (Paper prepared for the Study of the U.S. Presidential Selection Process sponsored by the Alfred P. Sloan Foundation, Alexander Heard, Director, February 1984), 27.

82. Ibid., 28.

83. Sidney Blumenthal, *The Permanent Campaign* (New York: Simon and Schuster, 1982), 20–26.

84. Wilson Carey McWilliams, "The Meaning of the Election," in *The Election of 1984: Reports and Interpretations,* Gerald Pomper et al., ed. Marlene Michels Pomper (Chatham, N.J.: Chatham House Publishers, Inc., 1985), 179.

85. Maxwell E. McCombs, "Newspapers versus Television: Mass Communication Effects across Time," in Shaw and McCombs, *Emergence of American Political Issues* (see n. 71), 105.

86. Jeff Greenfield, *The Real Campaign: How the Media Missed the Story of the 1980 Campaign* (New York: Summit Books, 1982), 11–33.

87. Nelson W. Polsby, "Interest Groups and the Presidency: Trends in Political Intermediation in America," in *American Politics and Public Policy,* ed. Walter Dean Burnham and Martha Wagner Weinberg (Cambridge: Massachusetts Institute of Technology Press, 1978), 45.

88. Page, Shapiro, and Dempsey, "What Moves Public Opinion?" (see n. 23), 39, 37, 40.

89. David H. Weaver, Doris A. Graber, Maxwell E. McCombs, and Chaim H. Eyal, *Media Agenda-Setting in a Presidential Election: Issues, Images, and Interest* (New York: Praeger, 1981), 206–8.

90. Rockman, *The Leadership Question* (see n. 12), 2.

91. Aaron Wildavsky, *Speaking Truth to Power: The Art and Craft of Policy Analysis* (Boston: Little, Brown, 1979), 57.

92. Lawrence D. Brown, *New Policies, New Politics: Government's Response to Government's Growth* (Washington, D.C.: Brookings Institution, 1983), 67, 68–69.

93. Cyrus Vance, *Hard Choices: Four Critical Years in America's Foreign Policy* (New York: Simon and Schuster, 1983), 13.

94. Undated releases. The address of the Committee for a Single Six-Year Term has been Suite 1010, 1019 19th Street, N.W., Washington, DC 20036. The extraordinary defense and world affairs burdens that have weighed on the U.S. government and its president are emphasized in Lynn Rusten and Paul C. Stern, *Crisis Management in the Nuclear Age* (Washington, D.C.: National Academy Press, 1987).

95. Ralf Dahrendorf, letter essay to Alexander Heard, December 13, 1983. See Bruce Buchanan, "The Six-Year One-Term Presidency: A New Look at an Old Proposal," *Presidential Studies Quarterly* xviii (Winter 1988): 129–42.

96. For a contribution to such, see Henry Kissinger and Cyrus Vance, "Bipartisan Objectives for American Foreign Policy," *Foreign Affairs* 66 (Summer 1988): 899–921.

97. Ernest R. May, "Changing International Stakes in Presidential Selection," in *Presidential Selection,* ed. Alexander Heard and Michael Nelson (Durham, N.C.: Duke University Press, 1987), 48, 45–47. Martin Tolchin reports anxieties stimulated by political action committees of U.S. subsidiaries of foreign corporations in "U.S. May Prohibit Foreign-Tied PAC's," *New York Times,* July 4, 1990, p. Y9.

Chapter Nine. Searching for Better Leadership

1. John H. Aldrich, *Before the Convention: Strategies and Choices in Presidential Nomination Campaigns* (Chicago: University of Chicago Press, 1980), 5.

2. Douglas W. Jaenicke, "The Jacksonian Integration of Parties into the Constitutional System," *Political Science Quarterly* 101 (1986): 102.

3. Richard P. McCormick, *The Presidential Game: The Origins of American Presidential Politics* (New York: Oxford University Press, 1982), 17.

4. Robert A. Dahl, "On Removing Certain Impediments to Democracy in the United States," *Political Science Quarterly* 92 (Spring 1977): 7.

5. Seymour Martin Lipset and William Schneider, *The Confidence Gap: Business, Labor, and Government in the Public Mind* (New York: Free Press, 1983), 390.

6. Louis Harris, "Despite Skepticism, Voters Say Government Can Be Made to Work," *Harris Survey,* no. 91 (November 13, 1978), 1, cited in ibid., 392.

7. Thomas E. Cronin, *The State of the Presidency,* 2d ed. (Boston: Little, Brown, 1980), 28.

8. John H. Aldrich, "Methods and Actors: The Relationship of Processes to Candidates," in *Presidential Selection,* ed. Alexander Heard and Michael Nelson (Durham, N.C.: Duke University Press, 1987), 165–66.

9. Ibid, 181. On effects of personal attributes within the present institutional structure, see Dean Keith Simonton, *Why Presidents Succeed—A Political Psychology of Leadership* (New Haven: Yale University Press, 1987).

10. Jeff Greenfield, *Playing to Win: An Insider's Guide to Politics* (New York: Simon and Schuster, 1980), 155–56. On the evolution of campaign technologies and practices, see J. Leonard Reinsch, *Getting Elected—From Radio and Roosevelt to Television and Reagan* (New York: Hippocrene Books, 1988), and on the increasing participation in partisan politics by entertainment celebrities, see Len Sherman, *The Good, the Bad, and the Famous* (New York: Carol Publishing Group, 1990).

11. John H. Aldrich, "On the Relationship between Methods of Presidential Nomination and Candidates Who Seek Nomination" (Paper prepared for the Alfred P. Sloan Foundation Study of the U.S. Presidential Selection Process, Alexander Heard, Director, 1983), 43.

12. Hugh Heclo, "Presidential and Prime Ministerial Selection," in *Perspectives on Presidential Selection,* ed. Donald R. Matthews (Washington, D.C: Brookings Institution, 1973), 32.

13. Erwin C. Hargrove, "What Manner of Man? The Crisis of the Contemporary Presidency," in *Choosing the President,* ed. James David Barber (Englewood Cliffs, N.J.: Prentice Hall, 1974), 32.

14. Robert C. Tucker, "Presidential Selection and the Superpower Relationship" (Paper prepared for the Study of the U.S. Presidential Selection Process sponsored by the Alfred P. Sloan Foundation, Alexander Heard, Director, March 1984), 6.

15. Ibid., 15–37.

16. McGeorge Bundy, "Notes on the Role of Nuclear Weapons Policy in Presidential Campaigns" (Letter essay prepared for the Study of the U.S. Presidential Selection Process sponsored by the Alfred P. Sloan Foundation, Alexander Heard, Director, 1984), 1.

17. Aldrich, "Methods of Presidential Nomination" (see n. 11), 12.

18. Peter Goldman and Tony Fuller, *The Quest for the Presidency 1984* (New York: Newsweek/Bantam Books, 1985), 74. See also Richard F. Fenno, Jr., *The Presidential Odyssey of John Glenn* (Washington, D. C.: CQ Press, 1990), 183-225. Senator Paul Simon, Democrat of Illinois, gave a relatively sanguine view of his experience in unsuccessfully seeking the Democratic nomination in 1988 in *Winners and Losers—the 1988 Race for the Presidency—One Candidate's Perspective* (New York: Continuum, 1989).

19. Michael J. Malbin, "Financing Presidential Nomination Campaigns" (Paper prepared for the Conference on Presidential Primaries, Gerald R. Ford Library, Ann Arbor, Mich., April 24–26, 1985), 6–7.

20. Herbert E. Alexander, "American Presidential Elections Since Public Funding, 1976–1984" (Paper delivered at the XIIth World Congress of the International Political Science Association, Paris, France, July 15–20, 1985), 13–14.

21. Rosalynn Carter, *First Lady from Plains* (New York: Fawcett Gold Medal, 1984), 115.

22. Aldrich, "Methods of Presidential Nomination" (see n. 11), 33.

23. Maxwell Glen, "Invading Michigan," *National Journal* 21 (May 24, 1986): 1248–49.

24. Elaine Ciulla Kamarck, "Momentum in the Presidential Nominating Process" (Paper presented in New York, April 26, 1985), sec. 4, 13.

25. Kamarck, ibid., is summarizing the history of the Goldwater campaign presented in John Kessel, *The Goldwater Coalition: Republican Strategies in 1964* (Indianapolis: Bobbs-Merrill, 1968); Robert Novak, *The Agony of the G.O.P., 1964* (New York: Macmillan, 1965); Stephen Shadegg, *What Happened to Goldwater? The Inside Story of the 1964 Republican Campaign* (New York: Holt, Rinehart, and Winston, 1965); and Theodore H. White, *The Making of the President, 1964* (New York: Atheneum, 1965).

26. Kamarck, "Momentum" (see n. 24) sec. 4, 13, 7.

27. Ibid., 14. For a detailed account of one experience, see Susan Berry Casey, *Hart and Soul—Gary Hart's New Hampshire Odyssey—and Beyond* (Concord, N.H.: NHI Press, 1986).

28. "Financing Presidential Campaigns: An Examination of the Ongoing Effects of the Federal Election Campaign Laws upon the Conduct of Presidential Campaigns" (Research report by the Campaign Finance Study Group to the Committee on Rules and Administration of the United States Senate, Institute of Politics, John F. Kennedy School of Government, Harvard University, January 1982), Sec. 1, 21, 28. See also Norman J. Ornstein, "A Tax Credit Worth Saving," *New York Times,* July 30, 1986, p. 23; and Jeffrey H. Birnbaum, "House Approves Historic Overhaul of Tax System That Would Slash Rates for Individuals and Business," *Wall Street Journal,* September 26, 1986, p. 3.

29. Elaine Ciulla Kamarck, "Democrats: Deregulate the Delegates," *Washington Post,* June 23, 1985, p. B1.

30. William Crotty, "Report on Presidential Nominations: Structure and Problems" (Paper prepared for the Study of the U.S. Presidential Selection Process sponsored by the Alfred P. Sloan Foundation, Alexander Heard, Director, 1983), sec. 5, 23.

31. Terry Sanford, *A Danger of Democracy—The Presidential Nominating Process* (Boulder, Colo.: Westview Press, 1981), 143.

32. Ibid., 143–53.

33. The Forum on Presidential Nominations, *A Statement of Purpose for Political Parties* (Durham, N.C.: Duke University Institute of Policy Sciences and Public Affairs, and Woodrow Wilson International Center for Scholars, 1981), 10–11.

34. *Report of the Commission on the Presidential Nominating Process,* White Burkett Miller Center of Public Affairs, University of Virginia (Washington, D.C.: University Press of America, 1982), 4.

35. For a discussion of this conclusion, see Jeane J. Kirkpatrick et. al., *The Presidential Nominating Process: Can It Be Improved?* (Washington, D.C.: American Enterprise Institute, 1980), 16–27.

36. David E. Price, *Bringing Back the Parties* (Washington, D.C.: Congressional Quarterly, 1984), 215.

37. Richard C. Wade, "Why Voters Have Grown Independent," *New York Times,* December 12, 1984, p. 31.

38. See "Mondale Captures Majority, But Party Triumph Eludes Him," *Congressional Quarterly* 42 (June 9, 1984): 1343–45.

39. Price, *Bringing Back the Parties* (see n. 36), 232, 214–15.

40. Steven J. Brams and Peter C. Fishburn, *Approval Voting* (Boston: Birkhauser, 1983), xi.

41. Nelson W. Polsby, *Consequences of Party Reform* (New York: Oxford University Press, 1983), 249, note 11.

42. A concurring appraisal appears in Jack H. Nagel, *Participation* (Englewood Cliffs, N.J.: Prentice-Hall, Inc., 1987), 107–8. See also Larry M. Bartels, *Presidential Primaries and the Dynamics of Public Choice* (Princeton: Princeton University Press, 1988), 282–83; and Samuel Merrill III, *Making Multicandidate Elections More Democratic* (Princeton: Princeton University Press, 1988).

43. Richard E. Neustadt, *Presidential Power—the politics of leadership* (New York: John Wiley & Sons, 1960), i.

44. Geofrey C. Ward, *A First-Class Temperament—The Emergence of Franklin Roosevelt* (New York: Harper & Row, 1989), 194.

45. Hedley Donovan, *Roosevelt to Reagan: A Reporter's Encounters with Nine Presidents* (New York: Harper and Row, 1985), 296.

46. Aldrich, "Methods of Presidential Nomination" (see n. 11), 42–43.

47. James David Barber, *The Presidential Character: Predicting Performance in the White House* (Englewood Cliffs, N.J.: Prentice Hall, 1972). See also Erwin C. Hargrove, "What Manner of Man?" (see n. 13), 31–32.

48. For variations on and extensions of this list, see Stephen Hess, *The Presidential Campaign,* rev. ed. (Washington D.C.: Brookings Institution, 1978), 27–38; and Donovan, *Roosevelt to Reagan* (see n. 45), chap. 22, "Job Specs for the Oval Office," 295–309.

49. Samuel Kernell, "Campaigning, Governing, and the Contemporary Presidency, in *The New Direction in American Politics,* ed. John E. Chubb and Paul E. Peterson (Washington, D.C.: Brookings Institution, 1985), 137.

50. Phillip G. Henderson, *Managing the Presidency—The Eisenhower Legacy—From Kennedy to Reagan* (Boulder, Colo.: Westview Press, 1988), 17–23.

51. Ronald A. Heifetz and Riley M. Sinder, "Political Leadership: Managing the Public's Problem Solving," in *The Power of Public Ideas,* ed. Robert B. Reich (Cambridge, Mass.: Ballinger Publishing Company, 1988), 179–203; and Nigel Bowles, *The White House and Capitol Hill—The Politics of Presidential Persuasion* (Oxford: Clarendon Press, 1987).

52. George C. Edwards III, *At the Margins—Presidential Leadership of Congress* (New Haven: Yale University Press, 1989), 213–24.

53. John Kenneth White, *The New Politics of Old Values* (Hanover, N.H.: University Press of New England, 1988), 1–6, 142–44.

54. Interview reported in Jeffrey Gale, *"BULLSHIT"—The Media as Power Brokers in Presidential Elections* (Palm Springs, Calif.: Bold Hawk Press, 1988), 114.

55. Doris A. Graber, "Press Coverage and Voter Reaction in the 1968 Presidential Election," *Political Science Quarterly* 89 (March 1974): 96–97.

56. Benjamin I. Page, *Choices and Echoes in Presidential Elections: Rational Man and Electoral Democracy* (Chicago: University of Chicago Press, 1978), 265.

57. Erwin C. Hargrove, *The Power of the Modern Presidency* (New York: Knopf, 1974), chap. 6. See also, Hargrove and Michael Nelson, *Presidents, Politics, and Policy* (Baltimore: The Johns Hopkins University Press, 1984), chap. 3.

Chapter Ten. Searching for Better Government

1. Henry Brandon, *Special Relationships—A Foreign Correspondent's Memoirs from Roosevelt to Reagan* (New York: Atheneum, 1988), viii; see also Hugh Heclo, "The Emerging Regime," in *Remaking American Politics,* ed. Richard A. Harris and Sidney M. Milkis (Boulder, Colo.: Westview Press, 1989), 315. A discerning, concise assessment of the performance and deficiences of contemporary U. S. government and of problems in addressing them through institutional change is given in John E. Chubb and Paul E. Peterson, "American Political Institutions and the Problem of Governance," in *Can the Government Govern?* ed. Chubb and Peterson (Washington, D. C.: The Brookings Institution, 1989), 1-43.

2. Bert A. Rockman, *The Leadership Question: The Presidency and the American System* (New York: Praeger, 1984), 66.

3. Samuel P. Huntington, *American Politics: The Promise of Disharmony* (Cambridge: Harvard University Press, 1981), 123.

4. Ibid., 125.

5. Ibid., 127.

6. Ibid., 129.

7. Ibid., 125.

8. Ibid.

9. Richard Rose, "Government Against Sub-Governments: A European Perspective on Washington," in *Presidents and Prime Ministers,* ed. Richard Rose and

Ezra N. Suleiman (Washington, D.C.: American Enterprise Institute, 1980), 299–300.

10. Lawrence D. Brown, *New Policies, New Politics: Government's Response to Government's Growth* (Washington, D.C.: Brookings Institution, 1983), 4–5.

11. Walter Dean Burnham, "The Reagan Heritage," in *The Election of 1988: Reports and Interpretations,* ed. Gerald M. Pomper (Chatham, N.J.: Chatham House Publishers, Inc., 1989), 14–25.

12. John W. Gardner, *On Leadership* (New York: Free Press, 1990), 121-37.

13. Richard Rose, *Do Parties Make a Difference?* (London: Macmillan, 1980), 119–21.

14. Sidney Blumenthal, *The Permanent Campaign,* rev. ed. (New York: Simon and Schuster, 1982), 301–34; Howard R. Penniman, "Campaign Styles and Methods," in *Democracy at the Polls: A Comparative Study of Competitive National Elections,* ed. David Butler, Howard R. Penniman, and Austin Ranney (Washington D.C.: American Enterprise Institute, 1981), 114–15.

15. G. Bingham Powell, Jr., *Contemporary Democracies: Participation, Stability, and Violence* (Cambridge: Harvard University Press, 1982), 208–12; and Edward Tufte, *Political Control of the Economy* (Princeton: Princeton University Press, 1978).

16. Rockman, *The Leadership Question* (see n. 2), 70.

17. Gary R. Orren, "The Changing Styles of American Party Politics," in *The Future of American Political Parties: The Challenge of Governance,* ed. Joel L. Fleishman (Englewood Cliffs, N.J.: Prentice Hall, 1982), 37–39. See also James L. Sundquist, *Constitutional Reform and Effective Government* (Washington, D.C.: Brookings Institution, 1986), 196–203.

18. Herbert E. Alexander, *Financing Politics,* 2d ed. (Washington, D.C.: Congressional Quarterly, 1980), 150–52.

19. Herbert E. Alexander, "Future Prospects for Presidential Campaign Finance" (Paper prepared for the Study of the U.S. Presidential Selection Process sponsored by the Alfred P. Sloan Foundation, Alexander Heard, Director, December 1983), 19; and Herbert E. Alexander and Brian A. Haggerty, *Financing the 1984 Election* (Lexington, Mass.: Lexington Books, 1987), 11–38.

20. James L. Sundquist, "Directions of Reform," in *Workbook for Constitutional System Review* (Washington D. C.: Committee on the Constitutional System, February 24, 1984), 274.

21. Roger H. Davidson, " 'Invitation to Struggle': An Overview of Legislative-Executive Relations," *Annals of the American Academy of Political and Social Science* 499 (September 1988): 17–19.

22. Sundquist, *Constitutional Reform* (see n. 17), 111–16.

23. Mattei Dogan, *Pathways to Power—Selecting Rulers in Pluralist Democracies* (Boulder, Colo.: Westview Press, 1989), 2. Elliot L. Richardson and James P. Pfiffner have proposed a restructuring of the American cabinet in "Our Cabinet System is a Charade," *New York Times,* May 28, 1989, p. E15.

24. Theodore J. Lowi, *The Personal President: Power Invested, Promise Unfulfilled* (Ithaca, N.Y.: Cornell University Press, 1985), 195–209.

25. Robert A. Dahl, "On Removing Certain Impediments to Democracy in the United States," *Political Science Quarterly* 92 (Spring 1977): 16.

26. Barbara Sinclair, "Building Coalitions in Congress," in *The New Congress,* ed. Thomas E. Mann and Norman J. Ornstein (Washington, D.C.: American Enterprise Institute, 1981), 217–20.

27. Bert A. Rockman, "The Modern Presidency and Theories of Accountability: Old Wine *and* Old Bottles" (Paper presented at the 1986 annual meeting of the American Political Science Association, Washington, D.C., August 28–31, 1986), 6–7.

28. Donald L. Robinson, *"To the Best of My Ability"—The Presidency and the Constitution* (New York: W. W. Norton & Company, 1987), 269–85.

29. Michael J. Malbin, "Looking Back at the Future of Campaign Finance Reform," in *Money and Politics in the United States,* ed. Michael J. Malbin (Chatham, N.J.: Chatham House Publishers, Inc., 1984), 242.

30. Lloyd N. Cutler, "Party Procedures for Presidential Nomination," in *Workbook for Constitutional System Review* (see n. 20), 269–70.

31. Ibid., 268.

32. Rockman, *The Leadership Question* (see n. 2), 165.

33. Michael X. Delli Carpini, *Stability and Change in American Politics: The Coming of Age of the Generation of the 1960s* (New York: New York University Press, 1986), 220.

34. Leon D. Epstein, *Political Parties in the American Mold* (Madison: University of Wisconsin Press, 1986), 39.

35. Edward Reingold, "Facing the 'Totally New and Dynamic,' " *Time,* January 22, 1990, 6.

36. Porter McKeever, *Adlai Stevenson—His Life and Legacy* (New York: William Morrow and Company, Inc., 1989), 420.

37. Gardner, *On Leadership* (see n. 12), 1.

Chapter Eleven. The Continuing Quest

1. L. H. Butterfield, ed., *Letters of Benjamin Rush, Volume I: 1771–1797* (Princeton: Princeton University Press, 1951), 475.

2. George F. Will, *The New Season—a spectator's guide to the 1988 election* (New York: Simon and Schuster, 1988), 13.

3. Eric Alterman, "G.O.P. Chairman Lee Atwater: Playing Hardball," *New York Times Magazine,* April 30, 1989, p. 31.

4. Herbert E. Alexander, "Parties, PACS, and Political Finance Reform: How and Why Has Election Financing Reform Gone Awry? What to Do about It?" *Vital Issues* 32 (September 1982).

5. Ibid. See also Michael J. Malbin, "Looking Back at the Future of Campaign Finance Reform," in *Money and Politics in the United States: Financing Elections in the 1980s,* ed. Michael J. Malbin (Chatham, N. J.: Chatham House Publishers, Inc., 1984), 256, 268.

6. F. Christopher Arterton, "Political Money and Party Strength," in *The Future of American Political Parties: The Challenge of Governance,* ed. Joel L. Fleishman (Englewood Cliffs, N. J.: Prentice Hall, 1982),139.

7. Joseph A. Schlesinger, "The New American Political Party," *American Political Science Review* 79 (December 1985): 1168.

8. Malbin, "Looking Back" (see n. 5), 270.

9. Michael Oreskes and Robin Toner, "Swamp of Political Abuse Spurs A New Constituency, for Change," *New York Times,* March 21, 1990, p. 1; Austin Ranney, *Channels of Power: The Impact of Television on American Politics* (New York: Basic Books, 1983), 180.

10. David Adamany, "Political Parties in the 1980s," in *Money and Politics in the United States,* ed. Michael J. Malbin (see n. 5), 82–83.

11. Elihu Katz, "Platforms and Windows: Broadcasting's Role in Election Campaigns," in *Sociology of Mass Communications,* ed. Denis McQuail (New York: Penguin, 1972), 367.

12. Jeane J. Kirkpatrick et al., *The Presidential Nominating Process: Can it Be Improved?* (Washington, D.C.: American Enterprise Institute, 1980), 6–27.

13. Pope McCorkle and Joel Fleishman, "Political Parties and Presidential Nominations," in *The Future of American Political Parties,* ed. Fleishman (see n. 6), 162.

14. Arterton, "Political Money," in *The Future of American Political Parties,* ed. Fleishman, 108–109. As noted in Chapter Six, Leon D. Epstein writes of changes in the legal status and regulation of parties in "Will American Political Parties Be Privatized?" *The Journal of Law and Politics* 5 (Winter 1989): 239–74. See also Timothy J. Conlan, "Politics and Goverance: Conflicting Trends in the 1990s?" *Annals of the American Academy of Political and Social Science,* 509 (May 1990): 128-38.

15. James I. Lengle, "Changing the Rules Changes the Game: An Assessment of Three Nomination Reforms for 1984," *Commonsense,* 1982, no. 2:18.

16. Nelson W. Polsby, *Consequences of Party Reform* (New York: Oxford University Press, 1983), 185.

17. Steven J. Brams and Peter C. Fishburn, *Approval Voting* (Boston: Birkhauser, 1983), 172.

18. David E. Price, *Bringing Back the Parties* (Washington, D.C.: Congressional Quarterly Press, 1984), 232.

19. Elaine Ciulla Kamarck, "Democrats: Deregulate the Delegates," *Washington Post,* June 23, 1985, p. B1. Two analyses of effects on delegate and candidate selection of characteristics of presidential primary rules, judged by explicit criteria, are John G. Geer, "Rules Governing Presidential Primaries," *Journal of Politics* 48 (November 1986): 1006-25, and Stephen Ansolabehere and Gary King, "Measuring the Consequences of Delegate Selection Rules in Presidential Nominations," *Journal of Politics* 52 (May 1990): 609-21.

20. *The Economist,* June 11, 1988, p. 10.

21. Howard R. Penniman, "U.S. Elections: Really a Bargain?" *Public Opinion* 7 (June-July 1984): 51–53. Precise comparisons are difficult, but see Herbert E. Alexander, ed., *Comparative Political Finance in the 1980s* (Cambridge: Cambridge University Press, 1989).

22. Senator David Boren (D-Okla.) led a spirited effort to limit federal campaign expenditures in early 1988; see David G. Goeller, "Democrats spurn foes, pledge cap on election costs," *Tennessean* (Nashville), February 28, 1988, p. 14-A. Efforts continued in 1990 to limit spending by candidates for Congress, e.g., Steven A. Holmes, "Bill on Senate Finance Clears the First of Many Hurdles," *New York Times,* March 9, 1990, p. A10.

23. "Financing Presidential Campaigns: An Examination of the Ongoing Effects of the Federal Election Campaign Laws upon the Conduct of Presidential Campaigns" (Research report by the Campaign Finance Study Group to the Committee on Rules and Administration of the United States Senate, Institute of Politics, John F. Kennedy School of Government, Harvard University, January 1982), sec. 1, 5.

24. Michael S. Berman, "Living with the FECA: Confessions of a Sometime Campaign Treasurer," *Annals of the American Academy of Political and Social Science* 486 (July 1986): 124.

25. Larry J. Sabato, *PAC Power: Inside the World of Political Action Committees* (New York: Norton, 1984), 176.

26. The recommendation of a conference of presidential finance officers sponsored by Citizens' Research Foundation, Washington, D.C., November 28, 1984, reported in Herbert E. Alexander and Brian A. Haggerty, *Financing the 1984 Election* (Lexington, Mass.: Lexington Books, 1987), 28; and Campaign Finance Study Group, Harvard University, "Financing Presidential Campaigns" (see n. 23), sec. 1, 25.

27. Herbert E. Alexander, "The Costs of the 1988 Presidential Campaigns" (typescript, December 1988), 2.

28. Alexander and Haggerty, *Financing 1984* (see n. 26), 28; Campaign Finance Study Group, Harvard University, "Financing Presidential Campaigns" (see n. 23), sec. 1, 20–22; Herbert E. Alexander, Testimony before the U.S. Senate Committee on Rules and Administration, January 26, 1983, 12; and *Financing Presidential Campaigns—Report of a Conference of Presidential Finance Officers* (Los Angeles, Calif.: Citizens' Research Foundation, 1989), 6. The conference was held in Washington, D. C., December 9, 1988.

29. Berman, "Living with the FECA" (see n. 24), 125. Extending the matching period was also recommended in *Financing Presidential Campaigns* (see n. 28), 7.

30. Alexander and Haggerty, *Financing 1984* (see n. 26), 28–29.

31. "Revised Check-off Fund Projections," staff memorandum to members of the Federal Election Commission, January 31, 1990; and Herbert E. Alexander, "Wide-Open Races Show Cracks in Fund System," *Los Angeles Times,* March 9, 1988.

32. Such legislation has been introduced by Senator Paul Laxalt (R-Nev.), Representative Bill Frenzel (R-Minn.), and others; and see campaign finance legislation proposed by Senator Charles Mathias (R-Md.), cited in *Commonsense* 1983, no. 1:77, 79–80.

33. Walter Shapiro, "Take it to the Limit—and Beyond," *Time,* February 15, 1988, 19.

34. Brooks Jackson, *Honest Graft—Big Money and the American Political Process* (New York: Alfred A. Knopf, Inc., 1988), 308.

35. Berman, "Living with the FECA" (see n. 24), 123.

36. "Soft-Money Decision," *Washington Post,* September 1, 1988, p. A–22.

37. "Soft Money? No—Sewer Money," *New York Times,* October 21, 1988, p. A-34; also, Herbert E. Alexander, "The Price We Pay For Our Presidents," *Public Opinion* 11 (March/April 1989): 48; and James A. Barnes, "Hard Questions on Soft Money," *National Journal* 21 (April 8, 1989): 864.

38. Alexander and Haggerty, *Financing 1984* (see n. 26), 29; and *Financing Presidential Campaigns* (see n. 28), 8–9. On tax exempt activities, see Richard E. Cohen and Carol Matlock, "All-Purpose Loopholes," *National Journal* 49 (December 7, 1989): 2980-87.

39. See *Financing Presidential Campaigns* (see n. 28), 9. See also Fred Wertheimer, "Campaign Finance Reform: The Unfinished Agenda," and William C. Oldaker, "Of Philosophers, Foxes, and Finances: Can the Federal Election Commission Ever Do an Adequate Job?" *Annals of the American Academy of Political and Social Science* 486 (July 1986): 101, 132–45.

40. Richard A. Watson and Norman C. Thomas, *The Politics of the Presidency*, 2d ed. (Washington, D.C.: CQ Press, 1988), 492–95.

41. Robert Shogan, "Democrat Group Campaigns for Changes in Delegate Laws," *Los Angeles Times,* May 9, 1990. Independent Republican Frank C. P. McGlinn of Pennsylvania has long advocated a district plan. Janet M. Martin has urged each state to consider doing so in light of its own circumstances—"Going as Maine goes would make popular vote more meaningful," *Philadelphia Inquirer,* November 8, 1988, p. 13A.

42. *Winner-Take-All: Report of the Twentieth Century Task Force on Reform of the Presidential Election Process* (New York: Holmes and Meier, 1978).

43. B. Drummond Ayers, Jr., "Electoral College's Stately Landslide Sends Bush and Quayle Into History," *New York Times,* December 20, 1988, p. 13.

44. A. James Reichley, "The Electoral System," in *Elections American Style,* ed. A. James Reichley (Washington, D.C.: Brookings Institution, 1987), 20.

45. For a discussion of the issue in 1988, see Dom Bonafede, "Fighting Off Lameness," *National Journal* 20 (May 7, 1988): 1188–91.

46. For a discussion of universal voter enrollment, see Kevin P. Phillips and Paul H. Blackman, *Electoral Reform and Voter Participation: Federal Registration—A False Remedy for Voter Apathy* (Washington, D.C.: American Enterprise Institute, 1975), 24–27; William Crotty, "The Franchise: Registration Changes and Voter Representation," in *Paths to Political Reform,* ed. William Crotty (Lexington, Mass.: Lexington Books, 1980), 103; and Gary R. Orren, "The Linkage of Policy to Participation," in *Presidential Selection,* ed. Alexander Heard and Michael Nelson (Durham, N.C.: Duke University Press, 1987), 112–13.

47. "One Reason Voters Didn't Vote," *New York Times,* November 25, 1988, p. 22.

48. Richard G. Smolka, *Election Day Registration: The Minnesota and Wisconsin Experience in 1976* (Washington, D.C.: American Enterprise Institute, 1977); and *Presidential Elections Since 1789* (Washington, D.C.: Congressional Quarterly Inc., 1987), 89–90.

49. Richard G. Smolka, *Registering Voters by Mail: The Maryland and New Jersey Experience* (Washington, D.C.: American Enterprise Institute, 1975).

50. Peverill Squire, Raymond E. Wolfinger, and David P. Glass, "Residential Mobility and Voter Turnout," *American Political Science Review* 81 (March 1987): 57.

51. Orren, "Linkage" (see n. 46), 114–16.

52. Ibid., 101–2.

53. "Former president Ford urges candidates to address issues," *Kenyon College Alumni Bulletin,* Spring 1988, 6.

54. Thomas E. Patterson and Robert D. McClure, *The Unseeing Eye: The Myth of Television Power in National Politics* (New York: G. P. Putnam's Sons, 1976), 128; Patterson and McClure, "Television and the Less-Interested Voter: The Costs of An Informed Electorate," *Annals of the American Academy of Political and Social Science* 425 (May 1976): 95; and Andrew Savitz and Mark Katz, "Sound Bites Have Teeth," *New York Times,* March 26, 1990, p. 15.

55. For a dissent expressing sharp anxiety over the expenditures of political action committees, see James Hunter Clinger, "The Clean Campaign Act of 1985: A Rational Solution to Negative Campaign Advertising Which the One

Hundredth Congress Should Reconsider," *Journal of Law and Politics* 3 (Spring 1987): 727–48.

56. Kathleen Hall Jamieson and David S. Birdsell, *Presidential Debates—The Challenge of Creating an Informed Electorate* (New York: Oxford University Press, 1988), 222.

57. Thomas E. Patterson, *The Mass Media Election: How Americans Choose Their President* (New York: Praeger, 1980), 103, 157.

58. Lee Hamilton, "How to Do It Better," *Time,* November 14, 1988, 22.

59. "Presidential Debates: Early and Often," *New York Times,* November 19, 1988, p. 14.

60. Edward J. Markey and Bob Graham, "Putting Their Mouths Where the Money Is," *New York Times,* July 19, 1989, p. 23.

61. John B. Anderson, *A Proper Institution—Guaranteeing Televised Presidential Debates* (New York: Priority Press Publications, 1988), 17–55.

62. Jamieson and Birdsell, *Presidential Debates* (see n. 56), 199.

63. Commission on National Elections, *Electing the President: A Program for Reform* (Washington: Center for Strategic and International Studies, 1986), 41–44.

64. Phil Gailey, "2 Parties to Run Political Debates; League of Women Voters Sees Threat to Minor Candidates," *New York Times,* October 21, 1985, p. A20; Steven J. Rosenstone, Roy L. Behr, and Edward H. Lazarus, *Third Parties in America: Citizen Response to Major Party Failure* (Princeton: Princeton University Press, 1984), 35.

65. John F. Burns, "Angry TV Debate in Canada Enlivens Election Campaign," *New York Times,* October 27, 1988, p. 1.

66. The Twentieth Century Fund, *With the Nation Watching: Report of the Twentieth Century Fund Task Force on Televised Presidential Debates* (Lexington, Mass.: Lexington Books, 1979), 93–94.

67. Elihu Katz, "Platforms and Windows: Broadcasting's Role in Election Campaigns," in *Sociology of Mass Communications,* ed. Denis McQuail (New York: Penguin, 1972), 367.

68. A. M. Rosenthal, "We Told You So," *New York Times,* October 25, 1988, p. 27. Jay G. Blumler enumerates inadequacies of media performance in election campaigns in "Election Communication and the Democratic Political System," in *Political Communication Research: Approaches, Studies, Assessments,* ed. David L. Paletz (Durham, N.C.: Duke University Press, 1987), 168. Timothy J. Russert, senior vice president and Washington bureau chief of NBC News, recommended five revisions of campaign coverage that networks themselves should make, "For '92, the Networks Have to Do Better," *New York Times,* March 4, 1990, p. E23.

69. Peter Nye, "Ron Brown and Lee Atwater: A Study in Contrasts," *The National Voter* 39 (April/May 1990): 7; also Michael Oreskes, "PBS Plans More Time for Candidates," *New York Times,* June 17, 1990, p. Y12.

70. Martin Schram, *The Great American Video Game—Presidential Politics in the Television Age* (New York: William Morrow and Company, Inc., 1987), 314.

71. For a discussion of this view, see Martin Landau, "A Self-Correcting System: The Constitution of the United States," *This Constitution: A Bicentennial Chronicle* 11 (Summer 1986): 4–10. For a discussion of a different perception and conviction, see James L. Sundquist, "Needed: A Political Theory for

the New Era of Coalition Government in the United States," *Political Science Quarterly* 103 (Winter 1988–89): 613–35.

72. James Q. Wilson, "Does the Separation of Powers Work?" *Public Interest* 86 (Winter 1987): 44–49.

73. James David Barber, "The Real World vs. Presidential Politics: The Myths of Politics in 1980" (Paper prepared for the Study of the U.S. Presidential Selection Process sponsored by the Alfred P. Sloan Foundation, Alexander Heard, Director, 1983), 1.

74. Robert C. Tucker explores issues of "Presidential Selection and the Super-power Relationship" but does not conclude that hope lies in basic structural change (Paper prepared for the Study of the U.S. Presidential Selection Process sponsored by the Alfred P. Sloan Foundation, Alexander Heard, Director, 1984).

75. William B. Quandt, "The Electoral Cycle and the Conduct of Foreign Policy," *Political Science Quarterly* 101 (1986): 836–37.

76. Michael Parenti, in *Inventing Reality—The Politics of the Mass Media* (New York: St. Martin's Press, 1986), is an especially harsh critic.

77. Hedley Donovan, *Right Places, Right Times—Forty Years in Journalism Not Counting My Paper Route* (New York: Henry Holt and Company, 1989), 394.

78. George C. Edwards III, *At the Margins: Presidential Leadership of Congress* (New Haven, Conn.: Yale University Press, 1989), 221.

79. Judith N. Shklar, *Ordinary Vices* (Cambridge: Harvard University Press, 1984), 220–21.

80. For one of many treatments of the general issue, see Roger H. Davidson, " 'Invitation to Struggle': An Overview of Legislative-Executive Relations," *Annals of the American Academy of Political and Social Science* 499 (September 1988): 9–21.

INDEX

260

Quandt, William B., 254
"Quantum Mechanics of Politics, The,"
214
Quemoy, 50
Quest for the Presidency 1984, The, 245
Quiet Revolution, 227
Quota system, 89

Rabinowitz, George, 225
Rachlin, Allan, 215
Radio. *See* Mass media
Ranney, Austin, 51, 63, 68–69, 88, 89, 91, 141,
213, 215, 216, 217, 218, 221, 222, 223,
227, 228, 232, 233, 239, 241, 242, 248,
249
Rasky, Susan, 235
Rationalist approach, to democracy, 227
Rationalizing agenda, 146
Reagan, Ronald, 28, 36, 37, 40, 41, 52, 60, 65,
70, 107, 108, 120, 121, 125, 132, 134,
142, 143, 151, 152, 154, 164, 165, 170,
174, 196, 202
"Reagan Heritage, The," 248
Reaganomics, 65
*Real Campaign: How the Media Missed the
Story of the 1980 Campaign, The,* 217,
222, 243
Reality, 9
Realpolitik, 148
"Real World vs. Presidential Politics: The
Myths of Politics in 1980, The," 254
"Reborn Political Center, The," 215
Reciprocal learning, and information, 28
Recommendations
and conclusions, 180–211
groupings of, 181
*Records of the Federal Convention of 1787,
The,* 217, 236
Reedy, George E., 31, 216
Rees, Albert, ix
Reference notes, 213–54
Referenda, national, 123
Reform
and frustration, 2–4
limits of, 171–72
"Reform and Alienation: The Decline of
Intermediation in the Politics of
Presidential Selection," 231
*Reforming American Government—The
Bicentennial Papers of the Committee
on the Constitutional System,* 224
*Reforming the Reforms: A Critical Analysis of
the Presidential Selection Process,* 226,
227
*Registering Voters by Mail: The Maryland
and New Jersey Experience,* 237, 252
Registration
easing, 124–28
and voting, 202–4
Rehnquist, William, 102
Reich, Robert B., 247
Reichley, A. James, 225, 232, 252
Reid, T. R., 241
Reingold, Edward, 249

Reinhold, Robert, 242
Reinsch, J. Leonard, 244
Reiter, Howard L., 233
"Relationship between the Presidential
Selection Process and Campaign
Finance and the Federal Election
Commission," 230, 231
Remaking American Politics, 247
*Report of the Commission on the Presidential
Nominating Process,* 246
"Report on Presidential Nominations:
Structure and Problems," 246
Representation
bases, 92–93
concepts, 87, 88–92
Representatives, House of. *See* United States
House of Representatives
Republic, The, 213
Republican Committee on Delegates and
Organization (DO), The, 89, 93
Republican National Committee (RNC), 120
"Republicans Show Gains in Loyalty," 216
"Residential Mobility and Voter Turnout,"
237, 252
Responsibility, and information, 18–20
*Responsible Electorate: Rationality in
Presidential Voting, 1936–1960, The,*
216
Responsible party system, 25
*Retrospective Voting in American National
Politics,* 25, 216
Revenue Act, 185
"Revised Check-off Fund Projections," 251
Rhetorical Presidency, The, 213, 238, 241
Richardson, Elliot L., 248
Riggs, Fred W., 215
*Right Places, Right Times—Forty Years in
Journalism Not Counting My Paper
Route,* 254
RNC. *See* Republican National Committee
(RNC)
Roberts, Richard P., 226
Roberts, Steven B., 230
Robertson, Marion G. (Pat), 155
Robinson, Donald L., 175, 224, 249
Robinson, Michael J., 217, 236
Rockman, Bert A., 37, 168, 176, 217, 218, 239,
243, 247, 248, 249
Rogers, Joel, 137, 240
Rohde, David W., 216, 233, 234, 236
"Role of Public Opinion Polls in Presidential
Selection, The," 241
Rolling Stone, 24, 216
"Rolling Stone Survey: Tuned Out, Turned
Off, The," 216
"Ron Brown and Lee Atwater: A Study in
Contrasts," 253
Roosevelt, Franklin D., 6, 8, 17, 151, 153, 165,
174, 178, 202, 210
Roosevelt, Theodore, 153, 164
*Roosevelt to Reagan: A Reporter's Encounters
with Nine Presidents,* 246
Rose, Richard, ix, 76, 132, 133, 169, 170, 225,
239, 242, 248